Twain in His Own Time

WRITERS IN THEIR OWN TIME

Joel Myerson, *series editor*

TWAIN

in His Own Time

A BIOGRAPHICAL
CHRONICLE OF HIS LIFE,
DRAWN FROM RECOLLECTIONS,
INTERVIEWS, AND
MEMOIRS BY FAMILY,
FRIENDS, AND
ASSOCIATES

EDITED BY

Gary Scharnhorst

University of Iowa Press
Iowa City

University of Iowa Press, Iowa City 52242
Copyright © 2010 by the University of Iowa Press
www.uiowapress.org
Printed in the United States of America

The University of Iowa Press is a member of Green Press Initiative
and is committed to preserving natural resources.

Printed on acid-free paper

Library of Congress Cataloging-in-Publication Data
Twain in his own time: a biographical chronicle of his life, drawn from recollections,
interviews, and memoirs by family, friends, and associates / edited by Gary Scharnhorst.
p.   cm.—(Writers in their own time)
Includes index.
ISBN-13: 978-1-58729-914-8 (pbk.)
ISBN-10: 1-58729-914-3 (pbk.)
ISBN-13: 978-1-58729-951-3 (e-book)
ISBN-10: 1-58729-951-8 (e-book)
1. Twain, Mark, 1835–1910.   2. Twain, Mark, 1835–1910—Friends and associates.
3. Authors, American—19th century—Biography.   1. Scharnhorst, Gary.
PS1333.T83 2010
818′4′09—dc22
[B]
2010013178

FOR
Emily, Germar, and Imani

Contents

Introduction   xiii

Chronology   xxi

Anonymous, "Mark Twain's Boyhood: An Interview with
Mrs. Jane Clemens" (1885)   1

[Laura Frazier], "Mark Twain's Childhood Sweetheart Recalls
Their Romance" (1918)   4

Homer Bassford, "Mark Twain as a Cub Pilot:
A Talk with Captain Horace Bixby" (1899)   8

Grant Marsh, "Mark Twain" (1878)   13

Tom Fitch, "Fitch Recalls Mark Twain in Bonanza Times" (1919)   14

C. C. Goodwin, From *As I Remember Them* (1913)   16

[Joseph T. Goodman], "Jos. Goodman's Memories of
Humorist's Early Days" (1910)   20

Arthur McEwen, "In the Heroic Days" (1893)   22

Dan De Quille, "Salad Days of Mark Twain" (1893)   25

Dan De Quille, From Archibald Henderson, *Mark Twain* (1910)   38

George E. Barnes, "Memories of Mark Twain" (1915)   40

Tom Fitch, "Fitch Recalls Mark Twain in Bonanza Times" (1919)   42

Tom Fitch, From *Western Carpetbagger:
The Extraordinary Memoirs of "Senator" Tom Fitch* (1978)   44

George E. Barnes, "Mark Twain as He Was Known during
His Stay on the Pacific Slope" (1887)   47

William R. Gillis, From *Memories of Mark Twain and
Steve Gillis* (1924)   50

Henry J. W. Dam, "A Morning with Bret Harte" (1894)   52

George E. Barnes, "Mark Twain as He Was Known during
His Stay on the Pacific Slope" (1887)   54

Franklin H. Austin, "Mark Twain Incognito—
A Reminiscence" (1926)   55

George E. Barnes, "Mark Twain as He Was Known during
His Stay on the Pacific Slope" (1887)   59

Tom Fitch, "Fitch Recalls Mark Twain in Bonanza Times" (1919)   63

Edward H. House, "Mark Twain as a Lecturer" (1867)   64

Noah Brooks, "Mark Twain in California" (1898)   67

Mary Mason Fairbanks, "The Cruise of the *Quaker City*" (1892)   69

Anonymous, "About Mark Twain" (1877)   71

William M. Stewart, From *Reminiscences of Senator
William M. Stewart of Nevada* (1908)   73

Noah Brooks, "Mark Twain in California" (1898)   77

J. N. Larned, "Mark Twain" (1910)   79

W. D. Howells, From *My Mark Twain* (1910)   80

Moncure D. Conway, "Mark Twain in London" (1872)   82

Moncure D. Conway, From *Autobiography* (1904)   87

Charles Warren Stoddard, "In Old Bohemia" (1908)   89

Henry Watterson, "Mark Twain—An Intimate Portrait" (1910)   92

Lilian Aldrich, From *Crowding Memories* (1920)   95

Annie Adams Fields, From *Memories of a Hostess:
A Chronicle of Eminent Friendships* (1922)   99

W. D. Howells, From *My Mark Twain* (1910)   105

Edmund Yates, From *Celebrities at Home* (1879)   112

Norman Hapgood, From *The Changing Years* (1930)   116

W. D. Howells, From *My Mark Twain* (1910)   118

Frank Harris, From *Contemporary Portraits,
Fourth Series* (1923)   123

Contents

Charles H. Clark, "Mark Twain at 'Nook Farm' (Hartford) and Elmira" (1885) — 127

Clara Clemens, From *My Father Mark Twain* (1931) — 131

Jervis Langdon, From *Samuel Langhorne Clemens* (1910) — 133

J. Henry Harper, From *I Remember* (1934) — 134

E. W. Kemble, "Illustrating *Huck Finn*" (1930) — 137

W. D. Howells, From *My Mark Twain* (1910) — 141

Will M. Clemens, "Mark Twain on the Lecture Platform" (1900) — 143

George Washington Cable, From Arlin Turner, *Mark Twain and George W. Cable: The Record of a Literary Friendship* (1960) — 145

Susy Clemens, From *Papa: An Intimate Biography of Mark Twain* (1985) — 148

George Cary Eggleston, From *Recollections of a Varied Life* (1910) — 150

W. D. Howells, From *My Mark Twain* (1910) — 152

Irving Bacheller, From *Opinions of a Cheerful Yankee* (1926) — 154

Brander Matthews, "Memories of Mark Twain" (1920) — 157

Dan Beard, From *Hardly a Man Is Now Alive* (1939) — 163

Daniel Frohman, From *Daniel Frohman Presents: An Autobiography* (1935) — 169

J. Henry Harper, From *I Remember* (1934) — 171

Dan Beard, From *Hardly a Man Is Now Alive* (1939) — 176

Grace King, From *Memories of a Southern Woman of Letters* (1932) — 178

William H. Rideing, "Mark Twain in Clubland" (1910) — 183

James B. Pond, From *Eccentricities of Genius* (1900) — 189

R. C. B., "Mark Twain on the Platform" (1896) — 202

Natalie Hammond, From *A Woman's Part in a Revolution* (1897) — 205

John Hay Hammond, From *Autobiography* (1935) — 207

Poultney Bigelow, From *Seventy Summers* (1925) — 210

Frank Marshall White, "Mark Twain as a Newspaper Reporter" (1910) — 213

James Ross Clemens, M.D., "Some Reminiscences of
Mark Twain" (1929)   222

Hamlin Garland, From *Roadside Meetings* (1931)   225

W. D. Howells, From *My Mark Twain* (1910)   229

Mary Lawton, From *A Lifetime with Mark Twain:
The Memories of Katy Leary* (1925)   233

Winston Churchill, From *A Roving Commission* (1930)   237

Andrew Carnegie, From *Autobiography of Andrew Carnegie* (1920)   238

James Montgomery Flagg, From *Roses and Buckshot* (1946)   241

W. D. Howells, From *My Mark Twain* (1910)   243

George Ade, From *One Afternoon with Mark Twain* (1939)   246

Hamlin Garland, From *Companions on the Trail:
A Literary Chronicle* (1931)   251

Henry M. Alden, "Mark Twain: Personal Impressions" (1910)   253

Norman Hapgood, From *The Changing Years* (1930)   255

Raffaele Simboli, "Mark Twain from an
Italian Point of View" (1904)   257

Samuel P. Davis, "Mark Twain on Friends and Fighters" (1906)   260

Dan Beard, From *Hardly a Man Is Now Alive* (1939)   263

Albert Bigelow Paine, "Innocents at Home" (1925)   266

W. D. Howells, From *My Mark Twain* (1910)   273

Archibald Henderson, From *Mark Twain* (1910)   275

Joseph G. Cannon and L. White Busbey,
From *Uncle Joe Cannon* (1927)   277

James B. Morrow, "Mark Twain's Exclusive Publisher
Tells What the Humorist Is Paid" (1907)   280

George Bernard Shaw, "Letters to the Editor" (1944)   282

Sir George Ian MacAlister, "Mark Twain,
Some Personal Reminiscences" (1938)   283

E. V. Lucas, "E. V. Lucas and Twain at a '*Punch* Dinner'" (1910)   285

Contents

Dorothy Quick, "A Little Girl's Mark Twain" (1935) 287

Elizabeth Wallace, From *Mark Twain and the Happy Island* (1914) 293

Dorothy Sturgis Harding, "Mark Twain Lands an
 Angel Fish" (1967) 296

Albert Bigelow Paine, "Mark Twain at Stormfield" (1909) 299

Dan Beard, From *Hardly a Man Is Now Alive* (1939) 305

Helen Keller, "Mark Twain" (1929) 308

Mary Louise Howden, "Mark Twain as His Secretary at
 Stormfield Remembers Him" (1925) 318

W. D. Howells, From *My Mark Twain* (1910) 326

Works Cited 329

Index 337

Introduction

MARK TWAIN ENJOYS A reputation unrivaled in American literary history, and, as one of his obituarists noted, he was the "architect" of that reputation (Budd, *Our Mark Twain,* 19). From the start of his career, Twain tried to control his public image. He understood intuitively the advantages of favorable publicity, and he was a "genius at dramatizing his celebrity" (Budd, *Our Mark Twain,* 240). To be sure, he was not dishonest, merely misleading. According to Huck Finn, "he told the truth, mainly. There was things which he stretched, but mainly he told the truth" (1). In *Roughing It* (1872), for example, he reminisced about his first public lecture, in San Francisco on 2 October 1866. On the afternoon of the lecture, as he recalled, he saw an empty box office. Expecting an empty theater that evening, he

> went down back streets at six o'clock, and entered the theatre by the back door. I stumbled my way in the dark among the ranks of canvas scenery, and stood on the stage. The house was gloomy and silent, and its emptiness depressing. . . . Then I heard a murmur; it rose higher and higher, and ended in a crash, mingled with cheers. It made my hair raise, it was so close to me, and so loud. . . . There was a pause, and then another; presently came a third, and before I well knew what I was about, I was in the middle of the stage, staring at a sea of faces, bewildered by the fierce glare of the lights, and quaking in every limb with a terror that seemed like to take my life away. The house was full, aisles and all! (534–35)

A pretty tale, perhaps, but demonstrably "stretched." The San Francisco newspapers had reported days in advance that the lecture was a sellout. In re-creating the event, Mark Twain simply indulged in some personal mythmaking.

This pattern of massaging the message holds throughout his life. Over the next forty years he sculpted his public persona and fiercely protected it. In 1873 he wanted his friend Ned House to puff *The Gilded Age* in the

New York Tribune,† and he ended his acquaintance with Whitelaw Reid, the editor of the *Tribune*, over Reid's refusal to assign the review to House (*Mark Twain's Letters* 5:367). Ironically, Twain was sued by House and the theatrical impresario Daniel Frohman seventeen years later for breach of contract when he vainly attempted to recover the dramatic rights to his novel *The Prince and the Pauper* (Scharnhorst 113–117; Fatout, "Mark Twain, Litigant").

A publicity hound under most circumstances, Twain usually refused to be interviewed unless he could direct the questioning. When his friend Maxim Gorky attracted unwelcome media attention in 1906 by traveling to New York with his mistress, Twain granted interviews for the sole purpose of damage control. In fact, he readily sat for interviews when they were to his advantage, as when he was on a lecture tour, but otherwise he was typically inaccessible. He praised his butler for learning to lie when turning away "the newspaper correspondent or the visitor at the front door" (Aldrich 144).† His silence was strategic: "a story about his turning down a reporter could assure the stiff-necked that he was no longer lapping up publicity" (Budd, *Our Mark Twain*, 151). On one occasion, he threatened a reporter not to "blackguard me in your paper," and he often admonished interviewers not to publish his exact words because he could sell them for up to thirty cents apiece rather than give them away. "Don't print a word of what I have said," he ordered a stringer for the *New York World* in November 1890. "It is my trade to gaggle, and if I talk to reporters for nothing where's my bread and butter coming in?" (Scharnhorst 69, 638, 375).

He sometimes urged his correspondents to destroy his private letters, such as one he sent his mother and sister in January 1868: "Read this *only* to the family, & then burn it—I do *hate* to have anybody know anything about my business" (*Mark Twain's Letters* 2:160). Ironically, this letter not only survives, but the text has been published. In 1882 Twain established his own publishing firm, Charles L. Webster and Co., which sold *Huck Finn* (1885), *A Connecticut Yankee in King Arthur's Court* (1889), and some of his other books by subscription. One of the advantages of this method of distribution was that it preempted reviews. The books were sold door-to-door, based upon a prospectus, prior to publication—and before the critics had an opportunity to comment. In 1896, after the demise of Webster and Co., Twain acknowledged authorship of *Personal Recollections of Joan of Arc* only after it had been published by Harper & Bros. and favorably received. He hired a clipping service, and the files of the Mark Twain Papers at Berkeley today are filled with the articles sent to him. Many of his speaking dates in Australia, New Zealand, India, and South Africa are known to scholarship only because clipped articles about them survive in his scrapbooks. He personally selected and approved his illustrators, such as E. W. Kemble and Dan Beard, as well as their illustrations for his books. Predictably, he refused to permit a single word of his writing to be revised without his consent. As Beard remembered, when an editor at *St. Nicholas* tampered with the text of *Tom Sawyer Abroad,* Twain stormed the offices of the magazine, "the sanctum sanctorum, the holy of holies," and declared, "Any editor to whom I submit my manuscripts has an undisputed right to delete anything to which he objects but . . . God Almighty Himself has no right to put words in my mouth that I never used!" (Beard 344).† Or as he told the journalist Frank Marshall White, he would rather editors "put street sweepings" in his manuscripts than "put words into my mouth" (White 961).† On the other hand, he also practiced a form of self-censorship, publishing the risqué *1601* (1882) without signature and suppressing "The War Prayer" during his life because, as he said, "no man dares tell the truth until after he is dead" (Beard 343).†

When on occasion he was publicly embarrassed, he backpedaled. In the case of the Whittier birthday speech in December 1877, he left the country with his family until the controversy blew over. Humiliated by his bankruptcy in 1895, he announced a plan to repay his creditors dollar for dollar four days before he left the country, and he did not return to the United States for five years—after the debt was paid in full. Meanwhile, he found a scapegoat for his failure in his publisher Charles Webster, who had conveniently died.

By the end of his life his pseudonym had become a brand name and his trademark. It was used to sell brands of whisky, cigars, and shirt collars, with his image appearing in the advertisements. He successfully sued publishing pirates on the grounds of trademark infringement. He founded the Mark Twain Company in 1908 in an ill-fated effort to obtain perpetual copyright to his works. His iconic white flannel suit, which he first wore as a publicity stunt in December 1906 while testifying before Congress on the need for an international copyright law, was from the first a theatrical costume, a form of self-promotion or self-dramatization. Budd allows that Twain was "fully conscious of creating a hubbub—for the immediate sake of copyright reform" (*Our Mark Twain* 207). "I don't like to be conspicuous," he told the artist James Montgomery Flagg, "but I *do* like to be the most noticeable person!" (Flagg 170).† Not surprisingly, at his open-casket funeral in New York, his body was dressed in one of his signature white suits. Laura Skandera Trombley has even suggested Twain arranged his daughter Clara's marriage to Ossip Gabrilowitsch in 1909 in order to prevent a public scandal that would have reflected badly on the family: "He was determined to depart this earth with a reputation as unstained as his white suits, universally recognized as a literary lion, highly regarded as an icon of integrity, and widely perceived as a loving husband and devoted father" (120).

Nor did his efforts to manage his legacy end with his death. The angry "Ashcroft-Lyon manuscript" he composed between May and October 1909 was nothing more or less than a weapon he entrusted to his daughter Clara to protect his reputation should she ever need to coerce his former business adviser Ralph W. Ashcroft and former secretary Isabel Lyon into silence. "He wrote out a full description of their entire story," Clara Clemens remembered, "which I was to publish if there was no other way to keep them quiet" (Hill, "Ashcroft-Lyon Manuscript," 44). Twain also left a note ordering Clara "to retain his lawyers at $1000 a year to maintain a constant vigilance over his assets"—not the least of which was his reputation (Skandera Trombley 130). True to the spirit of his wishes, Clara refused to authorize the publication of her father's *Letters from the Earth* until 1962, though Bernard De Voto had prepared them for the press in 1939, lest the controversial articles compromise the value of his literary estate.

Nor was this all. The list of his rearguard maneuvers goes on. In 1906 he commissioned Albert Bigelow Paine, a young author without much of a pedigree and who was something of a sycophant, to write his authorized biography. Of course, Twain tightly controlled Paine's access to materials. Twain's own rambling autobiography, mostly dictated between January 1906 and October 1909, settled some old scores and was originally planned to appear a century after his death. It was a time capsule, "a portrait gallery of contemporaries with whom he has come into personal contact" (Scharnhorst 333), the ultimate effort to protect his public image that guaranteed he would get the last word whatever his enemies might say about him. As Michael Kiskis adds, Twain expected his autobiography would be "admired a good many centuries" (xxv), and he hoped his heirs would receive royalties on it for as long as it was admired. Under the press of financial demands, Twain published a carefully crafted, self-serving fragment of his autobiography in the *North American Review* from September 1906 to December 1907 that served to burnish his image. "His flights had one eye on the compass while the other watched out for thunderheads," Budd concluded (*Our Mark Twain* 203). With the publication of Paine's official biography of Twain in 1912 and Paine's version of his autobiography in 1924, he "continued to help shape his own legend" (Budd, *Our Mark Twain,* 231). He never employed a publicist because he didn't need one or, more correctly, he already had an unsalaried one.

Whatever its other merits, *Twain in His Own Time* is largely immune from Twain's spin-doctoring and image-making. By the same token, it is not a debunking account of his life. Rather, it offers an alternative, anecdotal version of Twain's life over which he had virtually no control. (The only major exceptions to the entries in this book are the essays by Paine eventually incorporated into Twain's official biography and the excerpts from biographies of Twain written by two of his daughters.) It is a type of collaborative biography published incrementally over a period of eighty years, with most of the entries recorded by his friends and associates after his death. It gathers dozens of scattered sources about Twain's life and career, illustrating the complexity of his personality in a way no single biographer could; and it offers unsanitized glimpses of Twain, warts and all, with the public mask or facade stripped away. In 1923, for example, the iconoclastic Irish American author Frank Harris offered one of the most damning assessments of Twain's character ever published, which is included in this volume.

In the course of his long career, Mark Twain lost as many friends as he made. He did not suffer fools or rivals gladly, especially if they wore crinoline. He targeted them indiscriminately—from religious leaders (for example, Mary Baker Eddy, John Alexander Dowie, DeWitt Talmadge), to politicians (William McKinley, Tim Sullivan), to fellow writers and lecturers (Bret Harte, Kate Field), to literary pirates (John Camden Hotten), to military leaders (Frederick Funston). He feuded for years with C. C. Duncan, the captain of the *Quaker City,* the ship that carried him and the other "innocents" to Europe and the Holy Land in 1867. Though he and Henry James were both friends with W. D. Howells, neither of them could abide the other's work. James considered Twain vulgar, and, on his part, Twain declared he "would rather be damned to John Bunyan's heaven" than read *The Bostonians* (*Twain-Howells Letters* 534). If he was usually loved in public, he was sometimes loathed in private.

Twain exhibited a normal number of human foibles and contradictions. While *Huck Finn* is generally hailed as a great American novel, Twain also published his share of flops, such as *The American Claimant* (1892) and *Tom Sawyer Abroad* (1894). A consummate performer, he nevertheless co-authored (with Bret Harte) the play *Ah Sin* (1877), the most disastrous collaboration in the history of American letters. Ambitious to succeed, he was notoriously unwise in his investments, thinking the telephone a "wildcat speculation" while backing such inventions as a steam pulley, a carpet-pattern machine, and a powdered food supplement made from eggs called "plasmon." He was a practical joker who was quick to anger whenever he became the butt of a practical joke (Goodwin).† Blessed with an eye for the ironic or absurd, a harsh critic of cant and hypocrisy, he was also a master of poses who was notoriously prickly. A nineteenth-century progressive on most matters of race, he harbored an inexplicable hatred for American Indians. Depending on his mood, he could be either flamboyant or reclusive. He supported socialists and revolutionaries but counted such nabobs as Andrew Carnegie and Henry H. Rogers, vice president of the Standard Oil Company, among his dear friends. He was a popular lecturer who hated lecturing, especially in country villages. Near the end of his life he admitted he should have taken two pseudonyms, one for his humorous writings, the other for his more serious pieces (Harper).†

Few American authors have lived more eventful lives. The first major American writer born west of the Mississippi River, Samuel Clemens (1835–1910) was raised in the village (population 500) of Hannibal in the slave state of Missouri. If, as Herman Melville's Ishmael declares, the whale ship was his Harvard and his Yale, the print shop was Clemens's Princeton and Columbia. After working as a journeyman printer in St. Louis, New York, and Philadelphia, he decided to make his fortune in Brazil but changed his mind en route and learned riverboat piloting instead. When the Civil War destroyed the shipping business, he joined a county militia for two weeks before quitting in disgust because the young soldiers spent all their time drilling. He then joined his brother Orion in a move to the West, specifically Nevada, in 1861. He briefly prospected for gold and silver before beginning to write for local newspapers. "Six months after my entry into journalism," he remembered, "the grand 'flush times' of Silverland began, and they continued with unabated splendor for three years" (*Roughing It* 281). Returning to New York in 1867, he joined the first organized group tour to Europe and the Holy Land. He revised his newspaper reports of this trip into his first important book, *The Innocents Abroad.* Its success enabled him to marry Olivia Langdon, the daughter of a wealthy coal and timber merchant in Elmira, New York. With the financial help of his father-in-law, he bought one-third of a Buffalo newspaper and settled into a comfortable and conventional middle-class life.

But not for long. The routine chafed on him. He sold his share of the *Buffalo Express*; moved to Hartford, where his pre-Webster publisher was located; and launched his literary career in earnest. He finished *Roughing It* (1872); collaborated with his neighbor Charles Dudley Warner on his first novel, *The Gilded Age* (1873); and wrote *The Adventures of Tom Sawyer* (1876), *A Tramp Abroad* (1880), *The Prince and the Pauper* (1882), *Life on the Mississippi* (1883), *Adventures of Huckleberry Finn* (1885), and *A Connecticut Yankee in King Arthur's Court* (1889). Meanwhile, he invested huge amounts of money, as much as $6,000 a week, in a mechanical typesetting machine that was obsolete before it could be perfected. Five years after the publication of *A Connecticut Yankee,* he transferred ownership of his copyrights to his wife, declared personal bankruptcy, and set off on a round-the-world speaking tour to satisfy his creditors.

Though he paid his debts dollar for dollar, the final fifteen years of his life were not particularly happy ones. He was outraged by political developments in Africa and the Philippines, and the genocide by Germans and Belgians and Spanish of native peoples in those parts of the world. He became an outspoken critic of imperialism and an honorary vice president of the American Anti-Imperialist League. During these years, he lapsed into intermittent silence, beginning dozens of stories and novels and plays but rarely completing them. In April 1910, three years after he was awarded an honorary Litt.D. from Oxford University, he died of congestive heart failure at his home in rural Connecticut. He had survived his wife and three of their four children.

The texts reprinted in this volume are from the first printed versions. In preparing them for publication, I have silently corrected the obvious spelling and other typographical errors. In general, I have modernized the texts as little as possible. The complete bibliographical data for each entry is included in a source note following the text. I have indicated with a dagger (†) when a text cited in the introduction has been reprinted in this volume.

As usual, I have depended upon the kindnesses of strangers as well as friends in the compilation of this volume. I want to acknowledge in particular the help of Mark Woodhouse of the Gannett-Tripp Library at Elmira College, and Joe Lane, Frances Lopez, and the other staff in the interlibrary loan office of Zimmerman Library at the University of New Mexico.

The entries in this volume are organized chronologically by events, beginning with memories of Samuel Clemens's boyhood in Hannibal and ending with accounts of his death in 1910. It opens with an interview with his mother, Jane Clemens, perhaps the only one she ever granted, that has never been reprinted from its original appearance in the *Chicago Inter-Ocean*. It is followed by the recollections of Laura Frazier, the model for the character of Becky Thatcher in *The Adventures of Tom Sawyer;* an interview with Horace Bixby, the pilot who taught Twain the Mississippi River; and memoirs by several of the men who knew him while he was "roughing it" in Nevada and California in the 1860s, including Noah Brooks, Dan De Quille, Sam Davis, Joe Goodman, Bret Harte, George Barnes, and Jim Gillis. Twain's own account in *The Innocents Abroad* of the *Quaker City* voyage in 1867 is supplemented by comments reprinted in this volume by Captain Duncan and Twain's honorary "mother," Mary Mason Fairbanks. Also included are memoirs by members of his family: his daughters Susy and Clara; his brother-in-law, Jervis Langdon; his cousin, James Clemens; and the longtime Clemens family maid Katy Leary. Among the reminiscences of his friends and associates reprinted here are those of his two most famous illustrators, Kemble and Beard; several of his editors and publishers (for example, W. D. Howells, Henry M. Alden, Irving Bacheller, J. Henry Harper, George Harvey); his lecture manager James B. Pond; his official biographer and first literary executor Paine; two of his so-called adolescent angelfish (Dorothy Sturgis and Dorothy Quick); politicians (Senator William M. Stewart of Nevada, Congressman Tom Fitch of Nevada, Speaker of the House Joseph Cannon); several literary figures (George Washington Cable, Hamlin Garland, Brander Matthews, Grace King, George Bernard Shaw, George Ade); and some other prominent celebrities (Andrew Carnegie, Helen Keller, Winston Churchill).

Chronology

1823	6 May	Marriage of John Marshall Clemens (b. 1798) and Jane Lampton (b. 1803)
1825	17 July	Birth of Orion Clemens in Jamestown (now Gainesboro), Tennessee
1835	30 November	Birth of Samuel Langhorne Clemens (SLC) in Florida, Missouri
1838	13 July	Birth of Henry Clemens in Florida, Missouri
1839	November	Clemens family moves to Hannibal, Missouri
1840		Attends Hannibal school taught by Elizabeth Horr
1845	27 November	Olivia Susan Langdon born in Elmira, New York
1847	24 March	John Marshall Clemens dies of pneumonia in Hannibal
1848	spring	Begins work as an apprentice for the *Hannibal Courier*
1850	September	Works for brother Orion's *Hannibal Western Union*
1851	September	Orion Clemens buys *Hannibal Journal,* and SLC continues to work for him
1853		Works as a printer in St. Louis, New York, and Philadelphia
1855		Works as a printer for Orion's newspaper in Keokuk, Iowa

1857	March	Becomes a cub pilot on the lower Mississippi River under Horace Bixby
1858	21 June	Henry Clemens dies in Memphis, Tennessee, from burns suffered in the explosion of the steamboat *Pennsylvania* on 13 June
1859	9 April	Receives license to pilot steamboats between St. Louis and New Orleans
1861	June	Joins the Marion Rangers, a group of Confederate sympathizers, for two weeks
	18 July	Leaves for the West with his brother Orion, appointed by Abraham Lincoln to serve as secretary of Nevada Territory
	14 August	Arrives in Carson City, Nevada
1862	July	Joins the staff of the *Virginia City Territorial Enterprise* as a reporter
1863	3 February	First known use of his pseudonym "Mark Twain" in articles written from Carson City for the *Territorial Enterprise*
May		Becomes the Nevada correspondent of the *San Francisco Call*
1864	29 May	Leaves Nevada for California to become a reporter for the *San Francisco Call*
	10 October	Resigns from the *San Francisco Call*
1865	18 November	Publication of "Jim Smiley and His Jumping Frog" in the New York *Saturday Press*
1866	7 March	Sails for the Sandwich Islands as a correspondent for the *Sacramento Union*
	19 July	Leaves the Sandwich Islands to return to San Francisco
	2 October	Delivers his first lecture, on the Sandwich Islands, at Maguire's Academy of Music in San Francisco

	15 December	Leaves California for New York aboard the *America*
1867	12 January	Arrives in New York aboard the *San Francisco*
	30 April	Publication of *The Celebrated Jumping Frog of Calaveras County and Other Sketches,* SLC's first book
	6 May	Delivers his first lecture in the East, on the Sandwich Islands, at Cooper Union in New York
	10 June	Sails for Europe and the Holy Land aboard the *Quaker City*
	19 November	Returns to New York
	22 November	Arrives in Washington, D.C., to become Senator William Stewart's secretary
	27 December	Meets Olivia Langdon in New York
1868	9 January	Delivers his *Quaker City* lecture, "The Frozen Truth," in Washington, D.C.
	11 March	Sails for California to negotiate reprint rights to his fifty *Quaker City* letters originally published in the *San Francisco Alta California*
	2 April	Arrives in San Francisco
	14 April	Delivers his *Quaker City* lecture at Platt's Hall in San Francisco to an audience of over 1,600
	29 July	Arrives back in New York with completed manuscript of *The Innocents Abroad*
	September	First proposes marriage to Olivia Langdon
	26 November	Secretly engaged to Olivia Langdon
1869	4 February	Engagement to Olivia Langdon formally announced
	12 August	Purchases a one-third interest in the *Buffalo Express*

	15 August	Publication of *The Innocents Abroad*
	1 November	Begins to tour with his lecture "Our Fellow Savages of the Sandwich Islands"
1870	21 January	Ends lecture tour in Jamestown, New York
	2 February	SLC and Olivia Langdon (Livy) are married at the Langdon home in Elmira
	3 February	SLC and Livy settle in Buffalo in a house bought for them by Jervis Langdon
	6 August	Death of Jervis Langdon in Elmira
	7 November	Birth of son Langdon Clemens
1871	18 March	Leaves Buffalo for Elmira with Livy seriously ill with typhoid fever
	19 April	Completes the sale of his interest in the *Buffalo Express*
	2/3 October	Settles with his family in Hartford, Connecticut
	16 October	Begins a fall-winter lecture tour in Bethlehem, Pennsylvania
1872	February	Ends his lecture tour in Troy, New York
	29 February	Formal publication of *Roughing It*
	19 March	Birth of Olivia Susan (Susy) Clemens in Elmira
	2 June	Death of Langdon Clemens from diphtheria in Elmira
	21 August	Sails for Liverpool to prepare a proposed (but never completed) travel book about England
	25 November	Arrives back in New York
1873	13 February	Elected to membership in the Lotos Club of New York
	17 May	Sails for England with his family to secure British copyright of *The Gilded Age,* a novel written

		in collaboration with his Hartford neighbor Charles Dudley Warner
	22 June	Dines with Kate Field and Charles Dilke in London
	2 November	Arrives back in New York in company with his family
	8 November	Returns to England alone to await publication there of *The Gilded Age*
	1 December	Begins a three-week lecture season in London, first speaking on the Sandwich Islands and later "Roughing It"
	22 December	British publication of *The Gilded Age*
1874	26 January	Arrives back in Boston
	8 June	Birth of daughter Clara in Elmira
	16 September	New York premiere of SLC's play *The Gilded Age*
	19 September	Moves into his new house in the Nook Farm neighborhood of Hartford
1875	January	Publication of the first of eight installments of "Old Times on the Mississippi" in the *Atlantic Monthly*
	11 January	First performance of *The Gilded Age* in Hartford, starring John T. Raymond and Kate Field; SLC hosts them at lunch
	25 September	Publication of *Mark Twain's Sketches, New and Old*
1876	9 June	Publication of the British edition of *The Adventures of Tom Sawyer*
	8 December	Publication of the American edition of *The Adventures of Tom Sawyer*
1877	7 May	Washington, D.C., premiere of *Ah Sin,* a comic play written in collaboration with Bret Harte

	31 July	New York premiere of *Ah Sin*
	17 December	Delivers his (in)famous Whittier birthday speech at the Brunswick Hotel in Boston on the occasion of John Greenleaf Whittier's seventieth birthday
1878	11 April	Family sails for Europe
	6 May	Family arrives in Heidelberg
	August–November	Family travels through Baden, Switzerland, and Italy before settling in Munich
1879	28 February	Family settles in Paris
	July–August	Family travels through Belgium, Holland, and England
	3 September	Family arrives back in New York
1880	13 March	Publication of *A Tramp Abroad*
	26 July	Birth of daughter Jane Lampton (Jean) Clemens in Hartford
1881	1 December	Publication of *The Prince and the Pauper*
1882	April–May	Tour of Mississippi River valley with J. R. Osgood
1883	17 May	Publication of *Life on the Mississippi*
1884	5 November	Begins the "Twins of Genius" speaking tour with George Washington Cable in New Haven, Connecticut
	10 December	Publication of the British edition of *The Adventures of Huckleberry Finn*
	May	Founds the Charles L. Webster publishing company
1885	16 February	Publication of the American edition of *Adventures of Huckleberry Finn*
	28 February	Concludes the "Twins of Genius" tour, after 103 performances, in Washington, D.C.

	March	Removal of *Huckleberry Finn* from the shelves of the Concord Free Public Library for vulgarity
	December	Publication of "The Private History of a Campaign That Failed" in the *Century*
	1 December	Webster Co. issues first volume of Grant's *Memoirs*
1886	28 January	Testifies before Congress regarding international copyright
	February	Forms partnership with James Paige to produce an automated typesetter
1888	27 June	Awarded an honorary M.A. by Yale University
1889	August	Interviewed by Rudyard Kipling in Elmira
	10 December	American publication of *A Connecticut Yankee in King Arthur's Court*
1890	27 October	Jane Lampton Clemens (SLC's mother) dies in Keokuk; SLC attends her funeral in Hannibal on 30 October
	28 November	Olivia Lewis Langdon (Livy's mother) dies in Elmira
1891	6 June	Family sails for Europe after closing the house in Hartford
1892	20 February	SLC the guest of honor at a dinner hosted by Kaiser Wilhelm II in Berlin
	June–July	Travels to New York and Chicago to supervise his business interests
	September	Family settles near Florence, Italy
1893	22 March	Departs for New York and Chicago to oversee his business interests
	late May	Returns to Italy
	28 June	Family settles in Munich

	7 September	Returns to New York to oversee his business interests
1894	7 March	Sails for Europe to rejoin his family
	14 April	Returns to New York to declare the failure of his publishing company
	9 May	Returns to Paris to rejoin his family
	14 July	Returns to New York to oversee his business interests
	15 August	Sails for Europe on the *Paris* to rejoin his family in Normandy
	late November	Publication of *The Tragedy of Pudd'nhead Wilson*
1895	23 February	Sails for New York to arrange anonymous serial publication of *Personal Recollections of Joan of Arc* in *Harper's*
	4 April	Rejoins his family in France
	18 May	Arrives back in the United States with his family and repairs to Elmira
	15 July	First lecture in his round-the-world tour in Cleveland
	17 August	Publicly acknowledges his personal bankruptcy
	23 August	Embarks with Livy and Clara from Vancouver, B.C., for Australia
	16 September	Arrives in Sydney, Australia
	30 October	Sails for New Zealand
	17 December	Returns to Sydney
1896	14 January	Arrives in Colombo, Ceylon
	18 January	Arrives in Bombay, India
	25 March	Arrives in Calcutta
	15 April	Arrives in Mauritius

	6 May	Arrives in Durban, South Africa
	26 May	Meets Paul Kruger (aka "Oom Paul"), president of the South African Republic, to appeal for leniency for the Jameson Raiders
	31 July	Arrives in Southampton, England
	18 August	Daughter Susy dies of spinal meningitis in Hartford
	1 September	Receives news in England of Susy's death
1897	late July	Family repairs to Lake Lucerne, Switzerland
	28 September	Family arrives in Vienna, Austria
	November	Publication of *Following the Equator,* his final travel book
	11 December	Orion Clemens dies in Keokuk
1898	26 May	Family leaves Vienna for summer house in Kaltenleutgeben, Austria
1899	25 May	Received by Franz Josef, emperor of Austria and king of Hungary
	26 May	Leaves Vienna with his family for London
	mid-July	Family leaves London to travel in Scandinavia
	15 October	Returns with his family to London
1900	March	Invests $12,500 in plasmon, a food supplement
	15 October	Returns with his family to New York, where he takes a house at 14 West Tenth Street
	12 December	Introduces Winston Churchill before Churchill's first speech in New York
1901	21 June	Leaves New York with his family to summer in the Adirondacks
	October	Moves to Riverdale, New York
	23 October	Awarded an honorary Litt.D. by Yale University

	29 October	Introduces Seth Low, reform candidate for mayor of New York, at a campaign rally
1902	April	Buys a house in Tarrytown, New York
	29 May	Arrives in St. Louis and Hannibal on his final visit to Missouri
	4 June	Receives an honorary Doctor of Laws degree from the University of Missouri in Columbia
	8 June	Leaves St. Louis to return to New York
	24 June	Leaves Tarrytown to spend the summer in York Harbor, Maine
1903	22 October	Sells rights to all his books to Harper & Bros. in exchange for a minimum of $25,000 over five years
	24 October	Sails for Florence, Italy, in hopes Livy will recover her health
1904	5 June	Olivia Langdon Clemens dies in the Villa di Quarto near Florence
	28 June	Sails with Livy's body from Naples for New York aboard the *Prince Oskar*
	14 July	Livy buried in the family plot in Woodlawn Cemetery, Elmira
	summer	Vacations in the Berkshires
	August	Moves into a house at 21 Fifth Avenue, New York
1905	summer	Vacations with daughter Jean and his secretary, Isabel Lyon, in Dublin, New Hampshire
	5 December	Marks his seventieth birthday with a public celebration at Delmonico's in New York
1906	January	Anoints Albert Bigelow Paine his official biographer
	8 April	Meets H. G. Wells

	May	Returns to Dublin, New Hampshire, for the summer
	June	Publication of *Eve's Diary Translated from the Original Manuscript*
	August	Anonymous publication of *What Is Man?*
	September	The first of twenty-six monthly installments of his autobiography in the *North American Review*
	mid December	Lobbies Congress and President Theodore Roosevelt on behalf of international copyright
1907	2 January	Travels to Bermuda with Isabel Lyon and Joseph Twichell
	9 January	Arrives back in New York aboard the *Bermudian*
	16 January	Hosts a dinner for Helen Keller
	2 May	Attends the naval review at Jamestown, Virginia, with Henry H. Rogers; the same day SLC learns by telegram he has been awarded an honorary Litt.D. by Oxford University
	10 May	Addresses the Maryland House of Delegates while on a visit to Baltimore
	8 June	Sails for England with Ralph Ashcroft, his business adviser
	18 June	Arrives in London; meets George Bernard Shaw
	22 June	Guest of honor at a reception hosted by King Edward VII and Queen Alexandra at Windsor Castle
	25 June	Guest of honor at a dinner of the Pilgrim Club at the Savoy Hotel in London
	26 June	Receives the Litt.D. at Oxford

	22 July	Arrives back in New York aboard the *Minnetonka* after befriending Dorothy Quick en route
	15 November	Dorothy Quick visits him at his home in Tuxedo Park, New York
1908	22 February	Travels to Bermuda for his health with Henry H. Rogers
	13 April	Arrives back in New York aboard the *Bermudian* after befriending Dorothy Sturgis en route
	18 June	Moves into his new house near Redding, Connecticut, later christened "Stormfield"
	18 September	Redding house is burglarized
	13 October	Laura Frazer visits him in Redding
1909	18 March	Isabel Lyon and Ralph Ashcroft, his business manager, wed in New York
	April	Dismisses Lyon and Ashcroft, whom he believes have been cheating him
	6 October	Marriage of daughter Clara and the composer and musician Ossip Gabrilowitsch at Stormfield
	18 November	Travels to Bermuda for his health with Albert Bigelow Paine
	20 December	Arrives back in New York aboard the *Bermudian*
	24 December	Daughter Jean dies at Stormfield after suffering a seizure while bathing
1910	5 January	Travels to Bermuda for his health with Claude Beuchotte, his butler
	14 April	Arrives back in New York near death
	21 April	Dies of congestive heart failure at Stormfield

23 April   Funeral at Brick Presbyterian Church in New
                    York

24 April   Buried in the family plot in Woodlawn Cem-
                    etery, Elmira

"Mark Twain's Boyhood:
An Interview with Mrs. Jane Clemens" (1885)

ANONYMOUS

Samuel Langhorne Clemens, aka Mark Twain, was born in a cabin near Florida, Missouri, on 30 November 1835 and at the age of four moved with his slaveholding family thirty miles northeast to the port village of Hannibal on the Mississippi River. There his father, John Marshall Clemens, kept a store and served as a justice of the peace before dying of pneumonia in 1847 at the age of forty-eight. His widow, Jane Lampton Clemens (1803–90), lived in her later years with her oldest son, Orion (1825–97), and his wife, Mollie (1834–1904), in Keokuk, Iowa. "She was of a sunshine disposition," her son Sam remembered, "and her long life was mainly a holiday for her. She always had the heart of a young girl. Through all of the family troubles she maintained a kind of perky stoicism which was lighted considerably by her love of gossip, gaudy spectacles like parades and funerals, bright colors, and animals" (Skandera Trombley, *Company of Women,* 14). In 1885 she granted what is her only known interview on the subject of her famous son's hardscrabble boyhood.

IN AN UNPRETENTIOUS two-story brick dwelling, at the intersection of High and Seventh streets, Keokuk, Iowa, lives Orion Clemens and his wife. . . . With them resides Mr. Clemens's mother, who will be 82 years of age next June. The writer, being stranded in Keokuk for a few hours, improved the opportunity to make a call upon the venerable lady, and in the course of an hour's pleasant conversation, which followed, received from her lips many anecdotes concerning her most noted son, which will be new to the generality of readers.

"Sam was always a good-hearted boy," said Mrs. Clemens, "but he was a very wild and mischievous one, and do what we would we could never make him go to school. This used to trouble his father and me dreadfully, and we were convinced that he would never amount to as much in the world as his brothers, because he was not near so steady and sober-minded as they were."

"I suppose, Mrs. Clemens, that your son in his boyhood days somewhat resembled his own Tom Sawyer, and that a fellow feeling is what made him so kind to the many hair-breadth escapades of that celebrated youth?"

"Ah, no," replied the old lady with a merry twinkle in her eye. "He was more like Huckleberry Finn than Tom Sawyer. Often his father would start him off to school and in a little while would follow him to ascertain his whereabouts. There was a large stump on the way to the schoolhouse, and Sam would take his position behind that and as his father went past would gradually circle around it in such a way as to keep out of sight. Finally his father and the teacher both said it was of no use to try to teach Sam anything, because he was determined not to learn. But I never gave up. He was always a great boy for history and could never get tired of that kind of reading, but he hadn't any use for schoolhouses and textbooks."

"It must have been a great trial to you."

"Indeed it was," rejoined the mother, "and when Sam's father died, which occurred when Sam was 11 years of age, I thought then, if ever, was the proper time to make a lasting impression on the boy and work a change in him, so I took him by the hand and went with him into the room where the coffin was and in which the father lay, and with it between Sam and me I said to him that here in this presence I had some serious requests to make of him, and that I knew his word once given was never broken. For Sam never told a falsehood. He turned his streaming eyes upon me and cried out, 'Oh, mother, I will do anything, anything you ask of me except to go to school; I can't do that!' That was the very request I was going to make. Well, we afterward had a sober talk, and I concluded to let him go into a printing office to learn the trade, as I couldn't have him running wild. He did so, and has gradually picked up enough education to enable him to do about as well as those who were more studious in early life. He was about 20 years old when he went on the Mississippi as a pilot. I gave him up then, for I always thought steamboating was a wicked business, and was sure he would meet bad associates. I asked him if he would promise me on the Bible not to touch intoxicating liquors, nor swear, and he said, 'Yes, mother, I will.' He repeated the words after me, with my hand and his clasped on the holy book, and I believe he always kept that promise. But Sam has a good wife now who would soon bring him back if he was

[2]

inclined to stray away from the right. He obtained for his brother Henry a place on the same boat as clerk, and soon after Sam left the river Henry was blown up with the boat by an explosion and killed."[1]

The dear old lady gave me the last reminiscences in a trembling voice and with eyes filled with tears, but in a moment recovered her wonted serenity of expression and told many more incidents and entertaining stories of the then embryo humorist of which my memory is not sufficiently accurate to enable me to reliably reproduce, though the general idea will always remain in my mind as an indelible photograph of Mark Twain, not as the world knows him, but as he was and is to the mother whose idol he evidently is, and whose strong good sense and wise counsel in his youth undoubtedly has contributed largely to his success. Mrs. Clemens, aside from a deafness which necessitates the use of an ear trumpet, is well preserved and sprightly for her years.

Mark Twain inherited the humor and the talents which have made him famous from his mother, stated the younger Mrs. Clemens. "He is all 'Lampton,'" and resembles her as strongly in person as in mind. Tom Sawyer's Aunt Polly and Mrs. Hawkins in *Gilded Age* are direct portraits of his mother.

Mrs. Clemens was Miss Jane Lampton before her marriage, and was a native of Kentucky. Mr. Clemens was of the F.F.V.'s of Virginia.[2] They did not accumulate property, and the father left the family at his death nothing but, in Mark's own words, "a sumptuous stock of pride and a good old name," which, it will be allowed, has proved in this case at least a sufficient inheritance.

Notes

1. Twain's youngest brother, Henry Clemens (b. 1838), was a so-called mud clerk or purser's assistant on the steamboat *Pennsylvania* when its boiler exploded on 13 June 1858. Henry died of his burns eight days later in Memphis, Tennessee, with his brother Sam at his side.

2. Twain's paternal grandparents had lived in Campbell County and Mason County, Virginia, in the early nineteenth century and so were among the "First Families of Virginia."

Anonymous, "Mark Twain's Boyhood: An Interview with Mrs. Jane Clemens," *Chicago Inter-Ocean,* 5 April 1885, III 17.

"Mark Twain's Childhood Sweetheart Recalls Their Romance" (1918)

[Laura Frazier]

> Anna Laura Hawkins Frazier (1837–1938), whose name is sometimes spelled "Frazer" like it is in the following piece, was the model for the character of Becky Thatcher in *The Adventures of Tom Sawyer* (1876). She reminisced about their childhood in Hannibal some seventy-five years after Sam and Laura attended Samuel Cross's frame schoolhouse on the square and Elizabeth Horr (d. 1873) "taught the children in a small log house at the southern end of Main street" (Neider 31–32).

"YES, I WAS THE Becky Thatcher of Mr. Clemens's book," Mrs. Frazer said the other day as she sat in the big second-floor parlor of the old-time mansion in Hannibal, which is now the Home for the Friendless. Mrs. Frazer is the matron of the home.

"Of course I suspected it when I first read *The Adventures of Tom Sawyer*," she went on. "There were so many incidents which I recalled as happening to Sam Clemens and myself that I felt he had drawn a picture of his memory of me in the character of Judge Thatcher's little daughter. But I never confided my belief to anyone. I felt that it would be a presumption to take the honor to myself.

"There were other women who had no such scruples—some of them right here in Hannibal—and they attempted to gain a little reflected notoriety by asserting that they were the prototypes of the character. When Albert Bigelow Paine, Mr. Clemens's biographer, gathered the material for his life of the author he found no fewer than twenty-five women in Missouri and elsewhere, each of whom declared she was Becky Thatcher, but he settled the controversy for all time on Mr. Clemens's authority when the biography was published. In it you will find that Becky Thatcher was Laura Hawkins, which was my maiden name.[1]

[4]

"We were boy and girl sweethearts, Sam Clemens and I," Mrs. Frazer said with a gentle little laugh.

It was seventy years ago that her friendship with Mark Twain began, and her hair is gray. But her heart is young, and she finds in her work of mothering the twenty-five boys and girls in her charge the secret of defying age. On this particular afternoon she wore black-and-white striped silk, the effect of which was a soft gray to match her hair, and her placid face was lighted with smiles of reminiscence.

"Children are wholly unartificial, you know," she explained. "They do not learn to conceal their feelings until they begin to grow up. The court-ship of childhood, therefore, is a matter of preference and of comradeship. I liked Sam better than the other boys, and he liked me better than the other girls, and that was all there was to it. . . .

"I must have been six or seven years old when we moved to Hannibal," Mrs. Frazer said. "My father had owned a big mill and a store and a planta-tion worked by many negro slaves farther inland, but he found the task of managing all too heavy for him, and so he bought a home in Hannibal and was preparing to move to it when he died. My mother left the mill and the plantation in the hands of my grown brothers—I was one of ten children, by the way—and came to Hannibal. Our house stood at the corner of Hill and Main streets, and just a few doors west, on Hill Street, lived the Clem-ens family.

"I think I must have liked Sam Clemens the very first time I saw him. He was different from the other boys. I didn't know then, of course, what it was that made him different, but afterward, when my knowledge of the world and its people grew, I realized that it was his natural refinement. He played hooky from school, he cared nothing at all for his books, and he was guilty of all sorts of mischievous pranks, just as Tom Sawyer is in the book, but I never heard a coarse word from him in all our childhood acquaintance.

"Hannibal was a little town which hugged the steamboat landing in those days. If you will go down through the old part of the city now you will find it much as it was when I was a child, for the quaint old weather-beaten buildings still stand, proving how thoroughly the pioneers did their work. We went to school, we had picnics, we explored the big cave—they call it the Mark Twain Cave now,[2] you know."

In response to a query as to whether the story of the two children being lost in the cave were a record of actual fact, Mrs. Frazer replied in the negative. That is part of the fiction of the book, but the description of the cave is real enough—

"As a matter of fact, some older persons always went with us. Usually my elder sister and Sam Clemens's elder sister,[3] who were great friends, were along to see that we didn't get lost among the winding passages where our candles lighted up the great stalagmites and stalactites, and where water was dripping from the stone roof overhead, just as Mr. Clemens has described it."

Then she went on to explain that the "little red schoolhouse" was also one of the great humorist's interpolations, picturesque, but non-existent in her childhood days in Hannibal.

"In those early days we had only private schools," Mrs. Frazer said. "If there were public schools I never heard of them. The first school I went to was taught by Mr. Cross, who had canvassed the town and obtained perhaps twenty-five private pupils at a stated price for the tuition of each. I do not know how much Mr. Cross charged, but when I was older I remember that a young woman teacher opened a school after getting twenty-five pupils at $25 each for the year's tuition. I will never forget that Mr. Cross did not belie his name, however, or that Sam Clemens wrote a bit of doggerel about him."

She quoted it this way:

> Cross by name and Cross by nature,
> Cross hopped out of an Irish potato.

"The schoolhouse was a two-story frame-building with a gallery across the entire front," she resumed. "After a year together in that school Sam and I went to the school taught by Mrs. Horr. It was then he used to write notes to me and bring apples to school and put them on my desk. And once, as a punishment for some prank, he had to sit with the girls and occupied a vacant seat by me. He didn't seem to mind the penalty at all," Mrs. Frazer added with another laugh, "so I don't know whether it was effective as a punishment or not.

"We hadn't reached the dancing age then, but we went to many 'play parties' together and romped through 'Going to Jerusalem,' 'King William was King George's Son,' and 'Green Grow the Rushes—O.'"

She then told of the causes that led to the breaking off of the friendship between the two families and brought about the parting of the ways for Becky and Tom—

"Judge Clemens, Sam's father, died and left the family in straitened circumstances, and Sam's schooling ended there. He began work in the printing-office to help out and when he was seventeen or eighteen he left Hannibal to go to work in St. Louis. He never returned to live, but he visited here often in the years that followed."

Notes

1. In *Mark Twain: A Biography*, 68, Albert Bigelow Paine (1861–1937), Twain's authorized biographer, asserted unequivocally: "Becky Thatcher in the book was Laura Hawkins in reality."

2. Virtually everything known about McDowell's Cave, two miles below Hannibal and named for the St. Louis physician who owned it, appears in three sources. In chapter 29 of *Tom Sawyer*, Twain refers to the "vast labyrinth of crooked aisles" of the cave that "ran into each other and out again and led nowhere." The "massive oaken door" to the cave entrance routinely "stood unbarred," permitting visitors to explore at their whim and, as in the case of Tom and Becky Thatcher, to become lost (204). Twain reminisced in chapter 55 of *Life on the Mississippi* about the cave amid the bluffs downstream from Hannibal, and in his autobiographical dictation Twain remembered that the cave was "an uncanny place," with its "tangled wilderness of narrow and lofty clefts and passages" (*Mark Twain's Own Autobiography* 117).

3. Pamela Clemens Moffett (1827–1904).

[Laura Frazier], "Mark Twain's Childhood Sweetheart Recalls Their Romance," *Literary Digest*, 23 March 1918, 70, 73–75.

"Mark Twain as a Cub Pilot:
A Talk with Captain Horace Bixby" (1899)

HOMER BASSFORD

After working as a journeyman printer in St. Louis, New York, and Philadelphia, Twain embarked from Cincinnati aboard the steamboat *Paul Jones* on
16 February 1857, intending to sail to Brazil to seek his fortune. (Though he
later derided the steamer as an "ancient tub" in *Life on the Mississippi* [70], it
had in fact been launched only two years earlier.) Rather than travel to South
America, he soon asked the pilot, Horace Bixby (1826–1912), to take him on
as an apprentice and teach him the river. Before the boat arrived in New Orleans on 28 February, the two men had reached an agreement. Twain worked
for Bixby as a cub pilot for the next several months, a period he chronicled in
his series of essays "Old Times on the Mississippi" (January–August 1875).
On his part, Bixby was interviewed about his "cub" over forty years later.

CAPTAIN HORACE BIXBY, hard upon seventy years of age, is a pilot on the
Mississippi River. For half a century he has held the wheels on this and
other navigable streams in the West. Today he is quite as good a pilot
as he was twenty-five years ago. . . . In 1856—it may have been 1857—
Captain Bixby was in charge of the pilot-house of the *Paul Jones,* which
plied between Cincinnati and New Orleans. One day, as the boat was about
to leave Cincinnati, a tall young man, stooped of shoulders and shaggy as
to hair, stumbled up into the pilot-house and took a seat on the big bench at
the back. Pilots, as a rule, are not especially communicative. In those days
Captain Bixby was particularly slow to begin a conversation with his passengers. After the boat had steamed several miles on her muddy course the
young stranger began to talk. He asked twenty-five questions before Bixby
turned around. At length he got an audience by observing:

"I think I'd like to learn your trade."

"We hear that a good many times," replied Captain Bixby.

"But I'm in earnest," the young man continued.

"Are you in earnest enough to pay?" the pilot asked.

"I reckon. How much will you charge?"

"Well, in the first place, who are you?" inquired Bixby, his foot on the wheel, his eye squinting at the young man.

"My name's Samuel Clemens," the youth said, "and I'm a printer by trade."

"And where are you going?"

"I've started for Central America for my health, but I've thought I'd like to see how steamboating would go. There might be some health in that."

Captain Bixby asked Clemens to come over and stand by his side for a while. The young man from Missouri continued to talk, telling stories and making a running comment that was pleasing to the hearty, brusque pilot of the *Paul Jones*.

"That's a funny way you've got of pulling out your words," he said finally.

"Yaas!" Clemens responded. "Yaas, I reckon; but my maw, she pulls hers out, too."

"We were fast friends after that," Captain Bixby said, as he finished the story. "Later I met young Sam's mother; and, sure enough, there was the drawl, exactly as the boy had it."

Only a few weeks ago, on the Steamer [*Horatio G.*] *Wright*'s clean decks, Captain Bixby recounted the conversation here given.

"This is the bargain I drove with him," he said. "I told the boy that I would teach him the Mississippi River from St. Louis to New Orleans for five hundred dollars, not to include his expenses, except for meals on board. In port he was to look out for himself. Pilots were not particularly anxious to get cubs just then—they were more trouble than they were worth. When a steersman was needed there was no trouble to find one. Steamboating was a popular business in those days. Clemens said that he'd think it over, and I saw that he was very much in earnest. In fact, it was clear to me that he meant to learn the river. I liked him, and the more he talked the more anxious I got for him to try his hand. It was my custom, in taking what was called a cub, to ask questions affecting character and conduct. After I had learned all about the Clemens family—which was a good one, by the way (very old American stock, if I recollect)—I asked:

"'Do you drink?'

"'No-o.'

"'Do you swear much?'

"'Not very much.'

"'And do you chew?'

"'No—but I've got to smoke,' he answered, quicker than I ever heard him say any other thing. When I asked him what he thought of my offer he said:

"'Well, you see, I haven't got five hundred dollars in money. I might raise one hundred dollars, and if you'd take that much cash I would turn in one thousand acres of Tennessee land at twenty-five cents an acre. I don't know exactly where the land is, but I've got it.'[1]

"Well, I didn't want the real estate, but after a few days we drew up a contract. Clemens paid one hundred dollars in money. In six months he was to pay seventy-five dollars more. At the end of the year another seventy-five dollars, and the rest when he got his license. I have never seen that contract since the day it was signed. I put Sam to work right away. In all my time I never knew a man who took to the labor of piloting with so little effort. He was born for it, just as some men are born to make poetry and some to paint pictures.

"The next spring I planned to go up the Missouri River. I knew that I could make a lot more money in the mountain trade, and as Clemens had not wanted to learn the Missouri, I struck a new bargain with him and turned the teaching job over to a pilot named Brown, on the *Pennsylvania,* with Captain Klinefelter.[2]

"Clemens kept on improving, and from one boat he went to another, getting better all the time. Not very long after he left the *Pennsylvania* she blew up. Among the lives lost was that of one of Clemens's brothers, who was a clerk on board. After that Clemens was on the *Aleck Scott* and the *Falls City,* learning fast. It was on the *Alonzo Child,*[3] if I am not mistaken, that he was first employed as a full pilot. This was in the spring of 1859. In the same year he was my partner, although I was in charge. His pay, then, the first he earned as a regularly licensed officer, was two hundred dollars a month. His license was dated April 9, 1859, and was issued at St. Louis by Inspectors J. H. McCord and Henry Singleton. You can bet that Clemens was proud of it. In those days he did not use his middle name. I remember that the license merely said that 'Samuel Clemens was entitled to steer.' The license was renewed in March 1860 and again in the same month of 1861.

"After that my pilot went West. He had tasted a bit of the difficulties of war; blockades were to be run, and hazard was to take the place of another charm the river had. If I am not mistaken, I saw, down at Jefferson Barracks, just below St. Louis, some evidence of Clemens's war risks. His boat's smokestacks had bullet-holes in them—and the Civil War had only begun."

Captain Horace Bixby is one of the youngest old men I have ever seen. He is as spry as a boy of fifteen. If he wears glasses the fact is not generally known. Certainly he uses no such aid when steering his big steamboat. The day is never too gray, the night never too dark for his steady, blue eyes. In the old times of steamboating Captain Bixby was called a daring man.

"They said I was foolhardy," he remarked to me the other day; "but I was always sure of myself. Certainly I should have lost many a boat if it had not been so. I have many times brought my vessel through difficult places on bad nights when other Captains were tied to the bank; but the risk never seemed great. I always felt that it was the duty of a pilot to pilot. If ever such work is needed it is when the way is difficult. When I learned the river I had this feeling, and when I taught the river to others I always insisted upon the same thing. Mark Twain (the Sam Clemens as we knew him) was a good pilot. He was sure of himself and a safe man for his owners. I have heard men say that Clemens never held a license, that he was a mere steersman, but I am here to say that there was no better man of his years and experience on all the great Mississippi. If he had an accident I never heard of it, and if he ever wanted for a good professional name there is no record of it in the Government's books up at the customhouse."

At the veteran pilot's suggestion I walked with him to the inspector's office, and there we found, in a volume of filled-in blanks, the pilot license of Samuel Clemens, yellow in its forty years. Captain Bixby almost danced about the room as he talked about his famous "cub."

"There never was a better boy," he said. "He was bound to be great, whatever his course in life. I believe that he would have owned a line of steamboats had he kept to the river."

Notes

1. John Marshall Clemens purchased a tract of some 75,000 acres in Fentress County, Tennessee, for $400 in about 1830.

2. William Brown (d. 1858), pilot of the *Pennsylvania,* was killed in the same explosion that killed Henry Clemens. John S. Kleinfelter or Klinefelter (1810–85) was the captain of the steamboat when Twain served aboard it from 27 September until 26 November 1857, and from 17 February until 5 June 1858 (*Life on the Mississippi* 217–45).

3. Twain served aboard the *New Falls City* from 30 October until 8 December 1858; aboard the *Aleck Scott* from 13 December 1858 until 8 April 1859; and aboard the *Alonzo Child* from 19 September 1860 until 8 May 1861.

Homer Bassford, "Mark Twain as a Cub Pilot: A Talk with Captain Horace Bixby," *Saturday Evening Post,* 16 December 1899, 515.

"Mark Twain" (1878)

GRANT MARSH

> From 26 October 1859 until 24 February 1860 Twain piloted the *A. B. Chambers No. 2*. Grant Marsh (ca. 1834–1916), the first mate, reminisced years later about Twain's courage in a crisis. When the steamboat went aground north of Cairo, Illinois, where the Ohio and Mississippi rivers converge, Twain braved ice floes to lead a party scavenging for fuel. Less than a year earlier, he had recounted a similar experience in a letter to Orion and Mollie Clemens (*Mark Twain's Letters* 1:76–79).

"OH, YES! I knew Sam Clemens. I was on the boat *A. B. Chambers* with him the winter I was married, in '59 and '60. Sam was pilot and I was mate. He was not a great pilot, but he was a brave fellow. He didn't know what fear was. He never smiled, but was joking whenever he got a good chance. I believe he once saved my life, his own, and six others. Our steamer was lying above Cairo on a sandbar. We were out of wood and the captain ordered Sam, me, and the six roustabouts to get in a yawl and row up the river and bring down a flatboat loaded with wood. The river was full of floating lee. We rowed up on the opposite bank from the flatboat. The ice was running almost solid, with an occasional opening by the ice blocking up. We took advantage of these openings to shoot across the river. When we got into the channel a short distance I saw the danger we were encountering. The ice was liable to close in on us and drown the whole outfit. I appealed to Sam to row back. There was an opening in the rear. Sam resolutely: 'No.' In another minute the ice broke in the path behind the boat and crushed by with terrific force. Had we turned back when I suggested it, we would have been 'goners,' every mother's son of us. Sam's judgment was not questioned again on that trip."

Grant Marsh, "Mark Twain," *St. Louis Missouri Republican*, 8 December 1878, 7.

"Fitch Recalls Mark Twain
in Bonanza Times" (1919)

Tom Fitch

> In June 1861, after the start of the Civil War effectively ended steamboat traf-
> fic on the Mississippi River, Twain helped to organize the Marion Rangers, a
> home militia consisting of his Hannibal friends and classmates. He recorded
> a fictionalized version of his two-week stint as a soldier in "The Private His-
> tory of a Campaign That Failed," *Century* 31 (December 1885): 193–204. Tom
> Fitch (1838–1923), a future U.S. representative from Nevada (1869–71), often
> reminisced in later years about his famous friend.

MARK TWAIN DID NOT enlist in the Confederate service, as was erroneously
stated in a biography of him. At the outbreak of the war he joined a home
guard company which was raised in Hannibal, Mo., and became its Captain. This company was, as a part of the State militia, subject to the orders
of the Governor of Missouri. That official was a rebel, while the Lieutenant-
Governor was a Unionist. This Governor issued an order to the Home
Guard regiment at Hannibal to report for duty to the rebel Governor Price,[1]
whose forces were in Southern Missouri. Before this order reached Hannibal, the Governor, on account of the near approach of a Federal force to the
capital, fled to a point within the Confederate lines, and the Lieutenant-
Governor took charge.

The acting Governor[2] immediately sent an order to the Colonel of the
Home Guard at Hannibal to report for duty with his regiment to the Federal Governor at St. Louis. The fleeing Governor, being advised of this,
attempted, notwithstanding his absence from the State capital, to still exercise executive powers, and he sent to Hannibal another order directing
that the Home Guard be mustered into the Confederate service.

The three orders reached Hannibal within a day or two of each other
and were made public. Sam Clemens thereupon wrote a note to the Colo-

[14]

nel of the regiment saying: "Sir, I respectfully resign my membership of and my commission as Captain of Company B. Hannibal Home Guard. I am perfectly willing to fight for either the United States or the Confederacy, but this damned uncertainty as to which side I am on is killing me with anxiety. With assurances of my high consideration, I am, respectfully yours, etc."

Mark said: "I was troubled in my conscience a little, for I had enlisted, and was not clear as to my lawful right to disenlist. But I remembered that one of the conditions of joining was that the members of the guard should not be required to leave their home towns except in cases of invasion of the State by an enemy. The Confederate forces had invaded Southwest Missouri. I saw at once that in accordance with the terms of enlistment I was required to leave the State, and I left at once by the overland route for Nevada, of which territory my brother, Orion Clemens, had been appointed Secretary."[3]

Notes

1. H. Sterling Price (1809–67), governor of Missouri from 1853 to 1857, four years before the start of the Civil War.

2. Claiborne Fox Jackson (1806–62) was the governor of Missouri from January to August 1861. Jackson then served as first Confederate governor, replaced by Hamilton Rowan Gamble (1798–1864), who served as governor of the provisional state government from August 1861 until January 1864.

3. Orion Clemens was appointed by President Abraham Lincoln to the position of secretary of Nevada Territory in March 1861.

Tom Fitch, "Fitch Recalls Mark Twain in Bonanza Times," *San Francisco Chronicle*, 30 March 1919, 6F.

From *As I Remember Them* (1913)

C. C. GOODWIN

In July 1861 Twain left with his brother for the West, where he remained for the next five years. Twain tried mining in the Comstock, without much success, between the fall of 1861 and the summer of 1862. In July 1862, after writing a few squibs for local newspapers, Twain was offered a job by William H. Barstow as city editor of the *Virginia City Territorial Enterprise* at a salary of $25 a week. The co-owner and editor in chief, Joseph T. Goodman (1838–1917), and one of his co-workers, William H. Wright, aka Dan De Quille (1829–98), a popular western humorist and journalist, soon became two of his closest friends. In his autobiography, the Nevada journalist and jurist Charles Carroll Goodwin (1832–1917), editor of the *Washoe Times*, sketched Twain at this period of his life.

THE FIRST I EVER heard of him in Nevada was after the territory was organized. James W. Nye of New York[1] (the famous Nye) was appointed governor and Orion Clemens, a brother of Mark Twain, was appointed secretary of the territory. . . . With Nye, when he came from New York, came a young man named Robert Howland.[2] He was one of those "Don't-care-a-cent" young men, ready for any lark, afraid of nothing in the world; jolly, cordial, a man for men to like at first sight and for women to be charmed with. He and Mark Twain soon contracted a friendship for each other, and when the news came in from Aurora, one hundred miles south of Carson, of the great discoveries in that camp, these two men formed a partnership and in some way got to Aurora. There they bought or built a rude cabin and passed the cold winter therein. Years later Bob used to tell that in that bleak winter it was the wont of Mark Twain and himself to go out at night, steal the empty fruit cans, oyster cans, empty champagne bottles and bottles that once held booze from the rear of saloons and boarding houses, carry and put them up in the rear of their own cabin to give it an opulent look, that passersby in the daylight might say, "My, but those fellows must be flush with money!"

[16]

As the Fourth of July grew near, Mark wrote a Fourth of July oration, signed it "Mark Twain,"[3] and sent it to the local paper, in which it was copied. It began with the words, "I was sired by the great American Eagle and borne by a continental dam." This struck the fancy of Joseph T. Goodman, the owner and editor of the *Territorial Enterprise* in Virginia City, and he wrote to Mark that if he was not making more money mining than he would as local reporter on the *Enterprise,* he would hold a place for him. A few days later, when Mr. Goodman was entertaining some friends in the sanctum, a man walked in, shod in stogy shoes, wearing Kentucky jean pants, a hickory shirt, and a straw hat, all very much travel worn, and in addition had a roll of ancient blankets on one shoulder. He shrugged that shoulder, dropped the blankets, and staring from one man to another, finally drawled out, "My name is Clemens." That was Mark's introduction to real journalism in Nevada. . . .

That coming to the *Enterprise* was the making of Mark Twain. I doubt very much whether he ever would have been famous at all except for his experience there. He found an atmosphere different from what he ever dreamed of being in. The office was filled with bright young men, the town was filled with bright men. There he saw men that had made fortunes quickly, others who were trying to make fortunes quickly, and he saw other men who never had fortunes and never expected them. And he would hear them rail at the millionaires and say that the fact that they had money was a sure sign of how little God thought of money, judging by the men he gave it to. R. M. Daggett was on the *Enterprise,*[4] and from his example he learned that when it was necessary to call a man names, there were no expletives too long or too expressive to be hurled in rapid succession to emphasize the utter want to character of the man assailed. Dan De Quille was working with him, too. He used to write famous stories on almost any subject, and he knew all about the gift of using adjectives. It was contagious in that office. It reached to the composing room. There were typesetters who could hurl anathemas at bad copy which would have frightened a Bengal tiger. The news editor could damn a mutilated dispatch in twenty-four languages. . . .

That was the character of society that Mark was introduced to, and outside there were the brightest lawyers, doctors, and the shrewdest men of affairs in the world, and Mark got pointers from them all. If he wrote a good thing they would praise him and tell him to keep on, that there was something in him sure. If Homer nodded with him sometimes[5] they would hold him up to scorn the next day; but he noticed through all that nothing was too extravagant for them in the way of description, and nothing too fine.

Mark Twain did not like a joke a bit if he was the victim. The boys of the *Enterprise* office made him a formal presentation of a meerschaum pipe. He was exceedingly pleased, but when he found the next day that he could buy any number of such pipes at $1.50 each, it filled his soul with a desire to murder somebody, and he did not outgrow the feeling for a month. . . .

He was in San Francisco when that city suffered a severe shock of earthquake. It happened one Sabbath morning about ten o'clock and Mark wrote a description of it to the *Enterprise*.[6] The files of the *Enterprise* were burned and the letter, I believe, is lost to the world;[7] but some things about it seemed to me at the time about the jolliest writing that ever Mark Twain did. I believe I can recall a few paragraphs of it from memory almost word for word. He said:

"When that earthquake came on Sunday morning last there was but one man in San Francisco that showed any presence of mind, and he was over in Oakland. He did just what I thought of doing, what I would have done had I had any opportunity—he went down out of his pulpit and embraced a woman. The newspapers said it was his wife. Maybe it was, but if it was it was a pity. It would have shown so much more presence of mind to have embraced some other gentleman's wife.

"A young man came down from the fifth story of a house on Stockton street, with no clothing on except a knitted undershirt, which came about as near concealing his person as the tin foil does a champagne bottle. Men shouted to him, little boys yelled at him, and women besought him to take their sunbonnets, their aprons, their hoop skirts, anything in the world and cover himself up and not stand there distracting people's attention from the earthquake. He looked all around and then he looked down at himself, and then he went upstairs. I am told he went up lively.

"Pete Hopkins was shaken off of Telegraph Hill, and on his way down landed on a three-story brick house (Hopkins weighed four hundred and thirty pounds), and the papers, always misrepresenting things, ascribed the destruction of the house to the earthquake."

And so the letter ran on and on for a column and a half of the old, long, wide columns of the *Enterprise*, and every line was punctuated with fun.

Notes

1. James W. Nye (1815–76), governor of Nevada Territory 1861–64.

2. Robert Muir Howland (1838–90) eventually became the superintendent of several territorial mines.

3. Twain's earliest comic sketches from Nevada were signed with the pseudonym "Josh." He did not begin to sign his articles "Mark Twain" until February 1863.

4. Roland M. Daggett (1831–1901), one of the editors of the *Virginia City Territorial Enterprise.*

5. "Homer nodded": an explanation for the inconsistencies and errors in Homeric epic.

6. Twain reminisces about the San Francisco earthquake on 8 October 1865 in chapter 58 of *Roughing It* (398–403).

7. The last complete file of the *Territorial Enterprise,* in the San Francisco Public Library, was destroyed by the fire that followed the San Francisco earthquake in 1906.

C. C. Goodwin, from *As I Remember Them* (Salt Lake City: Special Committee of the Salt Lake Commercial Club, 1913), 252–56.

"Jos. Goodman's Memories of Humorist's Early Days" (1910)

[Joseph T. Goodman]

> Twain covered the second Nevada legislative session in Carson City, con-
> vened on 11 November 1862, for the *Territorial Enterprise.* "I was there every
> day in the legislature to distribute compliment and censure with evenly bal-
> anced justice and spread the same over half a page of the *Enterprise* every
> morning; consequently I was an influence" (*Autobiography* [1924] 2:307–8).
> After the close of the session on 20 December, Twain sent a series of letters
> from Carson to the newspaper, and in them he coined the pseudonym "Mark
> Twain."

JOSEPH T. GOODMAN of 1415 Benton street, Alameda, fifty years ago editor
and part proprietor of the *Territorial Enterprise,* published at Virginia
City, Nev., and in those pioneer times the biggest daily newspaper between
Chicago and San Francisco, was Samuel L. Clemens's first journalistic
"boss." The credit for discovering Mark Twain is due to Mr. Goodman,
though he is too modest to claim it. . . .

"Let me see—it was in 1862 that Sam Clemens came to work for us on the
Territorial Enterprise. He was prospecting in Esmeralda County and had
sent us some voluntary contributions. They struck us as so funny that we
sent him word to come to Virginia City and take a job on the paper.

"He came, and we put him to work reporting local affairs. Later on we
sent him to Carson to report a session of the legislature, and it was from
Carson that he sent us his first article signed 'Mark Twain.' He had asked
me if he might sign a name to some stories apart from the regular reports
of the daily proceedings in the legislature, and I had told him he might. So
he wrote a humorous series of letters on what he called 'The Third House,'
which described amusingly the carrying-on of a number of congenial leg-

islators that were in the habit of gathering for a jolly social time after both houses of the legislature had adjourned over night. . . ."

According to Mr. Goodman, Samuel Clemens did not originate "Mark Twain" as a *nom de plume.* He says that the author explained to him he had borrowed it from an old Mississippi river captain named Sellers who, after retiring from active service on the old-time stern-wheelers, had taken to writing the news of the river and its steamboating, and signed his stories "Mark Twain."[1] . . .

"We employed twenty-five of the best printers on the Coast, and Virginia City was a tremendously flourishing place in the days when Mark Twain's first articles were helping to make the *Territorial Enterprise* read by everyone. The town had a population of perhaps 25,000,[2] besides which there was a large floating population in the many camps and goldfields, and everyone bought the paper."

Notes

1. See Scharnhorst 153.

2. The combined population of Virginia City and nearby Gold Hill made it at the height of the mining boom the largest city in Nevada and the largest city between Chicago and San Francisco.

[Joseph T. Goodman], "Jos. Goodman's Memories of Humorist's Early Days," *San Francisco Examiner,* 22 April 1910, 3.

"In the Heroic Days" (1893)

ARTHUR McEWEN

Arthur McEwen (1851–1907) was a journalist on the Comstock, including a stint on the staff of the *Virginia City Chronicle* in the early 1870s. Later in his life he worked as the chief editorial writer for the *New York American*.

AN UNKNOWN NOBODY of a miner over at Aurora sent in items occasionally. He had humor in him, and Goodman offered him a salary to come over and assist Dan De Quille as a reporter. He came. It was Clemens—Mark Twain.

Than Goodman and Clemens no men could be more unlike outwardly. The first was handsome gallant, self-reliant, but not self-conscious, vehement of speech and swift in action. (He called out the silver-tongued Tom Fitch, then an editor, and shattered his knee with a pistol-ball, for instance, in return for an unpleasant article that appeared in the course of a controversy.) Clemens was sloth-like in movement, had an intolerable drawl, and punished those who offended him by long-drawn sneering speech. But the two were alike at bottom in one thing—both were genuine, and had the quality of brain that enables one man to understand another of opposite temperament and manner. They soon became friends.

Not many people liked Mark Twain, if one may judge by the tone of deprecation in which he is spoken of on the Comstock to this day. But go to any small place from which a celebrated man has sprung and the same phenomenon appears. It is the villager's way of impressing upon the stranger the villager's superior, intimate knowledge of the great man. They say that Mark was mean—that he would join in revels and not pay his share, and so on. Those who knew him well, who had the requisite intelligence to be more than surface companions, tell a different story. His salary was not large, and he sent a good part of it back to Missouri, where it was needed, instead of "spending it like a man" on his own pleasures. In brief, Mr. Clemens, while he enjoyed the rough-and-tumble, devil-may-care Comstock life, wasn't carried away by it. He knew there was a world outside. The first work that showed the stuff of which he was made was done on the *Enterprise.*

Mark, being a man of sense, never neglected his interests. The fact that to know a particular man might at some time be advantageous did not deter Mr. Clemens from making his acquaintance. He and the Episcopal clergyman became friends, and while the clergyman probably did not consider Sam Clemens a devout Christian, at least he regarded him as a promising young man whose leanings were in the right direction. Now the printers knew that to steal the shade of Mr. Clemens's lamp caused him to burn with a slow fury. So they stole it as often as they could for the pleasure of hearing him swear—an art at which he excelled. One evening at dusk he climbed to the deserted local room and found the shade gone. Thereupon he began to drag himself around in a leisurely but intense circle, as was his wont on such occasions, uttering oaths and calling down heaven's vengeance on the purloiners. While thus breathing maledictions, he passed the door and beheld the Episcopal minister standing therein transfixed with horror.

Mark paused not in his slow walk, but had the grace to drawl out in low ferocity this (expurgated) excuse: "I know you're shocked to hear me, Mr. Brown. It stands to reason you are. I know this ain't language fit for a Christian man to utter nor for a Christian man to hear, but if I could only lay my hands on the --- -- - ----- who stole my shade, I'd show you what I'd do to him, for the benefit of printers to all time. You don't know printers, Mr. Brown; you don't know them. A Christian man like you naturally can't come in contact with them, but I give you my word they're the --- ---- --- --- - --- that a body ever had anything to do with."

From that time on Mark's seat was not high in the synagogue.

The local department of the *Enterprise,* for which Mark Twain and Dan De Quille were responsible, was as unlike the local department of a city newspaper of the present as the town and time were unlike the San Francisco of today. The indifference to "news" was noble—nonetheless so because it was so blissfully unconscious. Either Mark or Dan would dismiss a murder with a couple of inches, and sit down and fill up a column with a fancy sketch. They were about equally good in the sort of invention required for such efforts, and Dan very often did the better work. But the one had reach and ambition; the other lived for the moment.

Arthur McEwen, "In the Heroic Days," *San Francisco Examiner,* 22 January 1893, 15.

"Salad Days of Mark Twain" (1893)

DAN DE QUILLE

Twain and his fellows enjoyed rollicking lives on the Comstock, as Dan De Quille remembered. "Much of my conduct on the Pacific Coast was not of a character to recommend me to the respectful regard of a high eastern civilization," Twain conceded several years later to his future father-in-law, Jervis Langdon (1809–70), "but it was not considered blameworthy there, perhaps. We go according to our lights" (*Mark Twain's Letters* 2:357). He learned to duel with a foil—this a decade before he observed fencing at a fraternity party in Heidelberg. He perpetrated hoaxes in the pages of the *Territorial Enterprise* that earned him a local reputation as a practical joker. Two of the hoaxes De Quille mentions in this piece have been recovered: "Petrified Man" (4 October 1862) and "Frightful Accident to Dan De Quille" (20 April 1864). Moreover, when Charles Farrar Browne, aka Artemus Ward (1834–67), visited Virginia City in November 1863, Twain struck up a friendship with the famous humorist. He crossed paths with the actress and poet Adah Isaacs Menken (1835–68), best known for her scandalous role in *Mazeppa* in which she appeared on stage in a flesh-colored body stocking. "The Menken" arrived in Virginia City on 27 February 1864, in company with her husband (the third of four), Robert Henry Newell, aka the humorist Orpheus C. Kerr (1836–1901). De Quille remembered in particular a dinner party he attended with Menken, Twain, and the American poet and actor Ada Clare, aka Jane McElhinney (1834–74)—while Newell strutted and fretted in the hallway outside the hotel room. Later, after drifting to San Francisco, Twain announced in "A Full and Reliable Account of the Extraordinary Meteoric Shower of Last Saturday Night" (*Californian*, 19 November 1864) that "the whole constellation of the Great Menken came flaming out of the heavens like a vast spray of gas-jets, and shed a glory abroad over the universe as it fell!" Some of Menken's vers libre, written under the influence if not in the style of Walt Whitman, appeared in both the *Territorial Enterprise* and the *Californian*. Much of her poetry was collected in *Infelicia* (1868), published two weeks after she died in Paris at the age of thirty-three.

THE COMSTOCK WAS YOUNG when I first met Mark Twain in the editorial rooms of the *Territorial Enterprise* in Virginia City. We were both young then, and the world seemed young and teeming to overflowing with wealth. The whole country was booming, and the *Enterprise* was booming equally with all else. It was undoubtedly at the time the most flourishing newspaper on the Pacific Coast. A tribal wave of gold rolled in upon its proprietors. The paper seemed to run itself—and in doing so ran all connected with it. It seemed to take the lead and go right along without thought or care on the part of anyone. All there was to do was to pile into the paper all the news it would hold. The money to pay for everything seemed to besiege the office.

Mark Twain and I were employed in the local department of the *Enterprise,* and there was no lack of matters of interest in our line. Improvements of all kinds, new discoveries in the mines, accidents, cutting and shooting affrays, fires and all manner of exciting events crowded themselves upon us. However, we went merrily along, joking and laughing, and never feeling the weight of the work we were doing in the whirl and excitement of the times.

Soon after we began working together Mark and I rented two rooms on the second floor of a large brick building on B street erected by R. M. Daggett and his partner W. F. Myers, the well-known operator in mining stocks. We had a large bedroom and a somewhat smaller room for use as a parlor or sitting room.

Joseph T. Goodman, editor and one-third owner of the *Enterprise,* bossed the job of furnishing these rooms, and piled into them several hundred dollars' worth of stuff. Mark said that as Goodman had been "so keen to do the ordering" of the things, we'd "just let him foot the bill." So, whenever the furniture man—good old Moses Goldman—came after us with his bill, we laughed at him, and referred him to Goodman. But one day old Moses sued us and we had to square up with him. Mark said we might have known better than to try such a trick with "a man whose front name was Moses and whose rear name was Goldman."

However, we had a huge double bed, piles of bedding, splendid carpets and the fine fittings of all kinds. This, in comparison with the bunks in which we roosted in an old tumble-down shed when I first began work on the *Enterprise,* was quite palatial.

Mark and I agreed well as roommates. Both wanted to read and smoke about the same length of time after getting into bed, and if one got hungry and got up to go downtown for oysters the other also became hungry and turned out.

We had in the building where we roomed a very agreeable and jolly lot of people. Tom Fitch, the "Silver Tongued," his wife, sister-in-law, and mother-in-law occupied a large suite of rooms just across the hall from us and were the best of neighbors. Often when Mark and I got home at night we found laid out for us in our rooms a fine spread of pie, cake, milk and the like. Mrs. Fitch's mince pies were perfection.

Envious reporters of other papers did not scruple to assert that we stole all these good things out of the Fitch pantry. We denied the charge, but it was labor lost. Worse than this was their story of our having hanged the pet cat of Tom's mother-in-law. It was said that we tied a cord about the neck of the cat and suspended it from a rear second-story window. As the good old lady had actually lost her cat, she was a little sour with us for a few days. It afterward appeared that R. M. Daggett, who was a great friend of the Fitch family, knew of the old lady's loss, and put reporters of the other papers up to publishing a sensational story on the "Secret Midnight Hanging." The explanation in the last line or two that the victim was a cat made it all the worse for us with the old lady. For about a fortnight mince pies did not flow in upon us.

A good deal has been said first and last of the stealing of Tom Fitch's fire-wood while Mark and I were rooming at the Daggett & Meyers building. Tom never lost much wood through us, but the boys would always have it otherwise. Wood was something of an object in those days, as in winter it sometimes boomed up to $40 a cord. We were in the habit of buying of the Chinese wood-peddlers by the donkey load. One bitterly cold night we found ourselves without wood. In the hall on the same floor stood Tom's well-filled wood box. Said Mark: "We are not going to freeze in here with plenty of wood just outside our door," and out he went and gathered up an armful of Tom's wood. Coming back to our door he threw a stick of wood upon the floor and made a great racket. This was to arouse Tom. Then, opening the door with a bang, he faced about in it as if he had just come from the inside and sang out in an angry tone, as though to me in the hall: "Dan, d—n it all, don't be taking Tom's wood! It ain't right, and wood so confounded high! It ain't a nice thing to do. Now take that wood right back or there'll be trouble!"

He went back to the wood box and made a big racket, but when he threw down one stick he picked up two, and presently he came into the room with wood piled up to his chin. This he put down so carefully that the sticks wouldn't have broken an egg. We soon had a rousing fire and wood to spare for the morning.

There was plenty of such fun in those times. A trick of outsiders was to place all manner of things in our rooms, the doors of which were never locked. Mark had a Japanese sword. One night when we got home we were startled to find standing before us a gigantic fellow who seemed in the dim light of an open window to threaten us with a drawn sword. The invader proved to be a huge dummy armed with Mark's sword. Of course it was expected we would turn loose upon the giant with our pistols. Luckily, however, we hailed the intruder, offering him a chance for his life, and by doing so discovered the hoax.

Occasionally buckets of water greeted us upon the opening of our door, and at times hidden bells and clappers were ringing and rapping half the night, while we searched in vain for the secret wires and strings.

An institution that was very popular for a time in 1863–64 among Comstock young men of leisure was a fencing school and gymnasium opened by M. Chauvel, a French restaurant keeper. Although he taught only fencing and the use of the broadsword, M. Chauvel kept a supply of boxing gloves for the accommodation of those who had a leaning toward the "manly art."

M. Chauvel's school was most liberally patronized by the reporters and editors of the newspapers then published in Virginia City. For an hour or two every afternoon this class of customers took possession of the gymnasium and several pairs of them were to be seen at it hammer and tongs with foils, broadswords, and boxing gloves.

Mark Twain, Joe Goodman, and some of the rest of us cared little for anything but fencing, and upon entering the gymnasium went at once for the foils; whereas Denis McCarthy, Steve Gillis, and several others immediately appropriated the boxing gloves.[1]

The boxing was decidedly rough sport compared with the foils—"you stoccado, your imbrocata, your passada and your montanto," as set forth by Captain Bobadil.[2]

Twain became quite an expert with the foils. In attack he was fiery and particularly dangerous for the reason that one could not watch his eyes, which he habitually wears about half closed. In defense he was not so good and would nearly always give ground when hotly pressed.

[28]

Among the boxers was George F. Dawson, a young Englishman who was at the time assistant editor on the *Enterprise*. Boxing was his hobby, and he particularly prided himself upon being a hard hitter. If no one could be found to put on the gloves and face him he would viciously tackle the sand bag or charge across the hall and "land one straight from the shoulder" against the wall.

Denis McCarthy, who was tall, strong, "long in the reach" and tolerably expert at boxing, was about the only newspaper man who was able to tackle Dawson, and they seldom had a set-to that did not result in anger on both sides and terminate in a wind-up that looked like a battle for blood.

One day some imp induced Mark Twain to put on a pair of boxing gloves, and with them all the airs of a knight of the prize ring. He had no thought of boxing with anyone. Having seen more or less sparring on the stage, a good deal of amateur boxing, and probably one or two prize fights, Mark had got some of the motions. No sooner had he the gloves on than he began capering about the hall. Dawson observed his antics with astonishment not unmixed with awe. He evidently considered that they were made for his special benefit and intimidation. Perhaps he may have thought he detected Mark regarding him interrogatively from beneath his bushy brows at the end of each series of cabezal rotations. At all events, in view of Mark's movements of supposed warlike import, Dawson kept a wary eye on him, never once suspecting that the ex-Mississippi pilot was merely making a bid for his admiration.

Presently Mark squared off directly in front of Dawson and began working his right like the piston of a steam engine, at the same time stretching out his neck and gyrating his curly pate in a very astonishing manner.

Dawson took this to be a direct act of defiance—a challenge to a trial of skill that could not be ignored. Desperately, therefore, and probably not without a secret chill of fear at heart, Dawson drew off and with full force planted a heavy blow squarely upon Mark's offered nose, the latter not making the least movement toward a guard. The force of the blow fairly lifted Mark off his feet and landed him across a settle that stood against the wall on one side of the hall, when Dawson, flushed with victory, ran up and, against all rule, began punching him in the head.

Dawson was hauled off by McCarthy, Gillis, and others and was sternly rebuked. There was a plentiful flow of claret and oaths as Mark staggered to his feet and began looking about for a club. He assured Dawson that the next time he undertook to entertain him it would be with a dray-pin.

With a hand and a handkerchief screening his wounded nose, Mark— "musing full sadly in his sullen mind" [3]—took his departure for our rooms up on B street, leaving a trail of blood across the hall, up the stairs, through the restaurant above, and all along his homeward route. His nose streamed blood.

An hour later I found him in our little parlor planted in front of a looking-glass. All the remainder of the day he stayed there and tenderly ministered to the wants of his ailing nose. [4]

Nothing the shelves of the apothecary contained was too good for that nose. It was indulged in towels saturated with sugar of lead and all manner of soothing lotions.

Notwithstanding the use of divers applications, Mark had a black eye and a prodigious nose. That wronged and wounded nose refused to submit to any restraining or ameliorating influence. It was a nose that need not have quailed in the presence of old Antiochus VIII, that of Mohammed, the great Frederick or Napoleon I; yet Mark was not proud of it. Mark would not venture forth to take his place at his desk until the shades of night had fallen. When he did arrive he was quite unamiable. A bear with a sore head was a lamb in comparison.

A printer who ventured into the sanctum in search of copy—gentle, amiable little William Henry Deane—seemed to be much struck by the bulbous and angry appearance of Mark's nose. He stared at the inflamed organ in big-eyed astonishment and then cried out: "Why, Mr. Clemens, what is the matter with your nose? It looks like an egg-plant!"

"Get out of here, blast you, or I'll make you look like a corpse!" yelled Mark, grabbing a paper-weight. "No printer has a d—n bit of right to come into this room, copy or no copy!"

Little Deane immediately became an absent man.

Just at that time the mines about Silver Mountain, Alpine county, California, were attracting attention. Goodman wanted to send a reporter up to Silver Mountain to write an article on the new mines. Mark volunteered to go. He wanted to get his nose out of town. He was well known in Carson City, but by going in the stage he could smuggle his nose through that place.

No sooner was Mark away than I wrote for the *Enterprise* a description of his arrival at Silver Mountain. In this it was said that as the stage was entering the town Mark placed himself at the window of the vehicle. The alert suburban inhabitants caught sight of his nose and raised a cry that a "freak" show was coming. The man with the big nose was in the coach.

At once the people of the town dropped everything and flocked about the stage, trying to peer within as it rolled along. They asked the driver if the nose was natural and where and when the show would take place. Men and boys ran ahead to the hotel at which the coach was to stop and took up positions in front of it. Three cheers were given as the nose was seen coming out of the stage. On the way from the coach to the hotel the supposed freak passed through a lane of admiring citizens.

An old lady who stood on the front of the veranda seemed quite fascinated by the phenomenal nose. As the owner of the nose was passing, the old dame asked permission to touch it. Being gratified in this desire she took off her spectacles, turned to the crowd and said it was the happiest moment of her life.

This was a mild and innocent squib for a Comstock newspaper in those days, but Mark said "it wasn't a d—n bit smart." He was hot about it when he got back to Virginia City. He said I had caused him to be annoyed by all the bums in Carson when he got back to that town as he was obliged to stand treat to shut their mouths.

A few days after his return to Virginia Mark got even with me. While riding on horseback my saddle turned, landing me on the ground and spraining one of my knees. That evening the bruised knee became so painful that I was obliged to go to our rooms, leaving Mark to "do the locals."

He got up a terrific story about my accident. He "concussed" me, and brought my remains into town on two drays.

Mark's notions as a nurse were rather peculiar. Coming up to our rooms to see me the evening of the accident, and finding me suffering, he went out and presently returned in triumph with an orange and a handful of cigars. He said as an orange was cooling and a cigar soothing, nothing could be better for a sprained knee.

Next morning, after looking at the *Enterprise,* I said to Mark: "Beware of the Greeks bearing gifts!"

"What is it now?" said he, trying to look innocent.

"I thought something was up last night," said I, "when you were so free with your cigars and oranges."

Mark chuckled and said: "Now, blast you, maybe you'll hereafter let my nose alone!"

But his item created greater alarm and grief in some quarters than he ever knew. It was headed "Terrible Accident to Dan De Quille,"[5] and rent me to fragments in the most serious and businesslike manner. Now the *Enterprise* went home to my wife and people who were then in the States. The moment that my wife saw that heading she dropped the paper and raised the death-howl. Some others of the womenfolk began to read the terrible story, but sickened and threw the paper aside when they came to where my hat was pulled out of the wreck of my liver. Not until the last line of the item was it shown that the story of the accident was a fake.

Mark Twain delighted in the horrible and shocking in those days. Not satisfied with the accidents happening in the mines, though many of them were sufficiently terrible, he would invent horrors of various kinds. These stories were generally in the way of finding human remains in out of the way places. He had a crow to pick with the Coroner, and delighted in placing him in ridiculous positions.

As an example, he told of going on one occasion with the Coroner to prospect for a dead body reported to be lying in an old tunnel. The Coroner entered the tunnel, which proved to be a very long one, while Mark remained outside to await results. Presently the official reappeared with one arm of the unknown dead man. In trying to drag out the decomposed body the limb had become detached. Intent upon business, the Coroner returned and brought out a leg, and so he continued the work until he accumulated at the mouth of the tunnel a pile of "remains" sufficient to justify him in holding an inquest and so earning his fee. Mark made the whole business as shocking and disgusting as possible.

A man who had at some time and in some way offended Mark was elected Justice of the Peace in Humboldt county. Mark got up a story of a petrified human body having been found out there under the roots of a pine tree of great size and age. After a full description of the appearance of the body and the place in which it was discovered, Mark brought in the Justice of the Peace and made him insist upon holding an inquest—in short, endowed him with the wisdom of a donkey.

Virginia City was booming when Artemus Ward arrived to deliver his lecture. Comstockers received Artemus as a brother, and he seemed as much at home as if he had all his life been a resident of Virginia City. He remained on the Comstock several days, making the *Enterprise* his head-quarters. Mark Twain and I had the pleasure of showing him the town, and a real pleasure it was—a sort of circus, in fact—as he constantly overflowed with fun. He was anxious to get hold of the lingo and style of the miners, and we made him acquainted with several old forty-niners. The greetings among these men struck him as something new, and he began practicing, playing himself off as an old-timer. The looks of astonishment which his efforts in this line called up in some quarters soon showed him that the half-horse half-alligator style of greeting was only good with a certain class. Mark Twain had a weakness for the clergy, and meeting one of his preacher friends on the street one day he introduced him to Ward without adding to the name the handle of "Reverend." Some twinkle in the eye of the reverend gentleman caused Artemus to think him one of the "old boys," so he greeted him with: "Well, old Two-Pan-One-Color, is the devil still in your dough-dish?"

Mark hastened to explain, and it all ended in a laugh, in which Ward joined very faintly.

Artemus Ward was full of curiosity about the Piute Indians and the Chinese. While he was here the Chinese had a powwow of some kind. A big tent was erected on a vacant lot in Chinatown, in which half a dozen yellow and purple-robed priests from San Francisco displayed their gods and received the vows of the faithful. One night Mark, Ward, and I "took in" this show and other Chinatown sights. We went to see Hop Sing, head of one company, and old Salt Sing, the champion of the opposition company. Both insisted upon our testing various fiery drinks, such as rice "blandy" and other kinds of "blandy."

We narrowly escaped being caught in the midst of a fight that started between the rival companies, a fight in which about fifty shots were fired, killing one man and wounding two or three.

In returning to the city from Chinatown we concluded to take a "near cut." Coming to a string of low frame houses, Artemus said the nearest cut was over the tops of the shanties, and crying "Follow your leader!" mounted a shed and then the roof of a house. "Come ahead," cried he, "and we'll go up into town over the roofs of the houses. Follow your leader."

The "China blandy" was venturesome—no wonder the Celestials fought—and soon we were all marching along over the roofs. We had not proceeded far before there came to our ears the command, "Halt there or I shoot," and we saw a man with a shotgun leveled at us. The man who had halted us was a watchman. He held his gun on us until we climbed down and marched up to him as ordered. Explanations followed and all was right as soon as our names were given.

"Right you are," said Artemus. "Take a few tickets and come to my show," and he poked over the fence to the man a handful of tickets.

"Thanks," said the watchman, and reaching behind into the tail of a long coat he drew forth a bottle that was almost as long as the barrel of his gun. "Good stuff," said he, as he poked the long bottle over the fence to us.

Mark and I feared to mix fighting American whisky with warlike Chinese "blandy," but Artemus took the bottle, and as he placed it to his lips and elevated it toward the North Star it looked like a telescope. "Splendid," said he, as he lowered the "instrument."

After his adventure we concluded to go to our rooms on B street and all three turn into our big bed together, "three saints," as Artemus put it, "Mark, Luke, and John." However, in going up Sutton avenue there was heard "a sound of revelry by night."[6] We were passing a huge barn of a building in which a couple of hurdy-gurdies were holding forth. Hurdies were something new to Ward, and he said he wanted to see this show.

On entering the dance hall Artemus announced our arrival by stating that we were "Babes in the Wood." As he was known by sight to most of those present there were at once "Cheers for Artemus Ward."

"Now," said Ward, "we three have got to have a dance together. It'll be a thing our offspring to the furthest generation will be proud of!"

So selecting three stalwart and capable girls as partners we danced to the unbounded admiration of a large and enthusiastic audience, headed by "Kettle-belly" Brown.

Artemus threw a twenty-dollar gold piece on the bar to pay for the dances and beer. The bartender took out about four times the usual rates and was raking Ward's double eagle into the till when "Kettle's" big hand came down upon the gold with a startling spat.

"No you don't!" said "Kettle,"—"these gentlemen are friends of mine. This twenty don't go into the till until you hand out the right change!" Instantly the correct change was passed over to Ward.

Immediately the whole heart and soul of Artemus Ward went out to "Kettle." Said he to Brown: "We are three mere 'Babes in the Wood'; come along with us. We need you to take care of us."

So instead of going to bed we went forth under the guidance of the genial "Kettle." We went to hear the Cornish singers, and to see some of the big games, meeting with still further adventures in our wanderings, but everywhere fathered and guided by the bulky, whole-souled and honest old Sonora miner, "Kettle-belly" Brown.

The first rays of the morning sun were gilding the peak of Mount Davidson. The "Babes" were out in front of Aaron Hooper's saloon—where happened to be some convenient packing cases—for a mouthful of fresh air. Seated upon one of the boxes Artemus was wrestling with a very active dose of mustard and water given him by the attentive "Kettle."

"You are early abroad, gentlemen," said staid old John A. Collins, out for his morning stroll. We would much preferred at the moment to have seen Beelzebub.

"Yes, Mr. Collins," said Mark, as he saw halted before us the moral patriarch of the Comstock. "It is beautiful to see the sun rise. As the poet says:

"Now fair Aurora lifts the golden ray
And all the ruddy Orient flames with day."

This little poetical outburst aroused Artemus. Lifting his head, with "Kettle's" assistance, he tearfully gazed up at the great moral reformer and, with much feeling and emphasis, said: "A man oppressed, dependent, yet a man!"[7]

In the old boom times, when we had all the big shows in Virginia City, Adah Isaacs Menken struck the Comstock with her play of *Mazeppa*. With her came Orpheus C. Kerr, her then husband, and, as a friend and guest, Ada Clare, "Queen of the Bohemians." Menken was delighted with the excitement and wild whirl of life as then seen in full swing on the Comstock. She said it was "in keeping with the wild shrieking of the many steam whistles and the thunder of the quartz mills."

She was taken through the lower levels of the mines, made an honorary member of Young America Engine Company No. 2, and presented a belt bearing the name of the company in large letters of solid silver bullion. She "took in" everything that was going, became smitten with the prevailing rage for speculating in mining stocks, and had half a notion to settle down on the Comstock and stay with the many congenial excitements in which Virginia City abounded.

"The Menken" at that time had half a mind to leave the stage and turn her attention to literature. She wrote for the *Enterprise* two or three poems—long ones in blankest of blank verse—and contemplated a realistic novel. Her bosom friend Ada Clare, on the contrary, thought of abandoning literature and taking to the stage.

Menken was very impulsive and full of all manner of notions and eccentricities. While here she took it into her head to give a big dinner, to which but four persons should sit down. These four were to be herself, Ada Clare, Mark Twain, and myself. Even Orpheus Kerr, her husband, was barred from the entertainment, a thing he apparently did not much relish.

The dinner was given in the Menken's rooms at the International Hotel. She kept a whole procession of waiters moving up and down the two flights of stairs between the kitchen and her rooms, many courses being no more than tasted before they were removed.

It seemed a little rough on Orpheus, glimpses of whom we caught as he patrolled the hall outside the rooms, that he should have only a smell of the good things as they were carried past him. For some reason he was just then in bad odor with his more energetic half.

The object of the dinner appeared to be, on Menken's part, a sort of literary consultation. She was full of her proposed novel. Aside from this talk, and some talk of getting up a new play for Clare, the dinner was rather dull. It was thought to enliven the occasion with

> Short swallow flights of song, that dip
> Their wings . . . and skim away.[8]

But the Menken was no nightingale, Clare was a sort of wren, and I was a screech owl. Mark enchanted us with his one and only song of:

> There was an old horse and his name was Jerusalem.
> And he came from Jerusalem,
> And he went to Jerusalem.
> There was an old horse . . .

And so on *ad infinitum.*

In the room were about nineteen dogs of as many breeds, "mongrel, puppy, whelps and hound, and curs of low degree,"[9] some Ada Clare's pets and others belonging to the Menken. These pampered beasts the pair continually fed upon cubes of sugar soaked in brandy and champagne. This provender made the animals howlingly hilarious, to the great delight of their mistresses, but to the disgust of Twain, who was seated on Menken's side of the table, where the canine carnival was most rampant.

Presently one of the dogs took an unwarranted liberty with Mark's leg. Guessing at the whereabouts of the cur under the table, Mark undertook to avenge the nip he had received with a sly kick. He missed the dog but hit the Menken's pet corn, causing her to bound from her seat, throw herself on a lounge and roll and roar in agony.

This mischance put a sort of damper on the festivities. Mark immediately became as sullen as if it had been his own corn that was wounded, and even when Menken came limping back to her chair and begged him not to mind, he refused to be conciliated.

Mark disliked the Menken and would have avoided the arrangement that seated him by her side had it been possible.

After this mishap nothing could propitiate Mark. He very soon imagined a pressing engagement and begged to be excused. As we took our departure we passed Orpheus, still on patrol duty in the hall. He was not in a good humor and scowled and muttered in reply to our salutations.

Notes

1. Steve Gillis (1838–1918) and Denis E. McCarthy (1841–85), typesetters for the *Virginia City Territorial Enterprise.*

2. De Quille alludes to a character in Ben Jonson's play *Every Man in His Humour.*

3. From Spenser's *The Faerie Queen.*

4. De Quille reported the incident the next day in "Mark Twain Takes a Lesson in the Manly Art," *Virginia City Territorial Enterprise,* April 1864.

5. "Terrible Accident to Dan De Quille," *Virginia City Territorial Enterprise,* 20 April 1864.

6. From Byron's "Revelry by Night."

7. Both Twain and Ward quote Alexander Pope's translation of Homer's *Odyssey.*

8. From section 48 of Tennyson's "In Memoriam."

9. From Oliver Goldsmith's "Elegy on the Death of a Mad Dog."

Dan De Quille, "Salad Days of Mark Twain," *San Francisco Examiner,* 19 March 1893, 13–14.

From Archibald Henderson, *Mark Twain* (1910)

DAN DE QUILLE

> De Quille reminisced elsewhere about another of Twain's famous hoaxes, "A Bloody Massacre Near Carson," published in the *Territorial Enterprise* on 28 October 1863. As Twain admitted at the time, "To find a petrified man, or break a stranger's leg, or cave an imaginary mine, or discover some dead Indians in a Gold Hill tunnel, or massacre a family at Dutch Nick's, were feats and calamities that we never hesitated about devising when the public needed matters of thrilling interest for breakfast. The seemingly tranquil *Enterprise* office was a ghastly factory of slaughter, mutilation and general destruction in those days" (*Virginia City Territorial Enterprise*, 7 March 1868).

MARK TWAIN WAS FOND of manufacturing items of the horrible style, but on one occasion he overdid this business, and the disease worked its own cure. He wrote an account of a terrible murder, supposed to have occurred at "Dutch Nick's," a station on the Carson River, where Empire City now stands. He made a man cut his wife's throat and those of his nine children, after which diabolical deed the murderer mounted his horse, cut his own throat from ear to ear, rode to Carson City (a distance of three and a half miles) and fell dead in front of Peter Hopkins's saloon.

All the California papers copied the item, and several made editorial comment upon it as being the most shocking occurrence of the kind ever known on the Pacific Coast. Of course rival Virginia City papers at once denounced the item as a "cruel and idiotic hoax." They showed how the publication of such "shocking and reckless falsehoods" disgraced and injured the State, and they made it as "sultry" as possible for the *Enterprise* and its "fool reporter."

When the California papers saw all this and found they had been sold, there was a howl from Siskiyou to San Diego. Some papers demanded the immediate discharge of the author of the item by the *Enterprise* proprietors. They said they would never quote another line from that paper while the reporter who wrote the shocking item remained on its force. All this worried Mark as I had never before seen him worried. Said he: "I am being burned alive on both sides of the mountains." We roomed together, and one night, when the persecution was hottest, he was so distressed that he could not sleep. He tossed, tumbled, and groaned aloud. So I set to work to comfort him. "Mark," said I, "never mind this bit of a gale, it will soon blow itself out. This item of yours will be remembered and talked about when all your other work is forgotten. The murder at Dutch Nick's will be quoted years from now as the big sell of these times."

Said Mark: "I believe you are right; I remember I once did a thing at home in Missouri, was caught at it, and worried almost to death. I was a mere lad, and was going to school in a little town where I had an uncle living.[1] I at once left the town and did not return to it for three years. When I finally came back I found I was only remembered as 'the boy that played the trick on the schoolmaster.'"

Mark then told me the story, began to laugh over it, and from that moment "ceased to groan." He was not discharged, and in less than a month people everywhere were laughing and joking about the "murder at Dutch Nick's."

Note

1. Twain's uncle John A. Quarles (1801–76) owned a seventy-acre farm in Rawls County, Missouri, where Twain spent summers as a child. It became the model for the Phelps farm in *Huck Finn*.

Dan De Quille, from Archibald Henderson, *Mark Twain* (New York: Stokes, 1910), 80–81.

"Memories of Mark Twain" (1915)

George E. Barnes

> The western journalist W. W. Barnes (b. 1837) worked in Virginia City during the 1860s for the rival newspaper, the *Union*. He reminisced half a century later about a series of fund-raisers in Nevada in 1863–64 for the U.S. Sanitary Commission, a forerunner of the American Red Cross, organized to assist wounded Union soldiers in the East. As Twain also recalled in chapter 45 of *Roughing It* (293–98), a sack of flour was repeatedly sold at auction until a total of $150,000 was raised: "This is probably the only instance on record where common family flour brought three thousand dollars a pound in the public market."

HEREWITH ARE SET DOWN some hitherto unpublished incidents culled from the recollections of Mr. W. W. Barnes, of Oakland, concerning Samuel L. Clemens while the great humorist was "Roughing It" in Virginia City, Nevada. . . . Barnes met Clemens in Virginia City, Nevada, during the later years of the Civil War. Barnes was then working on the *Union*, while Clemens was doing his first reportorial work on the rival paper, the *Enterprise*.

Real news was scarce in Virginia City at times in those days, and as readers of *Roughing It* will remember, the author frankly admits that many of his stories were fabrications. Clemens, it will be remembered, mentions the load of hay which was made to enter the town from many different directions and to encounter a wide variety of strange adventures so as to make "news" and fill space.[1] . . .

Mr. Barnes also well remembers the episode of the Sanitary Sack of Flour, which is a part of Nevada's annuals. A mayoralty election was to be held near the town of Austin. A man named Gridley[2] was the Republican candidate, while the Democratic candidate's name was Beal. It was agreed between the rivals that the unsuccessful aspirant was to carry a fifty-pound sack of flour to the top of a hill near the town.

Beal was elected, and Gridley cheerfully toted the sack of flour to the top of the hill, under the eyes of most of the town's population. Having done this, he proposed that the flour be sold to the highest bidder for the benefit of the National Sanitary Commission, which was the forerunner of the present International Red Cross Society.

This was agreed to by all parties, and the sack of flour was sold and resold many times. It was carried about all over Nevada and California, and sold again and again. It was the means of bringing many thousands of dollars to the humane cause represented by the Sanitary Commission. When it was sold in Virginia City the employees of the rival newspapers, the *Union* and the *Enterprise,* clubbed together and started bidding against each other. There was more or less feeling between the two publications, professional, political, and otherwise, and the employees of the *Enterprise* were in the habit of referring to the *Union* crowd as "Rebels," "Copperheads," etc. Nevertheless, the *Union* boys came to the bat with a purse of $100 for the sack of flour. Clemens passed the hat in the *Enterprise* office and raised the Union's bid by $50. Not to be outdone, the "Democrats" brought their bid up to $213, and carried off the prize. Incidentally, this historic sack of flour eventually came into the possession of Gridley, who first carried it up the hill at Austin. Gridley's descendants, who live in Modesto, are said to still have this sack of flour enclosed in a buckskin bag.

Something of the old rivalry between the "boys" of the *Union* and those of the *Enterprise,* in the historic days of the Comstock Lode, must still linger in the heart of one of them who, though feeble with age, yet maintains the spirit of the old days. For the old pioneer tells a story of Mark Twain which has never before seen print, and which, while a characteristic prank of the young fun-maker, and typical of the West that was all wild and very woolly, still was considered a rather coarse joke.

Notes

1. *Roughing It,* chapter 42 (274–77).
2. Reuel Colt Gridley (1829–70), from Hannibal, wagered on the mayoral election in Austin, Nevada, probably in fall 1863. He was not a candidate for the office.

George E. Barnes, "Memories of Mark Twain," *Overland Monthly* 66 (September 1915): 263–65.

"Fitch Recalls Mark Twain
in Bonanza Times" (1919)

TOM FITCH

Tom Fitch chronicles Twain's threatened duel with James Laird in May 1864, which Twain described in the installment of his autobiography in the *North American Review*, 21 December 1906 (repr. in *Mark Twain's Own Autobiography*, 73–76). The exchange of insults between Twain and Laird is reprinted in *Mark Twain's Letters* 1:290–96. Because dueling had been outlawed in Nevada, Twain and his "second," Steve Gillis, left Virginia City for San Francisco on 29 May to escape the inquiries of a grand jury.

MARK TWAIN, in an article published in the *North American Review*, told the story of his attempt at a duel with James L. Laird, who was then a one-third owner in the Virginia City *Union*. Mark yielded reluctantly to "the custom of the Comstock" in those days, which demanded imperatively that a person who had been subjected to a dose of personal journalism should challenge the editor of the sheet which had reviled him. The same custom required the challenged editor to either fight or leave the country.

Laird, or Laird's paper, had abused Mark editorially, and Mark challenged the offender. . . . Laird was an arrant coward. On receipt of the challenge from Mark Twain he called at my office. His face was white. He handed me the challenge. "I am up against it," said he. "I must either fight or quit the country. I will sell you my one-third interest in the *Union* for half its value, and sell it on credit, so that you can pay for it out of your share of the profits, and you assume the responsibility of my article and fight Sam Clemens."

"Can't I buy you out and then apologize to Sam?" said I.

"My partners wouldn't stand for that," said he. "Somebody has got to fight, or it will ruin the paper."

"Sam Clemens and I are personal friends," said I, "although we have been employed on rival papers. I decline to shorten his young and beautiful life, and I know that he would not like to be guilty of 'the deep damnation of my taking off.' I am willing to buy into your paper, but I decline to buy into your fight."

This ended the incident. Laird fled and went back to Illinois, where he was killed by a citizen whose domestic felicity he had invaded.

Tom Fitch, "Fitch Recalls Mark Twain in Bonanza Times," *San Francisco Chronicle,* 30 March 1919, 6F.

From *Western Carpetbagger: The Extraordinary Memoirs of "Senator" Tom Fitch* (1978)

TOM FITCH

> Twain disliked practical jokes when he was their butt, but his own humor was often self-deprecating. Tom Fitch elsewhere remembered several situations in Virginia City ripe with comedy, as in the case of the serial novel Twain planned to write for the *Virginia City Weekly Occidental* in collaboration with Roland Daggett, his wife, and Fitch himself. Unfortunately, the *Occidental*, published between 29 October 1864 and 15 April 1865, suspended publication before Twain could contribute his installment. Twain also discussed the collaborative novel in chapter 51 of *Roughing It* (339–47).

MARK TWAIN WAS as humorous in his private correspondence and private speech as in his published writings. He gave a friend a strong endorsement as an eloquent lecturer and accompanied it with a note saying, "Now try and not put the audience to sleep, and don't be the heedless cause of my first lie." A letter from his mother contained a pathetic appeal: "Samuel," said she, "why do you always begin your letters to me by asking conundrums? I am an old woman and have no taste for them."

He had such a dislike for pharisaical pretension that he was ever making mocking jests upon his own truthfulness, integrity, and habits. As a matter of fact, he was free from the vices of a frontier community and an honorable and upright man in his dealings—except in one particular. He was the most accomplished midnight mince pie thief that ever upset the calculations of our widow caterer. He had, besides, a habit, when things went wrong, of crashing together the crockery in his room, not so as to actually break it, but so as to make everyone nervous with apprehension.

One Christmas Eve all of us, except Mark, were seated in the smoking-room awaiting the announcement of dinner, when there arrived a lad with a package for Mr. Clemens, which he was directed to take to the smoking-room. After his departure we examined the bundle, for we were communists in spirit, and found that it contained a pretty knitted woolen scarf and a card bearing the inscription, "Mr. Samuel L. Clemens, from his friend Etta." "I can improve upon that message," suggested Daggett, who was the wag and philosophical disputant and cribbage player of the club, and, obtaining a sheet of note paper, he wrote in a fine female hand the following note:

"Mr. Clemens: The accompanying scarf having been prepared as a Christmas gift for you, it has been determined not to divert it from its original destination, although a knowledge of your late conduct having come to the ears of the writer your own conscience will tell you that this must close all communication between us, in which decision my father and mother concur. Your former friend, Etta."

The scarf was rewrapped and with this note tied to it was placed in Sam's room. Shortly afterward he made his appearance and proceeded to his room to prepare for dinner. Soon we heard the crockery going. "What is the matter, Sam?" said Daggett. Thereupon entered Mark Twain, with coat and collar off, and, throwing the package upon the table, he burst forth: "Read that," said he, flourishing the note from Etta, "read that. That's just my infernal luck. You hounds can run the town night after night and nobody ever says a word, but I am found out at once."

Mark Twain, Daggett, my wife and I agreed to collaborate in writing a novel. It was concluded that there should be no concert of action, plot, or plan between us; that either should have the right to introduce as many characters as he or she desired; that neither should have the right to kill, maim, imprison, or exile for life any character introduced by another, but might make such disposition as he pleased of characters of his own creation.

The novel was christened by me *The Silver Fiend, a Tale of Washoe,* and I began the great work with a thrilling description of a runaway team on a mountain road in the Sierras, stopped by a lariat in the hands of a college athlete, who, while on a prospecting tour, had camped on the mountain side.

Daggett commenced his chapter with the statement that while the horses stopped, the young man who held the lariat went on; that the sudden stop jerked him three miles over the mountain into a little valley where there was an Indian camp. Daggett, who was learned in savage lore, made an elaborate exposition of Indian customs and the intruder was given the choice of marrying an Indian squaw, eating roasted dog, or being tortured to death. He chose dog eating, was compelled to consume the ears of a spaniel and drumsticks of a bulldog before being permitted to depart.

Mrs. Fitch presented the third chapter, describing the home life and education, culture, and thought of a beautiful Vermont girl, who was compelled by her father's loss of fortune and death to come to the Pacific Coast and seek employment as a teacher.

Mark Twain was to write the fourth chapter, but the day before it was to appear the *Occidental* suspended and his part of the book was forever lost to the world. When questioned with regard to it he answered: "I should have kept the compact, but I intended to place that Vermont girl in a situation that she would have found difficult to explain to the satisfaction of her friends. I had her dealing monte in 'Dandy Pete's' saloon in Virginia City. I'm sorry the literary paper stopped before my turn came, but you couldn't expect that kind of a paper to be permanent here, could you? Can a lark sing in a cellar? Can summer abide on Mount Blanc? Will flowers blossom in hell?"

Tom Fitch, from *Western Carpetbagger: The Extraordinary Memoirs of "Senator" Tom Fitch* (Reno: University of Nevada Press, 1978), 52–56.

"Mark Twain as He Was Known during His Stay on the Pacific Slope" (1887)

George E. Barnes

> In early June 1864, after taking a room with Gillis in the Occidental Hotel in San Francisco, Twain joined the staff of the *San Francisco Morning Call*, edited and co-owned by George E. Barnes (d. 1897). Over the next several weeks Twain occasionally crossed swords with Martin G. J. Burke (d. 1906), the corrupt chief of the San Francisco police. Meanwhile, Twain's holdings of "feet," or stock, in Comstock mines, particularly the Hale & Norcross, crashed in value. In mid October, Barnes permitted him to quit before he was fired. As Twain explained in chapter 58 of *Roughing It,* "I neglected my duties and became about worthless as a reporter for a brisk newspaper. And at last one of the proprietors took me aside, with a charity I still remember with considerable respect, and gave me an opportunity to resign my berth and so save myself the disgrace of a dismissal" (404). As Barnes explained, Twain earned a living during the next few months by writing San Francisco "letters" to the *Territorial Enterprise* and contributing to the local literary weeklies, the *Golden Era* and the *Californian*. See also *Mark Twain in Eruption,* 254–60.

ABOUT 1864 MR. CLEMENS came to San Francisco. It cannot be said he made many friends in Nevada. There were some who affected his company on account of his writings, but he had not the faculty of winning friendship. Before he arrived in the city he had accumulated . . . a good deal of money, every stiver of which he sunk in Hale & Norcross.[1] Then he took up the burden of literary life again. He wrote San Francisco letters to his old paper, the *Territorial Enterprise,* and for some real or fancied cause attacked the local police so persistently and fiercely that Martin G. J. Burke, who was chief of the force at the time, brought a suit for libel against the paper. Such envenomed communications as Mr. Clemens wrote on this subject have rarely been penned. They made the official equanimity of the old City Hall boil like a caldron of asphaltum, the fume and stench being in proportion.

He also contributed for Charley Webb ("Inigo") to the *Californian,*[2] for the *Golden Era,*[3] and did all sorts of literary work whereby he could turn a cent. It was a terrible uphill business, and a less determined man than himself would have abandoned the struggle and remained at the base. Mr. Clemens was at Steamboat Springs, Nevada, for his health, when the letter was written offering him a place on the *Call.* He came down shortly after, but judging from his appearance, fortune had been playing scurvy tricks with him in the interim. Without doing the gentleman any injustice, it can be freely stated that although at the time a good general writer and correspondent, he made but an indifferent reporter. He only played at itemizing. Considering his experience in the mountains, he had an inexplicable aversion to walking, and in putting his matter on paper he was, to use his own expression, "slower than the wrath to come." Many funny and characteristic incidents occurred during his few months' stay on the *Call.* He only wanted to remain long enough, he said, when he engaged to go to work, to make "a stake," but on leaving, his purse was no heavier than when he came. The most notable thing he did, that can now be recalled, was a philippic against some undertaking employee, where the morgue happened to be—for the death house, in those days, like the old fashioned plan with the country schoolmistress and the villagers, was "boarded round," each undertaker accommodating the coroner in turn. It appears someone about the place refused to give Mr. Clemens information, or to let him see "the slate," and next morning he got such a dose, commencing "These body-snatchers," that a general apology was immediately made by every man in the establishment.[4] The proprietor was East at the time, but when he read the article he shivered, as he confessed afterward, and considered his business ruined. Mr. Clemens parted from the *Call* people on the most friendly terms, when it was found necessary to make the local department more efficient, admitting his reportorial shortcomings and expressing surprise they were not sooner discovered.

Notes

1. Twain soon filed a complaint about the fluctuations in the value of the stock in "What Goes with the Money?" *San Francisco Morning Call,* 19 August 1864; repr. in *Early Tales and Sketches,* 2:455. See also *Mark Twain's Own Autobiography,* 275n5.

2. Charles H. Webb, aka "Inigo" and "John Paul" (1834–1905), founded the *Californian* in 1864.

3. Roland Daggett founded the *Golden Era* in 1852.

4. The article probably was "A Small Piece of Spite," *San Francisco Call,* 6 September 1864; repr. in Branch 233–36.

George E. Barnes, "Mark Twain as He Was Known during His Stay on the Pacific Slope," *San Francisco Morning Call,* 17 April 1887, 1.

From *Memories of Mark Twain and Steve Gillis* (1924)

WILLIAM R. GILLIS

> In December 1864 Twain accompanied Steve Gillis on a trip to his brothers' pocket mine near Sonora, Jackass Hill, Tuolumne County. There he met Jim Gillis (1830–1907) and William R. Gillis (1840–1929), who remembered the visit.

THE NEAREST APPROACH TO any work that Mark Twain ever did at mining was when he became my partner at one time for about two weeks. One day when on my way home from Sonora I took a short cut across a parcel of land from which the surface dirt had been washed by the placer miners some years before. While walking over this ground I came to a spot where the croppings of a reef of very fine mineral slate had been uncovered, and upon closer examination discovered a small quartz vein with a clay casing running through this body of slate. The chances for finding a "pocket" here looked mighty good to me, and I determined to return the next day and give it a try-out. Putting a piece of the quartz in my pocket, I continued on my way home. On entering the cabin I found Sam just sitting down to supper.

"Hello, Billy," said he, "you are just in time for the feast. I won't sing the praises of the bacon, but I'll bet your stomach never entertained slapjacks like these in your life."

After supper I handed him the quartz and said, "Sam, the chances for finding a pocket where I got that rock look mighty good to me. Go over with me in the morning and we'll go snooks in anything we find."

"All right, if you are willing to take me in, knowing that I know nothing about pocket mining, I will go in with you and we'll try and dig out a million or two."

Next morning, on arriving on the ground, I said to him, "Sam, you sit down and rest while I shovel off some of this clay and see what the vein looks like where it is in place."

"All right, I'll take a smoke while you are doing that."

I took my pick and began digging. I had been at work only a short time when appearances were so favorable that I concluded to "take a pan." So, taking my crowbar, I began gouging the vein. I had filled the pan about half full when I saw color of gold.

"Sam," I called, "I guess we've struck it. There's gold in sight."

"That's bully," said he, and coming over to me, sat down and watched me gouging, all the while scratching the clay and quartz in the pan over with a small stick. When I had the pan sufficiently full, I shoved it over to him and said, "Here, Sam, take this over to the panhole and wash it, while I take out another."

"Billy," said he, "I wouldn't puddle in that confounded clay for all the gold in Tuolumne County. You pan it; I don't want any of it."

"Very well, Sam, just put it in the panhole to soak till I get out this other pan and I'll wash it myself." The result from that first pan was about five dollars in gold, and by quitting time I had panned out about one hundred dollars' worth. So it went for the next ten days, I doing the work and Sam superintending. At the expiration of that time I had extracted all the gold from the pocket, which amounted to about seven hundred dollars. When I received the returns from the mint I proffered Sam one-half of the money as his share as my partner in our mining venture. He refused to take any of it, saying, "The knowledge of mining I acquired while we were taking out that pocket, and the pleasure it gave me, is a better equivalent for my time and labor than that little dab of money."

William R. Gillis, from *Memories of Mark Twain and Steve Gillis* (Sonora, Calif.: Banner, 1924), 37–38.

"A Morning with Bret Harte" (1894)

Henry J. W. Dam

In January 1865 Twain traveled with Jim Gillis to Angels Camp in Calaveras County. Later in the year he was introduced to Bret Harte (1836–1902), editor of the *Californian,* soon to become the founding editor of the *Overland Monthly* and the author of "The Luck of Roaring Camp" (1868).

GEORGE BARNES, a well-known journalist and an intimate friend of mine, walked into my office one morning with a young man whose appearance was unmistakably interesting. His head was striking. He had the curly hair, the aquiline nose, and even the aquiline *eye*—an eye so eagle-like that a second lid would not have surprised me—of an unusual and dominant nature. His eyebrows were very thick and bushy. His dress was careless, and his general manner one of supreme indifference to surroundings and circumstances. Barnes introduced him as Mr. Sam Clemens, and remarked that he had shown a very original talent in a number of newspaper contributions over the signature of "Mark Twain." We talked on different topics, and about a month afterwards Clemens dropped in on me again.

He had been away in the mining district on some newspaper assignment in the meantime. In the course of conversation he remarked that the unearthly laziness that prevailed in the town he had been visiting was beyond anything in his previous experience. He said the men did nothing all day long but sit around the barroom stove, spit, and "swop lies." He spoke in a slow, rather satirical, drawl which was in itself irresistible. He went on to tell one of those extravagant stories, and half unconsciously dropped into the lazy tone and manner of the original narrator. It was as graphic as it was delicious. I asked him to tell it again to a friend who came in, and then asked him to write it out for the *Californian.* He did so, and when published it was an emphatic success. It was the first work of his that attracted general attention, and it crossed the Sierras for an Eastern hearing.[1] From that point his success was steady. The story was "The Jumping Frog of Calaveras." It is now known and laughed over, I suppose, wherever the English language is spoken; but it will never be as funny to anybody in print as it was to me, told for the first time by the unknown Twain himself, on that morning in the San Francisco Mint.

Note

1. "Jim Smiley and His Jumping Frog" originally appeared in the New York *Saturday Press,* 18 November 1865. Harte published it under the title "The Celebrated Jumping Frog of Calaveras County" in the *Californian,* 16 December 1865. A revised version subsequently appeared in Twain's *The Celebrated Jumping Frog of Calaveras County and Other Sketches* (1867).

Henry J. W. Dam, "A Morning with Bret Harte," *McClure's* 4 (December 1894): 47–48.

"Mark Twain as He Was Known
during His Stay on the Pacific Slope" (1887)

GEORGE E. BARNES

> George Barnes recalled that James Anthony (1824–76), one of the owners of
> the *Sacramento Union* (1852–74), sponsored Twain's voyage to the Sandwich
> Islands in exchange for a series of articles about the trip. Twain sailed for
> Honolulu aboard the *Ajax* on 7 March 1866.

ONE OF HIS FORTUNATE MOVES during his Pacific experience was the trip he
made to Hawaii soon after leaving the *Call*. He had a very firm friend in James
Anthony, one of the proprietors of the Sacramento *Union,* now merged into
the *Record-Union.* When Mr. Clemens mentioned to that gentleman his desire to visit the isles of tranquil delights means were at once furnished him,
the consideration being a specified number of letters to be published in the
Union, on the social, commercial, and political condition of the Kanaka
group. Mr. Clemens "changed his foot," to use a turf phrase, when he entered on this contract. While before he did nothing with his pen but provoke
a smile from his readers, and was considered by those who did not know
him personally to be merely a man in motley, an embodiment of "laughter
holding both his sides,"[1] he had the practical sense to conclude that this was
an occasion when the laughter could not gracefully come in. His work was,
accordingly, a series of solid and at the same time very readable articles on
the islands that attracted general attention. They were eagerly perused in
the *Union* and exhaustively discussed in our Chamber of Commerce.

Note

1. Barnes quotes John Milton's "L'Allegro" (1631).

George E. Barnes, "Mark Twain as He Was Known during His Stay on the Pacific Slope,"
San Francisco Morning Call, 17 April 1887, 1.

"Mark Twain Incognito—A Reminiscence" (1926)

FRANKLIN H. AUSTIN

> Judge Samuel L. Austin, the cofounder in 1863 of the Onomea sugar planta-
> tion seven miles north of Hilo, hosted Twain on a brief visit during his weeks
> in Hawaii. His son Franklin H. Austin later recalled the event.

MARK TWAIN CAME bearing an introduction to my father in the name of Samuel Clemens. (We did not know it was Mark Twain until afterwards.) The letter was addressed, Judge S. L. Austin, Onomea Plantation, Hilo, Hawaii, Sandwich Islands. . . .

Late one Friday afternoon we were sitting on the veranda laughing and talking when we spied two horsemen coming up the hill around the corner of the boiling house and wondered who they could be. . . . As the riders came up over the immediate rise, by the store, onto the green common in front, trotting up to the hitching rail, we saw that they were strangers. Father started down to the front gate to welcome them and I after him, while the horse boy came running from the store veranda to take charge of the horses. After they dismounted it could be seen that one of them was a tall immaculately dressed Englishman and the other, evidently an American, of medium height, rather slouchily dressed in a brown linen suit and a native lauhala straw hat pulled over his eyes. He had a flowing silky brown mustache, rather dark tanned complexion and bushy dark brown hair with bright hazel eyes. The shorter of the two men stepped up to father and handed him a letter while the boy unstrapped his sheepskin leggings and removed his big jingling Mexican spurs, which were all the vogue at the time. . . . After reading the letter father held out his hand and smiling said: "I am glad to see you Mr. Clemens. You are welcome anyway as all strangers are, but with this letter from my old friend, you are doubly welcome." (I cannot think who the letter was from, but probably Mr. Williams of Williams, Dimond & Co., our San Francisco agents.)[1] Clemens then turned to the Englishman:

"This is my friend Brown, Judge Austin."

"My name is not Brown. It is Howard," hastily interposed the English-man in some vexation as he shook hands. "My traveling companion per-sists in calling me Brown."[2]

"Well, it's easier to remember," drawled Mr. Clemens.

Father looked first at the vexed Englishman's face, then caught a teasing twinkle in the eyes of the shorter man, and laughed:

"Oh, well, what's in a name," and led the way up the slate blue walk through the garden to the house. . . .

[At dinner that evening] Mr. Clemens had discarded his ridiculously starched brown linen coat. . . . From the start [he] dominated the conver-sation, keeping the table in roars of laughter with anecdotes and jokes, so much so, in fact, that father could hardly carve the roast and had to stand up to his job, while mother nearly spilled the vegetables she dished out. He seemed pleased with his seat at the head of the table where he could see all of the faces and note the effect of his jokes. The only one who did not seem to appreciate the fun was Howard, the Englishman, who wore a bored expression. I may be mistaken, but I imagined that Clemens was a little annoyed that he could not make "his friend Brown" laugh. His slow, drawling voice for which he became famous was too funny for anything. (In *Roughing It* he mentioned this "drawl" as an impediment of speech, but I doubt it.)[3]

After the most hilarious and enjoyable dinner in my memory, at Ono-mea, we retired to the parlor while the men filed out to their lodgings. The first thing Clemens did was to slap father on the back in a familiar way and remark:

"Now, Judge, I want your strongest pipe and strongest tobacco."

Father was startled. He was a very dignified man, tall, an inch over six feet, weighing two hundred and forty pounds, and no one ever took such liberties with him. But a twinkle came into his eyes and I was sure he meant mischief—to have revenge on this fresh and familiar young man:

"Wait just a few minutes until I have my man cut up some tobacco and we will retire to my smoking room and enjoy smoking to our hearts' con-tent," father said.

Mahulualani had just come in with the baby for mother to nurse before putting it to bed and father told her to call Kekau. When his servant an-swered the call he instructed him to cut up a lot of the "paka eleele" (black tobacco). . . . In the meantime, Mr. Clemens had crossed over to the center table and was admiring it—a beautiful koa table inlaid with other native woods, made by Kaiser, the old German cabinet maker at Hilo, to match the massive koa bookcase which was also his handiwork. Mark Twain at this time had only published *The Jumping Frog* and we got the book soon after its publication. Mother was a splendid reader and it was her custom to read aloud to us for an hour or two every evening when no one was visiting. Clemens spied the volume lying on the table and picked it up.

"I know the man who wrote this book."

"Oh, do you?" exclaimed mother. "What is he like? We have just roared with laughter over his funny stories."

"Oh, he isn't much good—awful drunk."

Mother was up in arms at once. "I don't believe it. He stories are so clean and full of fun. I think you must be prejudiced against him."

"Oh, well, perhaps he may have some good in him." And he never even smiled.

Kekau reported the tobacco cut and we all adjourned to the smoking room. Father handed Clemens the big pipe, which he raved over, and the box of tobacco Kekau had just cut up.

"Where did you get that Navy Plug?" he exclaimed. "It can't be bought."

Father explained how he got it and gave him a piece. Mother did not like tobacco smoke but she braved it. She saw that father had some joke up his sleeve and did not want to miss it or Mr. Clemens's stories. She knew at once what father was up to when he brought out the big pipe and shook her head smiling. Howard filled himself a pipe of milder tobacco and kept on talking to Miss E., with whom he seemed to be getting on very well. Mother sent the children to bed, but on account of my eccentricity for requiring so little sleep, I was allowed to remain awake and hear this man talk. As soon as Mr. Clemens had filled the big meerschaum and settled himself comfortably in one of father's easy rocking chairs, he began his stories and jokes again. After smoking his pipe out Mr. Howard excused himself and said he would retire.

"Don't hurry in the morning," father called. "We never have family breakfast until eight o'clock."

Miss E. began also to see what father was driving at when she saw Mr. Clemens with the big pipe, for it was a standing joke that at last Judge

Austin had got a pipe too strong for him. But it did not phase Sam Clemens a bit. He filled pipeful after pipeful and kept us laughing until two o'clock in the morning.

Notes

1. Williams, Dimond & Co. was a San Francisco shipping agency established in 1862.

2. In a series of twenty-five letters dated between March and June 1866 and published in the *Sacramento Union,* Twain repeatedly skewered an imaginary traveling companion named Brown. See *Mark Twain's Letters from Hawaii.*

3. Twain mentions his "drawling infirmity of speech" in chapter 78 of *Roughing It* (534).

Franklin H. Austin, "Mark Twain Incognito—A Reminiscence," *Friend* 96 (September 1926): 201; 96 (October 1926): 250–52.

"Mark Twain as He Was Known during His Stay on the Pacific Slope" (1887)

George E. Barnes

While in Hawaii Twain interviewed the surviving crew members of the *Hornet*, recently rescued from a lifeboat after a disaster at sea and drifting some 4,000 miles. Not only did he submit material about the *Hornet* survivors to the *Sacramento Union*, he published an article based on their diaries in *Harper's Monthly* (34 [December 1866]: 104–13) entitled "Forty-three Days in an Open Boat." Ironically, his name was misspelled ("Mark Swain") at the top of the piece. He later reminisced about authoring this article in "My Debut as a Literary Person" (*Century* 59 [November 1899]: 76–88). After he returned to San Francisco on 13 August 1866, Twain planned a lecture about his trip and consulted with such friends as Harte, the California journalist James F. Bowman (1831–82), and the poet and travel writer Charles Warren Stoddard (1843–1909). He delivered his first lecture on the Sandwich Islands on 2 October 1866 at Maguire's Academy of Music in San Francisco.

FATE FAVORED HIM in another way while he was on the island of Oahu. The celebrated clipper ship *Hornet,* commanded by Captain Mitchell of Freeport, Me., and owned by Grinnell, Minturn & Co. of New York, was burned in the Pacific equatorial belt; and while Mr. Clemens was making love to the wahinas and doing the *dolce far niente* [the pleasure of leisure] act among the cocoa palms of the islands of the sea, a boatload of those who had escaped from the vessel arrived at one of the outlying points after forty-two days of perilous voyaging, and all but dead from starvation. So emaciated were the unfortunates that the natives carried them, with the ease they would handle children, up from their frail bark and laid them in the shade on the welcome greensward. Mr. Clemens interviewed these miserable survivors and sent such a graphic description of the disaster and the subsequent sufferings of that portion of the crew and passengers who had reached land that the whole reading world thrilled with pity. It was through him the first news of the terrible misfortune was made known to the owners of the *Hornet* and the public. He afterward published a more ample and revised account of this boat voyage, gathered from Captain Mitchell himself, in *Harper's Magazine*. . . .

When Mr. Clemens returned to San Francisco from Honolulu he was no better off than when he left, except in prestige, and quite in the dark as to his future course. His friends advised that he prepare a lecture, and he did so. Some, however, did not favor the idea of his appearing on the platform. The writer recollects the evening distinctly when he came to the *Call* editorial room to advise with the people there on the subject. It was raining heavily. Mr. Clemens entered in a sort of uncertain way, clad in a thin black frockcoat—his only protection from the storm. Buttoned up to the chin and soaked, he looked, and no doubt felt, as if he had just been fished out of the Dismal swamp. Taking a mass of manuscript from out of the breast-pocket of his soddened garment, where it had only been imperfectly protected from the rain, he threw it on the desk before one of the editors and said:

"I wish you'd read that and give me your opinion about it. I think it might do for a lecture."

"A lecture?"

"Yes; it's about the islands. I've been to Bowman, and I've been to Harte and Stoddard, and the rest of the fellows, and they say, 'Don't do it, Mark; it will hurt your literary reputation.' "

The editor had glanced over some of the pages in the meantime, and found a well-constructed piece of work. Mr. Clemens stood with his back to the fire that was burning in the grate, half concealed in the vapory haze arising from his drying clothes, but waiting anxiously for the verdict.

"Mark," asked the editor, after a while, looking up from his manuscript, "which do you need most at present, money or literary reputation?"

"Money, by ---!" We are sorry it is necessary to blank his full reply. Mr. Clemens could be profane, in those days, on occasion.

"Then go to Maguire, hire the Academy of Music on Pine street, and there deliver this lecture. With the prestige of your recent letters from the Hawaiian islands, you will crowd the theater."

He followed the advice, and also of two or three other newspaper men who were of the same opinion, delivered the lecture—his first appearance before the public as a speaker—and realized, if memory serves, some twelve hundred or fourteen hundred dollars, a small fortune to him then. Mr. Clemens had stage fright when he faced the large audience; but luckily caught them, in his confusion, by a few impromptu remarks at the opening.

"Ladies and gentlemen," said he, "this is the first time I have attempted to speak in public, and if I know myself as well when the lecture is over as I do now, it will be the last."

That lecture and its profits proved an epoch in Mr. Clemens's life. He repeated it at Platt's hall, but not with the same success as at the Academy. Afterward, he lectured in the interior and Nevada, taking a newspaper friend with him as agent and business man. When he returned he was asked what luck he had. He answered, smiling significantly at the same time:

"Oh, pretty good. We would have done much better only D[enis McCarthy] (mentioning his friend's name) made a slight mistake."

"How was that?"

"He mistook our trip for a spree."

Ten years after this occurrence the writer happened to be in Honolulu and dropped into Whitney's bookstore—Whitney was also proprietor of the *Commercial Advertiser*.[1]

"Do you know Sam Clemens—or 'Mark Twain,' as he signs himself?" Whitney asked.

"Perfectly."

"Then when you return to San Francisco I wish you'd ask him to send back that Methodist missionary's book on the islands I lent him one day. I see he helped himself liberally to the poor old preachers' labors in his lecture.[2] The graphic description of Mauna Loa in eruption belongs to the missionary entirely. Clemens had no opportunity to see it."

Notes

1. Twain met Henry M. Whitney (1824–1904) of the *Honolulu Pacific Commercial Advertiser* during his visit to Hawaii in 1866. He later praised Whitney as "one of the fairest-minded and best-hearted cannibals I ever knew" (*Galaxy* 10 [December 1870]: 884).

2. Twain no doubt derived some information for both his Sandwich Islands lecture and chapter 74 of *Roughing It* from Henry T. Cheever's *The Island World of the Pacific; Being the Personal Narrative and Results of Travel Through the Sandwich or Hawaiian Islands* (1855) and Rufus Anderson's *The Hawaiian Islands: Their Progress and Condition Under Missionary Labors* (1869). Both volumes are cited in *Mark Twain's Letters from Hawaii*

(211). In his lecture on the Sandwich Islands, Twain did not mention Mauna Loa, however, though he did refer in passing to "the progress of one eruption" of a volcano he did not name (Fatout, *Mark Twain Speaking*, 12).

George E. Barnes, "Mark Twain as He Was Known during His Stay on the Pacific Slope," *San Francisco Morning Call*, 17 April 1887, 1.

"Fitch Recalls Mark Twain in Bonanza Times" (1919)

TOM FITCH

Twain delivered his Sandwich Islands lecture on 4 November 1866 in the hometown of Tom Fitch, who later recalled the occasion. After touring with the lecture in the interior of the state for two months, Twain delivered a farewell performance in San Francisco on 10 December and left San Francisco for New York aboard the *America* five days later.

EVEN AS HE became locally famous as a humorous writer he distrusted his ability to entertain an audience as a speaker. In 1865 [*sic*] he was my guest for a week at my home in Washoe City, Nev., and while there he delivered his lecture on "The Sandwich Islands." I procured for him the use of the courtroom and I acted as doorkeeper. The admission fee was a dollar.

As we journeyed to my home I said to him, cheerfully: "I have taken in, Sam, over $200." "And I," said he, gloomily, "have taken in over 200 people." "Don't depreciate yourself, Sam," said I. "As a humorous writer you outrank Artemus Ward or Petroleum V. Nasby,[1] and you will before long enjoy as great a national reputation." "It may be," said he, "but as a lecturer I am a fraud, ain't I, now?" "Well," said I, "maybe you have a slight tendency that way." "I suspected as much," said he, with tears in his voice, but—" and he brightened up, "there are hundreds of towns in the United States of more than 5000 inhabitants, and maybe I can play them all—once."

Note

1. David Ross Locke, aka Petroleum V. Nasby (1833–88), American journalist, humorist, and political commentator.

Tom Fitch, "Fitch Recalls Mark Twain in Bonanza Times," *San Francisco Chronicle*, 30 March 1919, 6F.

"Mark Twain as a Lecturer" (1867)

Edward H. House

Twain arrived in New York on 12 January 1867 and delivered his Sandwich Islands lecture at the Cooper Institute on 6 May. The playwright and journalist Edward H. (Ned) House (1836–1901) reviewed the lecture for the *New York Tribune*.

ABOUT A YEAR and a half ago, a communication entitled "Joe [*sic*] Smiley and his Jumping Frog," with the hitherto unknown signature of "Mark Twain," appeared in the *Saturday Press* of this city. The name, though new, was not remarkable, but the style of the letter was so singularly fresh, original, and full of character as to attract prompt and universal attention among the readers of light humorous literature. Mark Twain was immediately entered as a candidate for high position among writers of his class, and passages from his first contribution to the metropolitan press became proverbs in the mouths of his admirers. No reputation was ever more rapidly won. The only doubt appeared to be whether he could satisfactorily sustain it. Subsequent productions, however—most of them reproduced from California periodicals—confirmed the good opinion so suddenly vouchsafed him, and abundantly vindicated the applause with which his first essay had been received. In his case, as in that of many other American humorous writers, it was only the first step that cost. Since that time he has walked easily—let us hope not too easily—over his special course.

His writings being comparatively new to the public, and his position having been so recently established, it might perhaps have been doubted whether his name would at present be sufficient to attract an audience of any magnitude to witness his debut as a lecturer. But the proof of the general good-will in which he is already held was manifested last Monday evening by his brilliant reception at the Cooper Institute. The hall was crowded beyond all expectation. Not a seat was vacant, and all the aisles were filled with attentive listeners. The chance offering of "The Jumping Frog," carelessly cast, eighteen months ago, upon the Atlantic waters, returned to him in the most agreeable form which a young aspirant for popular fame could desire. The wind that was sowed with probably very little calculation as to its effect upon its future prospects, now enables him to reap quite a respectable tempest of encouragement and cordiality. His greeting was such as to inspire the utmost ease and confidence, and it is pleasant to add that his performance in every way justified the favor bestowed upon him. No other lecturer, of course excepting Artemus Ward, has so thoroughly succeeded in exciting the mirthful curiosity, and compelling the laughter of his hearers.

The subject of his address, "The Sandwich Islands," was treated mainly from a comic standpoint, although scraps of practical information and occasional picturesque descriptions of scenery and natural phenomena peculiar to that region were liberally interspersed. The scheme of the lecturer appeared to be to employ the various facts he had gathered as bases upon which to build fanciful illustrations of character, which were furthermore embellished with a multitude of fantastic anecdotes and personal reminiscences. The frequent incongruities of the narration—evidently intentional—made it all the more diverting, and the artifice of its partial incoherence was so cleverly contrived as to intensify the amusement of the audience, while leaving them for the most part in ignorance of the means employed. As to the manner of the speaker, it is difficult to write explicitly. It was certainly peculiar and original. Perhaps no better idea of it could be conveyed than by saying it is in almost every respect the exact opposite to that of the late Artemus Ward. It suited that admirable lecturer's humor to exhibit a nervous quickness and a vivacity which always communicated itself to those who surrounded him, and his best "points" were made by the droll affection of complete unconsciousness with which he uttered the most telling jests. Mark Twain's delivery, on the other hand, is deliberate and measured to the last degree. He lounges comfortably around his platform, seldom referring to notes, and seeks to establish a sort of button-hole relationship with his audience at the earliest possible moment. He is even willing to exchange confidences of the most literal nature. Having made an accidental error in figures, last Monday evening, at which there was great laughter, he paused and requested to be informed "what he had said," and was indisposed to proceed until his curiosity should be gratified. Instead of manifesting indifference to his own good jokes, he appears to relish them as heartily as anybody—a characteristic, by the bye, which also belongs to

[65]

the most eminent "reader" now known to the British public. The only obvious preconcerted "effect" which he employs is a momentary hesitation or break in his narration before touching the climax of an anecdote or a witticism. But his style is his own, and needs to be seen to be understood.

Edward H. House, "Mark Twain as a Lecturer," *New York Tribune,* 11 May 1867, 2.

"Mark Twain in California" (1898)

Noah Brooks

The California journalist Noah Brooks (1830–1903) helped to arrange Twain's tour to Europe and the Holy Land aboard the *Quaker City* from 8 June to 19 November 1867. In exchange for the $1,250 price of the trip, Twain agreed to send the *San Francisco Alta California* a series of travel essays. In all, he contributed fifty-one letters to the newspaper between 2 August 1867 and 8 January 1868.

WHEN, IN 1867, the proprietors of the *Alta California,* a daily newspaper of which I was then the managing editor, came to me with a proposition that the office should advance to Clemens the sum needed to pay his expenses on a trip into the Mediterranean, on condition that he should write letters to the paper, I was not surprised that they should regard the scheme with grave doubt of its paying them for their outlay. But the persuasiveness of Clemens's fast friend and admirer, Colonel John McComb[1] (then a member of our editorial staff), turned the scale, and Mark Twain was sent away happy on his voyage of adventure and observation, sailing from New York on the steamer *Quaker City.*

His letters to the *Alta California* made him famous. It was my business to prepare one of these letters for the Sunday morning paper, taking the topmost from a goodly pile that was stacked in a pigeonhole on my desk. Clemens was an indefatigable correspondent, and his last letter was slipped into the bottom of a tall stack.

It would not be quite accurate to say that Mark Twain's letters were the talk of the town; but it was very rarely that readers of the paper did not come into the office on Mondays to confide to the editors their admiration of the writer, and their enjoyment of his weekly contributions. The California newspapers copied these letters, with unanimous approval and disregard of the copyrights of author and publisher.

Note

1. John McComb (1829–96), supervising editor of the *San Francisco Alta California*.

Noah Brooks, "Mark Twain in California," *Century* 57 (November 1898): 98.

"The Cruise of the *Quaker City*" (1892)

MARY MASON FAIRBANKS

Among Twain's fellow passengers aboard the *Quaker City* was Mary Mason (aka "Mother") Fairbanks (1828–98), wife of the co-owner of the *Cleveland Herald*, who remained his devoted friend and confidant to the end of her life. As her initial comment below suggests, Twain immediately became a thorn in the side of Charles C. Duncan (1821–98), the organizer of the *Quaker City* excursion and captain of the ship. A parody of genteel travel narratives, *The Innocents Abroad* (1868) was not only Twain's first important book, it was his best-selling book during his life. Some 70,000 copies were sold during its first year alone.

"CAPTAIN DUNCAN desires me to say that passengers for the *Quaker City* must be on board tomorrow before the tide goes out. What the tide has to do with us or we with the tide is more than *I* know, but that is what the *captain* says."

This was the introductory speech with which Mark Twain made his first bow, more than twenty years ago, to the party of "Innocents Abroad" who had gathered in New York awaiting the sailing of the *Quaker City*. . . .

"I am like an old, burned-out crater; the fires of my life are all dead within me," he said to a fellow traveler as they walked the deck together. But this was only a youthful cynicism, for he was then little past thirty. He did not know then that he had begun a voyage of discovery by whose circuitous route he was to find his inspiration and his opportunity. He had acquired some local prestige in California and Nevada as a humorous journalist, and was the author of a Gulliver sort of story, "The Jumping Frog," but as yet he had furnished little evidence of superior literary ability.

At first he lolled about the ship as one committed to utter indolence. His drolleries and moderate movements rendered him conspicuous among the passengers, while from his table would come frequent peals of contagious laughter, in the midst of which his own serious and questioning face and air of injured innocence were thoroughly mirth-provoking. Those who had the good fortune to share with him the adventures with which his remarkable and grotesque narratives have made the public familiar recall with interest the gradual waking up of this man of genius. His keen eyes discerned the incongruities of character around him, into which his susceptibility to absurdities gave him quick insight. Here in this goodly company of pilgrims, embracing men of mind and men of manners and their opposites, he put himself at school. With what result, let the unparalleled story of the *Innocents Abroad* bear witness.

It followed that in this journey of months, such a man as Mr. Clemens found his own *coterie* of congenial friends. With them he studied and discoursed of the strange countries at whose shores they were to anchor. He read their poets with inimitable pathos and he was the ship's oracle upon the Old Masters, whom later he ridiculed in his book.

To his preferred friends he revealed his true character, but, with a perversity on his part induced by the unmerited criticism of some of the company, he exaggerated his faults to others. Hence the conflicting estimates of Mark Twain's character, which often confound those who know him for what he is.

The appearance of *The Innocents Abroad,* which met with an unparalleled circulation, secured for its author a sudden notoriety. For an American ship to go cruising in foreign seas simply for pleasure was in those days a new departure, and although the witty author did not glorify the American traveler, his book was the event of the year. Its success attested its merit and at once he decided upon his career. It was manifest that he had found his calling, and had mined in a richer lode than California or Nevada could ever have opened to him. . . . The *Quaker City* sailed out of New York harbor with no celebrities on board. She brought back the Great American Humorist.

Mary Mason Fairbanks, "The Cruise of the *Quaker City*," *Chautauquan* 14 (January 1892): 429–30, 432.

"About Mark Twain" (1877)

ANONYMOUS

> On his part, Captain Duncan was not amused by Twain's portrayal of him in *The Innocents Abroad,* and he occasionally tried to retaliate over the years. In the end, of course, he was outmatched in the battle of wits.

AN AUDIENCE OF three hundred and odd people paid 25 cents apiece last evening for admission to the Tompkins Avenue Congregational Church in Brooklyn to hear from the lips of the *Quaker City*'s captain an accurate account of that ship's eventful trip to the Holy Land ten years ago, which accurate account the Captain, with some scorn, declares *Innocents Abroad* in no sense to be. . . . "One of the first persons," said the Captain, "who made application for a berth in the *Quaker City,* when in the spring of 1867 I organized this grand excursion, was a tall, lanky, unkempt, unwashed individual, who seemed to be full of whiskey or something like it, and who filled my office with the fumes of bad liquor.[1] He said he was a Baptist minister from San Francisco and desired to travel for his health. I knew him at once, it was Mark Twain, and I said, 'You don't look like a Baptist minister or smell like one either.' I don't intend to say much of Mark Twain, but I will just relate a single incident. We used to breakfast at 8 o'clock every morning, and everybody was always punctual except Mark Twain; he was always late. One morning he came straggling in tardy as usual, and picking up his cup began to abuse the coffee. He blamed the steward, he blamed everybody, and after all it turned out that the coffee he had found fault with for being so weak was an excellent cup of tea. In relating this experience in his book he says 'that passenger made an egregious ass of himself,' and I think as much." This cut appeared sufficient for the Captain, and he proceeded to pure history, only once more attacking Mr. "Twain," and this for an outrageously libelous paragraph in *Innocents Abroad,* wherein it is stated that Captain Duncan, at the great 4th of July dinner, made the following speech: "Ladies and gentlemen, may you all live long and prosper. Steward, pass up another basket of champagne."[2] "There is no truth in it," said the libeled Captain; "it was the speech Mark Twain was hankering for me to make, but if I had made any I would have said something sensible." (Applause.) "I used to be proud of *Innocents Abroad*," added the Captain, "until I discovered how unreliable it is."

Notes

1. Twain responded to Duncan in a letter to the *New York World* (18 February 1877, 5). To the charge that he seemed "full of whiskey" when he engaged passage, he replied, "I hope this is true, but I cannot say, because it is so long ago. . . . I was poor—*I* couldn't afford good whiskey. How could I know that the 'captain' was so particular about the quality of a man's liquor?"

2. *The Innocents Abroad,* chapter 10 (93): "Captain Duncan made a good speech; he made the only good speech of the evening. He said: 'Ladies and Gentlemen:—May we all live to a green old age and be prosperous and happy. Steward, bring up another basket of champagne.'"

Anonymous, "About Mark Twain," *New York World,* 12 January 1877, 5.

From *Reminiscences of Senator William M. Stewart of Nevada* (1908)

WILLIAM M. STEWART

After Twain returned to New York aboard the *Quaker City*, he began to "clerk" in Washington for William M. Stewart (1827–1909), a U.S. senator from Nevada (1863–75, 1887–1905), while he reworked his *Alta California* letters into a book. Stewart later reminisced about the vagaries of the arrangement in his autobiography. On his part, Twain recorded a humorous account of his Washington experience in "My Late Senatorial Secretaryship," *Galaxy* 5 (May 1868): 633–36.

ABOUT THE WINTER of 1867, I think, while my family was in Paris, I lived in a rather tumbledown building which at that time stood on the northwest corner of Fourteenth and F Streets, N.W., opposite the old Ebbitt House, where many of my Congressional cronies had quarters. The house was a weather-beaten old place, a relic of early Washington. . . .

I was seated at my window one morning when a very disreputable-looking person slouched into the room. He was arrayed in a seedy suit, which hung upon his lean frame in bunches with no style worth mentioning. A sheaf of scraggy black hair leaked out of a battered old slouch hat, like stuffing from an ancient Colonial sofa, and an evil-smelling cigar butt, very much frazzled, protruded from the corner of his mouth. He had a very sinister appearance. He was a man I had known around the Nevada mining camps several years before, and his name was Samuel L. Clemens.

I suppose he was the most lovable scamp and nuisance who ever blighted Nevada. When I first knew him he was a reporter on the *Territorial Enterprise*, which was otherwise a very reputable paper published in Virginia City. . . . I thought he had been hanged, or elected to Congress, or something like that, and I had forgotten him, until he slouched into my room, and then of course I remembered him. I said:

"If you put anything in the paper about me I'll sue you for libel." He waved the suggestion aside with easy familiarity.

"Senator," he said, "I've come to see you on important business. I am just back from the Holy Land."

"That is a mean thing to say of the Holy Land when it isn't here to defend itself," I replied, looking him over. "But maybe you didn't get all the *advantages*. You ought to go back and take a post-graduate course. Did you walk him?"

"I have a proposition," said Clemens, not at all ruffled. "There's millions in it.[1] All I need is a little cash stake. I have been to the Holy Land with a party of innocent and estimable people who are fairly aching to be written up, and I think I could do the job neatly and with dispatch if I were not troubled with other—more—pressing—considerations. I've started the book already, and it is a wonder. I can vouch for it."

"Let me see the manuscript," I said. He pulled a dozen sheets or so from his pocket and handed them to me. I read what he had written, and saw that it was bully, so I continued, "I'll appoint you my clerk at the Senate, and you can live on the salary. There's a little hall bedroom across the way where you can sleep, and you can write your book in here. Help yourself to the whiskey and cigars, and wade in."

He accepted all of my invitations, in the modest and unassuming manner for which he had been noted in Virginia, and became a member of my family, and my clerk.

It was not long before Clemens took notice of Miss Virginia.[2] Her timid, aristocratic nature shrank from him, and I think she was half afraid of him. He did not overlook any opportunities to make her life miserable, and was always playing some joke on her. He would lurch around the halls, pretending to be intoxicated, and would throw her into a fit about six times a day.

He would burn the light in his bedroom all night, and started her figuring up her expense account with a troubled, anxious face. Pretty soon he took to smoking cigars in bed.

She never slept after this discovery, but every night would lie awake, with her clothes handy on a chair, expecting the house to be burned down any minute, and ready to skip out at the first alarm; and she became so pale, and thin, and wasted, and troubled that it would have melted a pirate's heart to see her. She crept to my room one day, the mere shadow of her former self.

She no longer leaned over backward, as she usually did, because of being so straight and dignified, but was badly bent. I was shocked.

"Senator," she said, "if you don't ask that friend of yours to leave I shall have to give up my lodging-house, and God knows what will become of me then. He smokes cigars in bed all night, and has ruined my best sheets, and I expect to be burned out any time, but I can't keep it up much longer. I need sleep."

I told her to leave the room, and I called Clemens. He slouched in.

"Clemens," I said, "if you don't stop annoying this little lady I'll give you a sound thrashing—I'll wait till that book's finished. I don't want to interfere with literature—I'll thrash you after it's finished."

He blew some smoke in my face.

"You are mighty unreasonable," he replied. "Why do you want to interfere with my pleasures?"

I thought he would behave himself after that. But one day a week later Miss Virginia staggered into my room again, in a flood of tears. She said:

"Senator, that man will kill me. I can't stand it. If he doesn't go I'll have to ask you to give up your rooms, and the Lord knows whether I'll be able to rent them again."

This filled me with alarm. I was very comfortable where I was. I sent her away kindly, and called Clemens. He slouched in again.

"You have got to stop this foolishness," I said. "If you don't cease annoying this little lady I'll amend my former resolution, and give you that thrashing here and now. Then I'll send you to the hospital, and pay your expenses, and bring you back, and you can finish your book upholstered in bandages." He saw that I meant business.

"All right," he replied, "I'll give up my amusements, but I'll get even with you."

He did. When he wrote *Roughing It* he said I had cheated him out of some mining stock or something like that, and that he had given *me* a sound thrashing; and he printed a picture of me in the book, with a patch over one eye.[3]

Clemens remained with me for some time. He wrote his book in my room, and named it *The Innocents Abroad.* I was confident that he would come to no good end, but I have heard of him from time to time since then, and I understand that he has settled down and become respectable.

Notes

1. The mantra of Colonel Sellers in Twain's play *The Gilded Age*.

2. Stewart's landlady Virginia Wells, "an estimable lady about 70 years of age, prim, straight as a ramrod, and with smooth-plastered white hair" (Stewart 219).

3. Stewart refers to an illustration captioned "Portrait of Mr. Stewart" in chapter 44 of *Roughing It* (289).

William M. Stewart, from *Reminiscences of Senator William M. Stewart of Nevada,* ed. George Rothwell Brown (New York: Neale, 1908), 219–24.

"Mark Twain in California" (1898)

NOAH BROOKS

> After Twain contracted with the American Publishing Co. of Hartford to pub-
> lish his *Quaker City* book, he learned that the editors of the *Alta California*
> had copyrighted the travel letters he had sent them during the voyage. He
> sailed for San Francisco in March 1868—his final trip to California—to nego-
> tiate rights to them. In June, his rights to the articles secure, he asked Bret
> Harte to help him whip them into shape for republication. Later, he allowed
> that Harte "trimmed and trained and schooled me patiently until he changed
> me from an awkward utterer of coarse grotesquenesses to a writer of para-
> graphs and chapters that have found a certain favor" (*Mark Twain's Letters*
> 4:316). Noah Brooks chronicled the circumstances of Twain's travail/travel
> during these weeks. Twain returned to New York in late July.

DURING THE SUMMER of that year, while Clemens was in the Eastern
States, there came to us a statement, through the medium of the Associated Press, that he was preparing for publication his letters which had been
printed in the *Alta California*. The proprietors of that newspaper were
wroth. They regarded the letters as their private property. Had they not
bought and paid for them? Could they have been written if they had not
furnished the money to pay the expenses of the writer? And although up
to that moment there had been no thought of making in San Francisco a
book of Mark Twain's letters from abroad, the proprietors of the *Alta California* began at once their preparations to get out a cheap paper-covered
edition of those contributions. An advance notice in the press dispatches
sent from California was regarded as a sort of answer to the alleged challenge of Mark Twain and his publishers. This sent the perplexed author
hurrying back to San Francisco in quest of an ascertainment of his real
rights in his own letters. Amicable counsels prevailed. The cheap San
Francisco edition of the book was abandoned, and Mark Twain was allowed to take possession of his undoubted copyright, and his book of let-

ters, entitled *The Innocents Abroad,* was published in the latter part of that year—1869.

Noah Brooks, "Mark Twain in California," *Century* 57 (November 1898): 99.

"Mark Twain" (1910)

J. N. LARNED

> Twain dutifully courted Olivia Langdon (1845–1904), the daughter of a prominent and prosperous family in Elmira, New York, for nearly two years before they were married in February 1870. Twain purchased a one-third interest in the Buffalo Express for $25,000 in August 1869, partly with a loan from his father-in-law, Jervis Langdon, and sold it at a $10,000 loss in April 1871 after he realized he was ill suited to the grind of daily journalism. Perhaps his most memorable experience as an editor was the publication of a burlesque map he drew for the newspaper captioned "Fortifications of Paris," which appeared on 17 September 1870. Twain visually parodied a map entitled "The Defences and Environs of Paris" that had appeared on the front page of the New York Tribune four days earlier. Josephus Nelson Larned (1836–1913), part owner of the Buffalo Express with Twain, remembered the occasion forty years later.

MY ASSOCIATION WITH MARK TWAIN for about a year, during the period of his connection with the *Express,* when I worked in editorial fellowship with him, face to face across the table that we shared, gave me a close acquaintance which I count among the greater privileges of my life. . . . When Mark was writing he indulged himself in a frank enjoyment of his own humor that was interesting to see. He often stopped in his work to laugh at what had come into his mind, and his own relish of it was pretty certain to be prophetic of the zeal with which it would be read. I doubt if he ever enjoyed anything more than the jackknife engraving that he did on a piece of board for a military Map of the Siege of Paris, which was printed in the *Express* from his original "plate," with accompanying explanations and comments. His half day of whittling and the laughter that went with it are something that I find pleasant to remember. Indeed, my whole experience of association with him is a happy memory which I am fortunate in having.

J. N. Larned, "Mark Twain," *Buffalo Evening Express,* 26 April 1910, 5.

From *My Mark Twain* (1910)

W. D. HOWELLS

W. D. Howells (1837–1920), the foremost American literary critic of the late nineteenth century and one of the most important American novelists of the period, was associate editor of the *Atlantic Monthly* from 1866 to 1871 and its editor from 1871 to 1881. He also became Twain's closest literary friend. In his memoir of Twain, Howells remembered a luncheon in Bret Harte's honor at Ober's restaurant in Boston on 2 November 1871, hosted by the California journalist Ralph Keeler (1840–73). Among the other attendees were Twain; James T. Fields (1817–81), a prominent Boston publisher and Howells's predecessor as editor of the *Atlantic Monthly* (1861–71); and Thomas Bailey Aldrich (1836–1907), Howells's successor as editor of the magazine (1881–90).

IT WAS IN THE little office of James T. Fields, over the bookstore of Ticknor & Fields, at 124 Tremont Street, Boston, that I first met my friend of now forty-four years, Samuel L. Clemens. Mr. Fields was then the editor of the *Atlantic Monthly,* and I was his proud and glad assistant, with a pretty free hand as to manuscripts, and an unmanacled command of the book-notices at the end of the magazine. I wrote nearly all of them myself, and in 1869 I had written rather a long notice of a book just winning its way to universal favor. In this review I had intimated my reservations concerning *The Innocents Abroad,*[1] but I had the luck, if not the sense, to recognize that it was such fun as we had not had before. I forget just what I said in praise of it, and it does not matter; it is enough that I praised it enough to satisfy the author. He now signified as much, and he stamped his gratitude into my memory with a story wonderfully allegorizing the situation, which the mock modesty of print forbids my repeating here. Throughout my long acquaintance with him his graphic touch was always allowing itself a freedom which I cannot bring my fainter pencil to illustrate. He had the Southwestern, the Lincolnian, the Elizabethan breadth of parlance, which I suppose one ought not to call coarse without calling one's self prudish; and I was often hiding away in discreet holes and corners the letters in which he had loosed his bold fancy to stoop on rank suggestion; I could not bear to burn them, and I could not, after the first reading, quite bear to look at them. I shall best give my feeling on this point by saying that in it he was Shakespearian, or if his ghost will not suffer me the word, then he was Baconian.[2] ...

There is a gap in my recollections of Clemens, which I think is of a year or two, for the next thing I remember of him is meeting him at a lunch in Boston, given us by that genius of hospitality, the tragically destined Ralph Keeler, author of one of the most unjustly forgotten books, *Vagabond Adventures,* a true bit of picaresque autobiography. Keeler never had any money, to the general knowledge, and he never borrowed, and he could not have had credit at the restaurant where he invited us to feast at his expense. There was T. B. Aldrich; there was J. T. Fields, much the oldest of our company, who had just freed himself from the trammels of the publishing business, and was feeling his freedom in every word; there was Bret Harte, who had lately come East in his princely progress from California; and there was Clemens. Nothing remains to me of the happy time but a sense of idle and aimless and joyful talk-play, beginning and ending nowhere, of eager laughter, of countless good stories from Fields, of a heat-lightning shimmer of wit from Aldrich, of an occasional concentration of our joint mockeries upon our host, who took it gladly; and amid the discourse, so little improving, but so full of good fellowship, Bret Harte's fleeting dramatization of Clemens's mental attitude toward a symposium of Boston illuminates. "Why, fellows," he spluttered, "this is the dream of Mark's life," and I remember the glance from under Clemens's feathery eyebrows which betrayed his enjoyment of the fun. We had beefsteak with mushrooms, which in recognition of their shape Aldrich hailed as shoe-pegs, and to crown the feast we had an omelet souse, which the waiter brought in as flat as a pancake, amid our shouts of congratulations to poor Keeler, who took them with appreciative submission. It was in every way what a Boston literary lunch ought not to have been in the popular ideal which Harte attributed to Clemens.

Notes

1. "Reviews and Literary Notices," *Atlantic Monthly* 24 (December 1869): 764–66.
2. Twain believed that Francis Bacon wrote the plays attributed to William Shakespeare. See also Twain's *Is Shakespeare Dead?* (New York: Harper & Bros., 1909).

W. D. Howells, from *My Mark Twain* (New York: Harper & Bros., 1910), 3–4, 6–7.

"Mark Twain in London" (1872)

MONCURE D. CONWAY

Twain sailed on 21 August 1872 to research a book—never completed—on England. He spent the next two and a half months taking notes and occasionally lecturing. Twain spoke at the Savage Club in London on 22 September 1872 and was later elected to honorary membership in this historic "gentleman's club." Moncure Daniel Conway (1832–1907), an American Unitarian minister and author, described Twain's talk in one of his letters to the *Cincinnati Commercial*.

YOU MAY OBSERVE in the papers which will reach you from this side at the same time with this letter accounts of a lunar rainbow of extraordinary splendor and surpassing hues which has just occurred here. You may wonder what was the occasion of such an illumination in London. The thing will be explained when I announce that it occurred on the same evening in which Mark Twain was entertained by the Savage Club. . . . On the occasion of his first appearance at the Club he came attended by his publisher, the genial and clever Mr. [George] Routledge. Fortunately the chairman of the evening was the inimitable [John L.] Toole, the wittiest actor in London. Mark Twain was given the seat of honor at his side, and when the repast was over, Toole arose and invited us to fill our glasses. A large proportion of the fifty or sixty persons present did not know that any distinguished guest was present until this unusual invitation to fill glasses was given. The necessity of repairing to the theaters has made it the rule that there shall be no toasts or speeches to prolong the dinners, except at the Christmas or anniversary banquet. All now set themselves to know what was up. Toole then said: "We have at our table Mark Twain." At these words a roar of cheers arose, and for some moments the din was indescribable. Toole then proceeded in a penitent way to confess that for a year or two he had been cribbing from Mark Twain in a way that must now, he feared, suffer a humiliating exposure. When now and then he had indulged in an innocent "gag," he had had friends rush to him behind the scenes or on the streets with "Toole, that was capital; your own, I suppose?" Now invariably when he had been so greeted the thing happened to be Mark Twain's. So all he could say was: "Oh—ah—well—ahem—glad you liked it." He could not exactly make out how it was, but when he did put in a bit of originality, his friends seemed very rarely to come and inquire whether it was his own or not. Toole's deferential gravity and innocent look is always amusing, but his fooling in this speech was unusually funny. When Mark Twain arose, the contrast between him and the clever, comic actor beside him was singular. The one is small, with a jolly, blooming countenance, full of quickness, eye ever on the alert; the American tall, thin, grave, with something of the look of a young divinity student fallen among worldlings. Being one of the Savages, I have the happiness of laying before your readers Twain's speech, of which the Londoners are in hopeless ignorance, but, alas, it loses much by being transferred to paper. In its proper setting, related to its immediate environment and delivered with a solemn and dry suavity, quite indescribable, it struck others present besides myself as the best after-dinner speech we had ever heard.

The speaker had on full evening dress—swallow-tail coat, white cravat, and all that,—to wear which to the club dinner calls down upon the wearer considerable chaff, until it be meekly apologized for. This fact will explain the opening sentences of Twain's speech, which were uttered with deprecating lowliness. "Mr. Chairman and gentleman," he began, "it affords me sincere pleasure to meet this distinguished club, a club which has extended its hospitalities and its cordial welcome to so many of my countrymen. I hope"—and here the speaker's voice became low and fluttering—"you will excuse these clothes. I am going to the theater; that will explain these clothes. I have other clothes than these." The manner in which these words were uttered produced a great deal of merriment. "Judging human nature by what I have seen of it, I suppose that the customary thing for a stranger to do when he stands here is to make a pun on the name of this club, under the impression, of course, that he is the first man that that idea has occurred to. It is a credit to our human nature, not a blemish upon it; for it shows that underlying all our depravity (and God knows, and *you* know we are depraved enough) and all our sophistication, and untarnished by them, there is a sweet germ of innocence and simplicity still. When a stranger says to me, with a glow of inspiration in his eyes, some gentle innocuous little thing about 'Twain' and 'one flesh,' and all that sort of thing, I don't

[83]

try to crush that man into the earth—no. I feel like saying: 'Let me take you by the hand, sir; let me embrace you; I have not heard than pun for weeks.' We *will* deal in palpable puns. We *will* call parties named 'King' Your Majesty, and we will say to the Smiths that we think we have heard that name before somewhere. Such is human nature. We cannot alter this. It is God that made us for some and wise purpose. Let us not repine. But though I may seem strange, may seem eccentric, I mean to refrain from punning upon the name of this club, though I could make a very good one if I had time to think about it—a week.

"I cannot express to you what entire enjoyment I find in this first visit to this prodigious metropolis of yours. Its wonders seem to me to be limitless. I go about as in a dream—as in a realm of enchantment—where many things are rare and beautiful, and all things are strange and marvelous. Hour after hour I stand—I stand spellbound, as it were—and gaze upon the statuary in Leicester Square. [Great laughter—Leicester Square being a horrible chaos, with the relic of an equestrian statue in the center, the king being headless and limbless, and the horse in little better condition.] I visit the mortuary effigies of noble old Henry the Eighth, and Judge Jeffreys, and the preserved Gorilla, and try to make up my mind which of my ancestors I admire the most. I go to that matchless Hyde Park and drive all *around* it, and then I start to enter it at the Marble Arch—and—am induced to change my mind." [Cabs are not admitted in Hyde Park—nothing less aristocratic than a private carriage.] "It is a great benefaction—is Hyde Park. There, in his Hansom cab, the invalid can go—the poor sad child of misfortune—and insert his nose between the railings, and breathe the pure health-giving air of the country and of heaven. And if he is a well invalid, who isn't obliged to depend upon parks for his country air, he can drive inside—if he owns his vehicle. I drive round and round Hyde Park, and the more I see of the edges of it the more grateful I am that the margin is extensive.

"And I have been to the Zoological Gardens. What a wonderful place that is! I never have seen such a curious and interesting variety of wild animals in any garden before—except 'Mabille.'[1] I never believed before there were so many different kinds of animals in the world as you can find there—and I don't believe it yet. I have been to the British Museum. I would advise you to drop in there sometime when you have nothing to do for—five minutes—if you have never been there. It seems to me the noblest monument that this Nation has yet erected to her greatness. I say to her *our* greatness—as a Nation. True, she has built other monuments, and stately ones, as well; but these she has uplifted in honor of two or three colossal demigods who have stalked across the world's stage, destroying tyrants and delivering Nations, and whose prodigies will still live in memories of men ages after their monuments shall have crumbled to dust—I refer to the Wellington and Nelson columns, and—the Albert Memorial." [2]

[Sarcasm.—The Albert Memorial is the finest monument in the world, and celebrates the existence of as commonplace a person as good luck ever lifted out of obscurity.]

"The Library at the British Museum I find particularly astounding. I have read there hours together and hardly made an impression on it. I revere that library. It is the author's friend. I don't care how mean a book is, it always takes one copy." [A copy of every book printed in Great Britain must by law be sent to the British Museum, a law much complained of by publishers.] "And then, every day that author goes there to gaze at that book, and is encouraged to go on in the good work. And what a touching sight it is of a Saturday afternoon to see the poor toil-worn clergymen gathered together in that vast reading-room cabbaging sermons for Sunday!

"You will pardon my referring to these things. Everything in this monster city interests me, and I cannot keep from talking, even at the risk of being instructive. People here seem always to express distances by parables. To a stranger it is just a little confusing to be so parabolic—so to speak. I collar a citizen, and I think I am going to get some valuable information out of him. I ask him how far it is to Birmingham, and he says it is twenty-one shillings and sixpence. Now, we know that don't help a man any who is trying to learn. I find myself downtown somewhere, and I want to get some sort of idea of where I am—being usually lost when alone—and I stop a citizen and say: 'How far is it to Charing Cross?' 'Shilling fare in a cab,' and off *he* goes. I suppose if I were to ask a Londoner how far it is from the sublime to the ridiculous, he would try to express it in coin.

"But I am trespassing upon your time with these geological statistics and historical reflections. I will no longer keep you from your orgies. 'Tis a real pleasure for me to be here, and I thank you, for the name of the Savage Club is associated in my mind with the kindly interest and the friendly offices which you lavished upon an old friend of mine who came among you a stranger, and you opened your English hearts to him and gave him welcome and a home—Artemus Ward. Asking that you will join me, I give you his memory."

In deep silence and with much feeling, the company present rose and drank to this sentiment. Then, after some moments, the newcomer was heartily cheered, and the members went up to make his acquaintance. Soon after Mark Twain went off to the Gayety Theater with some friends, and saw Byron's play, "Good News," and "Ali Baba," (a new extravaganza,) in both of which Toole appeared, and in the latter of which he had the most absurd gag, crying out, "As Mark Twain says in the 'Jumping Frog,' 'Lie on, Macduff, and thingumbobbed be he," &c.

Note

1. Twain also refers to his brief visit to the Jardin Mabille pleasure garden in Paris in *The Innocents Abroad,* chapter 14 (133–37).

2. Prince Albert of Saxe-Coburg and Gotha (1819–1861) was the husband of Queen Victoria.

Moncure D. Conway, "Mark Twain in London," *Cincinnati Commercial,* 10 October 1872, 4.

From *Autobiography* (1904)

MONCURE D. CONWAY

> After Twain returned to England in May 1873 to work on his travel book on England, he agreed to deliver his Sandwich Islands lecture in the Queen's Concert Rooms on Hanover Square the week of 13–18 October. Conway remembered Twain's first performance that week in his autobiography.

HIS REPUTATION WAS WIDE in England, but it appeared singular that instead of appearing, like Artemus Ward and other American entertainers, at Egyptian Hall or some popular place, he should select the most fashionable hall in London, and charge high prices for admission. The hall was crowded with fashionable people in evening dress, of whom few if any had ever seen Mark. He came on the platform in full dress with the air of a manager announcing a disappointment, and stammered out apologies. "Mr. Clemens had landed at Liverpool, and had fully hoped to reach London in time, but," etc. The murmurs were deep and threatened to be loud, when Mark added that he was happy to say that Mark Twain was present and would now give his lecture. Loud applause and laughter greeted him, and he proceeded to mention several subjects he had thought of for his lecture. "But since my arrival I have found the English people so frantic in their interest in the—Sandwich Islands,"—the sentence was cut short by an explosion of laughter. "But before describing the Sandwich Islands," he resumed,—and that was the last we heard of the islands. The lecture was brimful of amusing inventions of far-western life, given with admirable gravity and action. After telling about a wild game of poker he suddenly became unctuous and added,—"All that was long ago. I never gamble *now*" (*sotto voce,* "unless I can make something by it"). So, after a narrative about a duel, he said in an exalted tone: "But I never fight duels now. If a man insults me, do I challenge that man? Oh, no! (uplifting his eyes piously) I take that man by the hand, and with soft persuasive words lead him to a dimly lighted apartment and—kill him!" The audience was in an ecstasy of delight and laughter from first to last.

Moncure Conway, from *Autobiography* (Boston: Houghton Mifflin, 1904), 2:142–43.

"In Old Bohemia" (1908)

CHARLES WARREN STODDARD

> During the winter of 1873–74, Charles Warren Stoddard, one of the so-called Golden State Trinity (along with Harte and Ina Coolbrith [1841–1928] in the late 1860s), worked as Twain's private secretary. Stoddard later reminisced about these months.

WHEN I WAS WITH Mark Twain in London . . . Mark found the London fog indigestible and six lectures a week at the Queen's Concert Rooms, Hanover Square, a burden. . . . About three o'clock of each afternoon—barring Sunday, which was a day of rest—Mark would begin to dread the approach of eight when he had to face a stolid British audience sitting up to its neck in the fog that had followed it into the hall. . . . As soon as Mark found himself before an audience he was absolutely at his ease; so were those who listened to him. Of course there was handshaking and albums to be written in after each lecture, but by the time Mark and I, and often Dolby,[1] had returned to the Langham Hotel the lecturer was in his glory, for there was a night and a day between him and his next appearance on the rostrum.

Our rooms were delightful; the fog was shut out of them; a cheerful English fireside is something never to be forgotten and I shall never forget that one. Perhaps just by way of opening the evening's entertainment Mark would go to the piano and, to his own accompaniment, sing in a very rich and musical voice some old negro melody, such as "Swing Low, Sweet Chariot." It was a joy to hear him and I did not have to be paid to listen.

Presently Mark would wander with a careless or unconscious air over to a table in the large reception room and begin to rearrange certain glasses, spoons, etc., that were always waiting there. A diligent search through London had resulted in the collection of ingredients almost unknown in the England of that day and certainly not generally recognized by the natives of the country.

We gathered by the fireside, he and I—that sounds like the opening line of some half-forgotten melody—a song of good fellowship and the merry days of yore. Mark brought with him two dainty glasses brimming with a delicately-tinted liquid. The glasses were equally divided between us. We drank in silence and were supremely happy for some moments. Then Mark, arousing from a revery, would turn to me and say in that mellow, slowly-flowing voice of his: "Now you make one, Charlie." With genuine embarrassment I would protest. I used to say: "Mark, you know that I cannot make one: I never could. It is not an art that can be acquired. It is a gift, a birthright, and there are not many who are so richly endowed as you. There is no recipe in the wide, wide world that even followed religiously would come within a thousand miles of that you lately offered me. Even if you were to stand over me with a club and tell me exactly what to do and I did just as you told me, the result would not be worthy of being mentioned in the same day with yours."

Then Mark—persuasively—"O! don't be afraid: I'll stand by you. If at first you don't succeed try, try again. Come now—it's your turn."

With fear and trembling I'd make an effort. Mark's reverie was longer than usual after I had done my best. I watched him furtively out of the corner of my eye, for I loved him and coveted his respect. Presently, as if arousing from a bad dream, he'd spring from his chair and gathering our glasses murmur, "Your's was so damned bad I'll have to make another one to take the taste out of my mouth." That was a happy thought of his: I needed a disinfectant as much as he did—but the end was not yet. He had hopes of me: he believed that eventually I might become the worthy apostle of a past master like himself. Again and again I'd try, but his verdict was ever the same. When my humiliation began to curdle my blood, and my depression of spirit was such that I could no longer disguise it, he would turn suddenly upon me and say, with unwonted severity: "You're going to sleep!" I could only meekly reply: "Dear Mark, let me go to my bed; you come and sit by me and talk." After this successful compromise, the last I could remember would be his mournful refrain of "Too much bitters! Too much bitters!"

That was a wonderfully interesting experience for me. Every night we talked till cock-crow; I leading him into the paths of the past and he recalling his youth with a charm and a freshness that was positively fascinating. I could have written his life just after our eight weeks together were over. I wish to heaven I had.

Note

1. George Dolby (d. 1900), who had been Charles Dickens's agent, managed Twain's lectures in England during the fall and winter of 1873–74.

Charles Warren Stoddard, "In Old Bohemia," *Pacific Monthly* 19 (March 1908): 262–63.

"Mark Twain—An Intimate Portrait" (1910)

Henry Watterson

> In early 1874 Twain drafted—or at least slightly rewrote and then copy-righted—a five-act play based on *The Gilded Age* (1873), a novel he wrote in collaboration with his Hartford neighbor Charles Dudley Warner (1829–1900), editor of the *Hartford Courant*. Twain sold rights to the play to the actor John T. Raymond (1836–1921), who regularly starred in the part of the daydreaming Colonel Sellers from 1874 until his death. Twain based the character on his "mother's favorite cousin, James Lampton. . . . The real Colonel Sellers, as I knew him in James Lampton, was a pathetic and beautiful spirit, a manly man, a straight and honorable man, a man with a big, foolish, unselfish heart in his bosom, a man to be loved; and he was loved by all his friends, and by his family worshipped" (*Mark Twain's Own Autobiography* 8). Henry Watterson (1840–1921), the influential editor and publisher of the *Louisville Courier-Journal,* recorded his and Twain's impressions of their mutual relative by marriage.
>
> Watterson also remembered a practical joke that he, Twain, and others played on Murat Halstead (1829–1908), editor of the *Cincinnati Commercial* and a stalwart Republican. Watterson impersonated Halstead in an interview with the *New York World* (4 May 1874, 1). In an unsigned and untitled editorial in the *New York Tribune* the next day (4), the writer (probably John Hay) quipped that Watterson "had the happy thought to make Mr. Halstead an old-line Democrat."

ALTHOUGH MARK TWAIN and I called each other "cousin" and claimed to be blood-relatives, the connection between us was by marriage: a great uncle of his married a great aunt of mine; his mother was named after and reared by this great aunt; and the children of the marriage were, of course, his cousins and mine; and a large, varied and picturesque assortment they were. We were lifelong and very dear friends, however; passed much time together at home and abroad; and had many common ties and memories. The last time I saw him, a little less than two years ago, he came to lunch with me at the Manhattan Club, in New York, where he greatly amused my son . . . by his intimate reminiscences of Col. Sellers, of the "Earl of Durham," and of other fantastic members of our joint family.

Just after the successful production of his one play, *The Gilded Age,* and the famous hit made by the late comedian, John T. Raymond, in its leading rôle, I received a letter from him in which he told me he had made in Col. Mulberry Sellers a close study of a certain mutual kinsman and thought he had drawn him to the life, "but for the love of Heaven," he said, "don't whisper it, for he would never understand, or forgive me, if he did not thrash me on sight." . . .

Another one of these mutual cousins was the "Earl of Durham." About the middle of the eighteenth century, before the War of the Revolution, there came to Virginia four brothers Lampton, younger scions of the House of Durham. From them the American Lamptons are sprung. Sam Clemens and I grew up on old wives' tales of estates and titles, which—maybe it was a kindred sense of humor in both of us—we treated with shocking irreverence.

It happened some forty years ago that there turned up, first upon the plains and afterward in New York and Washington, a straight descendant of the oldest of these Virginia Lamptons—he had somehow gotten hold of or had fabricated a full set of documents—who was what Theodore Roosevelt would call "a corker." He wore a sombrero, with a rattlesnake for a band, and a belt with a couple of six-shooters, and described himself and claimed to be the Earl of Dunham. "He touched me for a tenner the first time I ever saw him," drawled Mark Twain, "and I coughed it up and have been coughing them up, whenever he's around, with punctuality and regularity." The "Earl" was indeed a terror—especially when he had been drinking.

His belief in his peerage was as absolute as Col. Sellers's in his millions. All he wanted was money enough "to get across" and "state his case." During the Tichborne trial,[1] Mark Twain and I were in London, and one day he said to me, "I have investigated this Durham business down at the Herald's office. There's nothing to it. The Lamptons passed out of the Earldom of Durham a hundred years ago. There were never any estates. The title lapsed. The present earldom is a new creation—not the same family at all. But, I tell you what, if you'll put up five hundred dollars, I'll put up five hundred more, we'll bring our chap over here and set him in as a claimant, and, my word for it, Kenealy's fat boy[2] won't be a marker to him!" . . .

Mark Twain was the life of every company and of all occasions. I remember a practical joke of his suggestion played upon Halstead. A party of us were supping after the theatre at the old Brevoort House. A card was brought to me from a reporter of the *World*. I was about to deny myself, when Mark Twain said: "Give it to me, I'll fix it," and left the table.

Presently he came to the door and beckoned me to come to him. "I represented myself as your secretary and told this man," said he, "that you were not here, but that if Mr. Halstead would answer just as well, I would fetch him out. He is as innocent as a lamb and doesn't know either of you. I am going to introduce you as Halstead and we'll have some fun."

No sooner said than done. The reporter proved to be a little bald-headed cherub newly arrived from the isle of dreams, and I lined out to him a column or more of very hot stuff, reversing Halstead in every expression of opinion. I declared him in favor of paying the national debt in greenbacks. Touching the sectional question which was then the burning issue of the time, I made the mock Halstead say: "The 'bloody shirt' is only a kind of Pickwickian battle-cry. It is convenient during political campaigns and on election day. Perhaps you do not know that I am myself of good old North Carolina stock. My father and grandfather came to Ohio from the old North State just before I was born. Naturally, I have no sectional prejudices, but I live in Cincinnati and am a good Republican."

There was a good deal more of the same sort. How it passed through the *World* office I know not, but the next day it appeared. On returning to the table I had told the company what Mark Twain and I had done. They thought I was joking. It did seem inconceivable. Without a word to any of us, next day Halstead wrote a note to the *World* briefly repudiating the "interview," and the *World* printed his disclaimer with a line which said: "When Mr. Halstead talked with our reporter he had dined." It was too good to keep.

Notes

1. In one of the longest legal actions in U.K. history, Arthur Orton, aka Thomas Castro (1834–98), was tried for perjury in 1873–74 for impersonating Sir Roger Tichborne (1829–54?) in an effort to defraud the legitimate Tichborne heirs.

2. Orton's barrister was Edward Vaughan Kenealy (1819–80).

Henry Watterson, "Mark Twain—An Intimate Portrait," *American Magazine* 70 (July 1910): 372–75.

From *Crowding Memories* (1920)

LILIAN ALDRICH

Lilian Woodman Aldrich (1841–1927), the wife of Thomas Bailey Aldrich, remembered her first visit to the Clemenses in Hartford the weekend of 7–10 March 1874. The family was renting a house on Farmington Avenue in the Nook Farm neighborhood of west Hartford, near the site of the mansion Twain was having built (see also Andrews). Among the other visitors that weekend was James R. Osgood (1836–92), Twain's friend and future publisher. The Clemenses would move into their Hartford house on 19 September 1874.

LOOKING BACKWARD through the mist and dimness of the receding past, how happy are the memories of our first visit to Hartford! . . . The invitation of Mr. and Mrs. Clemens for this visit included Mr. Howells and Mr. Osgood. The little party of four who met that bright day at the station were fortunate in possessing the best life gives—happiness, health, freedom from care. As our train moved slowly into the station at Springfield, we saw on the platform Mark Twain and Charles Dudley Warner, waiting to join their guests, and go with them the rest of the short journey. Mark Twain was then in his golden dawn; he had friends in crowds; he had married the woman he loved, and fame had become a tangible asset. With the same slow and lengthened utterance that had made the old man at his lecture ask, "Be them your natural tones of eloquence?"—with his waving, undulating motion as he came towards us he said, "Well, I reckon I am prodigiously glad to see you all. I got up this morning and put on a clean shirt, and feel powerful fine. Old Warner there didn't do it, and is darned sorry—said it was a lot of fuss to get himself constructed properly just to show off, and that that bit of a red silk handkerchief on the starboard side of the pocket of his gray coat would make up for it; and I allow it has done it."

On the arrival at Hartford we were met by the same carriage and coachman that Mr. Clemens, after he had entered the enchanted land, described to Mr. Redpath,[1] who was urging lecture engagements: "I guess

I am out of the field permanently. Have got a lovely wife, a lovely house, a lovely carriage, and a coachman whose style and dignity are simply awe-inspiring—nothing less." Patrick McAleer[2] was accompanied by George,[3] who was both butler and guardian spirit of the house. George had been the body servant of an army general, and was of the best style of the Southern negro of that day. With much formality we were presented to him by Mr. Clemens, who said: "George came one day to wash windows; he will stay for his lifetime. His morals are defective; he is a gambler—will bet on anything. I have trained him so that now he is a proficient liar—you should see Mrs. Clemens's joy and pride when she hears him lying to the newspaper correspondent or the visitor at the front door."

We dined the evening of our arrival at the Warners' in a room so vivid in memory that the scent of the flowers still lingers. The conservatory was on the same level as the dining-room and opened out into it, and was as a midsummer out-of-door garden, with its tangle of vines and flowers. The plants were set in the ground, the vines climbed up and overhung the roof, and the fountain, with lilies at the base, made fairy music.

Never again can there be such talk as scintillated about the table that night. Howells, Clemens, Aldrich, and Warner made a quartette that was incomparable. . . . When the guests returned to the Clemens household, it was not until the small hours of the night that it was voted to adjourn and go to bed. But long before that, Mr. Howells, with eyes suffused with tears, had pleaded with Mrs. Aldrich to use her influence to make Mr. Aldrich abstain from any more provocative speech. Mr. Howells said he could not bear it longer, he was ill with laughter, and that for friendship's sake Aldrich must be muffled and checked. Let the others talk, but beg him to keep still.

The next morning, as we were dressing and talking of the pleasant plans of the day, there was a loud and rather authoritative knock at the bedroom door, and Mr. Clemens's voice was heard, saying, "Aldrich, come out, I want to speak to you." The other occupant of the room wrapped her kimono round her more closely, and crept to the door, for evidently something of serious import was happening, or about to happen. The words overheard were most disquieting. Twain's voice had its usual calmness and slowness of speech, but was lacking in the kindly, mellow quality of its accustomed tone, as he said: "In Heaven's name, Aldrich, what are you doing? Are you emulating the kangaroos, with hobnails in your shoes, or trying the jumping-frog business? Our bedroom is directly under yours, and poor Livy and her headache—do try to move more quietly, though Livy would rather suffer than have you give up your game on her account." Then the sound of receding footsteps.

Our consternation was as great as our surprise at the reprimand, for we had been unconscious of walking heavily, or of making unnecessary noise. The bedroom was luxurious in its appointments, the rugs soft on the floor; we could only surmise that the floor boards had some peculiar acoustic quality that emphasized sound. On tiptoe we finished our toilets, and spoke only in whispers, much disturbed in mind that we had troubled our hostess, and hoped she knew that we would not willingly have added to her headache even the weight of a hummingbird's wing. When the toilets were finished, slowly and softly we went down the stairs and into the breakfast room, where, behind the large silver coffee urn, sat Mrs. Clemens. With sorrowful solicitude we asked if her headache was better, and begged forgiveness for adding to her pain. To our amazement she answered, "I have no headache." In perplexed confusion we apologized for the noise we inadvertently made. "Noise!" Mrs. Clemens replied. "We have not heard a sound. If you had shouted we should not have known it, for our rooms are in another wing of the house." At the other end of the table Mark Twain sat, looking as guileless as a combination of cherubim and serephim—never a word, excepting with lengthened drawl, more slow than usual, "Oh, do come to your breakfast, Aldrich, and don't talk all day."

It was a joyous group that came together at the table that morning, and loud was the laughter, and rapid the talk, excepting Mrs. Clemens, who sat rather quiet, and with an expression of face as if she were waiting. Suddenly Mr. Clemens brought the laughter to a pause with his rap on the table, and then, with resonant and deep-toned voice, speaking even more slowly than usual, he asked God's blessing and help for the day. The words were apparently sincere, and spoken with reverent spirit, but we who listened were struck with the same surprised wonder as was the companion of his rougher days, Joe Goodman, who came East to visit them, and was dumbfounded to see Mark Twain ask a blessing and join in family worship. Nothing could have so clearly shown his adoration of Mrs. Clemens as this. He worshipped her as little less than a saint, and would have "hid her needle in his heart to save her little finger from a scratch."

[97]

Notes

1. James Redpath (1833–91), founder of the Boston Lyceum Bureau in 1869.
2. Patrick McAleer (1846–1906), the family coachman in Hartford.
3. George Griffin (1849?–97), Twain's butler from 1875 to 1891.

Lilian Aldrich, from *Crowding Memories* (Boston: Houghton Mifflin, 1920), 143–48.

From *Memories of a Hostess:*
A Chronicle of Eminent Friendships (1922)

ANNIE ADAMS FIELDS

Annie Adams Fields (1834–1915), American author, literary patron, and wife of James T. Fields, recorded in her diary the details of a visit to the Clemens's new house in Hartford.

Thursday, April 27, 1876.—We lunched, and at 3 p.m. were *en route* for Hartford. I slept and read Mr. Tom Appleton's journal on the Nile,[1] and looked out at the sunset and the torches of spring in the hollows, each in turn, doing more sleeping than either of them, I fear, because I seem, for some unexplained reason, to be tired, as Mrs. [Sophia] Hawthorne used to say, far into the future. By giving up to it, however, I felt quite fresh when we arrived, at half-past seven o'clock, Mr. Clemens's (Mark Twain's) carriage waiting for us, to take us to the hall where he was to perform, for the second night in succession, Peter Spyk in the *Loan of a Lover.*[2] It is a pretty play, and the girl's part, Gertrude, was well done by Miss Helen Smith;[3] but Mr. Clemens's part was a creation. I see no reason why, if he chose to adopt the profession of actor, he should not be as successful as [Joseph] Jefferson in whatever he might conclude to undertake. It is really amazing to see what a man of genius can do besides what is usually considered his legitimate sphere.

Afterward we went with Mr. Hamersley[4] to the Club for a bit of supper— this I did not wish to do, but I was overruled of course by the decision of our host. We met at supper one of the clever actors who played in a little operetta called *The Artful Mendicants.* It was after twelve o'clock when we finally reached Mr. Clemens's house. He believed his wife would have retired, as she is very delicate in health; but there she was, expecting us, with a pretty supper-table laid. When her husband discovered this, he fell down on his knees in mock desire for forgiveness. His mind was so full

[99]

of the play, and with the poor figure he felt he had made in it, that he had entirely forgotten all her directions and injunctions. She is a very small, sweet-looking, simple, finished creature, charming in her ways and evidently deeply beloved by him.

The house is a brick villa, designed by one of the first New York architects,[5] standing in a lovely lawn, which slopes down to a small stream or river at the side. In this spring season the blackbirds are busy in the trees and the air is sweet and vocal. Inside there is great luxury. Especially I delight in a lovely conservatory opening out of the drawing-room.

Although we had already eaten supper, the gentlemen took a glass of lager beer to keep Mrs. Clemens company while she ate a bit of bread after her long anxiety and waiting. Meantime Mr. Clemens talked. The quiet earnest manner of his speech would be impossible to reproduce, but there is a drawl in his tone peculiar to himself. Also he is much interested in actors and the art of acting just now, and seriously talks of going to Boston next week to the début of Anna Dickinson.

We were a tired company and went soon to bed and to sleep. I slept late, but I found Mr. Clemens had been re-reading Dana's *Two Years Before the Mast* in bed early, and revolving subjects for his Autobiography. Their two beautiful baby girls came to pass an hour with us after breakfast—exquisite, affectionate children, the very fountain of joy to their interesting parents. . . .

Returning to lunch, I found our host and hostess and eldest little girl in the drawing-room. We fell into talk of the mishaps of the stage and the disadvantage of an amateur under such circumstances. "For instance, on the first night of our little play," said Mr. Clemens, "the trousers of one of the actors suddenly gave way entirely behind, which was very distressing to him, though we did not observe it at all."

I want to stop here to give a little idea of the appearance of our host. He is forty years old, with some color in his cheeks and a heavy light-colored moustache, and overhanging light eyebrows. His eyes are gray and piercing, yet soft, and his whole face expresses great sensitiveness. He is exquisitely neat also, though careless, and his hands are small, not without delicacy. He is a small man, but his mass of hair seems the one rugged-looking thing about him. I thought in the play last night that it was a wig.

To return to our lunch table—he proceeded to speak of his Autobiography, which he intends to write as fully and simply as possible, to leave behind him. His wife laughingly said she should look it over and leave out objectionable passages. "No," he said, very earnestly, almost sternly, "*you* are not to edit it—it is to appear as it is written, with the whole tale told as truly as I can tell it. I shall take out passages from it, and publish as I go along in the *Atlantic* and elsewhere, but I shall not limit myself as to space, and at whatever age I am writing about, even if I am an infant, and an idea comes to me about myself when I am forty, I shall put that in. Every man feels that his experience is unlike that of anybody else, and therefore he should write it down. He finds also that everybody else has thought and felt on some points precisely as he has done, and therefore he should write it down."

The talk naturally branched to education, and thence to the country. He has lost all faith in our government. This wicked ungodly suffrage, he said, where the vote of a man who knew nothing was as good as the vote of a man of education and industry; this endeavor to equalize what God has made unequal was a wrong and a shame. He only hoped to live long enough to see such a wrong and such a government overthrown. Last summer he wrote an article for the *Atlantic,* printed without any signature, proposing the only solution of such evil of which he could conceive.[6] "It is too late now," he concluded, "to restrict the suffrage; we must increase it—for this let us give every university man, let us say, ten votes, and every man with common-school education two votes, and a man of superior power and position a hundred votes, if we choose. This is the only way I see to get out of the false position into which we have fallen."

At five, the hour appointed for dinner, I returned to the drawing-room, where our host lay at full length on the floor, with his head on cushions in the bay-window, reading, and taking what he called "delicious comfort." Mrs. Perkins[7] came in to dinner, and we had a cozy good time. Mr. Clemens described the preaching of a Western clergyman, a great favorite, with the smallest possible allowance of idea to the largest possible amount of words. It was so truthfully and vividly portrayed that we all concluded, perhaps, since the man was in such earnest, he moved his audience more than if he had troubled them with too many ideas. This truthfulness of Mr. Clemens, which will hardly allow him to portray anything in a way to make out a case by exaggerating or distorting a truth, is a wondrous and noble quality. This makes art and makes life, and will continue to make him a daily increasing power among us.

He is so unhappy and discontented with our government that he says he is not conscious of the least emotion of patriotism in himself. He is overwhelmed with shame and confusion, and wishes he were not an American. He thinks seriously of going to England to live, for a while, at least; and I think it not unlikely he may discover away from home a love of his country which is still waiting to be unfolded. I believe hope must dawn for us, that so much earnest endeavor of our statesmen and patriots cannot come to naught; and perhaps the very idea he has dropped, never believing that it can bring forth fruit, will be adopted in the end for our salvation. Certainly women's suffrage and such a change as he proposes should be tried, since we cannot keep the untenable ground of the present. . . .

It is most curious and interesting to watch this growing man of forty—to see how he studies and how high his aims are. His conversation is always earnest and careful, though full of fun. He is just now pondering much upon actors and their ways. Raymond, who is doing the *Gilded Age*, is so hopelessly given "to saving at the spigot and losing at the bung-hole" that he is evidently not over-satisfied nor does he count the acting everything it might be.

We sat talking, chiefly we women, after dinner and looking at the sunset. Mr. Clemens lay down with a book and J[amie] went to look over his lecture.[8] I did not go to lecture, but after all were gone I scribbled away at these pages and nearly finished Mr. Appleton's *Nile Journal.* They returned rather late, it was after ten, bearing a box of delicious strawberries, Mrs. Colt's gift from her endless greenhouses.[9] They were a sensation; the whole of summer was foreshadowed by their scarlet globes. Some beer was brought for Mr. Clemens (who drinks nothing else, and as he eats but little this seems to answer the double end of nourishment and soothing for the nerves) and he began again to talk. He said it was astonishing what subjects were missed by the Poet Laureate [Tennyson]. He thought the finest incident of the Crimean War had been certainly overlooked. That was the going down at sea of the man of war, *Berkeley Castle.* The ship with a whole regiment, one of the finest of the English army, on board, struck a rock near the Bosphorus. There was no help—the bottom was out and the boats would only hold the crew and the other helpless ones; there was no chance for the soldiers. The Colonel summoned them on deck; he told them the duty of soldiers was to die; they would do their duty as bravely there as if they were on the battlefield. He bade them shoulder arms and prepare for action. The drums beat, flags were flying, the service playing, as they all went down to silent death in the great deep.

Afterward Mr. Clemens described to us the reappearance before his congregation of an old clergyman who had been incapacitated for work during twelve years—coming suddenly into the pulpit just as the first hymn was ended. The younger pastor proposed they should sing the old man's favorite, "Coronation" *omitting* the first verse. He heard nothing of the omission, but beginning at the first verse he sang in a cracked treble the remaining stanza after all the people were still. There was a mingling of the comic and pathetic in this incident which made it consonant with the genius of our host. Our dear little hostess complained of want of air, and I saw she was very tired, so we all went to bed about eleven.

Saturday morning.— Dear J[amie] was up early and out in the beautiful sunshine. I read and scribbled until breakfast at half-past nine. It was a lovely morning, and I had already ventured out of my window and round the house to hear the birds sing and see the face of spring before the hour came for breakfast. When I did go to the drawing-room, however, I found Mr. Clemens alone. He greeted me apparently as cheerfully as ever, and it was not until some moments had passed that he told me they had a very sick child upstairs. From that instant I saw, especially after his wife came in, that they could think of nothing else. They were half-distracted with anxiety. Their messenger could not find the doctor, which made matters worse. However, the little girl did not really seem very sick, so I could not help thinking they were unnecessarily excited. The effect on them, however, was just as bad as if the child were really very ill. The messenger was hardly despatched the second time before Jamie and Mr. Clemens began to talk of our getting away in the next train, whereat he (Mr. C.) said to his wife, "Why didn't you tell me of that," etc., etc. It was all over in a moment, but in his excitement he spoke more quickly than he knew, and his wife felt it. Nothing was said at the time, indeed we hardly observed it, but we were intensely amused and could not help finding it pathetic too afterward, when he came to us and said he spent the larger part of his life on his knees making apologies and now he had got to make an apology to us about the carriage. He was always bringing the blood to his wife's face by his bad behavior, and here this very morning he had said such things about that carriage! His whole life was one long apology. His wife had told him to see how well we behaved (poor we!) and he knew he had everything to learn.

He was so amusing about it that he left us in a storm of laughter, yet at bottom I could see it was no laughing matter to him. He is in dead earnest, with a desire for growth and truth in life, and with such a sincere admiration for his wife's sweetness and beauty of character that the most prejudiced and hardest heart could not fail to fall in love with him. She looked like an exquisite lily as we left her. So white and delicate and tender. Such sensitiveness and self-control as she possesses are very, very rare.

Notes

1. *A Nile Journal* (1876) by Thomas Gold Appleton (1812–84).

2. Twain had slightly rewritten *The Loan of a Lover* (1834) by James Robinson Planché (1796–1880) and assumed the role in it of Peter Spyk.

3. Helen Yale Smith, daughter of a Hartford merchant.

4. Probably William Hamersley (1828–1920), state attorney for the Superior Court of Connecticut, president of the Hartford Club, and member of the Monday Evening Club, at whose bookstore tickets for *The Loan of a Lover* were sold. Less likely his son William Hamersley, one of the Hartford Club managers. The Monday Evening Club of Hartford was founded in 1869 and met every two weeks in members' homes. Twain was selected a member in 1873.

5. Edward Tuckerman Potter (1831–1904), the New York architect of Twain's Hartford home.

6. "The Curious Republic of Gondour," *Atlantic Monthly* 36 (October 1875), 461–63.

7. Lucy Maria Perkins (1833–93), wife of Charles Enoch Perkins (1832–1917), who was Twain's Hartford attorney from 1872 to 1882, a grandnephew of Harriet Beecher Stowe (1811–96) and Henry Ward Beecher (1813–87), a cousin of Alice Hooker Day (1847–1928), and an uncle of Charlotte Perkins Gilman (1860–1935).

8. On 28 April James T. Fields delivered his lecture in Hartford on Rufus Choate (*Hartford Courant,* 29 April 1876, 2).

9. Elizabeth Jarvis Colt (1826–1905), widow and heir of the inventor of the revolver and founder of Colt's Patent Fire Arms Manufacturing Company of Hartford.

Annie Adams Fields, from *Memories of a Hostess: A Chronicle of Eminent Friendships,* ed. M. A. DeWolfe Howe (Boston: Atlantic Monthly Press, 1922), 246–56.

From *My Mark Twain* (1910)

W. D. HOWELLS

> Howells also remembered a visit to Twain's new home in Hartford when his
> friend reminisced about the death from diphtheria of his son Langdon four
> years earlier.

THE VISITS TO HARTFORD which had begun with this affluence continued
without actual increase of riches for me, but now I went alone, and in Warner's European and Egyptian absences I formed the habit of going to Clemens. By this time he was in his new house, where he used to give me a
royal chamber on the ground floor, and come in at night after I had gone
to bed to take off the burglar alarm so that the family should not be roused
if anybody tried to get in at my window. This would be after we had sat
up late, he smoking the last of his innumerable cigars, and soothing his
tense nerves with a mild hot Scotch, while we both talked and talked and
talked, of everything in the heavens and on the earth, and the waters under the earth. After two days of this talk I would come away hollow, real-
izing myself best in the image of one of those locust-shells which you find
sticking to the bark of trees at the end of summer. Once, after some such
bout of brains, we went down to New York together, and sat facing each
other in the Pullman smoker without passing a syllable till we had occasion
to say, "Well, we're there." Then, with our installation in a now vanished
hotel (the old Brunswick, to be specific), the talk began again with the inspiration of the novel environment, and went on and on. We wished to be
asleep, but we could not stop, and he lounged through the rooms in the
long nightgown which he always wore in preference to the pajamas which
he despised, and told the story of his life, the inexhaustible, the fairy, the
Arabian Nights story, which I could never tire of even when it began to be
told over again. Or at times he would reason high—

"Of Providence, foreknowledge, will and fate,
Fixed fate, free will, foreknowledge absolute,"[1]

walking up and down, and halting now and then, with a fine toss and slant of his shaggy head, as some bold thought or splendid joke struck him.

He was in those days a constant attendant at the church of his great friend, the Rev. Joseph H. Twichell,[2] and at least tacitly far from the entire negation he came to at last. I should say he had hardly yet examined the grounds of his passive acceptance of his wife's belief, for it was hers and not his, and he held it unscanned in the beautiful and tender loyalty to her which was the most moving quality of his most faithful soul. I make bold to speak of the love between them, because without it I could not make him known to others as he was known to me. . . . She had been a lifelong invalid when he met her, and he liked to tell the beautiful story of their courtship to each new friend whom he found capable of feeling its beauty or worthy of hearing it. Naturally, her father had hesitated to give her into the keeping of the young strange Westerner, who had risen up out of the unknown with his giant reputation of burlesque humorist, and demanded guaranties, demanded proofs. "He asked me," Clemens would say, "if I couldn't give him the names of people who knew me in California, and when it was time to hear from them I heard from him. 'Well, Mr. Clemens,' he said, 'nobody seems to have a very good word for you.' I hadn't referred him to people that I thought were going to whitewash me. I thought it was all up with me, but I was disappointed. 'So I guess I shall have to back you myself.'"

Whether this made him faithfuler to the trust put in him I cannot say, but probably not; it was always in him to be faithful to any trust, and in proportion as a trust of his own was betrayed he was ruthlessly and implacably resentful. But I wish now to speak of the happiness of that household in Hartford which responded so perfectly to the ideals of the mother when the three daughters, so lovely and so gifted, were yet little children. There had been a boy, and "Yes, I killed him," Clemens once said, with the unsparing self-blame in which he would wreak an unavailing regret. He meant that he had taken the child out imprudently, and the child had taken the cold which he died of, but it was by no means certain this was through its father's imprudence. I never heard him speak of his son except that once, but no doubt in his deep heart his loss was irreparably present. He was a very tender father and delighted in the minds of his children, but he was wise enough to leave their training altogether to the wisdom of their mother. He left them to that in everything, keeping for himself the pleasure of teaching them little scenes of drama, learning languages with them, and leading them in singing. They came to the table with their parents, and could have set him an example in behavior when, in moments of intense excitement, he used to leave his place and walk up and down the room, flying his napkin and talking and talking. . . .

At that time I had become editor of the *Atlantic Monthly,* and I had allegiances belonging to the conduct of what was and still remains the most scrupulously cultivated of our periodicals. When Clemens began to write for it he came willingly under its rules, for with all his willfulness there never was a more biddable man in things you could show him a reason for. He never made the least of that trouble which so abounds for the hapless editor from narrower-minded contributors. If you wanted a thing changed, very good, he changed it; if you suggested that a word or a sentence or a paragraph had better be struck out, very good, he struck it out. His proof-sheets came back each a veritable "mush of concession," as Emerson says.[3] Now and then he would try a little stronger language than the *Atlantic* had stomach for, and once when I sent him a proof I made him observe that I had left out the profanity. He wrote back: "Mrs. Clemens opened that proof, and lit into the room with danger in her eye. What profanity? You see, when I read the manuscript to her I skipped that." It was part of his joke to pretend a violence in that gentlest creature which the more amusingly realized the situation to their friends.

I was always very glad of him and proud of him as a contributor, but I must not claim the whole merit, or the first merit of having him write for us. It was the publisher, the late H. O. Houghton, who felt the incongruity of his absence from the leading periodical of the country, and was always urging me to get him to write. I will take the credit of being eager for him, but it is to the publisher's credit that he tried, so far as the modest traditions of the *Atlantic* would permit, to meet the expectations in pay which the colossal profits of Clemens's books might naturally have bred in him. Whether he was really able to do this he never knew from Clemens himself, but probably twenty dollars a page did not surfeit the author of books that "sold right along just like the Bible."

We had several short contributions from Clemens first, all of capital quality, and then we had the series of papers which went mainly to the making of his great book, *Life on the Mississippi*.[4] Upon the whole I have the notion that Clemens thought this his greatest book, and he was supported in his opinion by that of the "portier" in his hotel at Vienna, and that of the German Emperor, who, as he told me with equal respect for the preference of each, united in thinking it his best; with such far-sundered social poles approaching in its favor, he apparently found himself without standing for opposition. At any rate, the papers won instant appreciation from his editor and publisher, and from the readers of their periodical, which they expected to prosper beyond precedent in its circulation. But those were days of simpler acceptance of the popular rights of newspapers than these are, when magazines strictly guard their vested interests against them. The *New York Times* and the *St. Louis Democrat* profited by the advance copies of the magazine sent them to reprint the papers month by month.[5] Together they covered nearly the whole reading territory of the Union, and the terms of their daily publication enabled them to anticipate the magazine in its own restricted field. Its subscription list was not enlarged in the slightest measure, and the *Atlantic Monthly* languished on the news-stands as undesired as ever.

. . . The part of him that was Western in his Southwestern origin Clemens kept to the end, but he was the most desouthernized Southerner I ever knew. No man more perfectly sensed and more entirely abhorred slavery, and no one has ever poured such scorn upon the second-hand, Walter-Scotticized, pseudo-chivalry of the Southern ideal.[6] He held himself responsible for the wrong which the white race had done the black race in slavery, and he explained, in paying the way of a negro student through Yale,[7] that he was doing it as his part of the reparation due from every white to every black man. He said he had never seen this student, nor ever wished to see him or know his name; it was quite enough that he was a negro. About that time a colored cadet was expelled from West Point for some point of conduct "unbecoming an officer and gentleman,"[8] and there was the usual shabby philosophy in a portion of the press to the effect that a negro could never feel the claim of honor. The man was fifteen parts white, but, "Oh yes," Clemens said, with bitter irony, "it was that one part black that undid him." It made him a "nigger" and incapable of being a gentleman. It was to blame for the whole thing. The fifteen parts white were guiltless. . . .

I go back to that house in Hartford, where I was so often a happy guest, with tenderness for each of its endearing aspects. Over the chimney in the library which had been cured of smoking by so much art and science, Clemens had written in perennial brass the words of Emerson, "The ornament of a house is the friends who frequent it," and he gave his guests a welcome of the simplest and sweetest cordiality: but I must not go aside to them from my recollections of him, which will be of sufficient garrulity, if I give them as fully as I wish. The windows of the library looked northward from the hillside above which the house stood, and over the little valley with the stream in it, and they showed the leaves of the trees that almost brushed them as in a Claude Lorraine glass. To the eastward the dining-room opened amply, and to the south there was a wide hall, where the voices of friends made themselves heard as they entered without ceremony and answered his joyous hail. At the west was a little semicircular conservatory of a pattern invented by Mrs. Harriet Beecher Stowe, and adopted in most of the houses of her kindly neighborhood. The plants were set in the ground, and the flowering vine climbed up the sides and overhung the roof above the silent spray of a fountain companied by callas and other water-loving lilies. There, while we breakfasted, Patrick came in from the barn and sprinkled the pretty bower, which poured out its responsive perfume in the delicate accents of its varied blossoms. Breakfast was Clemens's best meal, and he sat longer at his steak and coffee than at the courses of his dinner; luncheon was nothing to him, unless, as might happen, he made it his dinner, and reserved the later repast as the occasion of walking up and down the room, and discoursing at large on anything that came into his head. Like most good talkers, he liked other people to have their say; he did not talk them down; he stopped instantly at another's remark and gladly or politely heard him through; he even made believe to find suggestion or inspiration in what was said. His children came to the table, as I have told, and after dinner he was apt to join his fine tenor to their trebles in singing.

Fully half our meetings were at my house in Cambridge, where he made himself as much at home as in Hartford. He would come ostensibly to stay at the Parker House, in Boston, and take a room, where he would light the gas and leave it burning, after dressing, while he drove out to Cambridge and stayed two or three days with us. Once, I suppose it was after a lecture, he came in evening dress and passed twenty-four hours with us in that guise, wearing an overcoat to hide it when we went for a walk. Sometimes he wore the slippers which he preferred to shoes at home, and if it was muddy, as it was wont to be in Cambridge, he would put a pair of rubbers over them for our rambles. He liked the lawlessness and our delight in allowing it, and he rejoiced in the confession of his hostess, after we had once almost worn ourselves out in our pleasure with the intense talk, with the stories and the laughing, that his coming almost killed her, but it was worth it. . . .

I am surprised to find from the bibliographical authorities that it was so late as 1875 when he came with the manuscript of *Tom Sawyer,* and asked me to read it, as a friend and critic, and not as an editor. I have an impression that this was at Mrs. Clemens's instance in his own uncertainty about printing it. She trusted me, I can say with a satisfaction few things now give me, to be her husband's true and cordial adviser, and I was so. I believe I never failed him in this part, though in so many of our enterprises and projects I was false as water through my temperamental love of backing out of any undertaking. I believe this never ceased to astonish him, and it has always astonished me; it appears to me quite out of character; though it is certain that an undertaking, when I have entered upon it, holds me rather than I it. But however this immaterial matter may be, I am glad to remember that I thoroughly liked *Tom Sawyer,* and said so with every possible amplification. Very likely, I also made my suggestions for its improvement; I could not have been a real critic without that; and I have no doubt they were gratefully accepted and, I hope, never acted upon. I went with him to the horse-car station in Harvard Square, as my frequent wont was, and put him aboard a car with his MS. in his hand, stayed and reassured, so far as I counted, concerning it. I do not know what his misgivings were; perhaps they were his wife's misgivings, for she wished him to be known not only for the wild and boundless humor that was in him, but for the beauty and tenderness and "natural piety"; and she would not have had him judged by a too close fidelity to the rude conditions of Tom Sawyer's life. This is the meaning that I read into the fact of his coming to me with those doubts.

Clemens had then and for many years the habit of writing to me about what he was doing, and still more of what he was experiencing. Nothing struck his imagination, in or out of the daily routine, but he wished to write me of it, and he wrote with the greatest fullness and a lavish dramatization, sometimes to the length of twenty or forty pages, so that I have now perhaps fifteen hundred pages of his letters. They will no doubt some day be published,[9] but I am not even referring to them in these records, which I think had best come to the reader with an old man's falterings and uncertainties. With his frequent absences and my own abroad, and the intrusion of calamitous cares, the rich tide of his letters was more and more interrupted. At times it almost ceased, and then it would come again, a torrent. In the very last weeks of his life he burst forth, and, though too weak himself to write, he dictated his rage with me for recommending to him a certain author whose truthfulness he could not deny, but whom he hated for his truthfulness to sordid and ugly conditions. At heart Clemens was romantic, and he would have had the world of fiction stately and handsome and whatever the real world was not; but he was not romanticistic, and he was too helplessly an artist not to wish his own work to show life as he had seen it.

Notes

1. Howells quotes lines 559–60 from book II of Milton's *Paradise Lost.*

2. Joseph Twichell (1838–1910), minister of the Asylum Hill Congregational Church in Hartford from 1865 to 1910, was Twain's closest friend after 1868. He officiated at the marriage of Twain and Olivia Langdon in 1870, the marriage of their daughter Clara in 1909, and Twain's funeral in 1910.

3. Howells quotes Emerson's essay "Friendship."

4. Twain's "Old Times on the Mississippi" appeared serially in seven installments in the *Atlantic Monthly* between January and August 1875. These essays were subsequently reprinted in chapters 4–17 of *Life on the Mississippi* (1883).

5. The *New York Times* printed advance sheets of "Old Times on the Mississippi" on 16 December 1874, 21 January 1875, and 21 February 1875. The *St. Louis Democrat* printed advance sheets on 20 December 1874, 24 January 1875, 28 March 1875, and 30 May 1875.

6. In chapter 46 of *Life on the Mississippi* (467–69) Twain only half-facetiously blamed the Civil War on the cavaliers' infatuation with Walter Scott. Twain also named a half-sunken steamboat in chapters 12–13 of *Huck Finn* (80–91) the *Walter Scott.*

7. Twain paid the tuition of Warner McGuinn (1859–1937), a black student at Yale Law School.

8. Twain protested the court-martial and expulsion from West Point of Johnson C. Whittaker (1858–1931), a black cadet. See also Butcher.

9. See *Twain-Howells Letters.*

W. D. Howells, from *My Mark Twain* (New York: Harper and Bros., 1910), 9–12, 19–21, 35–38, 47–49.

From *Celebrities at Home* (1879)

EDMUND YATES

According to Twain's friend Edmund Hodgson Yates (1831–94), the editor of the London *World*, a society weekly, the so-called wild humorist of the Pacific Slope in middle age had become a genteel man of letters.

AMONG THOSE AMERICAN authors who, because they have had the courage to cut loose from the apron-strings of England, have achieved the greatest success both at home and abroad, Mark Twain is, in point of popularity, *facile princes*. Those who only know him as the author of *The Innocents Abroad* and *Roughing It* are apt to imagine he is a kind of frontier joker, of the type with which Bret Harte has made us familiar. It may be that there is even yet a vague suspicion of this bent, although his external person certainly shows no trace of it. If you see him in his charming house at Hartford, in the valley of the Connecticut, surrounded with every object which taste and wealth can procure, you feel that such a conception has been erroneous. The mansion with its quaint old English architecture and its exquisite tiles and mosaics, the rich ferneries and half-tropical hothouses, are no mere extraneous accumulations such as any man of wealth might create, but a gradual and organic outgrowth of the owner's mind which gives you a delightful peep into the inner recesses of his character. The main building, as well as the stables, is built of dark-red brick with dark-brown trimmings, interspersed with inlaid devices of scarlet-painted brick and black Greek patterns in mosaic. The whole has a most novel and pleasing effect— nothing gaudy and glaring, but all arranged with a rare artistic taste and a strict regard for harmony in colors and outlines. During the summer the outer window-sills are draped with hanging ferns and bright nasturtiums, and the woodwork of the broad East Indian portico is half-concealed beneath the foliage of clambering vines. But as winter reigns supreme during a good many months of the year in New England, Mark Twain has taken care to provide himself with summer vistas even while Nature does not afford them. His library, the place where the owner is most frequently to be found, opens into a miniature greenhouse, full of tall graceful ferns and blooming tropical plants. In the midst of all these luxuriant exotics a fountain is constantly playing, shedding its spray over the smooth white rocks at its base, and under the glass ceiling hangs a large cage in which a pair of California quails of brilliant plumage spend a brief season of happy captivity. Mark Twain cannot endure to see any bird or beast which Nature intended for freedom imprisoned within the narrow bars of a cage, and he bought these quails in the winter from a boy, meaning to set them at liberty in a neighboring forest as soon as spring should arrive.

In the pleasant city of Hartford he has gathered about him a delightful circle of friends, authors, business men, and lawyers, to whom his hospitable doors are always open. And he is, indeed, the prince of entertainers. Sitting in his richly-furnished library, to whose beauty and artistic completeness half the lands of Europe have contributed, he will tell an anecdote or discuss a literary or social question with a calm directness and earnestness, revealing to you an entirely new side of his character that has nothing in common with that which he is wont to display to the public who throng to his lectures. Even his drollest stories he related with this same earnest impressiveness, and with a face as serious as a sexton's. His brilliancy has a certain delightful quality which is almost too evanescent to be imprisoned in any one phrase. You have no oppressive consciousness that you are expected to laugh; you rather feel as if the talker had unexpectedly taken you into his confidence, and you feel your heart going out towards him in return. Throughout his house Mark Twain has indulged liberally his taste for wood-tints and quaint carvings. Each of the doors in the library is surmounted with carved cherubs and other biblical and mythical figures, spoils from some European pilgrimage. In his study on the second floor he revels in sphinxes and griffins, whose reclining bodies and capacious wings fashion themselves into luxurious lounges, easy-chairs, and sofas. The mantelpiece, with all its magnificent superstructure, had once adorned an old English or Scottish country seat, and Mark Twain was fortunate enough to pick it up during one of his many sojourns in England. Amid these surroundings Mark Twain spends the time between breakfast and dinner, composing with much serious reflection the sketches, novels, and dramas which have shaken the American public with laughter. After dinner the chances are that you will find him tranquilly smoking a cigar before the fire in the library, and chatting leisurely with some friend, who

[113]

addresses him plainly as "Mark," as his *nom de plume* somehow persists in clinging to him both in his private and public relations. His real name is Samuel L. Clemens. He is still a man in the prime of life, being now about forty-four years old. His rich and varied experiences in the past, as a Western editor, gold-digger, and pilot on the Mississippi, have stored his brain with abundant material for future works which have still to be written.

On such occasions as these he will dwell on his experiences while traveling in England. Once, while going by rail from London to Liverpool, he was shut up in a *coupe* with a fellow-traveler, who was deeply absorbed in a yellow-covered book, which, on further inspection, proved to be *Roughing It*. He evidently regarded the thing as a very serious business, for he hardly ever moved a muscle. "I presently began to feel very guilty," Mark Twain went on, "for having subjected a fellow-mortal to this prolonged torture. I gazed anxiously into his face in the hope of detecting some lurking shadow of a smile. But no, his gloom seemed rather to be deepening. With a guilty conscience and a dreadful sense of responsibility I watched him turning the leaves, and slowly and gradually, as he approached the end, my heart began to grow lighter. At last, as he closed the book, I heaved a huge sigh of relief. But my exultation was somewhat premature. The man quietly opened his satchel and pulled out the second volume. And now the same process was repeated, only with an intenser agony on my part. With deep anxiety I scrutinized his features, in the hope of finding some hidden trace of mirth. I would have been so grateful for the slightest fraction of a smile. But my friend was miserable. Before we reached Liverpool, I had serious thoughts of jumping out through the window."[1]

Mark Twain is a man of middle height; solidly built, but not stout; his features are all of a clear massive modeling, and the prevailing expression seems to be resolute courage and determination. His upper lip is covered with a thick brown moustache, and the broad territory of his forehead is usually encroached upon by his brown curly hair. His eyes are small and keen, but are by no means lacking in kindliness and humor. In his whole bearing there is a frank cordiality which is very winning. He is the father of two beautiful little girls, of whom he is very proud; and like the amiable prince of tradition he takes much pleasure, amid the serious business of his life, in playing with these two charming princesses. His library and his conversation testify to the excellence of his literary taste. Mark Twain is a devoted admirer of Macaulay, and has a habit of ever returning to him when the lighter literary pabulum of the day begins to pall upon his sense. The much-abused term, "professional humorist," can hardly apply to Mark Twain. He is rather a constitutional humorist, because his mind is so fashioned that, in dealing with any subject whatever, the humorous point of view first and most naturally presents itself to him. For all that he is very careful not to rush into publicity with a half-formed or half-perfected thought. His after-dinner speeches, which are probably read by a larger number of men and women in America than any public document, the President's Message not excepted, would no doubt have been very good and very laughable even if they had been entirely *impromptu;* but the careful and critical revision to which he subjects them before their public appearance certainly refines their quality.

When Mark Twain is not writing or making speeches he smokes, and if he feels any further need of recreation, he takes it in playing billiards. In the third story of his house there is an elegantly appointed billiard-room, where he often spends an evening with three or four masculine friends. Though he keeps handsome horses, housing them in a superb stable, and may be seen daily driving through the city with a fine pair of bays, he is not much of a connoisseur of horseflesh or a sportsman.

In politics he at first impresses you as an indifferentist, with perhaps a leaning towards pessimism; but if you happen to touch certain chords which never fail to respond in an American bosom, you soon discover that your first impression was very remote from the truth. The fact is, like many another thoughtful man, Mark Twain sees plainly the gravity of the present and future in the United States, and accordingly has very little patience with the spread-eagleism and cheap declamations of contending politicians. Probably his political creed is not very different from that of the Independents, a new and still unorganized party, which is daily growing among the citizens of the great Republic.

Note

1. Twain narrated a similar story in 1907 about his train trip from Liverpool to London on 2 September 1872, though in it the stoic passenger is reading *The Innocents Abroad,* not *Roughing It* (*Mark Twain's Letters* 5:153).

Edmund Yates, from *Celebrities at Home* (London: Office of the World, 1879), 3:135–41.

From *The Changing Years* (1930)

NORMAN HAPGOOD

> Norman Hapgood (1868–1937), American author, journalist, editor of *Collier's Weekly* (1903–12) and *Harper's Weekly* (1913–16), and the son of the industrialist Charles Hutchins Hapgood (1836–1917), reminisced in his autobiography about his friendship with Twain.

ALTHOUGH MY ACQUAINTANCE with Mark Twain, starting when I was eighteen, had much of the pleasantness of long-continued friendship, what it means in the plan of this book, with its emphasis on the search for intellectual truth, is that the humorist offered me, more than any other person I have known, the spectacle of sheer genius. As writing was my chosen trade, I felt as a young scientist might feel if he had the privilege of knowing the personal side of Einstein. . . . I am convinced he took as genuine a pleasure in some of his stereotyped farce as in the whitewashing of Tom Sawyer's fence. He was as assured of the inferiority of the painting of Titian, and generally of the Renaissance, as he was of the social truths behind Pap Finn's diatribe on negro suffrage.[1] He was absolutely sure that Bacon wrote Shakespeare, and that Jane Austen was of no importance. These irregularities need no accounting for; they were in the structure of his mind. . . .

Nook Farm, in Hartford, was a literary paradise not quite like anything I shall see again. There were no fences between the houses, the doors were not locked, and the members of the different families walked in and out of one another's dwellings without knock or ring. Mark Twain's house, the largest, stood at one corner of the grounds. Not many paces from it was the residence of Charles Dudley Warner. The house in which I used to stay was that of George Warner,[2] brother of the author, whose wife was the sister of William Gillette.[3] Richard Burton[4] had a house within the grounds, and once, although I no longer remember whether her house was there or not, I saw Harriet Beecher Stowe, the author of *Uncle Tom's Cabin,* wandering along the sidewalk adjoining Nook Farm, muttering to herself, her mind gone, but her happiness apparently remaining. I believe Joe Twichell, Mark

Twain's great friend, had his house there; it must have been across those well-known fields that Twichell came rushing to tell Mark Twain, who had been so proud to see his books on a little table by Darwin's bed, that the letters of the great biologist had just appeared and that Twichell reading them had come to the confession that after the heavy work of his middle age set in Darwin was not able to read any literary volumes except trash.

Notes

1. Pap excoriates black suffrage in chapter 6 of *Adventures of Huckleberry Finn* (33–34).

2. George Henry Warner (1833–1919), brother of Charles Dudley Warner.

3. William Gillette (1855–1937), American actor and playwright, a native of Hartford, and brother-in-law of Charles Dudley Warner, debuted in New York in Twain's play *The Gilded Age* in 1877.

4. Hartford poet Richard Burton (1861–1940).

Norman Hapgood, from *The Changing Years* (New York: Farrar & Rinehart, 1930), 202–5.

From *My Mark Twain* (1910)

W. D. HOWELLS

Howells's account of Twain's Whittier birthday speech on 17 December 1877 at the Brunswick Hotel in Boston on the occasion of John Greenleaf Whittier's seventieth birthday may not do entire justice to the complexities of that (in)famous cultural moment. Twain related a humorous, albeit bogus, anecdote about three California tramps, giving them the same names as Henry Wadsworth Longfellow (1807–82), the preeminent American poet; the American poet, novelist, and physician Oliver Wendell Holmes (1809–94); and Ralph Waldo Emerson (1803–82), the leading American intellectual of the nineteenth century. The initial reports of the dinner included no hints of audience dismay about Twain's speech, but soon local gossip indicated otherwise. According to some media accounts, the story fell flat, and it may even have troubled some of the men (the women had retired after the dinner) in the audience. Certainly the local Boston newspapers reported a growing scandal about Twain's indecorum at the dinner over the next several weeks, and Twain wrote letters of apology to Longfellow, Holmes, and Emerson. None of them took offense, as Howells remembered. Longfellow and Holmes dismissed the controversy as much ado about nothing, and, on his part, Emerson was suffering from dementia. For Twain's recollection of this episode, see *Mark Twain's Own Autobiography*, 233–37. See also Smith; Bush.

WHEN MESSRS. HOUGHTON & MIFFLIN became owners of the *Atlantic Monthly*, Mr. Houghton fancied having some breakfasts and dinners, which should bring the publisher and the editor face to face with the contributors, who were bidden from far and near. Of course, the subtle fiend of advertising, who has now grown so unblushing bold, lurked under the covers at these banquets, and the junior partner and the young editor had their joint and separate fine anguishes of misgiving as to the taste and the principle of them; but they were really very simple-hearted and honestly meant hospitalities, and they prospered as they ought, and gave great pleasure and no pain. I forget some of the "emergent occasions," but I am sure of a birthday dinner most unexpectedly accepted by Whittier, and a birthday luncheon to Mrs. Stowe, and I think a birthday dinner to Longfellow; but the passing years have left me in the dark as to the pretext of that supper at which Clemens made his awful speech, and came so near being the death of us all. At the breakfasts and luncheons we had the pleasure of our lady contributors' company, but that night there were only men, and because of our great strength we survived.

I suppose the year was about 1879 [*sic*], but here the almanac is unimportant, and I can only say that it was after Clemens had become a very valued contributor of the magazine, where he found himself to his own great explicit satisfaction. He had jubilantly accepted our invitation, and had promised a speech, which it appeared afterward he had prepared with unusual care and confidence. It was his custom always to think out his speeches, mentally wording them, and then memorizing them by a peculiar system of mnemonics which he had invented. On the dinner-table a certain succession of knife, spoon, salt-cellar, and butter-plate symbolized a train of ideas, and on the billiard-table a ball, a cue, and a piece of chalk served the same purpose. With a diagram of these printed on the brain he had full command of the phrases which his excogitation had attached to them, and which embodied the ideas in perfect form. He believed he had been particularly fortunate in his notion for the speech of that evening, and he had worked it out in joyous self-reliance. It was the notion of three tramps, three deadbeats, visiting a California mining-camp, and imposing themselves upon the innocent miners as respectively Ralph Waldo Emerson, Henry Wadsworth Longfellow, and Oliver Wendell Holmes. The humor of the conception must prosper or must fail according to the mood of the hearer, but Clemens felt sure of compelling this to sympathy, and he looked forward to an unparalleled triumph.

But there were two things that he had not taken into account. One was the species of religious veneration in which these men were held by those nearest them, a thing that I should not be able to realize to people remote from them in time and place. They were men of extraordinary dignity, of the thing called presence, for want of some clearer word, so that no one could well approach them in a personally light or trifling spirit. I do not suppose that anybody more truly valued them or more piously loved them than Clemens himself, but the intoxication of his fancy carried him beyond the bounds of that regard, and emboldened him to the other thing which he had not taken into account—namely, the immense hazard of working his fancy out before their faces, and expecting them to enter into the delight of it. If neither Emerson, nor Longfellow, nor Holmes had been there, the scheme might possibly have carried, but even this is doubtful, for those who so devoutly honored them would have overcome their horror with difficulty, and perhaps would not have overcome it at all.

The publisher, with a modesty very ungrateful to me, had abdicated his office of host, and I was the hapless president, fulfilling the abhorred function of calling people to their feet and making them speak. When I came to Clemens I introduced him with the cordial admiring I had for him as one of my greatest contributors and dearest friends. Here, I said, in sum, was a humorist who never left you hanging your head for having enjoyed his joke; and then the amazing mistake, the bewildering blunder, the cruel catastrophe was upon us. I believe that after the scope of the burlesque made itself clear, there was no one there, including the burlesquer himself, who was not smitten with a desolating dismay. There fell a silence, weighing many tons to the square inch, which deepened from moment to moment, and was broken only by the hysterical and blood-curdling laughter of a single guest, whose name shall not be handed down to infamy. Nobody knew whether to look at the speaker or down at his plate. I chose my plate as the least affliction, and so I do not know how Clemens looked, except when I stole a glance at him, and saw him standing solitary amid his appalled and appalling listeners, with his joke dead on his hands. From a first glance at the great three whom his jest had made its theme, I was aware of Longfellow sitting upright, and regarding the humorist with an air of pensive puzzle, of Holmes busily writing on his menu, with a well-feigned effect of preoccupation, and of Emerson, holding his elbows, and listening with a sort of Jovian oblivion of this nether world in that lapse of memory which saved him in those later years from so much bother. Clemens must have dragged his joke to the climax and left it there, but I cannot say this from any sense of the fact. Of what happened afterward at the table where the immense, the wholly innocent, the truly unimagined affront was offered, I have no longer the least remembrance. I next remember being in a room of the hotel, where Clemens was not to sleep, but to toss in despair, and Charles Dudley Warner's saying, in the gloom, "Well, Mark, you're a funny fellow." It was as well as anything else he could have said, but Clemens seemed unable to accept the tribute.

I stayed the night with him, and the next morning, after a haggard breakfast, we drove about and he made some purchases of bric-a-brac for his house in Hartford, with a soul as far away from bric-a-brac as ever the soul of man was. He went home by an early train, and he lost no time in writing back to the three divine personalities which he had so involuntarily seemed to flout. They all wrote back to him, making it as light for him as they could. I have heard that Emerson was a good deal mystified, and in his sublime forgetfulness asked, Who was this gentleman who appeared to think he had offered him some sort of annoyance! But I am not sure that this is accurate. What I am sure of is that Longfellow, a few days after, in my study, stopped before a photograph of Clemens and said, "Ah, he is a wag!" and nothing more. Holmes told me, with deep emotion, such as a brother humorist might well feel, that he had not lost an instant in replying to Clemens's letter, and assuring him that there had not been the least offence, and entreating him never to think of the matter again. "He said that he was a fool, but he was God's fool," Holmes quoted from the letter, with a true sense of the pathos and the humor of the self-abasement.

To me Clemens wrote a week later, "It doesn't get any better; it burns like fire."[1] But now I understand that it was not shame that burnt, but rage for a blunder which he had so incredibly committed. That to have conceived of those men, the most dignified in our literature, our civilization, as impersonable by three hoboes, and then to have imagined that he could ask them personally to enjoy the monstrous travesty, was a break, he saw too late, for which there was no repair. Yet the time came, and not so very long afterward, when some mention was made of the incident as a mistake, and he said, with all his fierceness, "But I don't admit that it was a mistake," and it was not so in the minds of all witnesses at second hand. The morning after the dreadful dinner there came a glowing note from Professor Child,[2] who had read the newspaper report of it, praising Clemens's burlesque as the richest piece of humor in the world, and betraying no sense of incongruity in its perpetration in the presence of its victims. I think it must always have ground in Clemens's soul, that he was the prey of circumstances, and that if he had some more favoring occasion he could retrieve his loss in it by giving the thing the right setting.

Notes

1. Twain to Howells, 23 December 1877 (*Twain-Howells Letters,* 212).
2. Francis James Child (1825–96), American rhetorician and folklorist, did not attend the dinner.

W. D. Howells, from *My Mark Twain* (New York: Harper & Bros., 1910), 58–62.

From *Contemporary Portraits, Fourth Series* (1923)

FRANK HARRIS

Twain and his family left for Europe on 11 April 1878 and settled in the Schloß Hotel on the bluff overlooking the Neckar River and the castle in Heidelberg, Germany, on 6 May. He described the town in chapter 2 of *A Tramp Abroad* (1880) as "the last possibility of the beautiful" (31). But the weeks in Heidelberg were not all peace and light. Twain learned that President Rutherford B. Hayes was considering a request to appoint his ex-friend Bret Harte to a diplomatic post in Germany. As Twain commented in a letter to Howells on 27 June, "Harte is a liar, a thief, a swindler, a snob, a sot, a sponge, a coward, a Jeremy Diddler, he is brimful of treachery" (*Twain-Howells Letters*, 235). Twain expressed similar sentiments in conversation with Frank Harris (1856–1931), an Irish American author, editor, and journalist who had been asked to invite him to address the Anglo-American Club in Heidelberg on the Fourth of July. Despite Harris's disdain for him, Twain in fact accepted the invitation and spoke to the club that day. However, given an opportunity to chat with Twain nearly thirty years later at the reception for him hosted by King Edward VII (1841–1910) in the gardens of Windsor Castle on 22 June 1907, Harris refused.

I WONDER WHY it is that I cannot force myself to like Mark Twain? I have never even told of my meetings with him, but I intend to do it now.

I remember when his *Gilded Age* came out, and soon afterwards his *Innocents Abroad* [*sic*]. I had hoped great things from him when I read the *Gilded Age*, with its exposure of the corruption in the Kansas legislature.[1] A few years later I met him, and thereafter all my interest in him vanished.

It was in Heidelberg. I was a member of the Anglo-American Literary Society when Mark Twain in the eighteen-seventies came to that city. I was chosen, one of two, to call upon him and ask him to address us.

My friend's name was, I think, Waldstein, brother of Sir Charles Wald-stein;[2] I am not certain; at any rate, two of us went and saw Twain in his hotel. He met us in a very friendly, human way, and promised to come and speak at one of our meetings if the evening could be settled to suit him. We told him we would make the necessary arrangements. He offered us cigars, and during our talk I told him how I had liked his *Gilded Age,* and how I liked Bret Harte. Thereupon, to our astonishment, he began inveighing against Bret Harte. "His talent," if you please, "was infinitely exaggerated, and he was not honest. He was a disgrace to literature, and had no real genius. He had cheated his publishers out of money. Had we never heard the story?"

I shrugged my shoulders. It did not matter to me whom Bret Harte had cheated. I knew that the man who had written "The Outcasts of Poker Flat" was throned in my admiration forever. . . . I found exquisite humor in this and in Bret Harte's parodies,[3] but Mark Twain would not have it. He became angry at once, declared that he did not care what a man wrote; a writer should pay his debts and be as honest as anybody else. "Bret Harte had played a disgraceful trick once on his publishers. They had fixed a price for a book of his at, say $3000 or $5000, the book to contain 100,000 words. Bret Harte wrote to them, saying that the book was well under way, and asked them for a payment on account. The publishers sent him a pay-ment on account, and did not hear from him for months. Finally they wrote to him about the book. He told them he would finish the book at once if he could rely on prompt payment. The publishers assured him that he would have a cheque as soon as they received the manuscript. A couple of weeks later they did receive what purported to be the manuscript, with a letter from Bret Harte begging for the money, as he was in dire need. Thereupon the publishers sent the cheque, without even opening the parcel. When they did open it, they discovered that only about the first twenty pages of the book were there; the whole of the rest of the parcel was made up of let-ters and stray scraps of paper, and that was all the book they ever got out of Bret Harte.[4]

"I told the publishers," Mark Twain concluded, "that they ought to have him put in prison. A man should be honest, above everything."

I ventured something about artists being insufficiently paid and getting anything but good treatment for supreme effort, but that brought no re-sponse from Twain. He declared that they did not need to write unless they wanted to; they could make shoes or do manual labor of some sort.

When we, the two envoys, came away we looked at each other. I was hurt to the soul. I said to my friend: "I never want to see that man again; never again do I want to talk with him. Fancy his running down Bret Harte on such paltry grounds!"

"At any rate," replied my friend, "he is going to speak for us, and so our mission has been successful."

"He may speak for you," I said, "but I won't be present at the meeting; I never want to hear his voice again; that is the man who thought 'The Jumping Frog' funny."

About a year before his death, I saw him at a garden party of King Edward. He walked across the lawn, all in white, with the American Ambassador,[5] who beckoned to me, but I drew out of the way; I did not want to meet Twain. . . .

I do not pretend to have exhausted Twain: the other day [George Bernard] Shaw wrote to me that I underrated him: "Mark Twain had humor in him," he says, and no doubt Shaw is right in this respect; but, speaking for myself, I simply cannot read him with any patience; his humor seems, to me, forced and unnatural; and his most recent biographer,[6] I really believe, has explained correctly his extraordinary shallowness of soul. Like all small men, he wanted success in the day and hour, and was willing to pay the price for it. He wrote for the market, and the million praised and paid him; he had a gorgeous and easy life, and was a friend of millionaires, and went about at the end like a glorified Hall Caine; but he wrote nothing lifeworthy, not a word that has a chance of living except his boys' books, *Tom Sawyer* and *Huckleberry Finn,* which may live for a generation, or perhaps even two, with *Treasure Island.* It amused me to see, the other day, that Swinburne classed Mark Twain with Martin Tupper; that's about his true place.

Notes

1. Twain and Charles Dudley Warner satirized the corruption of the U.S. Congress, not the Kansas legislature, in *The Gilded Age.*

2. The anthropologist Sir Charles Waldstein (1856–1927).

3. Harte had published a series of parodies of such writers as Dickens, Cooper, Dumas père, Charlotte Brontë, Victor Hugo, and Wilkie Collins in his *Condensed Novels* (1867).

4. A garbled composition history of Harte's novel *Gabriel Conroy* (1876). In 1907, in his

autobiographical dictation, Twain reflected on Harte's habit of working on this novel only when he needed money and on Bliss's niggardliness in advancing him money: "About once a month Harte would get into desperate straits; then he would dash off enough manuscript to set him temporarily free and carry it to [Elisha] Bliss and get a royalty advance. These assaults upon his prospective profits were never very large, except in the eyes of Bliss; to Bliss's telescopic vision a couple of hundred dollars that weren't due, or hadn't been earned, were a prodigious matter." Bliss "became alarmed" when he "realized that *Gabriel Conroy* was a white elephant. The book was nearing a finish, but, as a subscription book, its value had almost disappeared" so Bliss "sold the serial rights" in it to *Scribner's* (*Mark Twain in Eruption*, 280–81).

5. Whitelaw Reid (1837–1912), managing editor (1869–72) and editor in chief (1872–1905) of the *New York Tribune* and U.S. ambassador to England (1905–1912).

6. In *The Ordeal of Mark Twain* (1920), Van Wyck Brooks (1886–1963) contended that Twain's genius had been thwarted by his willingness to permit his wife, Howells, and other bourgeois custodians of culture to censor him—and so his life had been tragic.

Frank Harris, from *Contemporary Portraits, Fourth Series* (New York: Brentano's, 1923), 162–64, 173.

"Mark Twain at 'Nook Farm' (Hartford) and Elmira" (1885)

CHARLES H. CLARK

Charles Hopkins Clark (1848–1926), political editor of the *Hartford Courant* and one of the co-editors, with W. D. Howells, of *Mark Twain's Library of Humor* (1888), recorded his impressions of Twain in 1885. As Clark remembered, Twain spent some nine months of the year in Hartford and the summer months at Quarry Farm two miles from Elmira, where Susan Langdon Crane (1836–1924), Livy's sister, and her husband, Theodore W. Crane (1831–89), lived. Twain's octagonal study, on a bluff a hundred yards from the Victorian farmhouse overlooking Elmira and the Chemung River valley, was completed according to Susan Crane's instructions in June 1874. During many of his springs and summers between 1874 and 1889, Twain wrote most of *Tom Sawyer, Huck Finn, The Prince and the Pauper,* and *A Connecticut Yankee in King Arthur's Court* in his study at Quarry Farm.

OFF THE PLATFORM and out of his books Mark Twain is Samuel L. Clemens—a man who will be fifty years old at his next birthday, November 30, 1885. He is of a very noticeable personal appearance, with his slender figure, his finely shaped head, his thick, curling, very gray hair, his heavy arched eyebrows, over dark gray eyes, and his sharply, but delicately cut features. Nobody is going to mistake him for anyone else, and his attempts to conceal his identity at various times have been comical failures.[1] In 1871 Mr. Clemens made his home in Hartford, and in some parts of the world Hartford today is best known because it is his home. He built a large and unique house in Nook Farm, on Farmington Avenue, about a mile and a quarter from the old centre of the city. . . . In their travels in Europe, Mr. and Mrs. Clemens have found various rich antique pieces of household furniture, including a great wooden mantel and chimney-piece, now in their library, taken from an English baronial hall, and carved Venetian tables, bedsteads, and other pieces. These add their peculiar charm to the interior of the house. The situation of the building makes it very bright and cheerful. On the top floor is Mr. Clemens's own working-room. In one corner is his writing-table, covered usually with books, manuscripts, letters, and other literary litter; and in the middle of the room stands the billiard-table, upon which a large part of the work of the place is expended. By strict attention to this business, Mr. Clemens has become an expert in the game; and it is a part of his life in Hartford to get a number of friends together every Friday for an evening of billiards. He even plans his necessary trips away from home so as to be back in time to observe this established custom.

Mr. Clemens divides his year into two parts, which are not exactly for work and play respectively, but which differ very much in the nature of their occupations. From the first of June to the middle of September, the whole family, consisting of Mr. and Mrs. Clemens and their three little girls, are at Elmira, N.Y. They live there with Mr. T. W. Crane, whose wife is a sister of Mrs. Clemens. A summerhouse has been built for Mr. Clemens within the Crane grounds, on a high peak, which stands six hundred feet above the valley that lies spread out before it. The house is built almost entirely of glass, and is modeled exactly on the plan of a Mississippi steamboat's pilot-house. Here, shut off from all outside communication, Mr. Clemens does the hard work of the year, or rather the confining and engrossing work of writing, which demands continuous application, day after day. The lofty work-room is some distance from the house. He goes to it every morning about half-past eight and stays there until called to dinner by the blowing of a horn about five o'clock. He takes no lunch or noon meal of any sort, and works without eating, while the rules are imperative not to disturb him during this working period. His only recreation is his cigar. He is an inveterate smoker, and smokes constantly while at his work, and, indeed, all the time, from half-past eight in the morning to half-past ten at night, stopping only when at his meals. A cigar lasts him about forty minutes, now that he has reduced to an exact science the art of reducing the week to ashes. So he smokes from fifteen to twenty cigars every day. Some time ago he was persuaded to stop the practice, and actually went a year and more without tobacco; but he found himself unable to carry along important work which he undertook, and it was not until he resumed smoking that he could do it. Since then his faith in his cigar has not wavered. . . . While the life at Elmira is in the main seclusive and systematically industrious, that at Hartford, to which he returns in September, is full of variety and entertainment. His time is then less restricted, and he gives himself freely to the enjoyment of social life. He entertains many friends, and his hospitable house, seldom without a guest, is one of the literary centers of the city. Mr. Howells is a frequent visitor, as Bayard Taylor used to be. Cable, Aldrich, Henry Irving, and many others of wide reputation have been entertained there. The next house to Mr. Clemens's on the south is Charles Dudley Warner's house, and the next on the east is Mrs. Stowe's, so that the most famous three writers in Hartford live within a stone's throw of each other.

At Hartford Mr. Clemens's hours of occupation are less systematized, but he is no idler there. At some times he shuts himself in his working-room and declines to be interrupted on any account, though there are not wanting some among his expert billiard-playing friends who insist that this seclusion is merely to practice uninterruptedly while they are otherwise engaged. Certainly he is a skilful player. He keeps a pair of horses, and rides more or less in his carriage, but does not drive, or ride on horseback. He is, however, an adept upon the bicycle. He has made its conquest a study, and has taken, and also experienced, great pains with the work. On his bicycle he travels a great deal, and he is also an indefatigable pedestrian, taking long walks across country, frequently in the company of his friend the Rev. Joseph H. Twichell, at whose church (Congregational) he is a pew-holder and regular attendant. For years past he has been an industrious and extensive reader and student in the broad field of general culture. He has a large library and a real familiarity with it, extending beyond our own language into the literatures of Germany and France. He seems to have been fully conscious of the obligations which the successful opening of his literary career laid upon him, and to have lived up to its opportunities by a conscientious and continuous course of reading and study which supplements the large knowledge of human nature that the vicissitudes of his early life brought with them. His resources are not of the exhaustible sort. He is a member of (among other social organizations) the Monday Evening Club of Hartford that was founded sixteen years ago by the Rev. Dr. [Horace] Bushnell, Dr. Henry,[2] and Dr. J. Hammond Trumbull,[3] and others, with a membership limited to twenty. The club meets on alternate Monday evenings from October to May in the houses of the members. One person reads a paper and the others then discuss it; and Mr. Clemens's talks there, as well as his daily conversation among friends, amply demonstrate the spontaneity and naturalness of his irrepressible humor.

His inventions are not to be overlooked in any attempt to outline his life and his activities. "Mark Twain's Scrapbook"[4] must be pretty well known by this time, for something like 100,000 copies of it have been sold yearly for eight years or more. As he wanted a scrapbook, and could not find what he wanted, he made one himself, which naturally proved to be just what other people wanted. Similarly, he invented a notebook. It is his habit to record at the moment they occur to him such scenes and ideas as he wishes to preserve. All notebooks that he could buy had the vicious habit of opening at the wrong place and distracting attention in that way. So, by a simple contrivance, he arranged one that always opens at the right place; that is, of course, at the page last written upon. Other simple inventions of Mark Twain's include: A vest which enables the wearer to dispense with suspenders; a shirt with collars and cuffs attached, which requires neither buttons nor studs; a perpetual-calendar watch-charm, which gives the day of the week and of the month; and a game whereby people may play historical dates and events upon a board, somewhat after the manner of cribbage, being a game whose office is twofold—to furnish the dates and events, and to impress them permanently upon the memory.

Notes

1. When he returned to the Mississippi River valley in April–May 1882 to research his book *Life on the Mississippi* (1883), Twain sometimes traveled under a pseudonym. He wrote Howells on 16 April, for example, that he planned to register at his hotel in St. Louis under the name "S. L. Samuel" (*Twain-Howells Letters,* 401). See also Scharnhorst 38, 423, 467.

2. Caleb Sprague Henry (1804–84), former minister of the West Hartford Congregational Church.

3. The Hartford philologist James Hammond Trumbull (1821–97).

4. Twain patented a self-pasting scrapbook in 1872.

Charles H. Clark, "Mark Twain at 'Nook Farm' (Hartford) and Elmira," *Critic,* 17 January 1885, 25–26.

From *My Father Mark Twain* (1931)

CLARA CLEMENS

> Clara Langdon Clemens (1874–1962) was the only one of Twain's children to survive him, and she vigorously defended his genius and reputation until the end of her life, particularly in her biography of him.

THE MAJOR PART of Father's work was accomplished in the summer, which we spent with my mother's sister, Mrs. Theodore Crane. She lived on the top of a long hill overlooking Elmira, New York. The place was called Quarry Farm, and was a heavenly spot. On a sunny day one could see the Chemung River sparkling far below as it wound its way through the town of Elmira, nestled cozily between the hills surrounding it. At night the streets and houses, though at a great distance, seemed ablaze with artificial fire. It was a lovely sight.

The house in which my aunt lived was simple but very comfortable, with enough rooms to accommodate our family. Susy[1] and I slept together, my younger sister, Jean,[2] roomed with the nurse, and Father and Mother occupied a third room. Mrs. Crane often referred to her home as "Do as You Please Hall," for she wished everyone to feel complete liberty to act and think as he would. Her own nature was so sweet and gentle that one could not imagine a more suitable abode for her than this picturesque and peaceful farm elevated above the plane of ordinary mortals. She was as tranquil and lovable as the trees and flowers, her most constant companions.

Aunt Sue, for whom my elder sister was named, was the one person I have ever seen who appeared to be continually above and beyond the hurts inflicted by human existence. Father sometimes called her Sister Sue, and she returned the compliment by baptizing him Holy Samuel, though with a strong touch of humor in her tone of voice whenever she used this title. Aunt Sue adored Father's little bursts of temper and would laugh at him most heartily. Often he laughed with her, altering his vehement mood instantaneously to one of childlike mirth. These sudden changes from shadow to light, and from light to shadow, were perhaps one of Father's real charms, for the human race likes surprise.

There was a small rise of ground at the summit of the main hill, stretching off to one side like an extra branch to a tree. Halfway up this elevation stood the little octagonal cottage in which father did his writing. One reached it by a winding path and about twenty stone steps. It was a charming sort of Peter Pan house covered with ivy and surrounded by beautiful wild flowers and morning-glories. Through the tops of the trees an aperture had been made so that Father could enjoy the view of Elmira and the hills beyond—an inspiring place for creative work. In spite of the eight good-sized windows, the air was so permeated with tobacco smoke that it was almost stifling to one unused to it. Father seemed to thrive on it, notwithstanding, and in fact, the less he followed the good advice of physicians the better he seemed to feel. No exercise, little fresh air, constant inhaling of cigar smoke—all contributed to keep him in good health.

Once settled at the farm for the summer, he had no desire to leave it even for a short visit to town. He was devoted to some of Mother's friends and relatives there, but he very much preferred their coming to see him on the hill than calling on them in the valley. There was a fascination about the peace of the place that worked like a spell. Usually he went to his study about ten o'clock in the morning and remained until five in the afternoon, seldom taking anything to eat or drink in the middle of the day.

We dined at six o'clock, and the evening was spent in various ways. Often Father read aloud to the whole family the work he had accomplished during the day. Again, he and Theodore Crane, his brother-in-law, played games, either chess or cards, while Mother read aloud to the rest of us. No matter how engrossed Father might appear to be in the game he was playing, he managed to hear enough of the reading to throw out very humorous criticisms of the author's style, particularly if the author happened to be [George] Meredith (whom he thought too wordy) or Jane Austen, a pet aversion of his.

Notes

1. Olivia Susan (Susy) Clemens (1872–96).
2. Jane Lampton (Jean) Clemens (1880–1909).

Clara Clemens, from *My Father Mark Twain* (New York: Harper & Bros., 1931), 59–62, 64.

From *Samuel Langhorne Clemens* (1910)

JERVIS LANGDON

Charles Jervis Langdon (1849–1916) of Elmira, who met Twain aboard the *Quaker City* in 1867, was Livy's brother and so became Twain's brother-in-law in 1870.

IT HAS BEEN SAID he was given to swearing. I believe he was and that as a young man the habit had quite a hold on him. And yet I can remember hearing him swear only once, and that after I was grown up, which shows he was careful when the children were about. And what I did hear was entirely different from the heavy, guttural, vulgar thing we call profanity. It was so different I failed at first to recognize it. It came trippingly, almost musically, from the tongue. It was artistic compared with the ordinary variety. I can confirm one funny story that has been told about it. One day Mrs. Clemens was confined to her bed. She heard her husband in the distance. Something had happened. He was swearing. Soon he arrived at her door and before he had time even to greet her she repeated so far as she could remember it all of the language she had just heard. Mr. Clemens looked at her dumbfounded for a moment, then doubled over in mirth: "Livy, Livy," said he, "you have the words but not the tune."

Jervis Langdon, from *Samuel Langhorne Clemens* (Elmira, N.Y.: privately printed, 1910), 6–7.

From *I Remember* (1934)

J. HENRY HARPER

> Twain took time off from his usual summer routine in Elmira to return to the
> Mississippi River valley during the spring of 1882 with James R. Osgood and
> a shorthand secretary in tow and plans to expand his essays "Old Times on
> the Mississippi" (1875) into the book *Life on the Mississippi* (1883). He trav-
> eled to St. Louis, south by steamboat to New Orleans, then north to Hanni-
> bal and Quincy, Illinois. The journalist and humorist Opie Read (1852–1939)
> joined him on part of the trip.

ONE OF THE FEATURES of the cotton exposition was Mark Twain. I saw people turn away from the Chinese giant, eight feet high, to gaze upon a humorous philosopher who said that he was, though never tall, always short
along toward the first of the month. I heard that he was to board the *Kate
Adams* to steam around the bends and over the wide washes of his pilot
recollections. I made it a point to take passage on the same boat. The *Kate
Adams* was not crowded and for this I was thankful. I saw Twain talking
with an old friend, a pilot whose name I cannot recall; but I remember his
countenance, can see it at this moment. His eyes had a far-away expression
as if he were looking for a snag in the river, and his voice had the tone of a
negro tune. He and Twain were sitting forward on the upper deck, talking,
and courteously they invited me to join in with them. To listen to them was
like reading a "character" book.

"It was along about here where old Tim was drowned," said the pilot.

"That so? It was not the place that was interesting to me: it was the as-
surance that he had been drowned. About the only vital fact connected
with his life was that he was dead. When he slept he snored a lie. When he
awoke he blinked a falsehood. I saw Griswold smash his jaw for slandering
a young woman."

"Old Gris's daughter, wasn't it?"

"No, Gris had never seen the girl but took a swipe at him on general principles. Remember bow-legged Boyd?"

"Mighty well. He knew how to shuffle cards, but he died an honest death."

"It must have been sudden," said Twain.

"It was: fellow named Rankin shot him."

Up came a tall, bent man and introduced himself, Professor Wilkinson, of Columbia, if I remember rightly. I saw the humorist and the pilot wink at each other. The learned man sat down and picked a bit of cottonwood lint off his trousers. "Mr. Twain, you have helped to make this great waterway famous," he said.

The pilot tittered. Mark hated to be called Mr. Twain.

"Well, I didn't dry it up at any rate."

"Ah, very true, sir, and I might say very good. You will pardon me, I feel, but I have thought as to what you might have been had you received a systematic training at one of our universities."

"I might have been a professor," said Twain.

"Quite true, sir. Are you college bred?" he inquired of me.

"Well, I went through a classical institution and knew nearly as much when I came out as when I went in."

He looked at me. "Quite true, no doubt, yes sir. Well, we are making great strides in an educational way."

Mark Twain made fun of many phases of life, some of them endearments, but for learning he had a profound reverence. Not so with the pilot. "Education's all right in its way," he said, "but if Lincoln had rubbed shoulders with high-up school teachers do you reckon he ever would have been so close to the people?"

"My dear sir," Professor Wilkinson responded, inclining his head politely, "there is no element of novelty in your remark. I have often heard it or its like; but in answer to your question let me say that of itself, being close to the people has never exemplified the deepest of wisdom. When wisdom stands too close to the people it stoops to flattery. In our national house a senator is most impotent when he makes a speech for the state that elected him."

Up came a man with a message. "Gentlemen, Senator Zeb Vance[1] has just come aboard and by request is going to deliver a talk in the dining room. Won't you please come in and hear him?"

"Speak of the devil and—you know the rest," said Mark Twain. "Yes, we'll be pleased to hear him. But what's the use of his talking to us? We don't belong to his political household."

[135]

"I've been wanting to hear him for a long time," remarked the pilot, over-turning his chair. "In a speech he called an acquaintance of mine a liar and told the truth."

Old Zeb saw that a short-hand reporter was making ready not alone to catch his sentences but the shading of his words; and this has made more than one athlete of the rostrum limp and halt in his phraseology. The ora-tor began with Thomas Jefferson, in which all democrats know that there can be no mistake. He jumped over Hamilton, tiptoed lightly upon Henry Clay and then got down to himself. Like many a popular orator he was en-gaging while saying but little and the Professor, turning about remarked, "Periphrasis, nothing more: periphrasis."

Softly Mark Twain laughed, he and I looking at the pilot who heaved a sort of sigh and said: "You may think it's that, whatever the hell it is, but I call it damned bunk."

Note

1. Zebulon Baird Vance (1830–94), North Carolina politician.

J. Henry Harper, from *I Remember* (New York: Smith, 1934), 158–63.

"Illustrating *Huck Finn*" (1930)

E. W. KEMBLE

In April 1884 Twain selected Edward Windsor Kemble (1861–1933) to illustrate *Adventures of Huckleberry Finn*. Though Kemble insisted in "Illustrating *Huck Finn*" that he had never drawn any sketches of black characters before accepting the commission, he had in fact repeatedly contributed such sketches or caricatures to *Life*. Kemble was later selected to illustrate *Mark Twain's Library of Humor* (1888), also published by Charles L. Webster & Co. Indeed, he became well known for his caricatures of Southern blacks: he illustrated an edition of *Uncle Tom's Cabin* for Houghton Mifflin in 1892. He also published several books of racist caricatures: for example, *Coons* (1892), *A Coon Alphabet* (1898), and *Comical Coons* (1898). See also David, "The Pictorial *Huck Finn*."

WHILE CONTRIBUTING TO *Life* I made a small picture of a little boy being stung by a bee.[1] Mark Twain had completed the manuscript of *Huckleberry Finn* and had set up a relative, Charles L. Webster, in the publishing business.

Casting about for an illustrator, Mark Twain happened to see this picture. It had action and expression, and bore a strong resemblance to his mental conception of Huck Finn. I was sent for and immediately got in touch with Webster. The manuscript was handed me and the fee asked for—two thousand dollars—was graciously allowed. I had begun drawing professionally two years before this date, and was now at the ripe old age of twenty-three. Homeward I trod with nimble feet. . . .

Now began the important job of getting a model. The story called for a variety of characters, old and young, male and female. In the neighborhood I came across a youngster, Cort Morris by name, who tallied with my idea of Huck. He was a bit tall for the ideal boy, but I could jam him down a few pegs in my drawing and use him for the other characters.

From the beginning I never depended upon models but preferred to pick my types out of the ether, training my mind to visualize them. So I engaged my youthful model, and I remember that from the very start he became immensely popular among his feminine schoolmates as all of his income went for sweetmeats which were duly distributed on his homeward journeys from the seat of learning.

I had a large room in the top of our house which I used as a studio. Here I collected my props for the work. I spent the forenoon completing the drawing, using "Huck" as soon as he was released from school. He was always grinning, and one side of his cheek was usually well padded with a "sourball" or a huge wad of molasses taffy. Throwing his wool cap and muslin-covered schoolbooks on a lounge, he would ask what was wanted at this session. I would designate the character. "We will do the old woman who spots Huck as he is trying to pass for a girl." Donning an old sunbonnet and slipping awkwardly into a faded skirt, Cort would squat on a low splint-bottomed chair and become the most woebegone female imaginable. Forthwith he would relieve his extended cheek of its burden of taffy with a mighty gulp. I would make a simple outline sketch on yellow-toned paper and then take a rest, during which Cort would pop a "cocoanut strip" into his grinning mouth.

For the King, Cort wore an old frock coat and padded his waist line with towels until he assumed the proper rotundity. Then he would mimic the sordid old reprobate and twist his boyish face into the most outlandish expressions. If I could have drawn the grimaces as they were I would have had a convulsing collection of comics, but these would not have jibed with the text, and I was forced to forego them.

I used my young model for every character in the story—man, woman, and child. Jim the Negro seemed to please him the most. He would jam his little black wool cap over his head, shoot out his lips, and mumble coon talk all the while he was posing. Grown to manhood, "Huck" is now a sturdy citizen of Philadelphia, connected with an established business house.

This Negro Jim, drawn from a white schoolboy, with face unblackened, started something in my artistic career. Several advance chapters of *Huckleberry Finn* were published in the *Century Magazine*,[2] then under the able editorship of Richard Watson Gilder[3] and a select staff of assistants. My picture caught the fancy of Mr. Gilder and W. Lewis Fraser, the art director. I was asked to call and exhibit my wares. I went to *Life* and borrowed a few originals, but not one picture contained a Negro type.

"We want to see some of your Negro drawings," Mr. Frazer said.

"I have none," I replied. "I've never made any until this one in *Huck Finn*."

The art editor looked dubious. "I have several stories I would like to have you illustrate, but they are all of the South."

"Let me try," I urged, "and if they do not suit the text you need not use or pay for them."

I made the drawings. Mr. Frazer nodded his head as he looked at them.

"I guess they'll go. We'll strike off some proofs and send them to the authors and see what they say."

The proofs were sent and soon came back with the stamp of approval. One author went so far as to declare: "At last you have an artist who knows the South." I had, up to that time, never been further south than Sandy Hook. My coons caught the public fancy. The *Century* then engaged me to work exclusively for their magazine. This continued for several years, and all the stories from those charming writers of the South, Thomas Nelson Page, James Lane Allen, Harry Stilwell Edwards, Richard Malcolm Johnston, and George W. Cable, were placed in my hands for picture work. I was established as a delineator of the South, the Negro being my specialty, and, as I have mentioned, I had never been South at all. I didn't go for two years more. Then I told Mr. Gilder that it was high time for me to go and see what the real article looked like. He agreed with me. After visiting several plantations and noting the local color, a thing I had missed but had not attempted to carry out to any extent in my pictures, I found that my types were, in most cases, the counterparts of those surrounding me. I had seen the Negro of the city but he was a different bird from the plantation product, both in carriage and dress. It all seems so strange to me now that a single subject, a Negro, drawn from a pose given me by a lanky white schoolboy, should have started me on a career that has lasted for forty-five years, especially as I had no more desire to specialize in that subject than I had in the Chinaman or the Malay pirate.

Years later I sat beside Mark Twain at a luncheon in the home of Mrs. Clarence Mackay.[4] I had not seen him in all the intervening years. His face bore no trace of the siege he had been through when the firm of Charles L. Webster went bankrupt and he began his lecture tour, paying back every dollar of the indebtedness. We fell to talking of the past—its writers and illustrators. Abbey[5] had never been equaled, he contended. His delightful drawings for [Robert] Herrick's *Poems*, for *She Stoops to Conquer* and *The Quiet Life,* stamped him as a master of his craft. [A. B.] Frost stood alone in his humor. There were [W. T.] Smedley, [Charles S.] Reinhart, and [Frederic] Remington, a little group of shining lights undimmed by time. We spoke of *Huck Finn* and I told him of my model and of the various uses to which I had put him. He seemed greatly amused and wanted me to enlighten him about my beginnings as an illustrator.

Notes

1. I have been unable to locate any illustration in *Life* like the one Kemble describes here.

2. Three advance installments of *Huckleberry Finn* appeared in *Century:* 29 (December 1884), 268–79; 29 (January 1885), 456–59; and 29 (February 1885), 544–68; and one appeared in the *New York Tribune,* 11 January 1885, 9.

3. Richard Watson Gilder (1844–1909), editor of *Century* from 1881 until his death.

4. Katherine Duer Mackay (1880–1930), and her husband, the American financier Clarence Hungerford Mackay (1874–1938), lived at Harbor Hill, an estate designed by McKim, Mead & White, in Roslyn, New York, on the north shore of Long Island.

5. The painter and illustrator Edwin Austin Abbey (1852–1911) wed Mary Gertrude Mead, W. D. Howells's niece by marriage, in 1890.

E. W. Kemble, "Illustrating *Huck Finn*," *Colophon,* part 1 (1930): n.p.

From *My Mark Twain* (1910)

W. D. HOWELLS

> Twain and George Washington Cable (1844–1925) crisscrossed the country
> between 5 November 1884 and 28 February 1885 on what their agent, James B.
> Pond (1838–1903), called the "Twins of Genius" lecture tour. Together Twain
> and Cable performed 103 times in some eighty cities, from St. Paul in the
> west, to Louisville in the South, Montreal in the North, and Boston in the
> East. Twain often read excerpts from his forthcoming *Adventures of Huckle-*
> *berry Finn,* while Cable usually read excerpts from his novel *Dr. Sevier* (1884).
> Attendance averaged slightly over 500 per date, and Twain earned about
> $16,000 from the tour. Howells recalled how ambitious the original plans for
> the tour were.

THERE CAME A TIME when the lecturing which had been the joy of his prime
became his loathing, loathing unutterable, and when he renounced it with
indescribable violence. Yet he was always hankering for those fleshpots
whose savor lingered on his palate and filled his nostrils after his with-
drawal from the platform. The Authors' Readings when they had won their
brief popularity abounded in suggestion for him. Reading from one's book
was not so bad as giving a lecture written for a lecture's purpose, and he
was willing at last to compromise. He had a magnificent scheme for touring
the country with Aldrich and Mr. G. W. Cable and myself, in a private car,
with a cook of our own, and every facility for living on the fat of the land.
We should read only four times a week, in an entertainment that should not
last more than an hour and a half. He would be the impresario, and would
guarantee us others at least seventy-five dollars a day, and pay every expense of the enterprise, which he provisionally called the Circus, himself.
But Aldrich and I were now no longer in those earlier thirties when we so
cheerfully imagined *Memorable Murders* for subscription publication; we
both abhorred public appearances, and, at any rate, I was going to Europe
for a year.[1] So the plan fell through except as regarded Mr. Cable, who,
in his way, was as fine a performer as Clemens, and could both read and

[141]

sing the matter of his books. On a far less stupendous scale they two made the rounds of the great lecturing circuit together. But I believe a famous lecture-manager had charge of them and traveled with them.[2]

Notes

1. According to Twain, "Two years ago I got some such plan as this in my head. I wanted to get a larger menagerie together, Howells, T. B. Aldrich, 'Uncle Remus' [Joel Chandler Harris], Cable, and myself, so that we could all go on the stage together, and each read two minutes or so and pose as 'the happy family' between times. But Howells had to go to Italy on a commission from the *Century,* which will take him a year to fulfill; and the others couldn't join us for one reason or another, and so Cable and I started out alone" ("Clemens and Cable," *Minneapolis Tribune,* 25 January 1885, 3; repr. in Scharnhorst 77). Howells signed a contract with the Century Co. on 30 March 1882 to write ten to twelve articles about Italy, and he lived in Europe between July 1882 and July 1883.

2. Pond also organized the North American leg of Twain's round-the-world tour in 1895. See Twain to Howells, 3 July 1899 (*Twain-Howells Letters,* 704): "Pond is also a fool. I have seldom seen so complete & compact a one. But he is a most kindly & pleasant one, & I would not trade his society for that of the average wise man."

W. D. Howells, from *My Mark Twain* (New York: Harper and Bros., 1910), 53–54.

"Mark Twain on the Lecture Platform" (1900)

WILL M. CLEMENS

> William Montgomery Clemens (1860–1931)—no relation—remembered Twain and Cable's performance in Cleveland on 17 December 1884.

IN DECEMBER Twain and Cable appeared in Cleveland. They arrived one afternoon and registered at the Forest City House. I called to pay my respects. Was Mr. Clemens in? Yes, but he had just eaten dinner, it then being 3 o'clock, and had gone to bed, not to be disturbed until 7 o'clock, excepting in case Mr. John Hay, the author of "Little Breeches," called. Mr. Clemens would see Mr. Hay, but no other human being could entice him from his bed. In the evening occurred the entertainment. Mr. Cable read passages from his novel, *Dr. Sevier*. Mark Twain came upon the stage walking slowly, apparently in deep meditation. Those present saw a rather small man, with a big head, with bushy gray hair, heavy dark eyebrows, a receding chin, a long face, toothless gums visible between the lips, an iron-gray mustache, closely cut and stiff. The right hand involuntarily stroked the receding chin, and a merry twinkle came into his eyes, as he advanced to the front of the stage and began to recite, in his peculiar, drawling and deliberate way, "King Sollermun," taken from advance sheets of *Huckleberry Finn*.[1] When he had finished, he turned and boyishly ran off the stage, with a sort of dog trot. Then I remember that Mr. Cable came on, told us all about "Kate Riley" and "Ristofolo," and then, in imitation of Mark Twain, tried to run off the stage in the same playful manner. I remember also what a deplorable failure Mr. Cable made of the attempt, how his gentle trot reminded me of a duck going down hill, and how eventually he collided with one of the scenes, and lastly how the audience roared with laughter. Then Mark came forward again with his "Tragic Tale of the Fishwife," followed by Cable, who walked soberly now, like a Baptist deacon. Twain told us of "A Trying Situation," and finally concluded the entertainment with one of his inimitable ghost stories.[2]

Notes

1. Twain read the "King Sollermun" episode from chapter 14 (94–96) of *Huck Finn*.

2. Twain read "Tale of the Fishwife and Its Sad Fate" from "The Awful German Language," appendix D to *A Tramp Abroad* (608–9); "A Trying Situation" from *A Tramp Abroad*, chapter 22 (211–20); and "The Golden Arm" from *How to Tell a Story and Other Essays* (10–12).

Will M. Clemens, "Mark Twain on the Lecture Platform," *Ainslee's* 6 (August 1900): 25–32.

From Arlin Turner, *Mark Twain and George W. Cable: The Record of a Literary Friendship* (1960)

George Washington Cable

> At the memorial to Twain in New York on November 30, 1910, George Washington Cable reminisced about the "Twins of Genius" tour. He and Twain had performed in Paris, Kentucky, on 31 December 1884; in Cincinnati the evenings of 2 and 3 January 1885; in Toronto, Canada, on 14 February 1885; and in Rochester, New York, on 6 December 1884.

IT IS BECAUSE of that hold he has on all our hearts—and I speak for the whole American people—it was that spirit that caused an audience once in Paris, Kentucky, who had applauded him until their palms were sore and until their feet were tired, and who had laughed as he came forward for the fourth alternation of our reading together—the one side of him dragging, one foot limping after the other—the peculiar way known to us all—the house burst into such a storm of laughter, coming from so crowded a house, that Mark Twain himself, grim controller of his emotions at all times, burst into laughter and had to acknowledge to me, as he came off the platform: "Yes, yes"—still laughing with joy of it himself—"yes; they got me off my feet that time."

I remember the hold he had upon children's hearts, another field of his human kindness to all humankind. It is illustrated in an experience he had in Cincinnati when certain children were brought by their aunt to hear Mark Twain read from his pages in that great city, brought down from the town of Hamilton, and who went back home in the late hours of the night, beside themselves with the delight of their clear understanding and full appreciation of his humor, saying to their kinswoman: "Oh, Auntie! Oh, Auntie! It was better than Buffalo Bill!"

One point I should like to make to indicate the conscientiousness with which he held himself the custodian of the affections of the great mass of

[145]

the people who loved him in every quarter of the land. It was the rigor of his art, an art which was able to carry the added burden beyond the burden of all other men's art, the burden of absolutely concealing itself and of making him appear, whenever he appeared, as slipshod in his mind as he was in his gait. We were at Toronto, Canada. The appointment was for us to read two nights in succession, and we had read one night. The vast hall was filled to overflowing. I heard from the retiring room the applause that followed every period of his utterance, heard it come rolling in and tumbling like the surf of the ocean. Well, at last, as we were driving home to our hotel, I found him in an absolutely wretched condition of mental depression, groaning and sighing, and all but weeping, and I asked him what in the world justified such a mood—a man who had just come from such a triumph. "Such a triumph?" he said. "A triumph of the moment; but those people are going home to their beds, glad to get there, and they will wake up in the morning ashamed of having laughed at my nonsense."

"Nonsense?" I said.

"How is it nonsense?"

"I have spent the evening, and their time, and taxed them to the best of their ability to show appreciation of my wit and humor, and I have spent that whole time simply spinning yarns."

I said: "Don't mind; you are going to meet virtually the very same audience tomorrow, and tomorrow night you shall give them good literature, if any living writer in a living language has got that chance." I don't know if he slept that night, but I know he did what he did not often relish. He rehearsed, and rehearsed, and rehearsed, and the next night he gave them a program which he chose to begin, at my suggestion, with the *Blue Jay's Message*.[1] He left that house as happy as anyone ever saw Mark Twain, and that was with a feeling of acute joy because he had won friends he considered worthy, he had won every handclap and applause with a program worthy of honor.

One more point: every one knows that one of his passions was for history, and I assume that that passion for history was one of the demonstrations of his human kindness. It was the story of the human heart, and he loved history because it was the story of humanity.

One night we were in Rochester together. It was Saturday night, and for a wonder we were without an engagement that night, so we started out for a walk; we had gone a few steps when we found a bookstore, and at the same moment it was beginning to rain. I said: "Let us go in here." He said: "I remember I have not provided myself with anything to read all day tomorrow." I said: "We will get it here. I will look down that table, and you will look down this." Presently I went over to him and said I had not found anything that I thought would interest him, and asked him if he had found anything. He said no, he had not; but there was a book he did not remember any previous acquaintance with. He asked me what that book was.

"Why," I said, "that is Sir Thomas Malory's *Morte d'Arthur.*" And he said: "Shall we take it?" I said: "Yes; and you will never lay it down until you have read it from cover to cover."[2] It was easy enough to make the prophecy, and, of course, it was fulfilled. He had read in it a day or two, when I saw come upon his cheekbones those vivid pink spots which every one who knew him intimately and closely knew meant that his mind was working with all its energies. I said to myself: "Ah, I think Sir Thomas Malory's *Morte d'Arthur* is going to bear fruit in the brain of Mark Twain."[3] A year or two afterward, when he came to see me in my Northampton home, I asked him what he was engaged in, and he said he was writing a story of *A Yankee at the Court of King Arthur.* I said: "If that be so, then I claim for myself the godfathership of that book." He said: "Yes; you are its godfather."

Notes

1. "Baker's Blue-Jay Yarn," in chapter 3 of *A Tramp Abroad* (38–42).
2. On Twain's copy of Malory, see Roberts.
3. On Malory's influence on *A Connecticut Yankee,* see Bowden; Kordecki.

George Washington Cable, from Arlin Turner, *Mark Twain and George W. Cable: The Record of a Literary Friendship* (East Lansing: Michigan State University Press, 1960), 132–36.

From *Papa:*
An Intimate Biography of Mark Twain (1985)

SUSY CLEMENS

In her midteens, Susy Clemens wrote a biography of her father. In her entry for 12 February 1886, she touched on a variety of topics, including her mother's role as Twain's editor. The original misspellings are retained.

MAMMA AND I have both been very much troubled of late because papa, since he has been publishing Gen. Grant's book, has seemed to forget his own books and work entirely, and the other evening as papa and I were promonading up and down the library he told me that he didn't expect to write but one more book, and then he was ready to give up work altogether, die or do anything, he said that he had written more than he had ever expected to, and the only book that he had been pertickularly anxious to write was one locked up in the safe down stairs, not yet published.[1]

But this intended future of course will never do, and although papa usualy hold to his own opinions and intents with outsiders, when mamma realy desires anything and says that it must be papa allways give up his plans (at least so far) and does as she says (and she is usually right, if she disagrees with him at all). It was because he knew his great tendency to being convinced by her, that he published without her knowledge that article in the *Christian Union* concerning the government of children.[2] So judging from the proofs of past years, I think that we will be able to persuade papa to go back to work as before, and not leave off writing with the end of his next Story. Mamma says that she sometimes feels, and I do too, that she would rather have papa depend on his writing for a living, than to have him think of giving it up.

Ever since papa and mamma were married, papa has written his books and then taken them to mamma in manuscript and she has expergated them. Papa read *Huckleberry Finn* to us in manuscript just before it came out, and then he would leave parts of it with mamma to expergate, while he went off up to the study to work, and sometimes Clara and I would be sitting with mamma while she was looking the manuscript over and I remember so well with what pangs of regret we used to see her turn down the leaves of the pages which meant that some delightfully dreadful part must be scratched out. And I remember one part pertickularly which was perfectly fascinating it was dreadful, that Clara and I used to delight in, and oh with what dispare we saw mamma turn down the leaf on which it was written, we thought the book would be almost spoiled without it. But after it was published we changed our minds. We gradually came to feel as mamma did.

Notes

1. Susy Clemens refers to the manuscript novel subsequently published in part as "Extract from Captain Stormfield's Visit to Heaven," *Harper's Monthly* 116 (December 1907), 41–49; and 116 (January 1908), 266–76.

2. Twain's letter on the government of children, entitled "'What Ought He to Have Done?' Mark Twain's Opinion," appeared in the *Christian Union,* 16 July 1885, 4–5.

Susy Clemens, from *Papa: An Intimate Biography of Mark Twain,* ed. Charles Neider (Garden City, N.Y.: Doubleday, 1985), 187–89.

From *Recollections of a Varied Life* (1910)

GEORGE CARY EGGLESTON

> The author George Cary Eggleston (1839–1911) recalled the circumstances of an Authors' Club meeting, probably the one on 22 April 1886.

I PRESIDED, many years ago, at a banquet given by the Authors Club to Mr. William Dean Howells. Nothing was prearranged. There was no schedule of toasts in my hand, no list of speakers primed to respond to them. With so brilliant a company to draw upon I had no fear as to the result of calling up the man I wanted without warning.

In the course of the haphazard performance, it occurred to me that we ought to have a speech by some publisher, and accordingly I called upon Mr. J. Henry Harper—"Harry Harper,"[1] we who knew and loved him called him.

His embarrassment was positively painful to behold. He made no attempt whatever to respond but appealed to me to excuse him.

At that point Mark Twain came to the rescue by offering to make Mr. Harper's speech for him. "I'm a publisher myself," he explained, "and I'll speak for the publishers."

A roar of applause welcomed the suggestion, and Mr. Clemens proceeded to make the speech. In the course of it he spoke of the multitude of young authors who beset every publisher and beseech him for advice after he has explained that their manuscripts are "not available" for publication by his own firm, with its peculiar limitations. Most publishers cruelly refuse, he said, to do anything for these innocents. "I never do that," he added. "I always give them good advice, and more than that, I always do something for them—*I give them notes of introduction to [Richard Watson] Gilder.*"

Note

1. J. Henry Harper (1850–1938), an officer in the publishing firm of Harper & Bros. for most of his adult life and grandson of John Harper, one of the founders of the company. Twain often visited Harper at his summerhouse on Long Island.

George Cary Eggleston, from *Recollections of a Varied Life* (New York: Holt, 1910), 258–59.

From *My Mark Twain* (1910)

W. D. HOWELLS

As Howells remembered, Twain figured the *Life of Pope Leo XIII* by Father Bernard O'Reilly (1820–1907), published in 1887 by Charles L. Webster & Co., would be a surefire best seller.

ONE OF THE HIGHEST satisfactions of Clemens's often supremely satisfactory life was his relation to Grant. It was his proud joy to tell how he found Grant about to sign a contract for his book on certainly very good terms, and said to him that he would himself publish the book and give him a percentage three times as large. . . . The prosperity of this venture was the beginning of Clemens's adversity, for it led to excesses of enterprise which were forms of dissipation. The young sculptor who had come back to him from Paris modeled a small bust of Grant, which Clemens multiplied in great numbers to his great loss,[1] and the success of Grant's book tempted him to launch on publishing seas where his bark presently foundered. The first and greatest of his disasters was the *Life of Pope Leo XIII,* which he came to tell me of, when he had imagined it, in a sort of delirious exultation. He had no words in which to paint the magnificence of the project, or to forecast its colossal success. It would have a currency bounded only by the number of Catholics in Christendom. It would be translated into every language which was anywhere written or printed; it would be circulated literally in every country of the globe, and Clemens's book agents would carry the prospectuses and then the bound copies of the work to the ends of the whole earth. Not only would every Catholic buy it, but every Catholic must, as he was a good Catholic, as he hoped to be saved. It was a magnificent scheme, and it captivated me, as it had captivated Clemens; it dazzled us both, and neither of us saw the fatal defect in it. We did not consider how often Catholics could not read, how often when they could, they might not wish to read. The event proved that whether they could read or not the immeasurable majority did not wish to read the life of the Pope, though it was written by a dignitary of the Church and issued to the world with every sanction from the Vatican. The failure was incredible to Clemens; his sanguine soul was utterly confounded, and soon a silence fell upon it where it had been so exuberantly jubilant.

Note

1. The sculptor Karl Gerhardt (1853–1940) executed busts of both Twain and Ulysses S. Grant. Financially supported by Twain, he had studied at Ecole des Beaux-Arts in Paris with the instructor François Jouffroy.

W. D. Howells, from *My Mark Twain* (New York: Harper & Bros., 1910), 72–74.

From *Opinions of a Cheerful Yankee* (1926)

IRVING BACHELLER

> The journalist Irving Bacheller (1859–1950) founded the Bacheller newspaper syndicate in 1884.

I WENT TO SEE HIM one day at his home in Hartford. He was in a room upstairs. A billiard table was in the middle of it. I thought him one of the saddest-looking men I had ever met. Of course it was a serious matter to have a brave reporter break into the china shop of his meditations. He sat with his feet on a window sill and smoking a cob-pipe, looking out thoughtfully at the snow-covered landscape. He said that for weeks he had been unable to write anything fit for a better fate than feeding the fireplace. He had fed the fireplace until he was sick of it. His stuff burned well. That was all he could say for it. He was in a beautiful home with a devoted wife and a number of children and yet he did not look or talk like a happy man.

Some years later he came to luncheon with me at a little Bohemian club organized by myself and Stephen Crane and Edward Marshall[1] and Willis Hawkins,[2] all editors or special writers on the metropolitan press.

"It doesn't agree with me, therefore I'll eat it," he said of the mince pie. "I have always stuck to things that didn't agree with me until one or the other of us got the best of it. Of course I'm a fool. God made me so. Therefore if you cannot forgive me for my own sake, forgive me for God's sake."

In a drawling melancholy tone he said to me:

"Bacheller, I am careful about the ending of a story. I try to put a double snapper at the end—one to start the effect I am seeking, the other to prolong it. I have just thought of a story and I don't know how to end it. A man born on a farm in the country went to a great city and made a handsome success. He had never married. When the story begins he is a middle-aged bachelor. One day he is thinking of the old home and of the pretty girl he had played with and admired in his early school days. She had never married. Perhaps it was because she had been fond of him. He decided to return to the scenes of his youth and look her up. He went back to the familiar rustic neighborhood. Mary, the girl, was away on a visit but would be returning in a day or two. He tramped over the trails he had known as a boy. He visited the friends of his youth who were still to be found in that countryside. In his brother's top buggy he traveled the familiar roads and one day when he was driving on a lonely highway he saw the beloved brook and the old swimmin' hole. It was hard by the wayside, a little beyond a point where the old road came out of a strip of woods. He was hot and dusty. What would be the matter with having a swim in that deep clear pool where he had found one of the great joys of his boyhood? There was almost no travel on that back country road. Why shouldn't he do it? He was in a land where there were no bathrooms. The temptation was too much for him. He fell. Hitched the horse, took off his clothes, and dove in with the reckless abandon of a boy. He came out and dried himself with his hands in the old way. He got on his undershirt and his overshirt and his collar and necktie. He heard a team coming and voices back in the woods. They were near. He had not time to put on his drawers and trousers. So he jumped into the buggy and drew the lap robe over his nakedness and sat there waiting for the team to pass. In a minute he saw to his dismay Mary, the girl of his dreams, and other members of her family coming in a double wagon. She was returning to her home.

" 'Hello, Mary!' he called.

" 'Hello, Bill! where are you stopping?'

" 'Over at my brother's.'

"She got out of a wagon and came to greet him. To him she looked as charming as of old. Suddenly she asked:

" 'May I get in and ride with you?'

"Now, my question is: how is he going to answer her? What can he say with her standing eagerly at the side of the buggy and looking up into his face?"

"Perhaps he would say: 'Yes, if you will let me have all the lap robe,'" I suggested.

"But how about the trousers?" he demurred. "That is a valuable pair of trousers lying beside the brook and they are bound to increase in value as the day proceeds."

We who sat around him were roaring with laughter but his face and voice did not change. They would have become an undertaker at a funeral. Was he a consummate actor or was there behind his humor a background of melancholy never quite concealed? Well, undoubtedly he was a great actor, but the note of melancholy was no part of his acting. It was a part of *him*.

The next time I saw him he was lying in bed at his home on Fifth Avenue. I imagine it was the ex-bed of some old king or emperor. It was an immense thing of richly carved mahogany. He was propped on pillows with his meerschaum pipe in his mouth.

"Bacheller, I have been thinking of my nose," he said. "I hate the damn thing. It turns down so. It goes too far. It irritates me."

These were characteristic sentences. They carried the note of self-inspection. That was, I think, the keynote of his character. Intellectually he was a gigantic, if not quite a full-furnished man. In his own heart were the loves and passions and frailties of the great multitude of his brothers. Added thereto was a genius for self-expression the world has rarely seen. Mark Twain was his piece of soil and he worked it well. He was kind and just and noble-hearted.

Notes

1. Edward Marshall (1869–1933), American journalist.
2. Willis Brooks Hawkins (1852–1928), American journalist.

Irving Bacheller, from *Opinions of a Cheerful Yankee* (Indianapolis, Ind.: Bobbs-Merrill, 1926), 6–10.

"Memories of Mark Twain" (1920)

BRANDER MATTHEWS

Brander Matthews (1852–1929), the first professor of dramatic literature at Columbia University, was caught up in a dispute over copyright with Twain in the late 1880s. Matthews argued in favor of a robust international copyright agreement, while Twain, as Martin Buinicki explains (59–60), "saw property rights as matters of individual responsibility, rather than as divine or natural rights. He felt that one had to defend these rights actively to keep them."

IN 1882, Laurence Hutton and Lawrence Barrett, Frank Millet and E. A. Abbey, W. M. Laffan and I organized an intermittent and sporadic dining club, which we called The Kinsmen, because we intended to gather in the practitioners of the kindred arts, and which had no officers, no dues, and no rules, except that an invitation to one of our meetings was to be accepted as an election to membership. I gave the first dinner; and at the second, given by Hutton a full year later, I was delighted to find myself sitting by the side of Mark Twain.

Then began an intimacy which lasted until his death nearly thirty years thereafter. Later, when *Huckleberry Finn* was issued, I had the pleasure of reviewing it for the London *Saturday Review,* hailing it as one of the indisputable masterpieces of American fiction. This pleased Mark; and as he had somehow discovered that I had written the criticism he took occasion to thank me.[1]

Mark was also one of the earliest members of the Authors' Club, of which I had been one of the founders; and I served with him on the executive committee of the American Copyright League. It was during our eight-year campaign for international copyright that my relation with Mark was a little strained though fortunately only for a brief period. Until the passage of our bill in 1891 no foreign author had any control over the publication of his writings in the United States; an American publisher could reprint without payment anything any British man of letters wrote; and as a result every American man of letters had to see his books sold in competition with stolen goods. We all felt this keenly; but only a few of us knew that there were certain London publishers quite as willing to reprint American books without payment as certain New York publishers were to appropriate British books on the same terms. While we wanted the rights of the authors of the United Kingdom to be protected in the United States we also wanted the rights of the authors of the United States to be protected in the United Kingdom.

In 1887 I prepared a paper for the *New Princeton Review,* which I called "American Authors and British Pirates," and in which I collected examples of the cruel treatment accorded to certain of our writers, forced to behold their works reprinted in England without their permission and often with an offensive mutilation of the original in the vain effort to adjust it to the supposed prejudices of British readers.[2]

The facts in my article surprised many who had been ignorant of them; and the editor of the *New Princeton Review,* Prof. William M. Sloane, suggested that I might get together material for a second paper. So I wrote to half a dozen American authors who had been maltreated by British publishers, requesting them to supply me with particulars. One of my letters went to Mark; and a few days later Professor Sloane let me see Mark's reply, which he had sent not to me but direct to the editor for publication in the *New Princeton.* It was a vehement protest against my suggestion that the British law needed any alteration; and it held me up to scorn for making the needless suggestion.[3] Mark let his pen run away with him and poured ridicule upon me, in a fashion which was lacking in consideration for my feelings, even if it was not actually wanting in courtesy. It was a brilliant letter, certain to evoke abundant laughter from every reader—excepting only the one to whom it was addressed. It was also an unanswerable letter, so far as its inimitable manner was concerned; and yet it had to be answered somehow.

What had roused the sudden wrath which had blazed up in Mark's epistolary excoriation was my assertion that the British law could be improved, since it was perfectly satisfactory to Mark himself. Now the British law was better than the American in only one particular! No British author could get any protection in the United States, whereas the British courts had held that any book first published in Great Britain while its author was domiciled in any part of the British empire was entitled to the full protection accorded by the statutes to a book by a British subject.

In accord with an old rule of controversy—to answer earnest with jest and jest with earnest—I wrote a short and simple reply, strictly legal in tone. I pointed out that Mark having permanent relations with a satisfactory publisher in London could always run up to Canada or slip down to Bermuda so as to be under the British flag on the day when any new book of his was to be issued in England. Then I made it plain that this procedure was not possible for a young writer with his first book, often his best and often made up out of contributions to periodicals. There was no fun in my response and it must have seemed pretty pale in comparison with Mark's coruscating fireworks; but I had on my side both the facts and the law.[4]

I had cause to feel aggrieved that he had seen fit to pillory me in the marketplace; but I was unwilling to take offense and I was unable to see any reason why he should resent my studiously respectful retort. Yet I soon heard from more than one of our common friends that Mark was acutely dissatisfied; and when I next met him he was distant in his manner, and I might even describe him as chilly. Of course I regretted this, but I could only hope that his fundamental friendliness would warm him up sooner or later. . . .

I did not have to wait very long before our friendship was renewed, never again to be disturbed. We spent part of the summer of 1890 in the Catskills, at Onteora Park, the hilltop part dotted with unpretending cottages which housed a colony of workers in the several arts. . . . Within a week of our arrival Mark stepped up on our porch, as pleasantly as if there had never been a cloud on our friendship.

"I hear you play a French game called piquet," he began. "I wish you would teach me." And we taught him, though it was no easy task since he was forever wanting to make over the rules of the game to suit his whim of the moment—a boyish trait which I soon discovered to be entirely characteristic.

But we were all boys together that summer; and we invented new ways for discharging high spirits. On the Fourth of July we had a succession of sports, including a race round the clubhouse. Mark officiated as timekeeper, supplying a host of fanciful explanations why the runners took twice the time really necessary for the circuit of the building. He had to admit that the joke was on him when at last they did appear—running back on the side from which they originally started.

From the first he felt himself at ease with the friendly folk of Onteora; and I think he was appreciative of the high regard we had for him. He was a hard worker at intervals; and he was then worried by the difficulties in which his business as a publisher was becoming more and more deeply involved. But he liked to play, especially with his own children, making them accept him as of their own age; and he also could play with the grown-ups as if he were a child. . . .

As he was a consummate craftsman in his use of words when he wrote, so he was surpassingly dexterous in his management of his voice when he told an anecdote or when he made a speech. . . . In the course of forty years he delivered many after-dinner speeches in America and in Europe; and he made addresses more or less informal at many meetings in behalf of good causes.

When I urged him to gather the most durable of these into a book he wrote back: "I reckon it is a good idea to collect the speeches." When time passed and the promised book did not appear I repeated the suggestion; and this time he answered: "There isn't going to be any volume of speeches, because I am too lazy to collect them and revise them." After his death a volume of speeches was added to his complete works, a volume which was not too cautiously edited as it might have been.[5] The selection was uncertain; the arrangement was casual; and the reporting was often hopelessly unsatisfactory. Not a few of his least worthy efforts were included; and there were also not a few unfortunate repetitions. The volume does contain, however, some of the most amusing and most brilliant of his speeches, printed either from the manuscript, which he sometimes wrote out in advance, or from accurate shorthand reports.

It preserves for us the ill-received speech in Boston, that on his seventieth birthday, that on the horrors of the German language, and that on the weather of New England. But no matter how skillfully the selection might have been made, the reader could not get from the pale pages of a book the color and the flow that Mark bestowed upon his sentences by the skill of his own delivery and by the compelling power of his personality. Behind and beneath the words which have been preserved there was the presence of the man himself. Mr. Howells has told us that Mark "held that the actor doubled the value of the author's words." And those who had the pleasure and the privilege of listening to any one of these speeches will recognize that Mr. Howells did not overstate the case when he declared that Mark "was a great actor as well as a great author. He was a most consummate actor, with this difference from other actors, that he was the first to know the thoughts and invent the fancies to which his voice and action gave the color of life. Representation is the art of other actors; his art was creative as well as representative."

If this volume of his speeches had happily been arranged in the order of time I am inclined to think that it would have revealed a change in his tone as he grew older. Even in some of the earlier addresses, amid all the exuberance of his humorous exaggeration, there were to be noted, now and then, passages of exquisite word painting—like the truly poetic description of the ice storm in the speech on the weather of New England. Possibly these passages surprised most of those who heard them and who looked upon Mark as merely a fun maker, not suspecting the depth of his nature, his firmly controlled sentiment, his sustaining seriousness—and not recalling that the richest humor, that of Cervantes and Molière, is rooted in the profoundest melancholy.

Possibly again it was Mark's consciousness that this was the way he was regarded by the unthinking majority which led him to say more than once in the later years of his life that he had made a mistake in coming before the world at first as a humorist, as a man trying to make people laugh. In the beginning he may have been content with this reputation; but toward the end he was not. I remember going into the Players at the noon hour, half a dozen years before he died, and finding him at luncheon. Howells thinks that Mark did not greatly care for clubs and this may be so, but I can testify that he was completely at home in the house in Gramercy Park [the Players' Club], and he relished its friendly informality. He looked up as I came in and said; "Brander, I was just thinking of you. I'm glad that you and Howells have been telling people that I am serious. Now when I make a speech I find that they are a little disappointed if I don't say some things that are serious; and that just suits me, for I have so many serious things I want to say!"

Notes

1. Matthews's review of *Huckleberry Finn* in the London *Saturday Review*, 31 January 1885, 153–54; repr. in Budd, *Contemporary Reviews*, 260–63: "in no other book has the humorist shown so much artistic restraint, for there is in *Huckleberry Finn* no mere 'comic copy,' no straining after effect; one might almost say there is no wasted word in it."

2. Brander Matthews, "American Authors and British Pirates," *New Princeton Review* 4 (September 1887): 201–12.

3. Mark Twain, "American Authors and British Pirates: A Private Letter and a Public Postscript," *New Princeton Review* 5 (January 1888): 47–54.

4. Brander Matthews, "American Authors and British Pirates: An Open Letter to Close a Correspondence," *New Princeton Review* 5 (January 1888): 54–65.

5. *Mark Twain's Speeches* (New York: Harper & Bros., 1910) reprints the Whittier birthday speech in 1877; Twain's seventieth birthday speech delivered in New York on 5 December 1905 (Fatout, *Mark Twain Speaking,* 462–67); "Die Schrecken der Deutschen Sprache," delivered in Vienna on 31 October 1897, translated by Twain under the title "The Horrors of the German Language" (Fatout, *Mark Twain Speaking,* 314–18); and "The Oldest Inhabitant—The Weather of New England," first delivered before the New England Society of New York on 22 December 1876 (Fatout, *Mark Twain Speaking,* 100–103).

Brander Matthews, "Memories of Mark Twain," *Saturday Evening Post,* 6 March 1920, 14–15, 77–78, 81.

From *Hardly a Man Is Now Alive* (1939)

DAN BEARD

Twain selected the socialist Dan Beard (1850–1941) to illustrate *A Connecticut Yankee in King Arthur's Court* (1889). His drawings—over 200 of them executed in a week—were heartily approved by the author. The illustrations also offered an explicit leftist political interpretation of the text. Later, Beard illustrated Twain's novels *The American Claimant* (1892) and *Tom Sawyer Abroad* (1894), and he lived near Twain in rural Connecticut in 1909–10. He edited the wildlife magazine *Recreation* in 1905–6 and became one of the founders of the Boy Scouts of America in 1910. He remained an associate editor of *Boy's Life*, the Scouting magazine, until the end of his life. See also David, "The Unexpurgated *A Connecticut Yankee*."

MR. FRED HALL,[1] Mark Twain's partner in the publishing business, came to my studio in the old Judge Building and told me that Mark Twain wanted to meet the man who had made the illustrations for a Chinese story in the *Cosmopolitan*[2] and he wanted that man to illustrate his new book, *A Connecticut Yankee in King Arthur's Court*. The manuscript was sent to me to read. I read it through three times with great enjoyment. Then I met Mr. Clemens by appointment in his little office on Fourteenth Street, not far from the corner of Fifth Avenue.

Fourteenth Street was then the abode of artists, writers, and illustrators, whose studios seemed to be the pioneer fringe which pushed ahead of the business houses as they moved uptown. There was no elevator in this building. When I climbed to Mark Twain's office, if I was a little short of breath, it was not from the exercise so much as the awe I felt in the presence of a man who stood so high in my esteem. I stood before this shaggy-headed man, first on one foot and then on the other, not knowing how to open the conversation. He did not rise but turned his head slowly toward me, drawling, "Sit down. In regard to the illustrations you are to make," he said, "I only want to say this. If a man comes to me and wants me to write a story, I will write one for him; but if he comes to me and wants me to write a story

and then tells me what to write, I say, 'Damn you, go hire a typewriter,'"
meaning a stenographer. In saying this, he did not blow the smoke from his
mouth, but it seemed to roll out slowly like round, bulbous clouds, in perfect rhythm with his words, with which the smoke was so intimately connected that I remember it as if what he said were vocalized cumulus clouds
of tobacco smoke. If the building had been burning down it would not have
hurried him a bit. He would have leisurely arose and, while complaining of
the interruption, just as leisurely have found his way downstairs.

In making the illustrations for his book I referred to a collection of photographs of people of note. When I wanted a face or a figure to fit a character
in the story I looked over this collection of photographs and made free use
of them, not as caricatures or portraits of the people themselves, but for
the dress, pose, or their whole figure and features as best fitted the character I was to depict. The captain of our boat club, holding a halberd in his
hand, posed for one of the initial letters as a sentry dressed with a sealskin.
For the Yankee himself I used George Morrison, a real Connecticut Yankee
who was experimenting in a photoengraving establishment adjoining my
studio. The charming actress Annie Russell appears in the pages as Sandy,
the heroine. Sarah Bernhardt is there as a page. In fact no one held too lofty
a position to escape my notice if I thought he or she possessed the face or
figure suited to the character I wished to draw. I had more fun making the
drawings for that book than any other book I ever illustrated.

I made about four hundred illustrations in seventy working days. The
first illustration was that of a knight with lance set charging on the Yankee,
who was climbing a tree. This pleased Mr. Clemens very greatly. In the corner of the illustration there is a helmet as a sort of decoration with the visor
partly open, of which Mark said, "The smile on that helmet is a source of perennial joy to me." When I finished the book he wrote [11 November 1889]:

Dear Mr. Beard—
Hold me under everlasting obligations. There are a hundred artists who
could have illustrated any other of my books, but only one who could illustrate
this one. It was a lucky day I went netting for lightning bugs and caught a me-
teor. Live forever.

Sad to say, the illustrations which so pleased Mark Twain and delighted
people all over the world grievously offended some big advertisers. The offending illustrations were removed from further editions. . . .

[164]

Mark Twain was a humorist, but only enough so to put a visitor at ease, to take away the stiffness of formality. As soon as we settled down to conversation, no matter on what line of thought we had started, the discourse was on serious subjects. I never met a man who was a more earnest seeker for the truth in religion. He had evidently been brought up in a very orthodox atmosphere and rebelled at the inconsistencies taught him, thus giving people the impression that he himself was an unbeliever.

The death of his wife seemed to bow the old gentleman down with a load of sadness which he strove in vain to conceal by resorting to quaint expressions and humorous ideas. When his daughter Jean died he was crushed. His bushy brows had a tendency to give him a fierce look which sometimes reminded me of the expression of an eagle, yet all this was modified and softened by the sadness of his countenance when in repose.

He did not seem to be capable of understanding why fire should cause pain to a person. I tried to explain to him that it was protective, that otherwise one might go to sleep by a campfire and burn his legs off; and one had to learn not to put his finger in a gas jet.

"Yes," he said, "I can understand that, but why should it hurt a poor little baby?"

I said, "That is part of the baby's education. If it did not cause pain he would not learn to keep his head out of the fire."

"Why," he said indignantly as he paced up and down the living-room floor, "should it burn a poor dog?"

"Because that is part of the dog's education." Mark was so tenderhearted that he apparently thought there should be no suffering in the world at all. His heart always interfered with his reason. The reason why little children should suffer through no fault of their own was beyond his comprehension.

When he spoke bitterly of anything it was because of his righteous indignation over some act of oppression or injustice. Friendship to him was sacred. I never could quite decide in my mind whether or not he was personally vain or whether what some people took for vanity was simply the showman's instinct that he, like all public men, found necessary to use in his profession. He told me that the reason he wore white flannel was because he always did love white flannel clothes, that old age had mighty few privileges and he was going to take advantage of every darn one of them. One of these privileges was that an old man could dress as he pleased.

With his bushy head of white hair, the white flannel suit gave him a most handsome and distinguished appearance. In his own home, with a drawing room full of company, he was an ideal host—gracious, kindly, humorous and brilliant without condescension. He was fond of children, he loved his pipe and good companions. He had a very strong affection for [Richard] Watson Gilder of the *Century,* and toward the last he often complained because his friends were dying before him.

Above all things, Mark Twain was a humanitarian. Like Lincoln, he loved the common people and was always ready to take up swords and cudgels in their defense. In discussions with him over the suffering in this world I was never quite decided in my mind whether he seriously thought there should be no suffering or whether he took that side so that he might bring out the facts that could explain the mystery. I know that he often took an exceedingly positive stand on a subject in order to bring forth arguments against that stand, and whenever a good point was made he would smile with evident enjoyment.

Mark Twain's humor, like his character, was a product of his environment. Someday he will be remembered as a great philosopher who camouflaged his philosophy so that the public would understand it. It cannot be truly said that he administered sugar-coated pills, for some of his medicine was far from candied.

I once met Mr. Clemens up near the Waldorf-Astoria. He came swinging along the street in his white flannel suit and I joined him. He was in a very jovial mood. He said, "That little girl who was dancing along the street holding my hand came up without fear and greeted me, telling me she knew me as soon as she saw me. I acknowledged that I felt flattered, so when bidding her good-by at the end of the block I asked, 'So you know me?' 'Of course I do,' said the little girl, clapping her hands; 'Everybody knows you. You are Buffalo Bill.' I still feel flattered, Dan. She was a sweet little girl."

One morning Mark Twain came walking into my studio, as usual smoking a corncob pipe and wearing a tall silk hat. My studio then was located in the old Judge Building and my back window overlooked the roof of Ward McAllister's house. I gave Mark a place on the broad window seat with his back to Ward McAllister's roof, which brought to my mind the book McAllister had just published,[3] and I asked Mark if he had read it. "Yes," he drawled, "I have read it through three times and I wrote a parody on it.

Then I read McAllister's book again, read my parody once more and tore up my parody, convinced that some things are complete in themselves."

Laughingly I said, "Now, Mr. Clemens, you will pardon me if I continue work on this drawing which must be finished on time but here's a book that I know will interest you until luncheon time," and I handed him an ancient, large, thick volume on the history of the Bible, fully illustrated with copperplate cuts. The plates explained the construction of Noah's Ark in the most detailed fashion. Mark was immensely interested, and when lunchtime came he was still poring over the tome. To my query of, "How do you like it?" he replied, "It is grand, it is great. I never wrote anything as good as this in my life. I wish I had seen it years ago, for it explains many things which were mysteries to me. I always wondered where Noah got the food to feed the carnivorous beasts, but I was thoughtless. This book explains it all, and it is so simple. The book says these meat-eating beasts took on the vegetable habit." Then he became quite animated and, standing up and facing me, cried, "Imagine the Barbary lion bounding out on the deck of the Ark, each hair of his tawny mane standing on end, his eyes flashing green fire as he roars, 'Noah! Noah! Bring me another bale of hay!'"

"Since the lion has brought up the subject of food, suppose we go over to the Kensington and have some ourselves," I suggested.

"I never eat lunch," drawled Mark.

"Well, come drink a cup of coffee, then."

"No, I'll not do that, but I'll drink a bottle of beer."

"All right," I replied, and, putting on our hats, we crossed Fifth Avenue to the Kensington. Turning to the waiter, I remarked, "My guest never eats luncheon, Charles, so bring us a *dinner,* say a double porterhouse steak, very thick, two portions of lyonnaise potatoes, and two portions of Brussels sprouts." We also had a pot of coffee, roquefort cheese and a bountiful dessert. It was half-past three o'clock when we arose from the table. There is nothing very remarkable about that, but when I arose to pay my check I was somewhat startled to discover that we were the center of a circle of deeply interested people. I afterwards learned that after Mark Twain entered not a soul left the restaurant.

We started up Fifth Avenue to Scribner's Bookstore. It was a beautiful afternoon and all of Ward McAllister's four hundred clansmen and clanswomen were on dress parade. Choice seats in the clubroom windows were occupied by choice clubmen; the sidewalks were crowded with fashionable people, while the street itself was filled with the latest, up-to-date equipages drawn by proud, sleek, well-groomed, high-stepping horses. The open carriages were manned by liveried footmen. The overcoats of these haughty servingmen were carefully folded so that the double rows of shining brass buttons would be displayed as the coats hung stiffly over the backs of the seats. It was the Gay Nineties in full swing, and smiling ladies in the carriages were constantly bowing to acquaintances on the sidewalks as gentlemen lifted their hats. But it was not so with the liveried servants. They looked straight ahead, never changing their expressions, even when a fire engine came roaring by, leaving a stream of smoke and sparks in its trail.

But when Mark Twain came swinging along with white hair, white clothes, and long cigar it was different. The frozen servants melted and so far forgot their exalted position as to grin and nudge each other, while their masters and mistresses themselves cast aside their artificialities and became real human beings. The handsomely garbed ladies and gentlemen rivaled the street gamins, the pushcart men, and the policemen in their eagerness to get a good look at America's white philosopher.

I never felt so conspicuous in all my life. Of course they were not looking at *me;* they were interested only in Mark Twain, but I was with Mark Twain, and felt so embarrassed I would stumble over a shadow on the sidewalk. But Mr. Clemens himself did not act as if he knew there was anybody in the world but himself and his companion, and he continued his conversation, perfectly oblivious to the sensation he was creating. We were discussing the institution of slavery, and we were on our way to Scribner's to purchase a book on the subject which I had read and wanted to present to Mark. However, as much as I loved Mark Twain, I breathed a sigh of relief when I shook hands with him that afternoon and dodged between the vehicles across Fifth Avenue to the privacy of my studio.

Notes

1. Frederick J. Hall (1860–1926), Charles L. Webster's successor as manager of Charles L. Webster & Co.

2. Wong Chin Foo, "Poh Yuin Ko, the Serpent-Princess," *Cosmopolitan* 6 (December 1888), 180–91.

3. Ward McAllister, *Society as I Have Found It* (New York: Cassell, 1890).

Dan Beard, from *Hardly a Man Is Now Alive* (New York: Doubleday, 1939), 336–42.

From *Daniel Frohman Presents:*
An Autobiography (1935)

DANIEL FROHMAN

A dramatization of *The Prince and the Pauper* by Abby Sage Richardson (1837–1900) and produced by David Belasco (1853–1931) and Daniel Frohman (1851–1940) premiered on Christmas Day 1889 in Philadelphia and opened 20 January 1890 in New York. Edward House soon applied for an injunction to stop the production on the grounds that Twain had granted him exclusive dramatic rights to the novel. Eventually Frohman sued Twain to cover the cost of defending his rights against House. See also Fatout, "Mark Twain: Litigant."

I KNEW MARK TWAIN very well. He was a great friend of the theatre and often spoke at theatrical gatherings. He always had something interesting to say in his felicitous and dramatic manner.

His prescription for happiness has always appealed to me: "Good friends, good books, and a sleepy conscience. This is the ideal life."

The most intimate experience I ever had with him was when I produced one of his plays, "The Prince and the Pauper." It was an immediate success. On the first night at the old Broadway Theatre in New York City, he made a speech in acknowledgement of tumultuous applause.[1]

The next day, however, he came to me and said, "Mr. Frohman, this is the worst perversion of a story that I can imagine. The play hasn't my lines, scenes, or conversations over which I spent much time. Now I am going to rewrite the play. I will follow your structure of the story but I want you to substitute my version when it is ready."

In a few weeks he returned with the script, which I read. Thereupon, I said to him, "Mr. Clemens, if I produce this play as you have written it, it will take us two nights to present it. We have made a play out of the main events of the book and we have given it in pleasant and effective shape. We cannot possibly use all these lines."

After this unsatisfactory conversation, he left, and I heard no more from him. The play continued its run in New York and later went on tour as originally planned. No complaint was received from the author about the large royalties that accrued.

At one time I had a lawsuit with Mark Twain. During the day we sued each other in court. At night we played billiards together at the Players' Club.

Frequently I dined with him in his Fifth Avenue residence and with a friend we played billiards, for he was very fond of the game. But he found he lost every game, and so he said, "You fellows go on and play. I'm through."

We understood the reason and thereafter we arranged that he should win one game out of every three. This bolstered up his interest and enthusiasm so that he remained our friendly competitor during many succeeding sessions.

Note

1. The speech is reprinted in Fatout, *Mark Twain Speaking,* 256–57.

Daniel Frohman, from *Daniel Frohman Presents: An Autobiography* (New York: Claude Kendall & Willoughby Sharp, 1935), 141–42.

From *I Remember* (1934)

J. Henry Harper

In one of his autobiographies the publisher J. Henry Harper reminisced at
length about Twain during this period.

ONE DAY HE picked up the morning paper and saw that Jim Corbett, who
had just won the championship of the United States in New Orleans from
John L. Sullivan,[1] was to give an exhibition bout with him in Madison
Square Garden. He asked me if I thought I could get tickets?

"Easily," I said, and I forthwith secured front seats by the ring. But, as I
had already cautioned him, it proved a very mild affair.

After the bout was over, Clemens having expressed the desire to meet
Corbett, I sent my card to his dressing-room, and we were invited to come
in. Corbett was being rubbed down after his exercise. I introduced him
to Mr. Clemens, and Corbett seemed much pleased to meet him. Clemens
suggested that, in view of his recent success, he might be inclined to go
abroad and try for the championship of the world. Corbett acknowledged
that he had thought of doing so, whereupon Clemens remarked:

"It would hardly be fair, Corbett, unless you first put the gloves on
with me."

"That would not be quite just to me, Mr. Clemens," protested Corbett,
"because if you should get the better of me I would be down and out, while
if I managed to defeat you, you would still be Mark Twain."

Clemens turned to me and said, "Let's go!" . . .

We arranged with Mr. Clemens for the publication of his *Joan of Arc* as a
serial in the *Magazine*. He dropped into the office one day and asked if we
had started it. I told him that we were just about to go to press.

"That's fortunate," he remarked, "for I want to ask a favor of you; it is
not to include my name as the author, in serial form, but to publish it anon-
ymously." I protested, on the ground that his name was a most valuable
asset.

"I know all that," he agreed, "but I feel that it would be defrauding my public to have my name associated with it in serial form; of course, when it comes to book publication, that will be different." He went on to say that he felt he had made a grave mistake in not originally taking two *noms de plume,* one for his humorous writings, and one for his serious work. "As it is now," he went on, "my audience always looks for a laugh in whatever I publish, and it's a fact that in England, whenever I am called upon to make an after-dinner speech, the guests are all on the verge of laughter before I begin, afraid lest they might miss a salient bit of humor. I am getting old, and I find I become more and more inclined to write on serious subjects."

We left his name off the serial, although now, in re-reading the story with his name attached, it seems to me that in so many places it would hardly be possible to overlook his individual and masterly touch. Nevertheless, during its appearance in our *Magazine* it was attributed to several writers, no one hitting on Mr. Clemens as the author.

I asked him how he came to write the story of the Maid of Orleans. He replied that one day, as he was walking along the street, a clipping blew up to his feet; he stooped to retrieve it and found that it was an interesting article on Joan. As he read it he decided to write his own story of her life. He searched musty old libraries for authoritative material, and pored over old French documents which, although a French scholar, he was obliged to have translated. His novel seems to me the most convincing tale of her spiritual life. The trial scene, where Joan stands up alone, fighting for her existence and confuting the best legal talent of the day, is a superb picture, and it is all based upon the facts gleaned in his painstaking research.

Clemens loved to talk when he was in the humor and had a congenial audience, but he never would be paraded.

I remember attending a stag dinner at Hopkinson Smith's.[2] Smith sat opposite Mark Twain in the center of the table length and tried to draw him out. Clemens was not so inclined; in fact, he hardly spoke until we came to coffee and cigars. Then, all of a sudden, he brought his fist down on the table, making the glasses tinkle, and, turning to me, sitting next him, he said in a loud voice:

"They were just driving up to the cemetery, when the horses to the hearse took fright and ran away—"

It was a good story, and from then on he was the life of the party.

William Dean Howells was a close friend of Clemens's. He could not, however, stand a story that was at all off-color, and at a dinner I attended, where the two authors sat opposite each other, Clemens began a yarn which seemed to embarrass Howells. Finally, Clemens rose, and walking back and forth beside the table, told story after story until Howells burst out laughing. Clemens then sat down and said that was all he wanted to do—to make Howells laugh.

I remember another dinner at the Sub-Rosa Club in New York. It was a unique association made up of newspaper writers, and after the dinner was over, just before the speeches, two large paper roses were hung, a red and a white one, on the chandeliers at either end of the table. This was an indication that whatever was said thereafter would be strictly confidential.

Mark Twain was called upon to speak, and in response said:

"I am glad you have favored me, Mr. Toastmaster, because I have just copyrighted a new method of after-dinner speaking. I will give you a demonstration if you suggest a topic for me to talk about."

The toastmaster suggested "Egypt."

"That is a fine, juicy subject," remarked Clemens, and he went on to speak of the Egyptians, their monuments and customs.

He had not gone far when he introduced this entirely irrelevant story:

"Once, out West, I was riding in a four-horsed prairie schooner without springs. We were going at a good pace when we hit an obstruction, and I, being installed on the back seat, suddenly found myself bumped out in the middle of the road. The driver pulled up the team, and several of the party got out and hurried back to see if I had been much hurt.

"I'm all right," I answered, "but if ever I got to hell, I'd like to go just that way, I'd be so damned glad to get there."

He then went on about Egypt, working in several other good stories.

Shortly afterwards, General Horace Porter[3] was called on to speak, and the toastmaster gave him a subject. Porter, who was an excellent speaker and always replete with the best and most recent stories, began to warm up to his theme; then he stopped, saying: "That reminds me of a story."

Clemens interrupted him.

"Look here, General," he protested, "I have copyrighted that style of after-dinner speaking, and I can't have you infringing on my patent."

The result was that he got Porter all fussed up and the guests undoubtedly lost some choice yarns.

Clemens was somewhat psychic in his makeup. He told me that occasionally, when he was abroad, he had written letters home containing inquiries, and then, instead of mailing them, he had placed them in a pigeonhole of his desk. In due time he would receive a reply covering his questions.

He informed me that he was consistently unobserving. When he attended a reception or any similar affair, if Mrs. Clemens questioned him the next morning in regard to the gowns the ladies wore, the details would be absolutely blank in his mind. He declared that when absent he could not recall the charming view from his study window, although he had gazed at it hundreds of times.

On the other hand, he declared that in a dream, he once attended a grand *fête*. The next morning he could recall the brilliant surroundings and the ladies' attire in the minutest detail.

He had a recurring dream, which had begun with his youth, in which he met a girl walking in the country. They talked together as sympathetically as old friends. Every once in a while that dream would return, and as he grew older the girl also advanced in years.

The last time he saw her she was crossing a bridge. He recognized her from a distance, although she had grown old and somewhat feeble. When he caught up with her, they had a heart-to-heart talk, recalling other days. That was the last time she had been revealed to him.

Clemens came to lunch with us as he passed through New York on his way to Bermuda and we were surprised to see a big swelling adorning his forehead. We naturally asked him what had caused it, and he replied that the night before he had felt a cold coming on. Not wishing to be deprived of his Bermuda trip, he thought he would try the old remedy of his gold-digging days, which was to undress, get into bed, place a bottle of whisky beside him, and then drink until he was uncertain as to how much was left in the bottle. After the treatment, just as he was dropping off to sleep, he remembered an important message which he was obliged to give his servant, so he got up, and he had never imagined that a wooden floor could be so hard. The damned architect, instead of putting the bell next to the bed, had placed it across the room; he managed to crawl over to it, ring it, and somehow get back into bed. The result was the bump on his forehead.

He was then an old man.

One very hot summer day he was invited by a lady [Katherine Duer Mackay?] to go down to her residence on Long Island to spend the night. He was informed that his old friend Colonel George Harvey[4] was to be

[174]

there, and he accepted, provided there would be no one else invited to meet him.

During the afternoon Clemens learned that quite a number of her friends were coming to dinner that evening; so, after a short while, he excused himself, retired to his room, and went to bed. Later on, being notified that dinner would soon be served, he sent word that he was not feeling well and could not attend. That brought his hostess up in short order to find out what was the matter. He explained that he had been out walking in the grounds, and that a sheep had bitten him; of course, he couldn't possibly attend the dinner. Consequently, when dinner was over, the guests trooped up to see him, and he entertained them characteristically until they were obliged to leave. They all departed much impressed by his conversational charm.

When Clemens was in London, he thought he would like to meet [James McNeill] Whistler, so one morning he called at his studio. The door was opened by an attendant, who informed him that it would be impossible to see Mr. Whistler that morning, as he was working from a model.

Clemens instructed him to take in his card, and soon the man returned, saying that Mr. Whistler would be very pleased to see him. When Clemens entered the studio the two well-known wits eyed each other like skilled fencers waiting for an opening, each a trifle nervous. Clemens went over to the canvas on which Whistler had been working, and, with both hands uplifted, passing them to and fro in front of the picture, he remarked:

"This is a most charming effect you have produced."

Whistler cried out: "For God's sake, Clemens, be careful! I have just been working on it and the paint is wet."

"That's all right, old man," Clemens retorted, "I have my gloves on."

Notes

1. "Gentleman Jim" Corbett (1866–1933) won the American heavyweight boxing championship from John L. Sullivan (1858–1918) on 7 September 1892 in New Orleans. Corbett and Sullivan sparred at Madison Square Garden the evening of 17 September 1892.

2. Francis Hopkinson Smith (1838–1915), American engineer, author, and artist.

3. Horace Porter (1837–1921) was a Union general during the Civil War.

4. George B. M. Harvey (1864–1928) edited *Harper's Weekly* from 1901 until 1913 and was president of Harper & Bros. from 1900 until 1915.

J. Henry Harper, from *I Remember* (New York: Harper & Bros., 1934), 135–49.

From *Hardly a Man Is Now Alive* (1939)

DAN BEARD

> Dan Beard recorded some events in the early 1890s, when Twain was teetering on the edge of bankruptcy.

WHEN MARK TWAIN sent the manuscript of *Tom Sawyer Abroad* to *St. Nicholas,* there was a part of it which the editor thought might be improved, and the wording was consequently changed. Mark Twain was a gentle soul, but if Theodore Roosevelt stood for civic righteousness, Mark Twain stood for the unalienable rights of the author to his own statements. When Mark read the proof he was exceedingly wroth and, entering the sanctum sanctorum, the holy of holies, or the editorial department of *St. Nicholas,* he shocked the gentle creatures and terrified the associate editors by exclaiming, "Any editor to whom I submit my manuscripts has an undisputed right to delete anything to which he objects but"—and his brows knit as he cried—"God Almighty Himself has no right to put words in my mouth that I never used!"

After smelling salts were administered to the whole editorial staff, and the editor in chief was resuscitated, the mistake was remedied, the error rectified, and things went smoothly. I was not present, but some of the editorial staff themselves with great glee told me of the shocking incident as a profound secret. What prompted them to give this confidential information was that my illustrations of Huck Finn, Tom Sawyer, and Nigger Jim had been returned to me, the editor ruling that it was excessively coarse and vulgar to depict them with *bare feet*! I was asked to cover their nakedness with shoes. Of course I was working for *St. Nicholas* and it was only right that I should conform to *St. Nicholas'* idea of propriety, so I pinched the toes of those poor vagabonds with shoes they never wore in life, mentally asking their forgiveness as I did so.

Mr. Clemens sent the manuscript of *The Tragedy of Pudd'nhead Wilson* to the Century Company. He wrote to Fred Hall, "I mean to ship *Pudd'nhead*

Wilson to you—say tomorrow. It'll furnish me cash for a while. I reckon I am almost sorry it is finished. It was good entertainment to work at it and kept my mind away from other things." True to their fine traditions, the Century Company secured one of our best artists to make the illustrations. He came to my studio to learn in what sort of clothes he should dress the characters. I looked up the date and showed him a rough sketch of the costume. Then I dove down into my old cedar chest and found the very clothes of that date. The illustrations were made. They were dressed correctly and were a credit to the artist; but when Mark Twain was asked to come and look them over the great literary commoner carefully inspected all the pictures, murmuring as he did so, "Beautiful! Fine! Excellent!" Then looking up at the editorial group surrounding him, he innocently inquired, "But who are the people in the pictures?"

"Why, Mr. Clemens," they hastened to explain, "these are the illustrations for *Pudd'nhead Wilson*."

"They are beautiful," murmured Mr. Clemens, "but I don't know them! Dan Beard is the only man who can correctly illustrate my writings, for he not only illustrates the text, but he also illustrates my thoughts."

There is a constant effort on the part of one group to vulgarize Mark Twain's works, and as determined an effort on the part of another group to emasculate his writings. Posterity will be grateful that neither one nor the other party has fully succeeded. When I knew him, Mark Twain always excited my sympathy because he acted and looked so lonely, and as if he were concealing a heavy burden of sorrow, which is confirmed by his note to Fred Hall, "A Merry Christmas to you, and I wish to God I could have one myself before I die."

Dan Beard, from *Hardly a Man Is Now Alive* (New York: Doubleday, 1939), 344–45.

From *Memories of a Southern Woman of Letters* (1932)

GRACE KING

> The Clemens family moved into the Villa Viviani in the hills above Florence, Italy, in late September 1892. The New Orleans novelist Grace King (1851–1932) soon visited them there.

MR. CLEMENS WAS WAITING for us at the station in Florence, grumbling at the delay of the train "always late, except when you counted upon it to be late." His house, the Villa Viviani, lay on the road to Settignano, beyond the walls of Florence. The road was long and the evening dark. But there was a blaze of light awaiting us when the carriage stopped, and a warm welcome. The household was assembled in the doorway, Livy, Susy, and Jean; Clara had returned to Berlin to her music lessons.

There was no time to look around, dinner was served immediately. We talked as fast as we could, but dinner came to an end while we were still at the beginning of our experiences, so much more interesting when related to friends than we had found them in fact. Mr. Clemens sent us to bed soon, "Livy had to keep early hours."

The villa, described as a palace, was on the outside a plain, unadorned brick and stucco building, painted yellow, with green shutters. But the inside was a wonderful surprise. The salon, a "spacious and lofty chasm," as Mr. Clemens called it, was the center of the house, rising through two stories, and even above the rest of the building. All the rest of the house was built around it. There were long suites of bedrooms and endless corridors connecting them; lodgings planned for a court, so it seemed to our unsophisticated eyes. The numerous rooms had plenty of windows and sunlight; the marble floors were shiny and full of reflections.

The house seemed a fortress for strength. It stood in a commanding position on an artificial terrace, surrounded with walls of masonry. Tall trees and stately pines surrounded it. Pink and yellow roses overflowed the walls and the battered mossy stone urns at the gate posts. From the walls, the vineyards and olive orchards fell away toward the valley. The situation was perfect—three miles from Florence on the side of a hill. Beyond was Fiesole, built on its steep terrace. In the immediate front was the Ross Villa, with its wall and turrets. On the distant plain lay Florence, the huge dome of its Cathedral dominating the city. On the right and left of the Cathedral, the Medici Chapel and the tower of the Palazzo Vecchio.

The horizon, a rim of lofty blue hills, was white with innumerable villas. To Mr. Clemens this was the fairest picture on our planet, the most enchanting to look upon, the most satisfying to the eye. The sun sinking down with tides of color turned it all into a city of dreams, a sight to stir the coldest nature and make a sympathetic one drunk with ecstasy!

Mrs. Clemens's apartment was downstairs, to avoid the steps. She was very much amused at our voyages of discovery in the region of our apartments, particularly at our finding a chapel hidden away at the end of one wing, a perfect little *bijou,* with the frescoes fresh and bright and the smell of incense still about it. It had been reserved by the owners at the leasing of the villa; Americans were not supposed to be in need of such a retreat.

Mrs. Clemens did not appear at breakfast, and our truncated talk had to be deferred till lunch. Then it came in all its fullness. They had much to relate about their stay in the Black Mountains, and of a visit to Berlin, where the Kaiser was gracious in the extreme to them,[1] and they had a glimpse of court life. . . .

The Clemenses were all German in their sympathy. They spoke the language fluently and read the German newspapers. My sister and I, on the contrary, were hotly French in our feelings and had not been in Germany. They were not at all interested in our experience in Paris. Mr. Clemens had a poor opinion of French literature and would never concede that they had any sense of humor; and he spoke frankly of their ridiculous criticism of the "Jumping Frog." He, however, was not excitable in his feelings, and could laugh at himself first of all. Mrs. Clemens was full of interest in whatever interested us and urged us to talk of ourselves. We enjoyed one another very much, and it was always an interruption not welcomed when the carriage came to the door to take us into the city. . . .

The sunset moved our hearts; it seemed beyond anything that had ever gladdened our eyes in Nature. But Mr. Clemens, smoking his pipe after his cup of tea, said, "It cannot be compared to the sun on the Mississippi River." Nannie and I agreed with him, although it did seem incongruous to mention the Mississippi River in Florence, "heavenliest Florence," as Swinburne calls it. . . .

It was on such an afternoon that he confessed humorously to a fear of hell.

"But you don't believe in hell! Nobody believes in hell any longer!"

"I don't believe in it, but I'm afraid of it. It makes me afraid to die!" And from that he went on to recalling his childhood days under his mother's teaching. She was a firm Presbyterian and had no more doubts about hell than about redemption. "When I wake up at night," he said, "I think of hell, and I am sure about going there."

"Why, Youth," exclaimed Mrs. Clemens, using her pretty pet name for him, "who, then, can be saved?"

It was in our hearts, too; but we could say nothing; and he smoked his pipe in silence until sunset colors faded and we had to go into the house.

As Faust said, when at last Mephistopheles claimed his soul, "It is enough, let the moment stay!" It has stayed, in memory.

Susy Clemens was at this time exquisitely pretty, but frail-looking. Her health was always an anxiety to her mother and father. She had been sent to Bryn Mawr, a maid accompanying her, to unpack her trunk and make her comfortable. But a very short time proved the utter impossibility of hard study for Susy. She did not care for what she experienced and merely submitted to a slow torture by remaining. She was brave enough to offer to stay and suffer till the end of the term, but the maid was sent to pack her trunk and fetch her home.

In Berlin, where her father and mother were received by the Kaiser, she was taken to a court ball, a most brilliant function. She showed the pretty silk dress that she had worn, made by a great modiste, but she had not enjoyed the function. It had bored her, in fact. She loathed the memory of it and hated her pretty dress. She had received no attention save as the daughter of Mark Twain.

"How I hate that name! I should like never to hear it again! My father should not be satisfied with it! He should not be known by it! He should show himself the great writer that he is, not merely a funny man. Funny! That's all the people see in him—a maker of funny speeches!"

Thus she walked in the clouds, like a goddess.

[180]

At the time, Mr. Clemens was writing his *Joan of Arc,* and he too complained, as Susy did, that he could not be taken as a serious writer, and he shuddered at the idea that his Joan might be considered funny, when it was meant to be serious history. And he would not sign his name to it—vain precaution!

He was troubled about Joan's voices, fearing, it seemed to me, to confess a belief in them and shrinking from avowing that Joan could never have done what she did without supernatural guidance. I had just read Michelet's *Histoire de France,* and was under the influence of his mystical handling of Joan. I told Mr. Clemens about it, and he promised to get it and read it; but I knew that what Michelet could write with perfect confidence and dignity, Mark Twain would shrink from.

He read aloud several chapters from his manuscript one night after dinner, watching our faces anxiously. But in spite of our assurances to the contrary, he wrote as Mark Twain, not as Michelet. Mrs. Clemens did not share his doubts nor Susy's criticisms. Her great eyes shone with emotion and admiration as he read. Whether right or wrong, he rested in full confidence on her judgment. She was to him what Joan's voices were to her. To be with them was to know the strength and beauty of a perfect marriage.

Some evenings were given over to pure fun, when Susy, an inimical mimic, would parody scenes from Wagner's operas and Mr. Clemens would give an imitation of a ballet dancer, posturing, throwing kisses, and making grimaces, while Susy played a waltz on the piano. . . .

It was during the summer of 1896, while we were staying in the mountains of North Carolina, that I learned by chance through a newspaper that Susy Clemens had died in Hartford. I could not believe it! It seemed impossible! How did it happen? I telegraphed at once to Hartford but received as answer only the bare facts. I learned, however, that Mrs. Clemens was in New York, and when I wrote to her the answer came a month later, a heartbroken, distracted letter that I destroyed.

She told me that she had left Susy behind at Elmira when she, Clara, and Jean[2] started with Mr. Clemens on his "around the world lecture tour." Susy herself had begged to remain in America. She hated travel and was always afraid of the sea. Her health was good and her parents had no misgivings. The lectures had assumed an almost holy purpose, and seemed absolutely necessary to pay off the load of debt that had accumulated against them.

"But I should not have left her," was the sad refrain breaking through every other sentence. "She was not a child to be left."

She was very happy at the family home in Elmira, but as summer came, she grew restless and nervous and unlike herself in many ways. She had gone over to Hartford to see her old friends, and stayed at the home of the Warners, with "Cousin Charlie" and "Cousin Susie," as she called them. Her health, Mr. Warner wrote me, seemed to be failing. Nevertheless, she worked hard at her singing. She refused to see a doctor, but as she grew worse, one was sent for. He did not think her case serious, advised perfect quiet and that she should be taken to her old home. A letter was written to her mother in England and her relatives were summoned from Elmira.

She became rapidly worse, and the doctor pronounced her ailment meningitis. Her fever increased. She walked through the deserted rooms of her old home with her tortured mind in delirium and pain. Her sight left her. At last she lay down in her own room, put her hands on her nurse's face and called her "Mamma!" and spoke no more, but sank into unconsciousness.

Notes

1. Twain dined with Kaiser William II on 20 February 1892.
2. Jean did not accompany her family on her father's round-the-world speaking tour.

Grace King, from *Memories of a Southern Woman of Letters* (New York: Macmillan, 1932), 169–74, 201–2.

"Mark Twain in Clubland" (1910)

WILLIAM H. RIDEING

> During the panic of 1893, Twain's finances worsened. He left his family in Europe and sailed to New York in late August to try to raise money. On 29 September he rented a room at the Players' Club on Gramercy Park South, where he was visited by the editor William Henry Rideing (1853–1918).

FOR SEVERAL MONTHS "Mark," as his intimates were allowed to call him, lived at The Players in one of the two best rooms which had been occupied at the opening of the club by Edwin Booth and Lawrence Barrett, and I, then the managing editor of the *North American Review,* went there one morning to ask him whether he would write an article for us on the origin of the most famous of his stories, "The Celebrated Jumping Frog." We were fellow-members, and I had already known him several years.

He pointed amiably to a chair, in which I sat while he paced the floor and puffed at a slow-burning pipe, using it much as an artist uses a brush or his hand in swings and curves when he describes the tremendous things he intends to do with an almost untouched canvas. He talked more slowly than usual—I never heard him talk fast—and at intervals stopped altogether, now resting midway, then striding from wall to wall, shaking his head at what he disagreed with or nodding it in concurrence.

All the typographical dashes in the printer's case would be insufficient if I used them to indicate the long-drawn pauses between his words and sentences. Every syllable was given its full value, distinctly and sonorously. To me his voice was beautiful. It was not a laughing voice, or a light-hearted voice, but deep and earnest like that of one of the graver musical instruments, rich and solemn, and in emotion vibrant and swelling with its own passionate feeling.

"I didn't write that story as fiction," he said, after a delay, tirelessly but slowly moving his head from side to side; "I didn't write it as fiction," he repeated in the way he had of repeating everything he desired you to understand he stood by, and that there could be no mistake about, "I wrote it—."

To and fro again and a sweep of his arm. A pause in the middle of the room.

"I wrote it as—not as fiction, not as fancy, not out of imagination—I wrote it as a matter, a matter of h-i-s-t-o-r-y. I can remember now at this very minute, I can remember now, right here, just how that story happened, every incident in it."

Here there was another pause, as if the curtain had been drawn on an interlude in a play. He never under any circumstances was precipitous, or to be driven. Nobody could ever hasten him out of his excogitations. His face was serious, reflective and reminiscent. That was its prevalent expression. I knew him for nearly thirty years, and cannot remember hearing him laugh in all that time, even when he must have been amused and others were laughing around him—Howells, for instance, bubbling with the freshest, merriest, sincerest, and most contagious laugh in the world, Howells, who, though so different in many ways, was one of the dearest and most congenial of his friends, Howells and Aldrich, both of whom he especially delighted in. A smile, an engaging, communicative, penetrative smile, which wrapped one in its own liquid and suffusing satisfaction, was his nearest approach to risibility, save perhaps a shrug or a scarcely audible chuckle.

I could see that some unexpected thing was coming, while I listened to those clear but halting sentences, which dropped from him like pebbles breaking the silence of a lonely pool. His face, that aquiline, almost occipital face, was as grave as if life and death had been in the balance.

"Well," he drawled, "what do you suppose happened last night? Don't be in a hurry. It's no good being in a hurry."

I did not presume a guess, and he emitted a cloud from the reviving pipe as if to symbolize the impenetrability of his mystery. Again he paced the room before he explained himself.

"A fellow sitting next to me at dinner last night said to me, 'How old do you suppose that story of yours about the Jumping Frog is, Mark?' I stopped to think, quite in earnest, and I said, recalling all the circumstances, 'That story is just about forty-five years old. It happened in Calaveras County in the spring of 1860.' 'No, it isn't,' said he, 'no, it isn't. It's more than that; it's two thousand years old.' And since then that fellow has shown me a book, a Greek textbook, and there it is, there it is, my Jumping Frog, in Bœotia t-w-o t-h-o-u-s-a-n-d years ago."

Two thousand years never seemed so long to me, nor could they have sounded longer to anybody than they did in his enunciation of them, which seemed to make visible and tangible all the mystery, all the remoteness and all the awe of that chilling stretch of time. His way of uttering them and his application of them often gave the simplest words which he habitually used a pictorial vividness, a richness of suggestion, a fullness of meaning with which genius alone could endue them.

The mystery of the Bœotian was soon solved. He had been translated into the Greek textbook by Professor Henry Sidgwick, Mr. Balfour's brother-in-law, and History was restored to the pedestal on which she had tottered. I got the article I wanted, and a very good price was paid for it. Mark was not an easy contributor to manage. He knew his own value, and had no unbusiness-like indifference to the substantial recognition of it by editors and publishers. He would have his pound of flesh, and insisted on it as strongly as he insisted that no changes should be made in what he wrote, though occasionally elisions would have saved him from the criticisms of fastidious readers, especially from the criticisms of women. I believe the only critic he ever listened to with patience, and respected and obeyed, was his wife.

How mistaken were the people who not knowing him imagined that everywhere and on all occasions his attitude and point of view were those of the jester! I never knew a more earnest man than he was, or one whose aroused indignation was so overwhelming. When anger moved him you could see his lean figure contract and his eyes ominously screw themselves into their sockets. Every fiber in him quivered, and for the moment his voice became acid and sibilant and out of tune—almost a whine. Then he would let himself out in a break, like that of a dam unable to hold the flood, in language as candid and unshrinking as the vernacular of the Elizabethans. Epithet would be piled on epithet, one following another with cumulative vigor, distinctness and the disclosing and illuminative effect of explosives. And not a word missed its mark, not a word seemed superfluous or exchangeable for any other word; each fitted the use he made of it as a cartridge fits a rifle or a revolver; each told. When he disliked anybody or any thing, whether it was the Czar, General Funston,[1] Leopold of Belgium,[2] apologists for Shelley, or the Reverend Mr. Sabine,[3] whose refusal

[185]

to bury an actor led to the glory of "the little church round the corner," he would not compromise or extenuate what offended him for months or years afterwards, if at all. It took years to soften the bitterness which while fresh was implacable. Nor were his animosities petty or spiteful or unreasonable. Hypocrisy, deceit, sanctimoniousness and cruelty were among the cardinal sins for him. You might think he had forgotten particular instances of them, but he would surprise you by springing them back on your memory, in moods and circumstances to which they had no relation, in biting phrases which showed how they still rankled.

His attitude toward the ordinary foibles of humanity was parentally indulgent and benevolent. He admired women and met them with all the grace and complaisance of an ancient courtier, and he loved children and all things simple, beautiful, and true. His affability exposed him to flocks of bores, and out of sheer courtesy he would endure them and hide his impatience while they flattered themselves that they were impressing him and establishing an intimacy, the legend of which should be boasted of while they lived and cherished by all their descendants when they were gone. He would smile on them and wag his head and murmur in a sort of purr acquiescence in their talk, and when he at last released himself by some ingenious strategy or through the intervention of a friend, who had been watching his unmistakable and comically pitiful signs of weariness, they would fly off to repeat what he hadn't said or jumble what he had, and thereafter ever speak of him as "Mark." It was a lesson in saintly fortitude to observe him and hear the unfathomable sigh which came out on his escape from them.

Usually there was no end to his patience, but I remember him losing it at a little dinner given at The Players, when by some mischance he was seated next to an impossible person, a guest, not a member of the club, who may be called Bounder. Bounder gave him no rest, but Clemens stood the strain for a long time without a protest, and merely swayed his head in the leisurely half-drowsy, ponderous way an elephant has. That was another little peculiarity of his. Some of us could see that his restraint could not last much longer, however, and presently he beckoned the host, much to that gentleman's bewilderment, into the anteroom.

"David," he said when he got him there, "David—do you love me, David?" His voice quavered with pathos; it was a voice that always had more pathos in it than mirth: it shook with the melancholy of trees in the wind and pleaded. As I have already intimated, it was seldom he revealed any consciousness of his own humor. "Do you love me, David?"

David was the late Mr. David Alexander Munro,[4] a close and dear friend of his and of all of us. "Love you? Of course I do, old boy. What's the matter?"

"Then for the love of heaven if you love me save me from Bounder, save me from Bounder, save me from Bounder!" repeated thrice like the tragic wail of a soul doomed and immured in the nethermost depths of despair.

Difficult explanations had to be made, and another than he sacrificed for the rest of the evening to the confident and voluble Mr. Bounder.

He always conveyed to me the sense of music, not lively music *con vivace,* but the slower movements like the *andante* of a symphony. There were exquisite cadences in his voice, and his gestures harmonized with them. He did not sparkle as Aldrich sparkled; he glowed. Have you seen Vesuvius when quiescent, throbbing in the dark, its ruddy fire diminishing one moment and the next burning scarlet like the end of a Gargantuan cigar? In that one could find by a stretch of fancy a resemblance to his passages from coolness to heat. He was more like a frigate than a torpedo boat, and he deliberated before he touched his guns.

He confessed to me once that at gatherings when speech-making was expected, he preferred to do his part after others had done theirs, for what was said before made opportunities for him later on. An instance of this occurred at a breakfast in London given during his last visit to England. Augustine Birrell, the Irish Secretary, preceded him, and referring to the demands made on him in what is probably the most irritating and laborious of all parliamentary offices, declared, "I am sure I don't know how I got here."

That gave Clemens the chance he had waited for, and he lost no time in making the most of it. No other American who ever visited London received half the applause bestowed on him, not Henry Ward Beecher, Dr. [Oliver Wendell] Holmes, General Grant, or even Mr. [Joseph Hodges] Choate.

"Mr. Birrell," he began very slowly and with a more expansive smile than usual, "Mr. Birrell has just said he doesn't know how he got here." Then he bent over the Irish Secretary, and looked into his wine glasses. "Doesn't know how he got here"—very significantly. Mr. Birrell was puzzled behind his spectacles, and everybody was on the *qui vive* just as the speaker liked to have them; it was a part of his game.

"Well, he hasn't—had—anything—," a prolonged pause. "Anything—more—to—drink—since he came, and we'll at least see that he gets home all right."

The inflection breathed encouragement; it said by implication what many more words could not have said better, that Mr. Birrell was in the hands of a self-sacrificing friend who would look out for him. It surely was not the sort of humor they were used to, but bishops in their frocks, deans, cabinet ministers and judges—they, as well as the rest of us, yielded to it in uncontrollable laughter, while the speaker demurely shook his head as if he were compassionating the frailty of humanity. Nor was this the sort of humor, accepted though it was as the essence of him, by which he should be measured. Sunshine in water is not a gauge of its depths. Only those who knew him well discovered his profundity, and how impassioned and militant (a little quixotic, too) he could be in good causes.

Notes

1. Frederick Funston (1865–1917) had engineered the removal of *Adventures of Huckleberry Finn* from the shelves of the Denver Public Library, apparently in retaliation for Twain's ironic "A Defense of General Funston," *North American Review* 174 (May 1902): 613–24.

2. Twain's *King Leopold's Soliloquy* (1905), a satirical dramatic monologue that indicts King Leopold of Belgium (1835–1909) for profiting by a system of forced labor in the Congo.

3. Rev. William T. Sabine (1838–1913), rector of the Episcopal Church of the Atonement in New York, refused to permit the funeral of the actor George Holland (1791–1870) in his church, explaining that "there is a little church around the corner where they do that sort of thing." The Church of the Transfiguration on East Twenty-ninth Street thus earned its nickname and became the site of many theatrical weddings and funerals.

4. David Alexander Munro (1844–1910), assistant editor of the *North American Review*.

William H. Rideing, "Mark Twain in Clubland," *Bookman* 31 (June 1910): 379–82.

From *Eccentricities of Genius* (1900)

JAMES B. POND

> In order to repay his creditors, Twain reluctantly agreed to a round-the-world speaking tour. James B. Pond, who had managed Twain and Cable's "Twins of Genius" tour in 1884–85, managed the North American leg of Twain's tour in 1895. In all, Twain hosted two dozen "At Homes" across the continent before embarking from Victoria, British Columbia, for Australia on 23 August.

SAMUEL L. CLEMENS (Mark Twain) I consider one of the greatest geniuses of our time, and as great a philosopher as humorist. I think I know him better than he is known to most men—wide as his circle of acquaintances is, big as is his reputation. He is as great a man as he is a genius, too. Tenderness and sensitiveness are his two strongest traits. He has one of the best hearts that ever beat. One must know him well fully to discern all of his best traits. He keeps them entrenched, so to speak. I rather imagine that he fights shy of having it generally suspected that he is kind and tenderhearted, but many of his friends do know it. He possesses some of the frontier traits—a fierce spirit of retaliation and the absolute confidence that life-long "partners," in the Western sense, develop. Injure him, and he is merciless, especially if you betray his confidence. Once a lecture manager in New York, whom he trusted to arrange the details of a lecture in Steinway Hall, swindled him to the amount of $1,500, and afterward confessed it, offering restitution to that amount, but not until the swindle had been discovered. They were on board ship at the time, and "Mark" threatened to throw the fellow overboard, meaning it, too, but he fled ashore. In *The Gilded Age* "Mark" immolated him.[1] The fellow died soon afterward, and James Redpath, who was a witness to the scene on the steamboat, and who knew the man well, insisted that "Mark's" arrow killed him; but he would have fired it all the same had he known what the result would be. . . .

In his tour around the world "Mark Twain" earned with his voice and pen money enough to pay all his creditors (Webster & Co., publishers) in full, with interest, and this he did almost a year sooner than he had originally calculated. Such a triumphal tour has never before been made by any American since that memorable tour around the world by General Grant. Samuel L. Clemens has been greeted in France, Switzerland, Germany, and England almost like a crowned head.

He wrote me from Paris, May 1, 1895: "I've a notion to read a few times in America before I sail for Australia. I'm going to think it over and make up my mind." On May 18th he arrived in this country, and I made arrangements for him to lecture in twenty-one cities on his way to the Pacific, beginning in Cleveland, July 15th, and ending in Vancouver, British Columbia, August 15th. . . .

June 11th he wrote me from Elmira . . . "I like the approximate itinerary first rate. It is *lake* all the way from Cleveland to Duluth. I wouldn't switch aside to Milwaukee for $200,000." His original idea was to lecture in nine cities, besides two or three others on the Pacific Coast. I was to have one-fourth of the profits except in San Francisco, where he was to have four-fifths. But we did not go to San Francisco.

There were five of us in the party: Mr. and Mrs. Clemens, Clara (one of their daughters), Mrs. Pond and myself. During the journey I kept a detailed journal, from which I shall quote:

Cleveland, July 15, 1895.
. . . Reporters from all the morning and evening papers called and interviewed him. It seemed like old times again, and "Mark" enjoyed it.

The young men called at 3 p.m. and paid me the fee for the lecture, which took place in Music Hall. There were 4,200 people present, at prices ranging from 25 cents to $1. It was nine o'clock before the crowd could get in and "Mark" begin. As he hobbled upon the stage, there was a grand ovation of cheers and applause, which continued for some time. Then he began to speak, and before he could finish a sentence the applause broke out again. So it went on for over an hour on a mid-July night, with the mercury trying to climb out of the top of the thermometer. "Mark Twain" kept that vast throng in convulsions.

Cleveland, Tuesday, July 16th.
Ninety degrees in the shade at 7:30 a.m. Good notices of "Mark Twain's" lecture appear in all the papers.[2] "Mark" spent all day in bed until five o'clock, while I spent the day in writing to all correspondents ahead. If Sault Ste. Marie, the next engagement, turns out as well in proportion as

this place, our tour is a success. "Mark" and family were invited out to dinner with some old friends and companions of the *Quaker City* tour.[3] He returned very nervous and much distressed. We discover a remarkable woman in Mrs. Clemens. There's a good time in store for us all. . . .

Friday, July 19th, Grand Hotel, Mackinac.

. . . We reached the Grand Hotel at 4:30. I saw one of "Mark's" lithographs in the hotel office, with "Tickets for Sale Here" written in blue pencil on the margin. It seemed dull and dead about the lobby, and also in the streets. The hotel manager said the Casino, an adjoining hall, was at our service, free, and the keeper had instructions to seat and to light it. Dinner time came; we all went down together. It was "Mark's" first appearance in a public dining room since we started. He attracted some attention as he entered and sat down, but nothing especial. After dinner the news-stand man told me he had not sold a ticket, and no one had inquired about the lecture. I waited until eight o'clock and then went to the hall to notify the man that he need not light up as there would be no audience. The janitor and I chatted until about half-past eight, and I was about to leave when a man and woman came to the door and asked for tickets. I was on the point of telling them that there would be no lecture when I saw a number of people, guests of the hotel, coming. I suddenly changed my mind and told them: "Admission $1; pay the money to me and walk right in." The crowd kept rushing on me, so that I was obliged to ask everybody who could to please have the exact amount ready, as I was unable to change large bills without a good deal of delay. It was after nine o'clock before the rush was over, and I sent a boy for "Mark." He expressed his pleasant surprise. I asked him to walk to the platform and introduce himself, which he did, and I don't believe an audience ever had a better time of an hour and a half. "Mark" was simply immense. . . .

Saturday, July 20th, Mackinac to Petoskey [Michigan].

"Mark" is feeling better. He and I left the ladies at the Grand, in Mackinac, and went to Petoskey on the two o'clock boat and train. The smoke, from forest fires on both sides of the track, is so thick as to be almost stifling. There is a good hotel here.

There was a full house, and for the first time in a number of months I had a lecture room so crowded at one dollar a ticket that many could not get standing room and were obliged to go away. The theatre has a seating capacity of five hundred, but over seven hundred and fifty got in. "Mark's" program was just right—one hour and twenty minutes long. He stopped at an hour and ten minutes, and cries of "Go on! Go on!" were so earnest that he told one more story. George Kennan was one of the audience. He is going to give a course of lectures at Lake View Assembly, an auxiliary Chautauqua adjoining Petoskey, where about five thousand people assemble every summer. Mr. Hall, the manager, thought that "Mark Twain" would not draw sufficient to warrant engaging him at $250, so I took the risk outside, and won. . . .

Monday, July 22d.

. . . We landed in Duluth at just 9 p.m. . . . "Mark" was the first passenger to land. Mr. Briggs hurried him to the church, which was packed with twelve hundred and fifty warm friends (100 degrees in the shade) to meet and greet him. It was a big audience. He got through at 10:50 and we were all on board the train for Minneapolis at 11:20. . . .

Tuesday, July 23d, Minneapolis.

We are stopping at the West Hotel; a delightful place. Six skilled reporters have spent about two hours with "Mark." He was lying in bed, and very tired I know, but he was extremely courteous to them and they all enjoyed the interview. The Metropolitan Opera House was filled to the top gallery with a big crowd of well-dressed, intelligent people. It was about as big a night as "Mark" ever had to my knowledge. He introduced a new entertainment, blending pathos with humor with unusual continuity. This was at Mrs. Clemens's suggestion. She had given me an idea on the start that too much humor tired an audience with laughing. "Mark" took the hint and worked in three or four pathetic stories that made the entertainment perfect. The "show" is a triumph, and "Mark" will never again need a running mate to make him satisfactory to everybody.

The next day the Minneapolis papers were full of good things about the lecture. The *Times* devoted three columns and a half of fine print to a verbatim report of it.[4] The following evening in St. Paul "Mark" gave the same program, which was commented on in glowing terms by St. Paul papers.

Friday, July 26th, Winnipeg—The Manitoba.

We have had a most charming ride through North Dakota and southeastern Manitoba. It seems as if everything along the route must have been put in order for our reception. The flat, wild prairies (uninhabited in 1883) are now all under cultivation. There are fine farmhouses, barns, and vast fields of wheat—"oceans of wheat," as "Mark" said. . . .

We had a splendid audience. "Mark" and I were entertained at the famous Manitoba Club after the lecture—a club of the leading men of Winnipeg. We did not stay out very late, as "Mark" feared Mrs. Clemens would not retire until he came, and he was quite anxious for her to rest, as the long night journey in the cars had been very fatiguing. . . .

Tuesday, July 30th, en route.

We left Crookston at 5:40 a.m.; were up at 4:30, everybody was cheerful; there was no grumbling. This is our first unseasonable hour for getting up, but it has done us all good. Even Clara enjoyed the unique experience. It revived her memory. She recollected that she had telegraphed to Elmira to have her winter cloak expressed to Crookston. Fortunately the agent was sleeping in the express office, near the station. We disturbed his slumbers to find the great cloak, which was another acquisition to our sixteen pieces of hand baggage. Our train was forty-five minutes late. "Mark" complained and grumbled; he persisted that I had contracted with him to *travel* and not to wait about railway stations at five o'clock in the mornings for late trains that never arrived. He insisted on traveling, so he got aboard the baggage truck and I *traveled* him up and down the platform, while Clara made a snapshot as evidence that I was keeping to the letter of my contract.

When we boarded the train, we found five lower berths (which means five sections) ready for us. There was a splendid dining car, with meals *a la carte,* and excellent cooking. All the afternoon there were the level prairies of North Dakota wheat just turning, the whole country a lovely green; then came the arid plains, the prairie-dog towns, cactus, buffalo grass, jack rabbits, wild life and the Missouri River—dear old friend that had borne both of us on her muddy bosom many a time. It was a great day for both "Mark" and me. The ladies were enthusiastic in proportion as they saw that "Mark" and I were boys again, traveling upon "our native heath."

Wednesday, July 31st, Great Falls, Montana.

We arrived at the Park Hotel here at 7:30 a.m. after a good night's sleep. Interest grows more and more intense as we come nearer to the Rocky Mountains. . . . "Mark" is improving. For the first time since we started he appeared about the hotel corridors and on the street. He and I walked about the outskirts of the town, and I caught a number of interesting snap-shots among the Norwegian shanties. I got a good group including four generations, with eight children, a calf, and five cats. "Mark" wanted a photograph of each cat. He caught a pair of kittens in his arms, greatly to the discomfort of their owner, a little girl. He tried to make friends with the child and buy the kittens, but she began to cry and beg that her pets might be liberated. He soon captured her with a pretty story, and she finally con-sented to let them go. Few know "Mark's" great love for cats, as well as for every living creature. . . .

August 2d, Butte, Montana.

We enter the Rocky Mountains through a canyon of the Upper Missouri; we have climbed mountains all day, and at Butte they are nearly 8,000 feet high. It tells on me, but the others escape. The ladies declare it has been one of the most interesting days of their lives, and "Mark" has taken great interest in everything, but kept from talking. After reaching the hotel, he kept quiet in bed until he went to the hall. He more than made up for last night's disappointment and was at his best. I escorted Mrs. Clemens and Clara to a box in the theatre, expecting to return immediately to the hotel, but I found myself listening, and sat through the lecture, enjoying every word. It actually seemed as if I had never known him to be quite so good. He was great. The house was full and very responsive.

After the lecture many of his former Nevada friends came forward to greet him. We went to a fine club, where champagne and stories blended until twelve, much to the delight of many gentlemen. "Mark" never drinks champagne. His is hot Scotch, winter and summer, without any sugar, and never before 11 p.m.

Friday, August 2d.

Today "Mark" and I went from Butte to Anaconda without the ladies. We left the hotel at 4:30 by trolley car in order to have plenty of time to reach the train, but we had gone only three blocks when the power gave out and we could not move. It was twelve minutes to five and there was no carriage in sight. We tried to get a grocery wagon, but the mean owner refused to take us a quarter of a mile to the depot for less than ten dollars. I told him to go to ----. I saw another grocery wagon near by and told its owner I would pay any price to reach that train. "Mark" and I mounted the seat with him. He laid the lash on his pair of broncos, and I think quicker time was never made to that depot. We reached the train just as the conductor shouted "All aboard!" and had signaled the engineer. The train was moving as we jumped on. The driver charged me a dollar, but I handed him two. . . .

A little incident connected with our experience here shows "Mark Twain's" generosity. The local manager was a man who had known "Mark" in the sixties, and was very anxious to secure him for a lecture in Anaconda. He, therefore, contracted to pay the price asked. Anaconda is a small city, whose chief industry is a large smelting furnace. There were not enough people interested in high-class entertainments to make up a paying audience, and the manager was short about sixty dollars. I took what he had, and all he had, giving him a receipt in full. As "Mark" and I were not equal partners, of course the larger share of the loss fell to him. I explained the circumstances when we had our next settlement at the end of the week, hoping for his approval.

"And you took the last cent that poor fellow had! Send him a hundred dollars, and if you can't afford to stand your share, charge it all to me. I'm not going around robbing poor men who are disappointed in their calculations as to my commercial value. I'm poor, and working to pay debts that I never contracted; but I don't want to get money in that way."

I sent the money, and was glad of the privilege of standing my share. The letter of acknowledgment from that man brought out the following expression from "Mark": "I wish that every hundred dollars I ever invested had produced the same amount of happiness!" . . .

Monday, August 5th, Missoula, Montana.

. . . We had a large audience in a small hall, the patrons being mainly officers of the fort and their families. As most of the ladies who marry army officers come from our best Eastern society, it was a gathering of people who appreciated the occasion. After the lecture, the meeting took the form of a social reception, and it was midnight before it broke up. The day has been one of delight to all of us. As we leave at 2:30 p.m. tomorrow, all have accepted an invitation to witness guard-mounting and lunch early at the fort.

August 7th.

. . . It was an enjoyable ride to Spokane, where we arrived at 11:30, and put up at the Spokane House, the largest hotel I ever saw. It was a large commercial building, covering an entire block, revamped into a hotel. A whole store was diverted into one bedroom, and nicely furnished, too. Reporters were in waiting to interview the distinguished guest. "Mark" is gaining strength and is enjoying everything, so the interviewers had a good time.

We spent all day, August 8th, in Spokane. The hotel was full. The new receiver and his gay party are also spending the day here, but all leave just before the time set for the lecture.

In the forenoon "Mark" and I walked about this remarkable city, with its asphalt streets, electric lights, nine-story telegraph poles, and commercial blocks that would do credit to any Eastern city. There were buildings ten stories high, with the nine top stories empty, and there were many fine stores with great plate-glass fronts, marked "To Rent." . . .

We found here a magnificent new theatre—the Opera House. It has cost over $200,000 and was never yet a quarter filled. The manager was greatly disappointed at the receipts for the lecture; he had counted on a full house. Where he expected the people to come from I don't know. The receipts were not much better than in Missoula. "Mark" didn't enjoy it, and manifested no delicacy in so expressing himself. . . .

That night at 11:30 we went aboard the sleeper on the Great Northern Road. Everything was in readiness for us. The next day was one full of interest as we rode over the Rockies on the zigzag road, traveling over thirty miles to make seven. "Mark" rode on the engine, greatly to the delight of the engineer.

We transferred at Seattle to the little "Greyhound of Puget Sound"—*The Flyer*—said to be the fastest steamer in the world. "Mark" sat on the deck of *The Flyer* watching the baggage-smashers removing our trunks from the baggage car to the truck which was to convey them to *The Flyer*, and exclaimed: "Oh, how I do wish one of those trunks were filled with dynamite and that all the baggage-destroyers on earth were gathered about it, and I just far enough off to see them hurled into Kingdom Come!"

We arrived in Tacoma at five o'clock, and have sumptuous apartments at The Tacoma, a grand caravansary built by the Northern Pacific Railroad Company. . . . Here in Tacoma the ladies are to remain and rest, while "Mark" and I take in Portland and Olympia.

Friday, August 9th, Portland, Oregon.
At Tacoma early this morning Mr. S. E. Moffett, of the *San Francisco Examiner*, appeared. He is "Mark's" nephew and resembles his uncle very

much.[5] On his arrival "Mark" took occasion to blaspheme for a few minutes, that his relative might realize that men are not all alike. He cursed the journey, the fatigues and annoyances, winding up by acknowledging that if everything had been made and arranged by the Almighty for the occasion, it could not have been better or more comfortable, but he "was not traveling for pleasure," etc.

He and I reached Portland on time, 8:22, and found the Marquam Grand packed with a waiting audience and the sign "Standing Room Only" out. The lecture was a grand success. After it "Mark's" friend, Colonel Wood,[6] formerly of the United States army, gave a supper at the Portland Club, where about two dozen of the leading men were entertained for two hours with "Mark's" storytelling. They will remember that evening as long as they live. There is surely but one "Mark Twain."

Saturday, August 10th, Portland to Olympia.

Smoke, smoke, smoke! It was not easy to tear ourselves away from Portland so early. *The Oregonian* contains one of the best notices that "Mark" has had. He is pleased with it, and is very jolly today.

We left for Olympia at eleven o'clock via Northern Pacific Railroad. Somehow "Mark" seems to grow greater from day to day. Each time it seemed as though his entertainment had reached perfection, but last night surpassed all. A gentleman on the train, a physician from Portland, said that no man ever left a better impression on a Portland audience; that "Mark Twain" was the theme on the streets and in all business places. A young reporter for *The Oregonian* met "Mark," as he was boarding the train for Olympia, and had probably five minutes' talk with him. He wrote a two-column interview which "Mark" declared was the most accurate and the best that had ever been reported of him.[7] . . .

Monday, August 12th, Tacoma, Wash.—The Tacoma.

. . . The Tacoma Press Club gave "Mark" a reception in their rooms after the lecture, which proved to be a very bright affair. "Mark" is finding out that he has found his friends by the loss of his fortune. People are constantly meeting him on the street, at halls, and in hotels, and telling him of the happiness he has brought them—old and young alike. He seems as fresh to the rising generation as he is dear to older friends. Here we met Lieutenant-Commander Wadhams,[8] who is executive officer of the *Mohi-*

can, now in Seattle harbor. He has invited us all on board the man-of-war to dine tomorrow, and we have all accepted.

"Mark" had a great audience in Seattle the next evening. The sign "Standing Room Only" was out again. He was hoarse, but the hoarseness seemed to augment the volume of his voice. After the lecture he met many of his friends and admirers at the Rainier Club. Surely he is finding out that his misfortunes are his blessings. He has been the means of more real pleasure to his readers and hearers than he ever could have imagined had not this opportunity presented itself.

Wednesday, August 14th, Seattle to Whatcom [Bellingham, Wash.].

"Mark's" cold is getting worse (the first cold he ever had). He worried and fretted all day; two swearing fits under his breath, with a short interval between them, they lasted from our arrival in town until he went to sleep after midnight. It was with great difficulty that he got through the lecture. The crowd, which kept stringing in at long intervals until half-past nine, made him so nervous that he left the stage for a time. I thought he was ill, and rushed back of the scenes, only to meet him in a white rage. He looked daggers at me, and remarked:

"You'll never play a trick like this on me again. Look at that audience. It isn't half in yet."

I explained that many of the people came from long distances, and that the cars ran only every half hour, the entire country on fire causing delays, and that was why the last installment came so late. He cooled down and went at it again. He captured the crowd. He had a good time and an encore, and was obliged to give an additional story.

Thursday, August 15th, Vancouver, B.C.—The Vancouver.

"Mark's" throat is in a very bad condition. It was a great effort to make himself heard. He is a thoroughbred—a great man, with wonderful will power, or he would have succumbed. We had a fine audience, a crowded house, very English, and I think "Mark" liked it. Everything here is English and Canadian. There is a rumor afloat that the country about us is beautiful, but we can't see it, for there is smoke, smoke everywhere, and no relief. My eyes are sore from it. We are told that the *Warrimoo*[9] will not sail until Wednesday, so I have arranged for the Victoria lecture Tuesday.

Friday, August 16th, Vancouver.

Our tour across the continent is virtually finished, and I feel the reaction. "Othello's occupation gone."[10] This morning "Mark" had a doctor, who says he is not seriously ill. . . .

Monday, August 19th.

We are at Vancouver still, and the smoke is as firmly fixed as we are in the town. It is bad. "Mark" has not been very cheerful today. He doesn't get his voice back. He and I took a walk about the streets, and he seemed discouraged, I think on account of Mrs. Clemens's dread of the long voyage, and because of the unfavorable stories we have heard of the *Warrimoo*. We leave Vancouver, and hosts of new friends, for Victoria, B.C., and then we part. That will not be easy, for we are all very happy. It makes my heart ache to see "Mark" so downhearted after such continued success as he has had.

On August 20th the boat for Victoria arrived half an hour late. We all hurried to get on board, only to be told by the captain that he had one hundred and eighty tons of freight to discharge, and that it would be four o'clock before we left. This lost our Victoria engagement, which I was obliged to postpone by telegraph. "Mark" was not in condition to relish this news, and as he stood on the wharf after the ladies had gone aboard he took occasion to tell the captain, in very plain and impious language, his opinion of a passenger-carrying company that, for a few dollars extra, would violate their contract and obligations to the public. They were a lot of—somethings, and deserved the penitentiary. The captain listened without response, but got very red in the face. It seems the ladies had overheard the loud talk. Soon after "Mark" joined them he came to me and asked if I wouldn't see that captain and apologize for his unmanly abuse, and see if any possible restitution could be made. I did so, and the captain and "Mark" became quite friends. . . .

Wednesday, August 21st, Victoria, B.C.—The Driad.

"Mark" has been in bed all day; he doesn't seem to get strength. He smokes constantly, and I fear too much also; still, he may stand it. Physicians say it will eventually kill him.

We had a good audience. Lord and Lady Aberdeen, who were in a box, came back on the stage after the lecture and said many very nice things of the entertainment, offering to write to friends in Australia about it. "Mark's" voice began strong, but showed fatigue toward the last. His audience, which was one of the most appreciative he ever had, was in great sympathy with him as they realized the effort he was obliged to make, owing to his hoarseness.

A telegram from Mr. George McL. Brown says the *Warrimoo* will sail at six o'clock tomorrow evening. This is the last appearance of "Mark Twain" in America for more than a year I know, and I much fear the very last, for it doesn't seem possible that his physical strength can hold out. . . .

Thursday, August 22d.

We are in Victoria yet. The blessed "tie that binds" seems to be drawing tighter and tighter as the time for our final separation approaches. We shall never be happier in any combination, and Mrs. Clemens is the great magnet. What a noble woman she is! It is "Mark Twain's" wife who makes his works so great. She edits everything and brings purity, dignity, and sweetness to his writings. In *Joan of Arc* I see Mrs. Clemens as much as "Mark Twain."

Friday, August 23d, Victoria.

"Mark" and I were out all day getting books, cigars, and tobacco. He bought three thousand Manila cheroots, thinking that with four pounds of Durham smoking tobacco he could make the three thousand cheroots last four weeks. If perpetual smoking ever kills a man, I don't see how "Mark Twain" can expect to escape. He and Mrs. Clemens, an old friend of "Mark's" and his wife, now living near here, went for a drive, and were out most of the day. This is remarkable for him. I never knew him to do such a thing before.

The *Warrimoo* arrived about one o'clock. We all went on board and lunched together for the last time. Mrs. Clemens is disappointed in the ship. The whole thing looks discouraging, and our hearts are almost broken with sympathy for her. She tells me she is going to brave it through, for she must do it. It is for her children. Our party got out on the deck of the *Warrimoo,* and Mr. W. G. Chase, a passenger, took a snapshot of our quintet. Then wife and I went ashore, and the old ship started across the Pacific Ocean with three of our most beloved friends on board. We waved to one another as long as they kept in sight.

Notes

1. J. Adolphe Griller, lecture agent in chapter 58 of *The Gilded Age*. Twain: "He was a falsehood done in flesh and blood. Actually a caricature of Brelsford, an agent of the American Lecture Bureau" (French 199).

2. For example, "Mark Twain: His Scheme for the Regeneration of the Human Race," *Cleveland Plain Dealer,* 16 July 1895, 8.

3. Among the friends from the *"Quaker City* tour" Twain visited in Cleveland was Mary Mason Fairbanks.

4. See "Twice Told Tales," *Minneapolis Times,* 24 July 1895, 1–2: "Rambling on from one story to another, the lecture-reading, as he himself calls his program, reveals Twain at his best in all of his most various phases." According to "Mark Twain's Lecture," *Minneapolis Journal,* 24 July 1895, 4, Twain's program consisted of the following readings: the "Jumping Frog" story, "My First Theft," "Jim Blaine and His Grandfather's Old Ram," find corpse in his father's office, excerpts from *Huck Finn* and *Tom Sawyer Abroad,* and "The Whistling Story" as an encore. The reviewer also called the performance "a judicious blending of the pathetic and homely with those occasional scintillations of wit that flashed like dew drops in the morning sun."

5. Samuel E. Moffett (1860–1908), the son of Clemens's sister Pamela.

6. Charles Erskine Scott Wood (1852–1944), a former soldier and author who resided in Portland, Oregon.

7. See Lute Pease's interview, "Mark Twain Talks," *Portland Oregonian,* 11 August 1895, 10; repr. in Scharnhorst 172–75.

8. Albion V. Wadhams (1847–1927), a U.S. naval officer, later a rear admiral.

9. In the first chapter of *Following the Equator* (1897), Twain referred to the *Warrimoo,* built in 1892, as "a reasonably comfortable ship, with the customary sea-going fare—plenty of good food furnished by the Deity and cooked by the devil" (26).

10. *Othello,* act III, scene iii, lines 347–57.

James B. Pond, from *Eccentricities of Genius* (New York: Dillingham, 1900), 197–225.

"Mark Twain on the Platform" (1896)

R. C. B.

> Twain arrived in Sydney on 16 September 1895, and he remained in Australia,
> after a side trip to New Zealand, until early January 1896.

UNFORTUNATELY, PERHAPS, for himself, but decidedly fortunately for the people who have the pleasure of listening to him, Mark Twain has been dragged out of his American study by pecuniary losses to the footlights of the lecture-platform and the admiring gaze of his multitudinous readers. It is quite twenty years since the author of *Huck Finn* spoke across the footlights, and even at that distant date his lectures were very few in number, so that the people who have seen or heard the humorist in public prior to his present lecturing-tour must be very limited indeed. Perhaps it is a good thing that Mark Twain has been compelled to take to lecturing for a time, as it will enable him to visit countries previously unknown to him, and, as he has already promised, result in *Tramp Abroad,* Vol. II, being published. In fact, Mark Twain has so arranged his tour that he will not revisit any of the countries which formed such excellent scope for witty observation in his well-known book. Mark Twain placed himself unreservedly under the care of that well-known Colonial lecture-agent, Mr. R. S. Smythe, who has negotiated so many big "stars" through the Colonies. Crossing from San Francisco [*sic*], the humorist opened his tour in Sydney in the middle of September. His tour, which will last a year, extends over all the Australian Colonies, New Zealand, Mauritius, Ceylon, and South Africa. He had an offer of £2000 for ten lectures in London, but for the present had to refuse it. He will finish his Colonial tour, and get the resultant book off his hands before thinking of a trip to England.

As a lecturer—or rather, storyteller, for the author objects to be called a lecturer—Mark Twain is, and has proved himself to be, in his opening Australian "At Homes," a decided success. Like Charles Dickens, he relies entirely on his old books for the pabulum of his discourses, but, unlike the author of *Pickwick,* he does not read long extracts from these books.

He takes some of his best stories—"The Jumping Frog," *Huck Finn,* the difficulties of the German language, *par example*—and re-tells them, with many subtle additions of humor and some fresh observations, in the most irresistibly amusing manner. He is in no sense a disappointment as a humorist. He starts his audience laughing in the very first sentence he utters, and for two hours keeps them in a continual roar. The only serious moments occur when, with the unutterable pathos of which the true humorist alone is capable, he interpolates a few pathetic touches which almost make the tears mingle with the smiles. Every story he tells serves the purpose of illustrating a moral, and, although, for the most part, he talks in low, slow, conversational tones, at times he rises to real bursts of eloquence—not the polished, grandiloquent eloquence of the average American speaker, but the eloquence conveyed in simple words and phrases, and prompted by some deep and sincerely felt sentiment. The author has the power of seeming to jest at his serious side, just as in his books; but there is no mistaking the seriousness with which, for example, he is moved by the remembrance of the iniquities perpetrated on liberty in the old slavery days amid which Huck Finn and Jim the slave lived. He makes the most unexpected anecdotes point the most unexpected morals, but it is the recital of the old, familiar stories without any moral attaching to them which pleases most, coming as they do warm from the brain of the man who invented them.

Mark Twain steals unobtrusively onto the platform, dressed in the regulation evening-clothes, with the trouser-pockets cut high up, into which he occasionally dives both hands. He bows with a quiet dignity to the roaring cheers which greet him at every "At Home." Then, with natural, unaffected gesture, and with scarcely any prelude, he gets under weigh [*sic*] with his first story. He is a picturesque figure on the stage. His long, shaggy, white hair surmounts a face full of intellectual fire. The eyes, arched with bushy brows, and which seem to be closed most of the time while he is speaking, flash out now and then from their deep sockets with a genial, kindly, pathetic look, and the face is deeply drawn with the furrows accumulated during an existence of sixty years. He talks in short sentences, with a peculiar smack of the lips at the end of each. His language is just that of his books, full of the quaintest Americanisms, and showing an utter disregard for the polished diction of most lecturers. "It was not" is always " 'twarn't" with Mark Twain, and "mighty fine" and "my kingdom" and "they done it" and "catched," and various other purely transatlantic words and phrases crop up profusely during his talk. He speaks slowly, lazily, and wearily, as a man dropping off to sleep, rarely raising his voice above a conversational tone; but it has that characteristic nasal sound which penetrates to the back of the largest building. His figure is rather slight, not above middle height, and the whole man suggests an utter lack of physical energy. As a matter of fact, Mark Twain detests exercise, and the attention must be very strong to induce him to go very far out of doors. Rolf Boldrewood[1] called on him in Melbourne, and had the greatest difficulty in the world to persuade him to take a drive. With the exception of an occasional curious trot, as when recounting his buck-jumping experiences, Mark Twain stands perfectly still in one place during the whole of the time he is talking to the audience. He rarely moves his arms, unless it is to adjust his spectacles or to show by action how a certain thing was done. His characteristic attitude is to stand quite still, with the right arm across the abdomen and the left resting on it and supporting his chin. In this way he talks on for nearly two hours; and, while the audience is laughing uproariously, he never by any chance relapses into a smile. To have read Mark Twain is a delight, but to have seen and heard him is a joy not readily to be forgotten.

Note

1. Thomas Alexander Browne, aka Rolf Boldrewood (1826–1915), an Australian author best known for the novel *Robbery Under Arms* (1882).

R. C. B., "Mark Twain on the Platform," *Critic* 25 (April 1896): 286.

From *A Woman's Part in a Revolution* (1897)

NATALIE HAMMOND

> A few weeks after his arrival in South Africa in early May 1896, Twain visited the Jameson raiders in their prison in Pretoria. A group of about 600 British irregulars under the command of Leander Starr Jameson (1853–1917) had tried and failed to spark a rebellion against the Boer government in South Africa in late December 1895–early January 1896. The raid was supported by Cecil Rhodes (1853–1902), British financier and African colonialist. Twain was welcomed to Pretoria by the wife of one of the "reformers," Natalie Harris Hammond: "I found she and I had much in common. She was born in Missouri; so was I. She had lived a long time in California; so had I; and we were therefore fellow Americans" (Scharnhorst 307). The raiders were subsequently released upon payment of an indemnity by the British government.

MARK TWAIN CAME TO the Rand. He visited the men at Pretoria. My husband did the honors of the prison, and introduced him to the Reformers. He talked a long while to them, sitting on a dry goods box. Expressed his satisfaction at finding only one journalist in the crowd, and no surprise that the lawyers were largely represented. He assured them that they were to be congratulated and envied, although they did not know it. There was no place one was so safe from interruption as in a jail. He recalled to their minds Cervantes[1] and Columbus—it was an honor to share captivity with such men as these.

Note

1. According to tradition, Miguel de Cervantes Saavedra (1547–1616) wrote the first part of *Don Quixote* (1605) while in prison at Argamasilla in La Mancha. See also "Mark Twain Home Again," *New York Times*, 16 October 1900, 3; repr. in Scharnhorst 352–64: "At this time the Jameson raiders were in jail, and I visited them and made a little speech trying to console them. I told them of the advantages of being in jail. 'This jail is as good as any other,' I said, 'and, besides, being in jail has its advantages. A lot of great men have

been in jail. If Bunyan had not been put in jail, he would never have written *Pilgrim's Progress.* Then the jail is responsible for *Don Quixote,* so you see being in jail is not so bad, after all.'"

Natalie Hammond, from *A Woman's Part in a Revolution* (New York: Longmans, Green, 1897), 152.

From *Autobiography* (1935)

JOHN HAY HAMMOND

> John Hay Hammond (1855–1936), mining engineer, collaborator with Cecil Rhodes in gold and diamond mining in South Africa, and the husband of Natalie Harris Hammond, was one of the Jameson raiders whom Twain visited in the Pretoria prison.

"THE STAR OF THE STARS AND STRIPES," as the Johannesburg *Times* called Mark Twain, was on a round-the-world lecture tour, and took advantage of an engagement in nearby Johannesburg to pay a social call on the American prisoners. I had great hopes for the effects of this afternoon on our spirits as I was familiar with Mark Twain's genial personality and witty conversation. While I was a student at Yale, I met him a number of times at Hartford, Connecticut, where I often went to spend weekends with General Franklin, president of the Colt Arms Company.[1]

In the glare of the South African sun which beat into the courtyard, Samuel Clemens, with his white hair and spotless linen suit, was a refreshing sight. I grasped his hand warmly in both of mine. "Mr. Clemens, I'm certainly glad to see you again. How did you ever find your way into this God-forsaken hole?"

"Getting into jail is easy," replied the humorist. "I thought the difficulties arose when it came to getting out."

I smiled appreciatively and introduced him to the rest of our company. He was particularly struck with the martial demeanor of Colonel Bettington,[2] who had been one of the Committee's military commanders.

"This is a pretty dull sort of place, Colonel. Killing time, eh?"

"I suppose so," replied Bettington. "I'm a soldier and must kill something."

"You've got all the big bugs here, haven't you?"

"Yes, two hundred million were in my cell last night."[3] The colonel rubbed his shoulders.

"What! Two hundred million big bugs?"

"Good Lord, no! Two hundred million pounds in good hard English money."

"Where do you keep it?"

The colonel pointed to Solly Joel,[4] leaning against the wall. "There's some of it standing over there. Barnato Brothers, you know."

"And what's he doing in here? Hasn't he enough money to buy himself out?"

"So far he hasn't had any success, but we still have hopes."

After an hour or so of amusing conversation, Mr. Clemens prepared to depart, refusing our invitation to wait until we were ready to leave.

As he left the prison, a cub reporter accosted him. "Mr. Clemens, how did you find living conditions in the prison?"

"Why do you ask?"

"Some of the prisoners have complained to Krüger[5] that the jail was no fit place for gentlemen. Although the president replied he was not aware that jails were intended for gentlemen, just the same we'd like to have your impressions."

"Has Mr. Hammond, or any of the other Americans, made any complaint?"

"No," admitted the youth; "the grievances were urged by their friends."

"Well," said Mark Twain, "I am not surprised that Mr. Hammond has made no complaint. I knew him as a young engineer out in Nevada where he used to spend a good deal of his time in mining camp hotels, and compared with those accommodations Hammond is now living in luxury."[6]

The reporter carefully noted this down on his pad and Mark Twain went on to say that he was really greatly pleased with the jail; he had found some very charming gentlemen there, and he thought it was an ideal rest cure for these tired businessmen. He only regretted his stay was so short that he could not take advantage of the peaceful conditions of the jail to rest his own tired nerves. He said he could not imagine a place where one would be less troubled by the importunities of his creditors and the only feature he did not like about the jail was that there were too many lawyers among the prisoners, and somehow or other he never could hit it off with lawyers.

Next morning a very sharp criticism of the jail authorities appeared in this Boer paper, which was one of the Joubert[7] papers hostile to Krüger. The article declared the jail was supposed to be a place for punishment and *not* a pleasant rest cure, and the paper called upon the government to take drastic measures of a punitive nature. The prison authorities responded by diminishing our rations, which had been none too liberal before.

None of the prisoners had seen this news item, and we could not account for the increased severity of our jailers' treatment of us; conditions had seemed intolerable before. Some friends on the outside, however, learned the reason and at once sent a deputation to Bloemfontein, several hundred miles south, to intercept Mark Twain, who was on his way to Cape Town to sail for England. As soon as he saw the paper containing his interview, and realized its unfortunate consequences, he hastened back to Pretoria to make clear to President Krüger that he had merely been trying to be humorous. In truth, he considered our quarters disgraceful and quite unfit for political prisoners. His explanation was apparently satisfactory; the severity of the discipline was once more relaxed.

Notes

1. William Buel Franklin (1823–1903), U.S. Army general during the Civil War and vice president of the Colt Arms Company from 1866 until 1888.

2. Rowland Albemarle Bettington (1852–1933) immigrated to South Africa in 1872 and fought on behalf of the British in the Boer War (1899–1902).

3. Natalie Hammond 52: "The four leaders were put into a cell 11 feet by 11 feet, which was closed in by an inner court. There was no window, only a narrow grille over the door. The floor was of earth and overrun by vermin."

4. Solomon Barnato Joel (1865–1931), South African financier.

5. Paul Krüger, aka Oom Paul (1825–1904), a prominent Boer resistance leader against British rule and the first president of the Transvaal Republic in 1880.

6. "Mark Twain in Port Elizabeth: An Interview," *Port Elizabeth Eastern Province Herald and Port Elizabeth Commercial News*, 19 June 1896, 3; repr. in Scharnhorst 310. To the question "Did you hear any complaints from the prisoners as to their treatment?" Twain replied, "Oh, no; I have been in many worse jails in America."

7. Petrus Jacobus (Piet) Joubert (1831–1900), one of Krüger's political rivals.

John Hay Hammond, from *Autobiography* (New York: Farrar & Rinehart, 1935), 2:398–400.

From *Seventy Summers* (1925)

POULTNEY BIGELOW

Twain arrived in Johannesburg, South Africa, on 17 June 1896, where he was greeted by an old friend, the American journalist and historian Poultney Bigelow (1855–1954).

MARK TWAIN ARRIVED in Johannesburg whilst I was the guest of my Jew friend Goerz[1] and his winsome Viennese *bonne à tout faire* [literally, "maid of all work"]. Goerz was mad to make Mr. Clemens's acquaintance, and gladly placed at my disposal his victoria and pair for afternoon drives. . . .

Mark Twain was a sick man, but he made his audiences roar with laughter. He was good at a laugh himself, when in his normal health, but never laughed at his own stories. Indeed, his very sepulchral solemnity when perpetrating a violently comical tale was not the least part in its ultimate success. His audiences crowded every square inch of the largest hall, and, if I might believe a miner under oath, everyone who pressed upon him at the close of his talk had known him in early California or Nevada days. Every one of that pressing party reached eagerly for Mr. Clemens's reluctant hand, and if I boiled down a hundred greetings they would sound something like this: "Put it there, old man! Don't you remember me?—don't you remember Bill Bloodgood that night in Jim Dusenburg's cabin? and that Chinaman who poured our whiskey into the oilcan? Dear old Mark! those were happy days! Put it there, old hoss—I knew you'd know me again, etc., etc." And to all these affectionate friends Mark Twain nodded his head slowly and sympathetically like Royalty on a balcony, murmuring the while "Of course—why, of course!"—and thus disposing of one after another in a comparatively short space of time, thanks to the rough pressure from the rear that brooked no monopoly of the great humorist. After each lecture I carried him swiftly to Goerz's house, where Fräulein Vienna had always a bright wood-fire on the hearth and a kettle of boiling water, plus lemons, sugar, and rum. Then came the real day of joy for him—an easy chair and outstretched legs, pockets full of cigars, a long tumbler of steaming toddy, and lots to talk about.

Goerz congratulated Mr. Clemens on meeting so many of his early friends! To which the answer of Mark Twain was: "I never thought there could be so many *G-d d—d* liars in any one town! They were not even intelligent liars—they gave dates when I was not even in America and they named places that I never heard of before—the blank-blank damned liars!" But Mark Twain was gentle—he did not expose them to the public—these men had for weeks been jacking up their professional prestige by professing to have been pals with Mark in his early Western days. Maybe they did persuade themselves that they had actually lived the scenes whereof they dreamed. At any rate all were made happy at a comparatively small sacrifice of truth and time.

Goerz passed out of my life three years afterwards—in London. Mark Twain was there also, undergoing treatment for his persistent nervous dyspepsia and general debility. He lived near me in Chelsea, and would stroll around on a sunny morning for a smoke and chat—sometimes for a stroll on the Embankment. No one had his address but myself and his business manager—for he needed rest. Mrs. Clemens was then a semi-invalid, and his two daughters absorbed in their studies—especially Clara, who is now a star in concerts. Goerz had a splendid establishment, whose presiding divinity was a beautiful Danish damsel who had left the stage to become his ostensible wife. Now Mark Twain professed great breadth insofar as tobacco, toddy, profane language, and poker were concerned, but in domestic relations he was a saint, and adored his lovely wife as legendary knights paid homage to the Queen of Heaven. Goerz begged me to bring Mr. Clemens to his house for an evening. I told him it was impossible. However, when I broached the matter to Mr. Clemens, he consented, on condition that there be no company—a purely family affair—no dress—and an early escape. Goerz, of course, promised that it should be a strictly "family" affair—only us two plus Goerz and his "wife"—as he styled her to Mark Twain.

When we arrived we found twenty guests, all Jews. Now Mr. Clemens to me was ever a champion of the downtrodden race of Israel—he even gave one of his daughters to a Jew.[2] But as he gazed glumly at Goerz and his "Chosen," methinks he was ready to recall much that he had ever said in favor of Hebrews. However, the dinner came and went; Mark Twain was placed next to his host, whilst I had a merry time with his Danish nymph, whose nature was amiable and frankly amorous. Doubtless Goerz dreaded lest his guest of honor discover the identity of his alleged bride—and he succeeded for that evening. But as a "family" dinner-party it was a failure. Mr. Clemens was annoyed, and showed it by an almost unbroken silence. One of the Jews, who was evidently rated as the funny member of the "family," attempted to raise our spirits to his own level by reciting a very long and very well-worn American story. He directed his chuckles and German gutturals directly at the guest of honor, who from chuckle to chuckle assumed an expression more and more weary. At the close of the tale, the teller laughed loudly, and the whole of the "family" with him. I had not listened to the long story, have been vastly more probably employed by the fascinating daughter of Thespis. But when the loud laughter announced the climax I glanced in the direction of Mark Twain and saw that he alone showed no sign of merriment. The funny man of this Trimalchion feast now craned across and queried: "What for you do not laugh, Mr. Clemens? It is a very good story, don't it."

Mark Twain merely gazed somberly at his questioner, drew a few puffs, and drawled out very distinctly these words: "At one time that *was* a good story. I invented that story forty years ago!"

Notes

1. The mining engineer Adolf Goerz (1857–1900) was not Jewish.
2. Clara Clemens married Ossip Gabrilowitsch on 6 October 1909.

Poultney Bigelow, from *Seventy Summers* (London: Edward Arnold, 1925), 2:165–68.

"Mark Twain as a Newspaper Reporter" (1910)

Frank Marshall White

> Twain and his family sailed from Cape Town on 15 July and arrived in England
> on 31 July 1896. The American journalist Frank Marshall White (1861–1919),
> the European correspondent of the *New York Journal,* interviewed Twain in
> the spring of 1897, a few months after the death of Susy on 18 August 1896 in
> Hartford of spinal meningitis. Jean Clemens had meanwhile joined her par-
> ents and surviving sister in London. White inadvertently became the source
> of the story that Twain was dying in London. Later in 1897 Twain was a first-
> hand witness to the riots in the Austrian Reichsrath in Vienna.

IN 1897 I WAS the European representative of an important New York newspaper, and it occurred to me that it would be legitimate journalistic enterprise to engage Mark Twain, who was then living in London, to report the
Diamond Jubilee procession that was to be the feature of the celebration of
the sixtieth anniversary of Queen Victoria's reign, to occur in June. Perhaps I might not have ventured to make the proposition to one whom many
regarded as America's first man of letters had I not believed that money
would be an object to him, for it was soon after the failure of the publishing
firm that involved him in financial disaster, and he was then engaged in the
courageous struggle that resulted in his paying the debts of the concern
single-handed and acquiring another fortune.

Although this was about the time that the rumor was circulated in
America that the great humorist was dying in poverty in a London gar-
ret, he was living with Mrs. Clemens and their two daughters in a comfortable home in Chelsea, was in good health, and working ten or twelve
hours per day. It was a house of mourning, however, for only a few months
before death had removed the oldest daughter from the family of five . . .
and the visitor felt a prevailing sadness in the atmosphere, in the subdued
voices of the servants, in the silence of the darkened rooms. Mrs. Clemens had not left her own apartment for many days, and her daughters were

constant in their attendance upon her. In the great tragedy that had come into their lives, the pecuniary calamity was realized only by the head of the family.

Nevertheless, although his face was lined with care and sorrow, Mark Twain was as whimsical as usual when I made my errand known. I told him, to start with, that the exigencies of the situation were such, with a greater amount of work devolving upon telegraph wires and cables in every direction from London during the Jubilee than had ever deluged them before, that he would be compelled after the procession had passed to "rush" whatever he might write with the utmost speed in order to insure its transmission to New York.

"That's one reason why I don't like to write for newspapers—the hurry," he drawled, shaking his shaggy head that was just beginning to turn gray. "I wrote something for a New York newspaper not long ago, and made up my mind not to write for one again. They asked me to write a humorous article, and I thought it was humorous when I sent it in. It may not have been that, but at least it was more humorous than when it appeared. They put words into my mouth. I'd rather they had put street sweepings there. I want to see proofs of things I write before they are published."

Upon being assured that he might depend on anything he might write appearing word for word as he wrote it in the columns of the sheet I represented, although the correction of the proofs was impracticable in the circumstances, since the process would occupy some three weeks, he had another objection to present. "You see," he said, "with the great crowds there will be in London during the celebration—on the day of the procession probably the most tremendous crowds of all—I couldn't possibly get home to write my report in time."

I told him that I proposed to secure a seat for him to view the procession on the Hotel Cecil stand, and that I would also get him a room in the hotel in which he could write his article.

"But I couldn't have my wife there," he protested. "I wouldn't think, in her condition, of asking her to leave the house."

Observing that I was puzzled, he explained in all seriousness: "Ever since we have been married I have depended on my wife to go over and revise my manuscript. I have written scarcely anything in twenty-five years that she hasn't edited. Not but that I can do the spelling and grammar alone—if

I have a spelling-book and a grammar with me—but I don't always know just where to draw the line in matters of taste. Mrs. Clemens has kept a lot of things from getting into print that might have given me a reputation I wouldn't care to have, that I wouldn't have known any better than to have published." . . .

On being brought back to the subject of the proposed Jubilee article, the humorist suddenly became businesslike—and he had the reputation of being an efficient man of business, although he did pay his debts when he might have shuffled out of it through the bankruptcy courts. "Of course," he said, "I prefer to write for the magazines rather than the newspapers, and to take my time about it, and have my wife censor it, and correct my proofs. However, we can't always consult our preferences. Now, if you can offer me a sufficient inducement, I might consider writing a newspaper article in a hurry, without my wife seeing it, and allowing a cable operator to have the first hack at it, with the printer to mangle what the operator left of it."

I named a sum larger than I had ever heard of any publication paying for an article of the nature and length I had suggested to Mark Twain. He shook his head. I doubled the amount. He nodded.

It was early in June that I made the bargain with Mark Twain (which, by the way, was not secured on either side by so much as the scratch of a pen), and he did not stick to the strict letter of the agreement, but gave more than he had agreed. On an occasion when I had called on him about another matter, he remarked: "I have decided to illustrate that Jubilee article. I think that appropriate illustrations would be portraits of the Duke of Orleans, the Duke of Bourbon, King Henry V, and myself, and I have almost finished them, so that you can send them by mail, to be ready when the cable article comes along."

He handed me four sheets of manuscript, each containing what he termed a description of one of the forthcoming portraits, fair illustrations of his own peculiar vein of amusing nonsense, which ran thus:

Duke of Orleans.—I have represented the Duke of Orleans in the battlefield. He is looking surprised at the way things are going. I got that effect by waving his hair and working up his eyelashes. At first he was looking too much surprised, but that was because his coat tail was too long. I took off a little and rounded the corners; this makes him calmer. I got that look of regret which you see in him by putting those shoes on him, which are too small for him.

Duke of Bourbon.—I have represented the Duke of Bourbon in the act of trying to escape from the Tower of London disguised as a gentleman. I tried to make his handkerchief stick up a little more out of his coat pocket, so as to express horror and surprise, but there was not enough white paint left when I got to that part. But it is no matter. I got it in another way; by striping his pants. I gave them that trembly look and got the same effect.

Henry V.—In the original the king had a crown on. That is no kind of thing for a king to wear when he comes home on business; he ought to wear something he can collect taxes in. You will find this representation of Henry V accurate and full of feeling, full of sublimity. I have painted him looking over the field of Agincourt and studying where to begin.

Mark Twain, by Clemens.—I do not wear whiskers, but I painted them on to get that look of purity and elevation you see in the picture, so as to give the general scheme of the portrait a look of courtliness and wealth.

I got the "portraits" a day or two later. I had supposed that he would send nonsensical sketches by his own hand. Perhaps he had attempted something of the sort, but what he sent me was three dummy figures from a tailor's advertisement, labeled respectively "The Duke of Orleans," "The Duke of Bourbon," and "King Henry V," and a newspaper cut of Dr. Chauncey M. Depew to represent "Mark Twain, by Clemens." A note accompanying these works of art said: "The president of the Royal Academy thinks that if I should throw these pictures up life size and put them in the National Gallery they would attract attention, but perhaps that is because of his good heart."

The week before the Jubilee was celebrated there was a rehearsal at daybreak of the big procession over the route from Buckingham Palace to the Tower, and across London Bridge and back over Westminster Bridge, in order to insure a smooth performance for the actual event. The entire street program was carried through, without the participation of the principals, of course, the Queen and attendant royalties with the other guests of the occasion being represented by dummies. Mark Twain thought that it would be worthwhile to see the rehearsal in order to gain an idea beforehand of what he was going to write about. He had received a "tip," from what he considered a reliable source, as to the morning the earlier show was to take place (a profound secret), and I had agreed to call for him early that day and drive him over the course. During the week I received the following note from him [dated June 11, 1897]:

Dear Mr. White:

Do you think there will be room for my two daughters to go with us the morning of the 19th? If there should be room & no objection they might be useful to me in helping notice details.

I called at the Clemens residence at half-past three o'clock (the hour of sunrise in England in June) on the morning of the 19th, and the four of us drove up and down between Buckingham Palace and the Tower for two or three hours, but no sign of a processional rehearsal could we discover. Many picturesque and complicated aspersions did the humorist cast upon the character of his informant as to the potential occurrence of the morn. Playfully chided by his offspring as to the futility of losing his temper, which he really had not lost at all, he drawled, pensively: "I don't know about that. Sometimes when a man is in a thoroughgoing temper he finds things to say that are worth preserving."

On the day of the Jubilee procession, Wednesday, the 23d of June, Mark Twain had one of the best seats from which to view the show along the entire route, the front corner seat facing the head of the line of march on the stand erected before the Hotel Cecil in the Strand. . . . As our star reporter was not particularly robust, and we could not afford to take any chances on his becoming lost or incapacitated, I had appointed a member of our staff, Dr. [E. H.] Graham-Dewey, as his escort and body-guard, and he brought him safely from Chelsea by the underground road and through the Embankment Gardens into the rear entrance of the Hotel Cecil. Dewey had the next seat to his charge on the Cecil stand, accommodating two or three hundred, which—the hotel being filled by guests from the various parts of the British Empire—was occupied by representatives of many nations, most of whom knew our famous humorist by reputation and recognized him from portraits they had seen in distant lands, and it was all that his companion could do to prevent his being mobbed. In fact, Dewey declared that Mark Twain attracted more attention in his immediate vicinity than did the procession itself. He sat with a large pad on his knee and made many notes. He was cordial to the English reporters who tried to interview him, but firm in his refusal.

"No, no. You mustn't ask me to talk," he said to them. "We reporters mustn't quote one another."

[217]

He relented, however, after the procession had passed, so far as to remark: "I was not dreaming of so stunning a show. All the nations seemed to be represented. It was a sort of an allegorical representation of the Last Day, and some of us who live to see that day will probably recall this one—if we are not too much disturbed in mind at the time."

A group of English and Australian notables now formed a guard about the distinguished American writer and cheerfully helped Dewey to fight a way for him across the Strand and to a friend's chambers in Henrietta Street, Covent Garden. Here he deftly turned out his copy, which reached the cable office and eventually the newspaper in ample time.

Later in the same year Mark Twain did some journalistic work in Vienna, where he attended many of the stormy sessions of the Reichsrath growing out of the German-Czech controversy in the fall and winter, being, indeed, dragged out with the others when the soldiery arrested Dr. Wolf and cleared the Parliamentary halls in November. His permanent record of those events is to be found in his article in *Harper's Magazine* for March 1898, entitled "Stirring Times in Austria,"[1] but he also sent occasional dispatches to American newspapers. That the perfidious editor of a contemporary had the audacity to employ his services, disregarding priority of claim on my part, is indicated by the following letter I received from him in January, which also presents his views as to where the line should be drawn between a literary correspondent and a mere reporter:

Vienna, Sunday night.
[26 December 1897]

Dear Mr. White:

There is nothing to telegraph to-night—I sent it to the *World* last night. I expected a request from you, but the *World*'s request reached me 17 hours ahead of yours.

There is nothing new to-day but Badeni's resignation,[2] but I should not care to telegraph an ordinary and foregone event like that, & it wouldn't pay you to have me do it anyway.

The other time that you wanted a telegram it was good magazine matter if detailed fully, but in condensed form it was merely matter for a reporter.

I was sorry I didn't hear from you this time, & was half minded to send you 500 words anyhow without waiting.

Yrs sincerely,
S. L. Clemens

[218]

You see, it was a *special* occasion. I haven't any use for the telegraph on any *but* that sort. . . .

It was on the last day of May 1897 that my paper had cabled me from New York the information that a report was current in the American press that Mark Twain was dying in poverty in London. I had seen him only a day or two before, and knew that he was in good health and living in comfort; but the following morning I sent a reporter to his house to show him the cable from New York. He was writing in bed that day, and a servant took the cable to his bedroom, whence he sent down the following note, out of which grew one of the most famous of his later witticisms. The note read:

> James Ross Clemens, a cousin of mine, was seriously ill two or three weeks ago in London, but is well now.
> The report of my illness grew out of his illness; the report of my death was an exaggeration.
> Mark Twain.

I called on Mark Twain later in the day, when he told me that he did not know whether to be more amused or annoyed by the New York rumor. "Of course I'm dying," he said; "but I'm not dying any faster than anybody else. I can understand perfectly how the report of my illness got about; the report of my poverty is harder to deal with. My friends might know that unless I were actually dying I should not live in poverty when I am receiving offers to lecture by every mail. The fact is that I was under contract to write the book I have just finished [*Following the Equator*], or I should have accepted these offers."

I sent a dispatch about Mark Twain's financial and physical condition to my paper that night, in which I embodied in his own words what he had written about his cousin in the morning. The operator who cabled it left out all punctuation marks, as is usual unless they are specifically marked for transmission. The copyeditor in New York, preparing the dispatch for the printer, began a paragraph with the last clause of the second and last paragraph of the note he had written in bed, "The report of my death is an exaggeration," and this by process of repetition became, "The reports of my death are grossly exaggerated."[3]

A couple of weeks after sending the above-mentioned dispatch I received the following note [dated 12 June 1897]:

Dear Mr. White:

Come down, now, & let us see if we can invent some way to repair the enormous damage which your cablegram has done me.

Sincerely, Clemens.

I might have been surprised, had I not the same morning received a telegram from my paper to the effect that the *New York Herald* had started a subscription for the pecuniary relief of Mark Twain,[4] and asking me to ascertain whether he approved it. As I surmised, this movement having brought him a mass of cablegrams from all parts of America inquiring if he was in need of financial assistance, he had attributed the sensation to something in my dispatch of a fortnight before. The *Herald* had evidently not informed the object of its prospective beneficence beforehand that it was about to raise a subscription for him, for he was taken entirely by surprise when I showed him the cable from the office of my paper. He also was very much pleased, and said: "You can say in reply that if it is true, it is pleasanter news than I have been accustomed to receive for some time past. I was expecting a monument by and by, but if my friends wish to pay my debts I will do without the monument."

Mark Twain might not have objected to having his friends pay off his debts. It was when the *Herald* announced that the fund it proposed to raise was to meet his personal necessities, and not for the relief of his creditors, that he put a stop to the project.

Notes

1. "Stirring Times in Austria," *Harper's Monthly* 96 (March 1898): 530–40.

2. Kasimir Felix Badeni (1846–1909), prime minister of the Austrian half of the Austro-Hungarian empire since 30 September 1895, resigned on 28 November 1897 after enraging the German-Austrians by offering political concessions to the Young Czechs in the Reichsrath.

3. See Frank Marshall White, "Mark Twain Amused," *New York Journal,* 2 June 1897, 1: "I can understand perfectly how the report of my illness got about. I have even heard on good authority that I was dead. James Ross Clemens, of St. Louis, a cousin of mine, was seriously ill two or three weeks ago in London, but is well now. The report of my illness grew out of his illness. The report of my death was an exaggeration."

4. After reporting that Twain was in desperate straits ("Mark Twain Is Ill in London," 1 June 1897, 9), the *New York Herald* began to solicit funds to relieve his distress on 13 June 1897. Less than a week later, the *Herald* explained that subscribers were not contributing

to Twain's debt relief but to his personal support ("For Twain Himself: The Herald Fund Is Designed to Meet the Personal Wants of the Writer, Not for the Creditors," 19 June 1897, 5). The *Herald* shut down the fund on 27 June 1897 at Twain's insistence ("Mark Twain Declines Help," I 8). Over the period of two weeks, only $928 was given to the fund, an average of about $65 per day, in addition to the $2,000 the *Herald* and Carnegie contributed.

Frank Marshall White, "Mark Twain as a Newspaper Reporter," *Outlook* 96 (December 1910): 961–67.

"Some Reminiscences of Mark Twain" (1929)

JAMES ROSS CLEMENS, M.D.

> Ironically, James Ross Clemens, M.D. (1866–1948), a distant cousin from
> St. Louis with whom Twain had been confused, learned of Twain's ostensible
> distress and offered to help him.

IN THE WINTER OF 1898, when a medical student at St. Thomas's hospital,
London, I chanced to read in the London *Evening Globe* that Mark Twain
was residing in London in straitened circumstances. A letter was forthwith
dispatched by me to him, care of Chatto and Windus, his London publishers, in which I introduced myself as another of the Clemens tribe and asked
for the honor and privilege of being allowed to aid him in his distress.

Several days passed and then one evening there came a knock at my
street door and in walked Clemens himself. Fortunately the report of his
bankruptcy proved false but he seemed altogether at a loss how to express
adequately his appreciation of my letter and was visibly touched. From
that time on to the day of his death I was always his "Dr. Jim." I was often
invited to his home in Cheyne Walk, Chelsea, and met at his table all of
England's literary lions.

The following story bears repeating: On a certain wet Sunday Mr. Clemens found himself stranded in the country and obliged to put up at a village
inn. Man-like he gravitated to the smoking room and there met a brother
derelict and after the time of day had been passed a desultory conversation commenced between the two men. It was but natural that Mr. Clemens
soon had literary subjects to the fore and began to attack England's latest
giant, Thomas Hardy, but the little man with the broken nose across the
table did not seem somehow to concur as heartily as Mark Twain had expected in his diatribes against the author of *Tess of the D'Urbervilles*. When
the little man arose to go, after paying his score, he gave Mark Twain a look
that can best be described as "dirty" and stalked from the room with the
hauteur of a Spanish grandee. Vaguely ill at ease, Mr. Clemens asked the
waiter the name of the gentleman. "Mr. Thomas 'Ardy, sir."

I can still hear Mr. Clemens's delighted chuckle as he scored the point against himself.

At the Strand Theater—William Gillette in *Secret Service* and Mr. Clemens and myself, as Gillette's guests, were occupying a stage box. In the second act a black cat walked across the stage although its name was not on the program. "Mark my words, Dr. Jim," exclaimed Clemens excitedly, "poor Gillette is in for some misfortune or other this evening." And sure enough, when we went behind the scenes at the end of that act we found Gillette binding up a forefinger which he had cut about to the bone on the telegraph key.

I happened to quote to Mr. Clemens a London saying that there were only three really funny sayings in the world and that two of them were not fit for the drawing room. "O why didn't I know of that when I was writing *Pudd'nhead Wilson*," exclaimed Mr. Clemens feelingly. "I should have headed one of the chapters with it as a caption."

Mark Twain, like Dr. Johnson, hated getting up in the morning and on one occasion entering his bedroom long past the hour of noon I found him in bed, luxuriously propped up on pillows and busily skimming through a crowd of books he had entrenched himself among. "I have to make some after-dinner remarks tonight although I am not supposed to know that I am to be called upon so I am doing my 'improvising' now" was his explanation. . . .

"Dr. Jim," said Mr. Clemens to me one day in his most solemn manner, "I have in a safe deposit box the manuscript of an unpublished work of mine which is the best thing by far I ever did and I give you the following excerpt as a sample of its quality. Being last summer in Germany in the company of a crowd of German research scholars I was fired by their example to do a little research of my own and the piece of work I attempted was to answer the question as to whether or not ants have intelligence. And to this end I first had made about a dozen little toy churches and labeled them 'Presbyterian,' 'Catholic,' 'Methodist' and so on. Then I rang a church bell and turned loose a crowd of ants I had caught. I found the ants paid no attention whatever to my churches. This was experiment No. 1. Experiment 2 consisted in placing a little honey, say in the Episcopal Church, and ringing the bell. Before its notes had ceased every last one of the ants had entered the portals of the Episcopal Church. Experiment 3 was the transferring of the honey to the Methodist Church and ringing for service. The former devout Episcopalians now went over in a body to the Methodist Church. In short, in whatever church I placed the honey, there I would find the ants before I had done ringing the church bell. From these experiments there could be but one deduction, viz: that ants have intelligence." . . .

I was the innocent cause of Mr. Clemens's famous cablegram: "The report of my death is greatly exaggerated." I happened to be taken desperately ill with pneumonia whilst a house surgeon at St. Thomas's hospital and was visited daily by my famous kinsman. Somehow or other the report got out that it was Mark Twain himself who had pneumonia and that he had died and the news was duly cabled to America. When shown the cable of condolence from America to his London publishers the famous reply was sent by him.

Protection of American copyright in England was a matter very close to his heart and it was in the spirit of '76 that he fought its battles against the British publishers. "There should be an eleventh commandment: Thou shalt not plagiarize," was his frequent comment.

The story of Mark Twain and the old lady in the Pullman should not be let die. Exhausted to the point of extinction by a very full day in Chicago, Mark boarded the night train for New York and retired to his berth at once for (as he fondly thought) a long night of blissful repose; but just as he was slipping over the borderline between waking and sleeping he heard an old lady's voice wistfully soliloquizing and telling herself how thirsty she was with the regularity and persistence of the ticking of a clock. "Oh, I am so thirsty." At last, unable to bear the nuisance any longer, Mark got up in his night clothes and groped his way the length of the cold, dark car to where the drinking water was kept. Filling a glass he carried it back to the elderly victim of loquacity and thirst. This good deed done and a payment in heartfelt thanks from the old lady duly pocketed, Mark got back into his berth and pulling the blankets up over his head with a deep sigh of relief and content snuggled down to sleep. But just as the Sandman was bending over him a now all too familiar and accursed voice began to exclaim and kept it up at minute intervals the rest of the night. "Oh, I was so thirsty."

James Ross Clemens, M.D., "Some Reminiscences of Mark Twain," *Overland Monthly and Out West Magazine* 87 (April 1929): 105, 125.

From *Roadside Meetings* (1931)

Hamlin Garland

> Hamlin Garland (1860–1940), the American author of *Main-Travelled Roads* (1891) and *Ulysses S. Grant: His Life and Character* (1898), also visited Twain in London, and Twain reminisced with him about his negotiation with Grant for rights to his memoirs in 1885.

I LEARNED THAT Mark Twain had returned to London, and I hastened to write him. "There are several points in the *Life of General Grant* upon which I would like to have your comment."

He replied at once, inviting me to call upon him at his hotel.

Up to this time I had never met him, although I knew a great deal of him through his friends, and had heard him speak several times. He had been living in Europe for four or five years and had been highly successful both as a writer and lecturer. According to report, kings and queens had been quick to do him honor and many critics considered him to be the largest and most significant figure in American literature. His fame, based no longer upon his eccentricities but upon the rugged force and New World flavor of everything he said and wrote, was worldwide. I was keenly eager to see him and talk with him.

As I came upon him in a small but exclusive hotel in the West End, I was shocked by the changes which had come to him. His shaggy hair was white and a stoop had come into his shoulders. It appeared that in growing old he had diminished. He appeared smaller than I had remembered him on the platform, but his fine head and rough-hewn features were more impressive than ever before.

He had heard of my book on Grant, probably through Brander Matthews, but I think he would have been courteous without either of these aids. After putting his small hand in mine he motioned me to a chair and began to speak in the rhythmic drone which had been so large a factor in his success as an after-dinner speaker. It was made up of peculiar stresses difficult to describe, and was interrupted here and there by sudden pauses, corresponding to a dash in print—a most dramatic device, as when he wrote, "Be good—and you'll be lonesome." These, and a curious aloofness of glance (as though he spoke from out a mask) made it difficult for me to take his serious statements at their full value. Most people expected him to be funny, a fact which he was accustomed to curse regretfully. As he talked to me he appeared to forget me. He looked over my head at some far-off landscape. His eyes, hidden by his bushy eyebrows, were half closed and I saw them only occasionally. I was surprised to find them blue and keen.

I asked him if he had any objections to telling me how he came publish the Grant memoirs and he replied, "None at all, but before you print it you'll have to get Mrs. Clemens's consent."

His story was something like this:

"One night as I was a-comin' away from the theater, I chanced to hear one man say to another, 'Do you know that General Grant is about to publish his memoirs?' And the other said, 'No; who is the publisher?' That was enough for me. I went the very next day to see the general. I found him in his library with his son, Colonel Fred. 'General,' I began, 'is it *true* that you are about to publish your memoirs?' 'It is,' he replied. 'I am at this moment considering an offer for the manuscript.' 'General,' I said, 'that interests me. Would you mind telling me exactly what that offer *is*?' 'Not at all,' he replied. 'The Century Company is willing to assume all the expenses and risk and pay me ten per cent on all copies sold.' 'Good God, general,' I exclaimed, 'you are *giving* them the book. You should have *three times* that amount.' . . . You know how modest the old general was; well, he showed that phase of his character now. 'Oh, no,' he answered, 'you are mistaken. I think they are treating me very handsomely. My book will not sell largely.'

"'*You* are the one mistaken, general,' I retorted, 'the book will sell largely, and just to show you how I feel about it, I will offer you twenty-five per cent royalty, and draw you a check for fifty thousand dollars advance royalty *right now*!' This staggered the old soldier, but he shook his head. 'That's very fine of you, Mr. Clemens, but I can't accept it. I am committed to these other men.' At this point Colonel Fred put in his oar. 'Why, no, you're not, father. You're only *considering* their offer. You're under no obligation to them. You have a perfect right to lay Mr. Clemens's proposition over against theirs.'

"In the end I convinced the general that I was a publisher and not a philanthropist, and I got the book. I published it. It sold enormously, as you know—more than a half-million copies—and I had the high satisfaction of visiting the old commander on his deathbed at Mt. McGregor,[1] when he could no longer utter a word or lift a hand, and of saying to him, 'General, there *is* in the bank in New York City—subject to *your* order or the order of Mrs. Grant—the sum of three hundred thousand dollars, and there'll be more—much more.'"

As he ended on this note of reminiscent emotion, I shared his conception of what that message must have meant to The Great Commander whose later days had been so quietly heroic, and so filled with mental and physical pain.

When this matter was cleared away, Clemens fell into talk of his failure as a publisher. "I am going home soon—as soon as I have made a little more money. I am nearly clear of those obligations I assumed as a partner in Webster & Co.," he said, and this brought up the subject of his arrangement with his creditors. He cursed with heart-felt fervor and Oriental magnificence Charles Webster, "who chiseled me out of fifty thousand dollars, thus bringing about the ruin of my publishing house." With cold malignity he then said in level monotone, "For many years I have been writing a kind of diary in which I have set down from time to time exactly what I think of the men and women I have met. It can't be published while *I* am alive. It can't be published while *Mrs. Clemens* is alive. It can't be published while *any of the people mentioned* are alive; but when it *is* published, that blankety blank blank will turn in his grave!"

He ended with such deadly hatred in face and voice that I was able to share in some degree the disgrace he had been called upon to bear and the burden he had voluntarily assumed. In my notebook that night I outlined this conversation and added, "He has accomplished a tremendous task—A really great soul."

As I was going away I again said: "*McClure's Magazine* wants to print this story. Shall I send it to them?"

"Certainly. Go ahead! But they'll have to get Mrs. Clemens's O.K. on the proof."

The most curious sequel to this interview (which by the way Mrs. Clemens would not let us publish) is the fact that Webster, whom Clemens accused of "chiseling" him out of fifty thousand dollars, was not in any way connected with the business at that time. He had been ill and out of the firm for several years. The failure of the firm was due to Mark's own unwise investments in a typesetting machine.[2] Albert Bigelow Paine, his biographer,[3] told me this some ten years after this meeting, and added, "When I had convinced Clemens of his error he sat for a few moments in silence, then remarked in a musing tone, 'Albert, there *was* a time when my memory was reliable. There was a time when I could remember a great many things *that were so* and some that were *not* so—now I remember only the latter!' "[4]

Notes

1. Twain had visited Grant at his home at Mount McGregor, New York, from 29 June to 2 July 1885.

2. The Paige typesetting machine, invented by James W. Paige, failed practicality tests at the *Chicago Herald* in 1894. In all, Twain lost an estimated $200,000 on the project.

3. Twain hired Albert Bigelow Paine to write his biography in January 1906.

4. Compare Twain's *Autobiography*, 3: "When I was younger I could remember anything, whether it had happened or not; but my faculties are decaying now, and soon I shall be so I cannot remember any but the things that never happened."

Hamlin Garland, from *Roadside Meetings* (New York: Macmillan, 1931), 449–53.

From *My Mark Twain* (1910)

W. D. Howells

Twain returned to the United States on the *Minnehaha*, landing in New York on 15 October 1900. He soon leased a house near Washington Square Park at 14 W. Tenth Street. Howells soon visited him there.

IN THE BRIEF LETTER I got from him in the Western city, after half a dozen wakeful nights, he sardonically congratulated me on having gone into "the lecture field," and then he said: "I know where you are now. You are in hell."[1]

It was this perdition which he re-entered when he undertook that round-the-world lecturing tour for the payment of the debts left to him by the bankruptcy of his firm in the publishing business. It was not purely perdition for him, or, rather, it was perdition for only one-half of him, the author-half; for the actor-half it was paradise. The author who takes up lecturing without the ability to give histrionic support to the literary reputation which he brings to the crude test of his reader's eyes and ears invokes a peril and a misery unknown to the lecturer who has made his first public [*sic*] from the platform. Clemens was victorious on the platform from the beginning, and it would be folly to pretend that he did not exult in his triumphs there. But I suppose, with the wearing nerves of middle life, he hated more and more the personal swarming of interest upon him, and all the inevitable clatter of the thing. Yet he faced it, and he labored round our tiresome globe that he might pay the uttermost farthing of debts which he had not knowingly contracted, the debts of his partners who had meant well and done ill, not because they were evil, but because they were unwise, and as unfit for their work as he was. "Pay what thou owest." That is right, even when thou owest it by the error of others, and even when thou owest it to a bank, which had not lent it from love of thee, but in the hard line of business and thy need.

Clemens's behavior in this matter redounded to his glory among the na-

tions of the whole earth, and especially in this nation, so wrapped in commerce and so little used to honor among its many thieves. He had behaved
like Walter Scott,[2] as millions rejoiced to know, who had not known how
Walter Scott had behaved till they knew it was like Clemens. No doubt
it will be put to his credit in the books of the Recording Angel, but what
the Judge of all the Earth will say of it at the Last Day there is no telling.
I should not be surprised if He accounted it of less merit than some other
things that Clemens did and was: less than his abhorrence of the Spanish
War, and the destruction of the South-African republics, and our deceit of
the Filipinos, and his hate of slavery, and his payment of his portion of our
race's debt to the race of the colored student whom he saw through college
[Warner McGuinn], and his support of a poor artist for three years in Paris
[Karl Gerhardt], and his loan of opportunity to the youth who became the
most brilliant of our actor-dramatists [William Gillette], and his eager pardon of the thoughtless girl who was near paying the penalty of her impertinence with the loss of her place, and his remembering that the insolent
brakeman got so few dollars a month, and his sympathy for working-men
standing up to money in their Unions, and even his pity for the wounded
bird throbbing out its little life on the grass for the pleasure of the cruel
fool who shot it. These and the thousand other charities and beneficences
in which he abounded, openly or secretly, may avail him more than the
discharge of his firm's liabilities with the Judge of all the Earth, who surely
will do right, but whose measures and criterions no man knows, and I least
of all men. . . .

When Clemens returned to America with his family, after lecturing
round the world, I again saw him in New York, where I so often saw him
while he was shaping himself for that heroic enterprise. He would come to
me, and talk sorrowfully over his financial ruin, and picture it to himself as
the stuff of some unhappy dream, which, after long prosperity, had culminated the wrong way. It was very melancholy, very touching, but the sorrow to which he had come home from his long journey had not that forlorn
bewilderment in it. He was looking wonderfully well, and when I wanted
the name of his elixir, he said it was plasmon.[3] He was apt, for a man who
had put faith so decidedly away from him, to take it back and pin it to some
superstition, usually of a hygienic sort. Once, when he was well on in years,
he came to New York without glasses, and announced that he and all his
family, so astigmatic and myopic and old-sighted, had, so to speak, burned

their spectacles behind them upon the instruction of some sage who had found out that they were a delusion. The next time he came he wore spectacles freely, almost ostentatiously, and I heard from others that the whole Clemens family had been near losing their eyesight by the miracle worked in their behalf. Now, I was not surprised to learn that "the damned human race" was to be saved by plasmon, if anything, and that my first duty was to visit the plasmon agency with him, and procure enough plasmon to secure my family against the ills it was heir to for evermore. I did not immediately understand that plasmon was one of the investments which he had made from "the substance of things hoped for," and in the destiny of a disastrous disappointment. But after paying off the creditors of his late publishing firm, he had to do something with his money, and it was not his fault if he did not make a fortune out of plasmon. . . .

At Riverdale[4] they kept no carriage, and there was a snowy night when I drove up to their handsome old mansion in the station carryall, which was crusted with mud as from the going down of the Deluge after transporting Noah and his family from the Ark to whatever point they decided to settle at provisionally. But the good talk, the rich talk, the talk that could never suffer poverty of mind or soul, was there, and we jubilantly found ourselves again in our middle youth. It was the mighty moment when Clemens was building his engines of war for the destruction of Christian Science,[5] which superstition nobody, and he least of all, expected to destroy. It would not be easy to say whether in his talk of it his disgust for the illiterate twaddle of Mrs. Eddy's book,[6] or his admiration of her genius for organization was the greater. He believed that as a religious machine the Christian Science Church was as perfect as the Roman Church and destined to be more formidable in its control of the minds of men. He looked for its spread over the whole of Christendom, and throughout the winter he spent at Riverdale he was ready to meet all listeners more than half-way with his convictions of its powerful grasp of the average human desire to get something for nothing. The vacuous vulgarity of its texts was a perpetual joy to him, while he bowed with serious respect to the sagacity which built so securely upon the everlasting rock of human credulity and folly.

Notes

1. Twain wrote Howells on 19 October 1899 (*Twain-Howells Letters* 710): "*I* know how you feel! I've been in hell myself. You are there tonight."

2. After the failure of his publisher John Ballantyne and Co. in 1826, Scott pledged to repay the firm's indebtedness of £130,000.

3. A food supplement of powdered skim milk.

4. Twain rented the Appleton mansion overlooking the Hudson River in Riverdale, New York, from the summer of 1901 until the spring of 1903.

5. "Christian Science and the Book of Mrs. Eddy," *Cosmopolitan* 27 (October 1899): 585–93. See also Twain's *Christian Science* (1907).

6. *Science and Health* (1875) by Mary Baker Eddy (1821–1910), the founder of the Church of Christian Science.

W. D. Howells, from *My Mark Twain* (New York: Harper & Bros., 1910), 54–55, 81–84.

From *A Lifetime with Mark Twain: The Memories of Katy Leary* (1925)

MARY LAWTON

Within six weeks Twain was in the news again for protesting the excessive fare of a cabman who carried his maid from Grand Central Station to his home near Washington Square. Catherine (Katy) Leary (1856–1934) worked for the Clemens family from 1880 until Twain's death in 1910.

IT WAS ABOUT THIS TIME [November 1900] that I had trouble with a cabman. I'd been up to Hartford to get some things, and when I got back into the Grand Central Station, I didn't know enough to take a cab inside (they used to have cabs on the inside then); I went outside and called the first cab I seen. I didn't have no baggage—just a little satchel in my hand. I told the cabman to take me down quick to 14 West Tenth Street. Well, he just took me all over New York instead! I didn't know the city very well then, but I did know that I shouldn't be ridin' all through Central Park! Up and down he took me, all over Central Park! Finally, after I hollered to him, he took me down to Tenth Street.

I was pretty mad, but I only said, "How much is it?" Then he said, very sharp, "Seven dollars!" Well, I nearly fainted! I didn't have only two dollars in my purse, so I says: "Just you wait a minute. I'll go and get the money for you." I rang and the butler let me in, but Mr. Clemens, it happened, was standin' right there in the hall when I opened the door, so I just burst out and says:

"Oh, Mr. Clemens! That cabman outside wants to charge seven dollars for bringing me down here."

"What?" said Mr. Clemens. "Bring him right inside, Katy." Then he put his head out the front door and shouted to the man, "Bring in your tariff!"

Well, the cabman brought it in and Mr. Clemens looked at it and says, "Young man, you're entitled to exactly seventy-five cents—for bringing this woman down here—just seventy-five cents," he says.

[233]

"Yes," I said, "and you told me it would be *seven dollars!*"

The cabman was pretty scared by that time, for he said: "Oh, you didn't understand me! I only said *five* dollars."

"Well," says Mr. Clemens, "we can't hear no more about it," he says. "You can just take this dollar and be off! But," he says, "I think I'd better know who you work for." The cabman was mad, but he told him, of course. Then Mr. Clemens says, "Is this your own cab?"

"No," says the man, "I'm working for my boss."

"Well," says Mr. Clemens, "you take this dollar and if your boss ain't satisfied with that, report to me in the morning." And then Mr. Clemens added, "If you don't report to me, I'll report *you,* for the way you've acted."

The man started to go and he kind of muttered to himself, "The old damned fool!"

Oh! Then Mr. Clemens said, "I heard you, I heard you, and you'll hear in the morning from me!"

Of course the man never came back, but Mr. Clemens was pretty mad at his ridin' me all over the park and trying to cheat me; so he had the cabman arrested and his license taken away. Oh, we had a great time! The trial was down at the City Hall and the judge was a friend of Mr. Clemens, and they said I'd have to appear, too. But they didn't ask me a word, so I didn't have to say anything. Of course, by that time everybody heard about it and the room with just crowded. Lots and lots of reporters. They was even settin' up on the windows and on everything, these reporters was, while the trial was going on. The cabman told his story—Bock was his name—how I'd engaged him and that the regular fare was five dollars; and then Mr. Clemens spoke right up and says: "He's a regular pirate! A pirate and no mistake!"[1]

I can't remember all the trial, but they pointed me out and says the man was guilty; that they would take his license away; how he'd insulted Mr. Clemens at his door, and the whole thing. Then the cabman says: "Well, I have to stand outside the station while them cabs inside get all the first jobs, the best ones; and sometimes I have to stand outside for hours and don't get anything; so when I do get a job, I have to make it pay!"

"That's enough," said Mr. Clemens. "That's all I want to know. That's all you need to say. Didn't I tell you that they was regular pirates? Here is this poor woman," says Mr. Clemens, "that he tried to cheat out of all that money. She's workin' for me and I pay the bills; but I wasn't goin' to pay such a pirate bill as *that*! I paid that man one dollar and he was only entitled to seventy-five cents."

Well, Mr. Clemens read the riot act after that, said what pirates these cab drivers was, how they robbed people, and it made a great impression in New York. There was a lot in the papers about it, and it really made the cab drivers look out a little bit and behave themselves after that.

When the trial was over, Mrs. Clemens and Miss Clara came down there, and I says: "Well, it's over and it's all beautiful and I didn't have to say a word! Mr. Clemens, he done all the talking." So we all got into a cab and they brought me home in triumph!

A little while after that, I was going down the street and a man who had been watching me come out of the house, stepped up, and says, "Is your name Leary, and are you the woman who had trouble with the cab driver?"

I says, "Yes, and Mr. Clemens took his license away from him."

"Well," this man says, "that cab driver is really a nice young man but his boss is a rascal, and he has to turn in just so much money or else lose his job. And his mother is a widow and he's her only support."

Oh, that made me feel awful, thinkin' I was the cause of it! "He hasn't any work now," this man says, "and don't know where to get any work, because he's a cabman and can't do anything else."

Of course, I went right home and told Mr. Clemens.

"Why, I'll get his address," said Mr. Clemens. "I'll fix that up all right, Katy." So Mr. Clemens sent for the man and paid him for the time he'd been idle since he was arrested, and had the judge or whoever it was took the license away, give it back, and he got a new job. Now, wasn't that lovely of Mr. Clemens? He gave him good advice and talked to him for about an hour, Mr. Clemens did—had the cabman up in the Billiard Room, talking to him, and I guess he made a real good man of Mr. Bock. But that was always Mr. Clemens's way. He never could bear to see anybody in trouble.

Note

1. According to news accounts of the trial, the owner of the cab company, Michael Byrne, misconstrued Twain's language. To Byrne's claim that cabbies deserved "special privileges," Twain "bristled up. His eyes flashed. 'The pirate can make that argument,' he interjected. This caused laughter. The cab owner did not take it as a joke. His face became livid. 'We have been repeating parrot talk yourself,' he exclaimed. Mark Twain did not no-

tice that 'pirate' had been twisted into 'parrot'" ("Mark Twain Bests a Grasping Cabman," *New York World,* 23 November 1900, 12; repr. in Scharnhorst 380–81).

Mary Lawton, from *A Lifetime with Mark Twain: The Memories of Katy Leary* (New York: Harcourt, Brace, 1925), 196–200.

From *A Roving Commission* (1930)

WINSTON CHURCHILL

> When Winston Churchill (1874–1965), the hero of the second Boer War and future British prime minister, lectured the evening of 12 December 1900 in the grand ballroom of the Waldorf-Astoria in New York, Twain was invited to introduce him. He began by acknowledging that "Mr. Churchill and I do not agree on the righteousness of the South African war, but that is of no consequence. There is no place where people all think alike—well, there is heaven; there they do, but let us hope it won't be so always" (repr. in Fatout, *Mark Twain Speaking*, 367–69). Churchill later remembered the occasion.

MY OPENING LECTURE in New York was under the auspices of no less a personage than "Mark Twain" himself. I was thrilled by this famous companion of my youth. He was now very old and snow-white, and combined with a noble air a most delightful style of conversation. Of course we argued about the war. After some interchanges I found myself beaten back to the citadel, "My country right or wrong." "Ah," said the old gentleman, "when the poor country is fighting for its life, I agree. But this was not your case." I think however I did not displease him; for he was good enough at my request to sign every one of the thirty volumes of his works for my benefit; and in the first volume he inscribed the following maxim intended, I daresay, to convey a gentle admonition: "To do good is noble; to teach others to do good is nobler, and no trouble."

Winston Churchill, from *A Roving Commission* (New York: Scribner's, 1930), 360.

From *Autobiography of Andrew Carnegie* (1920)

ANDREW CARNEGIE

> Twain also befriended the American industrialist and philanthropist Andrew Carnegie (1835–1919).

NONE OF MY FRIENDS hailed my retirement from business more warmly than Mark Twain. I received from him the following note, at a time when the newspapers were talking much about my wealth.

> [6 February 1901] Dear Sir and Friend:
>
> You seem to be prosperous these days. Could you lend an admirer a dollar and a half to buy a hymn-book with? God will bless you if you do; I feel it, I know it. So will I. If there should be other applications this one not to count.
>
> Yours
Mark
>
> P.S. Don't send the hymnbook, send the money. I want to make the selection myself.
>
> M.

When he was lying ill in New York I went to see him frequently, and we had great times together, for even lying in bed he was as bright as ever. One call was to say good-bye, before my sailing for Scotland. The Pension Fund for University Professors was announced in New York soon after I sailed. A letter about it from Mark, addressed to "Saint Andrew," reached me in Scotland, from which I quote the following:

> You can take my halo. If you had told me what you had done when at my bedside you would have got it there and then. It is pure tin and paid "the duty" when it came down.

Those intimate with Mr. Clemens (Mark Twain) will certify that he was one of the charmers. . . . The public only knows one side of Mr. Clemens— the amusing part. Little does it suspect that he was a man of strong convictions upon political and social questions and a moralist of no mean order. For instance, upon the capture of Aguinaldo by deception,[1] his pen was the most trenchant of all. Junius was weak in comparison.

The gathering to celebrate his seventieth birthday was unique. The literary element was there in force, but Mark had not forgotten to ask to have placed near him the multi-millionaire, Mr. H. H. Rogers, one who had been his friend in need.[2] Just like Mark. Without exception, the leading literary men dwelt in their speeches exclusively upon the guest's literary work. When my turn came, I referred to this and asked them to note that what our friend had done as a man would live as long as what he had written. Sir Walter Scott and he were linked indissolubly together. Our friend, like Scott, was ruined by the mistakes of partners, who had become hopelessly bankrupt. Two courses lay before him. One the smooth, easy, and short way—the legal path. Surrender all your property, go through bankruptcy, and start afresh. This was all he owed to creditors. The other path, long, thorny, and dreary, a life struggle, with everything sacrificed. There lay the two paths and this was his decision:

"Not what I owe my creditors, but what I owe to myself is the issue."

There are times in most men's lives that test whether they be dross or pure gold. It is the decision made in the crisis which proves the man. Our friend entered the fiery furnace a man and emerged as a hero. He paid his debts to the utmost farthing by lecturing around the world. "An amusing cuss, Mark Twain," is all very well as a popular verdict, but what of Mr. Clemens the man and the hero, for he is both and in the front rank, too, with Sir Walter.

He had a heroine in his wife. She it was who sustained him and traveled the world round with him as his guardian angel, and enabled him to conquer as Sir Walter did. This he never failed to tell to his intimates. Never in my life did three words leave so keen a pang as those uttered upon my first call after Mrs. Clemens passed away. I fortunately found him alone and while my hand was still in his, and before one word had been spoken by either, there came from him, with a stronger pressure of my hand, these words: "A ruined home, a ruined home." The silence was unbroken. I write this years after, but still I hear the words again and my heart responds.

Notes

1. Twain was severely critical of American military strategy in the Philippines. See the *New York Times Saturday Review of Books,* 17 November 1900, 789. See also Twain's unfinished review of Edwin Wildman's biography of Emilio Aguinaldo, first published in Zwick 88–108.

2. Henry Huttleston Rogers (1840–1909), vice president of Standard Oil Co. and one of Twain's best friends since 1893, helped to sort out Twain's finances after his bankruptcy.

Andrew Carnegie, from *Autobiography of Andrew Carnegie* (Boston: Houghton Mifflin, 1920), 294–97.

From *Roses and Buckshot* (1946)

JAMES MONTGOMERY FLAGG

> The American artist and illustrator James Montgomery Flagg (1877–1960)
> executed a portrait of Twain for permanent exhibition in the Lotos Club of
> New York, a literary association founded in 1870. Twain once referred to it as
> "the ace of clubs." See also "Lotos Dinner to Mark Twain," *New York Times,*
> 10 November 1893, 8.

WHEN DR. [WILLIAM WALLACE] WALKER said that the Lotos Club would give
me a life membership for my portrait of Twain, it was in the bag. Willie
had to do some tall talking to get Twain to pose for a portrait, but in spite
of the old gent's saying he would "rather have smallpox than sit for his picture" he finally consented. So I spent several Sunday mornings with Twain
painting and listening. He told me stories in his drawl and I got laughing so
I couldn't paint. We were in his room at the back of the old house on West
10th Street, which was connected with the front room by a long passage.
He could tip his chair back and see Mrs. Clemens sewing in her room in
the front. He had been cussing softly, then he said to me:

"My wife cusses too, not the same words. *She* says 'Sugar!' and the Recording Angel will give her just as black marks as he does me!"

William Dean Howells and Poultney Bigelow, the pal of Willie Hohenzollern,[1] would come in and they'd all get talking. I found it so interesting I'd forget all about painting. I had just enough sense to keep my trap
shut and listen. I have a hazy remembrance that these men were planning
some scheme for a vast celebration which involved Queen Victoria. Mark
Twain had just come back from a lecture tour of the world from which he
had made $100,000 in order to pay the debts of his publisher—debts he
wasn't responsible for. And all this in his old age. The creditors were paid
in full.

He had a funny way of spreading his mail in a long row on the floor,
walking down the line and choosing letters he thought he wanted to look
at. He said he was glad I hadn't given him "society" eyebrows. One of his

longhorn eyebrows turned up and the other one turned down. Howells, looking at my finished portrait, said:

"You've got Sam at his stormiest!"

He had a house on the [Fifth] Avenue in later years, and I often saw him standing in his area, or areaway, as old New Yorkers called the sunken space leading to the tradesman's entrance. Occasionally he would be talking to his old Negro butler. He always was dressed in white, and with his white mane he wasn't a figure to forget. He explained his clothes by saying:

"I don't like to be conspicuous, but I *do* like to be the most noticeable person!"

Maisie La Shelle,[2] years later, told me the best story about Mark Twain. Mark and Howells were in the front row at the old Academy hearing Adelina Patti in some opera. Howells noticed the wicked leer in Mark's eye and questioned him. Mark, heaving a big sigh, said through his teeth in Howells's ear:

"I would rather sleep with that woman *stark naked* than with General Grant in full uniform!"

Mark himself told me a story about an Englishman in a tough saloon in the Far West, a tenderfoot; there was only one other customer, a beefy, unself-conscious, uninhibited cow-person who leaned on the bar and ran the gamut of animal noises. Starting with a sneeze, a cough, and an expectoration, he startled the Britisher, who edged down the bar with astonished and popping eyes. The cow-person went blandly through his astounding repertory, closing with a burping arpeggio closely followed by the finale—a blast as deep and as rounded as the lowest note of the trombone in mating season, and so loud that the bottles and glasses clinked on the shelves. A cryptic, conceited smile combined with an unfocused gleam of satisfaction spread on the cow-person's red face. The Britisher had by now edged right up to the virtuoso and had leaned forward to look with stark admiration into the Westerner's puss. "I sa-a-y! Tell me, my good fellow," murmured the astonished Britisher, "can you do something with your navel?"

Notes

1. Prince William of Hohenzollern (1882–1951), the last crown prince of Prussia and the German empire, abdicated in 1918.

2. Maisie La Shelle, wife of the theatrical producer Kirke La Shelle (1862–1905).

James Montgomery Flagg, from *Roses and Buckshot* (New York: Putnam's, 1946), 168–70.

From *My Mark Twain* (1910)

W. D. HOWELLS

> Howells remembered his visits with Twain early in the new century.

HE HAD BEGUN . . . to amass those evidences against mankind which eventuated with him in his theory of what he called "the damned human race." This was not an expression of piety, but of the kind contempt to which he was driven by our follies and iniquities as he had observed them in himself as well as in others. It was as mild a misanthropy, probably, as ever caressed the objects of its malediction. But I believe it was about the year 1900 that his sense of our perdition became insupportable and broke out in a mixed abhorrence and amusement which spared no occasion, so that I could quite understand why Mrs. Clemens should have found some compensation, when kept to her room by sickness, in the reflection that now she should not hear so much about "the damned human race." He told of that with the same wild joy that he told of overhearing her repetition of one of his most inclusive profanities, and her explanation that she meant him to hear it so that he might know how it sounded. The contrast of the lurid blasphemy with her heavenly whiteness should have been enough to cure any one less grounded than he in what must be owned was as fixed a habit as smoking with him. When I first knew him he rarely vented his fury in that sort, and I fancy he was under a promise to her which he kept sacred till the wear and tear of his nerves with advancing years disabled him. Then it would be like him to struggle with himself till he could struggle no longer and to ask his promise back, and it would be like her to give it back. His profanity was the heritage of his boyhood and young manhood in social conditions and under the duress of exigencies in which everybody swore about as impersonally as he smoked. It is best to recognize the fact of it, and I do so the more readily because I cannot suppose the Recording Angel really minded it much more than that Guardian Angel of his. It probably grieved them about equally, but they could equally forgive it. Nothing came of his pose regarding "the damned human race" except his invention of the Human

Race Luncheon Club. This was confined to four persons who were never all got together, and it soon perished of their indifference. . . .

During the summer he spent at York Harbor [1902] I was only forty minutes away at Kittery Point, and we saw each other often; but this was before the last time at Riverdale. He had a wide, low cottage in a pine grove overlooking York River, and we used to sit at a corner of the veranda farthest away from Mrs. Clemens's window, where we could read our manuscripts to each other, and tell our stories, and laugh our hearts out without disturbing her. At first she had been about the house, and there was one gentle afternoon when she made tea for us in the parlor, but that was the last time I spoke with her. After that it was really a question of how soonest and easiest she could be got back to Riverdale; but, of course, there were specious delays in which she seemed no worse and seemed a little better, and Clemens could work at a novel he had begun. He had taken a room in the house of a friend and neighbor, a fisherman and boatman; there was a table where he could write, and a bed where he could lie down and read; and there, unless my memory has played me one of those constructive tricks that people's memories indulge in, he read me the first chapters of an admirable story. The scene was laid in a Missouri town, and the characters such as he had known in boyhood; but as often as I tried to make him own it, he denied having written any such story; it is possible that I dreamed it, but I hope the MS. will yet be found.[1] . . .

My perspectives are not very clear, and in the foreshortening of events which always takes place in our review of the past I may not always time things aright. But I believe it was not until he had taken his house at 21 Fifth Avenue that he began to talk to me of writing his autobiography. He meant that it should be a perfectly veracious record of his life and period; for the first time in literature there should be a true history of a man and a true presentation of the men the man had known. As we talked it over the scheme enlarged itself in our riotous fancy. We said it should be not only a book, it should be a library, not only a library, but a literature. It should make good the world's loss through Omar's barbarity at Alexandria; there was no image so grotesque, so extravagant that we did not play with it; and the work so far as he carried it was really done on a colossal scale. But one day he said that as to veracity it was a failure; he had begun to lie, and that if no man ever yet told the truth about himself it was because no man ever could. How far he had carried his autobiography I cannot say; he dictated the matter several hours each day; and the public has already seen long passages from it,[2] and can judge, probably, of the make and matter of the whole from these. It is immensely inclusive, and it observes no order or sequence. Whether now, after his death, it will be published soon or late I have no means of knowing. Once or twice he said in a vague way that it was not to be published for twenty years, so that the discomfort of publicity might be minimized for all the survivors. Suddenly he told me he was not working at it; but I did not understand whether he had finished it or merely dropped it; I never asked.

Notes

1. Probably the so-called Schoolhouse Hill version of "The Mysterious Stranger," written in November–December 1898.

2. Twain published twenty-five installments of his *Autobiography* in the *North American Review* between September 1906 and December 1907.

W. D. Howells, from *My Mark Twain* (New York: Harper & Bros., 1910), 76–77, 90, 92–93.

From *One Afternoon with Mark Twain* (1939)

GEORGE ADE

The American humorist and journalist George Ade (1866–1944) remembered a visit with Twain in 1902 in company with Clarence C. Rice (1855–1935), a family friend and the Clemens family physician.

IT WAS IN THE LATE SUMMER or early autumn of 1902, as nearly as I can fix the date, when Dr. Clarence C. Rice, a long-time friend and traveling-companion of Mark Twain's, came to me at my hotel in New York City and invited me to accompany him on a pilgrimage to the One and Only.

Of course I accepted the invitation. Probably no person then alive and gifted with a pair of movable legs would have done otherwise. And especially so myself. For a good many years I had been waiting and hoping to meet Mark Twain. I think I had read everything he ever wrote. With great admiration and respect I had witnessed his "comeback" in the early nineties, during which he repaid a mountainous debt as a matter of honor, not of personal legal responsibility.

How unappreciative we often are, at the time, of the red-letter days in our lives! I cannot say that I was not impressed with the importance of the invitation to visit Mark Twain. I certainly was. But what was in my mind at the time was the belief that he would live for many more years; and that, having met him on this occasion with Dr. Rice, I would later visit him alone and at greater length.

My recollection is that I planned to have the next visit take the form of a newspaperman's interview. I knew that such an article would be in ready demand at a good price. But it was not the money I wanted; it was the honor of having written an article about Mark Twain, all-time Dean of American Literature, commanding figure in this country and throughout the world. Kipling had done a fine job of his interview with Twain in Elmira in 1890, as published in *From Sea to Sea* in 1899.[1] Probably I was just enough conceited in those days to make a try at outdoing Kipling. I can't remember as to this. Time mercifully blots from our memories any of the follies of early life.

Although, at that time, I was regarded in some quarters as being a bit of a humorist myself, I do definitely recall that I had no thought of conferring with Mark Twain as a fellow fun-maker. Beside his towering fame, my own stature was something like that of a child's mud-pie man, placed alongside the statue of Rodin's "Thinker."

And thus it happened that I made no notes recording the details of the most momentous meeting of my life. I went; I saw and heard; I came away. The tragic events of the few remaining years of Mark Twain's life made it impossible for me ever to talk with him again. I never wrote that master-piece of an interview I was going to write. I have never before set down on paper the few impressions of our one meeting that still remain fixed in my mind.

Yes, if I had known that I was never again to meet Mark Twain, I would have come provided with a handful of pencils and my pockets bulging with copy paper. I would have carefully recorded the date, the state of the weather—every word he spoke, every trifling detail of that pilgrimage to the shrine of this immortal American.

Vaguely, I can recall that Dr. Rice and I journeyed up the Hudson by rail and alighted at a station which should have been named Riverdale. I was being escorted by Dr. Rice and paid little attention to the route. I don't even remember what kind of a vehicle it was that met us at the station and carried us up to a delightful, rambling, homey-looking old house on a hill-side, surrounded by huge, wide-branching trees.

He stood alone on the porch, waiting to greet us. I can recall that he wore a white or tan-colored suit, loose and comfortable-looking, but not ill-fitting. From the moment that he took my hand in his firm clasp, he was the soul of kindliness, cordiality, and affability. I can recall only his eyes. I lack words to describe them. Probably the word "imperious" comes close to describing the calm, penetrating, unwavering gaze he enveloped me with during the first few moments of our meeting. I was several inches taller than he, so that he must have looked upward into my eyes: yet I did not sense the difference in height. It seemed, indeed, as if he were looking downward on me.

We seated ourselves in roomy rocking-chairs on the porch. Courteously, Mark Twain asked about my trip to New York. He remarked that he and I would have been born in adjacent states if the damned geographers had not maliciously thrust Illinois between Indiana and Missouri. From then on,

Dr. Rice and I did little talking. Our host was happy, expansive. He began his discourse by warning me that I was soon to be made the victim of a fantastic plan, evolved by a woman of family acquaintance, to translate some of my "Fables in Slang" into French.

"She cannot possibly find any French equivalents for your specimens of American vernacular," said Mr. Clemens, "but she is determined to make the effort and I am waiting until it is done so that I can watch some Frenchman go crazy while trying to read it."

I mentioned to him the fact that the "Jumping Frog" had been done into French, with disastrous results, and I said that I would not be a party to turning the "Fables" into that language.

Mr. Clemens advised me to keep quiet and let her go ahead and tackle what he, too, knew to be the impossible. Somehow, I gained the impression that, by keeping the lady occupied, indefinitely, with the task of turning the "Fables" into French, Mr. Clemens would be grateful to me. Possibly she had been pressing him hard to turn some of his own tales, in the vernacular, into that language. . . .

We must have spent a couple of hours there on the front porch, rocking and smoking. Dr. Rice and I answered an occasional question, but our answers served only to start Mr. Clemens on a new train of thought. He dwelt for some time on the theme of the great middle west. In me he knew he had an appreciative listener; a product of Mississippi Valley soil like himself; one who spoke his language and who was in full understanding of his tales of life on the River.

We talked for a time about William Dean Howells, in whom Mr. Clemens and I had a mutual friend. Probably no man was closer to Mark Twain, during his active writing career, than was Howells. And it chanced that I had formed an overwhelming regard for Mr. Howells because it was he who "discovered" me and who was the first to encourage me at the time when my realistic little yarns in the *Chicago Record* first began to appear. I have sometimes wondered if it were not Mr. Howells who secretly engineered that surprise invitation given me by Dr. Rice to visit Mark Twain.

Then, drawling and puffing slowly on his pipe, Mark Twain was again in Hannibal. I wish I could remember only a few of the many tales he poured forth with scarcely a pause between them. Never was there a show of haste or evidence of a desire to speed the arrival of the point of a story. That was reserved (frequently for several slow puffs) until the listener became half-maddened with curiosity. Twain was the world's supreme master of suspense in oral delivery. He knew how to make one second of silence outweigh a hundred words. But the trick is to know just how to build up to that period of silence; and to inject it between exactly the right words. I suppose in these days it is called "timing." I tried the device once at a banquet in telling an anecdote. The audience is still wondering as to where the point of the tale came in.

One boyhood escapade he told us about that afternoon I do remember. It concerned Sam Clemens and his associate Tom Sawyers and Huck Finns. I have since seen the story in some of Twain's books,[2] but at that time it was new to me and no presentation of the tale, in cold type, can picture the incident as did Mark Twain in his oral recitation of it.

Atop a high hill that hangs over Hannibal there was a large boulder, partly imbedded in the earth. Sam Clemens and his gang, after hours of labor, managed to loosen this boulder and topple it over the edge of the hill. Down it went, a huge, irresistible engine of destruction. It hurdled a half-sunken roadway on which a horse and wagon were then passing. It kept on until it crashed into one wall of a planing-mill and came out through the other.

Mr. Clemens here paused in his recital, his eyes narrowed to slits, his gaze fixed on the shining expanse of the Hudson River that lay before us. He seemed to be thinking of those far-off days of his boyhood on the Mississippi. Dr. Rice and I waited until the silence had endured beyond the point where it could be regarded as the familiar suspense device. We were burning with curiosity to learn the rest of the story.

"Where did the boulder stop?" I ventured to ask.

"I lost so much interest in that boulder after it hit the planing mill that I never took the trouble to ask," answered Mr. Clemens.

"Anybody killed?" asked Dr. Rice.

"Not in the mill," he answered, "but it has brought a lingering death to those boys on the hill. Several of us half-died with fright right on the spot. Others have since completely died. I will probably be cut down somewhere around my one-hundredth birthday. We were so frightened that we entered into a solemn vow never to reveal the source of the agitation causing that boulder to act the way it did. I have kept my vow to this day."

If any other members of the Clemens family were at home during the period of our visit, we did not have the pleasure of meeting them. We merely sat and listened to that matchless, unhurried recital of fact, fancy, and philosophizing on men and affairs as it issued from Mark Twain.

Why can't I recall more of the things he said! I can explain my failure only by saying that I must have fallen completely under the spell of his bewitching personality. And I was a traveled citizen of the world at that time. I had met many celebrities in this country and abroad. I came into Mark Twain's presence with the realization that I was to meet an exceptional individual. I came away with the realization that I had just met and talked with *the* individual then alive.

In one respect, Mark Twain did not conform to my expectations. Like all the rest of the world, I had come to regard him as an ever-jovial humorist, judging him solely by his writings. But Mark Twain in the flesh was grave, almost solemn. His flashes of wit, the tales that he told that afternoon, were unaccompanied by the slightest trace of a smile. Except occasionally, when his eyes seemed to be afire in discussing some incident of man's inhumanity to man, his slow, thoughtful manner of speaking was tinged with plaintiveness, almost sadness.

Notes

1. Originally printed in "Rudyard Kipling on Mark Twain," *New York Herald*, 17 August 1890, 5; repr. in Scharnhorst 117–26.

2. Ade apparently had read about the episode in chapter 58 of *The Innocents Abroad*.

George Ade, from *One Afternoon with Mark Twain* (Chicago: Mark Twain Society, 1939), 5–13.

From *Companions on the Trail:*
A Literary Chronicle (1931)

Hamlin Garland

> Hamlin Garland fondly recalled an evening with Twain in Riverdale when Livy
> was in frail health and his daughter Jean had begun to suffer from seizures.

LATE IN FEBRUARY 1903, Clemens, who had taken a house in Riverdale, invited my wife and me to dinner, an invitation which we instantly and joyously accepted, for we had never seen him in his home. We reached the Riverdale station about seven of a rainy night, and as the only conveyance in sight was a musty hack, we took it. As we clattered up the hill and through a dark wood, we seemed a thousand miles from Manhattan. We came at last to an old-fashioned mansion surrounded by tall, bare-branched elm trees—a drab and lonesome place, with which I could not associate Mark Twain. As we entered the bright hall, however, he came running down the stairway with amazing agility to meet us. He presented us to his daughters with a wave of his hand—ceremony and conventions did not much count with him.

We were the only guests, and at dinner he did all of the talking, for we were there to listen. Like Roosevelt, he monologued to some purpose, and his purpose that night appeared to be our entertainment. He touched upon cockroaches, June bugs, Mississippi River steamboats, and other subjects of humorous exaggeration, then described his recent trip to St. Louis and Hannibal,[1] all in characteristic drawl. "I was provided with an old sweetheart in every town," he said. "They seated these candidates beside me on the platform, nice old ladies who firmly believed they were Becky." We laughed until our sides ached when he most deftly fought an imaginary beetle. Every sentence he uttered was salable. He loved to turn a neat phrase and his remarks were often deliciously unexpected. Our laughter appeared to stimulate him. That his daughters were almost equally amused was evi-

[251]

dent, although I wondered how they could retain their ability to laugh in the midst of such abounding, unending humor.

After the ladies rose, Mark's delightful fooling ceased. With somber intonation he said, "We are only a kind of private hospital here. Mrs. Clemens is shut away from us by the doctor's orders—I'm allowed to see her only a few minutes each day—and Jean is not well."

He led the way to his library, and after he had lighted his pipe, I started him on another tack by asking, "What are you doing?"

"I am still investigating Mrs. Eddy and her papacy," he replied. Fetching a book from his table he handed it to me. "Examine that. It's one of the early copies of her book. Did you ever see a worse job of printing? It has the quality of a seed catalogue. I'm not objecting to her theory of mental healing—I'm inclined to believe in it—but I intend to expose her business methods." He then passed into a scathing denunciation of the "close corporation" which she or her advisors had formed to exploit her book. "She has a genius for monopoly," he said, a statement which has since been amplified by Dakin's biography.[2]

Knowing very little about this publishing scheme, I listened to his scorching diatribe without comment, but I could see that he was deep in the problem and in characteristic fashion was "making it smoke." He talked to me without seeing me—I was only an excuse for his thinking out loud. I never once saw his eyes—so deeply hidden were they under his shaggy eyebrows—and I cannot say even now what their color was.

Notes

1. In late May–early June 1902 Twain returned for the final time to Missouri, specifically to St. Louis, Hannibal, and Columbia, where he was awarded an honorary Doctor of Laws degree by the University of Missouri on 4 June 1902.

2. Twain refers to Edwin Franden Dakin's *Mrs. Eddy: The Biography of a Virginal Mind* (1929).

Hamlin Garland, from *Companions on the Trail: A Literary Chronicle* (New York: Macmillan, 1931), 192–94.

"Mark Twain: Personal Impressions" (1910)

Henry M. Alden

> Henry Mills Alden (1836–1919), the editor of *Harper's Monthly* from 1869 until his death, remembered a dinner in Twain's honor at the Metropolitan Club in New York on 23 October 1903.

AT A DINNER celebrating his birthday, though not on the exact date—only men being present, and all of them his personal friends—after having recounted in his most humorous vein many vivid and laughter-provoking early experiences of his in the West, he spoke of his approaching departure to Italy with his wife, in terms that clearly indicated his apprehension as to her health, and his hopes of its restoration through the change of scene and climate, concluding with these words: "This is *her* birthday."

I thought then of this homely side of the man's nature, of which the world at large knew scarcely anything; I thought of what he had suffered, in reverses of fortune, in private griefs and solicitudes, and how these sorrows had developed those sweeter traits of the man's personality which bind all men more closely to him, and which should yield new graces and values to his imaginative work.

Years before, I had seen him in his Hartford home. Up in his billiard-room, in the twilight, he chatted familiarly about his little ones—two of his girls were then quite young. The family circle was as yet unbroken. I do not know what storms may even then have been gathering, threatening material security, but I think those Hartford years must have been the happiest of Mark Twain's life. All know what followed—bankruptcy, the brave struggle to pay all creditors in full, seventeen years of homelessness, the loss of all but one member of his family, and that one married, till, at the opening of the present year—his seventy-fifth—we behold him utterly alone, though closely pressed by the whole world's sympathy.

One thing he has never lost, even in the most restless moments of his life—his love of children. Wherever I have seen him, where these little ones were, he has sought them out, as if finding in them a restful solace—a refuge from all worldly conceits and masks and even from the grandeurs of his own imagination. What delicate entertainment he offers them, subduing his naïve grotesquery to meet their dainty imaginings, is their secret and his. His latest sketch—that of Marjorie Fleming[1]—betrays something of it.

Surely the last vintage of such a life must be the most exquisite. The *Autobiography* is yet to be completed. From the glimpses hitherto published—such, for instance, as he has given of "Susy's Diary"[2]—we may hope for rare disclosures of the more intimate side of his nature: also for disclosure equally rare of his speculation concerning life and the world.

Notes

1. Marjorie Fleming (1803–11), Scots child writer.
2. Twain quoted liberally from "Susy's Diary" in the installments of his *Autobiography* published in the *North American Review*.

Henry M. Alden, "Mark Twain: Personal Impressions," *Book News Monthly* 28 (April 1910): 582.

From *The Changing Years* (1930)

NORMAN HAPGOOD

Norman Hapgood's parents sailed across the Atlantic in company with Twain and Livy aboard the *Princess Irene,* which sailed from New York for Naples on 24 October 1903, the day after the farewell dinner and seven months before Livy's death. For the record, the report of their sailing in the *New York American* includes the detail that "Mr. and Mrs. Charles H. Hapgood, of Alton, Ohio," were "lifelong friends of the Clemenes" (25 October 1903, 40). Certainly they remained friends the remainder of Twain's life. The elder Hapgood and his wife, Fanny Powers Hapgood, were guests at Clara Clemens's wedding in 1909.

BEFORE HIS WIFE DIED there occurred an incident that brought into relief the kindly side that was always a large part of the man. My father and mother were crossing the ocean on the same ship as Mr. Clemens and his wife. Mrs. Clemens was in poor health, and her husband had requested my father not to talk with her when she was in her chair on deck. My father, who was the most scrupulous of men about the rights of other people, on the second day out found himself in a predicament. As he took his regular walk around the deck, Mrs. Clemens intentionally catching his eye, motioned him to come and speak to her. His decision had to be made quickly. The warning of Mr. Clemens was in his mind, but merely to bow and pass on, after so definite a request from Mrs. Clemens, would have looked like rudeness; so he decided to stop a mere instant, say a pleasant word or two, make an excuse, and continue his walk. By a coincidence, such as those that occur in fiction and in experience, at that very moment Mr. Clemens happened to come up. With all his calm and drawling manner, he was a man of sharp impulse, temper, and emotion. "I told you no one was to speak to her," he spoke out, almost or quite angrily. My father raised his hat, said merely, "I am sorry," and passed on.

Of course a word with his wife showed to Mark Twain the mistake he had made; and the result was what might have been expected by one who understood his moral nature. Every remaining evening of the voyage he sought out my father, asked him for a walk, and in order to make amends for his error called out all the resources of his sometimes wonderful conversation, resulting in an atonement that was more than complete.

Another example of human consideration was almost Quixotic. . . . It happened that I had a box for one of the plays of Eleonora Duse, and Mr. Clemens had accepted an invitation for himself, though not for his wife, as her health did not permit her to make the trip from Riverdale, where they were living, to New York. The worst snowstorm of the winter burst into the situation; it was hard enough even for New Yorkers to get to the theater; and it was only what I expected when the curtain went up without Mr. Clemens having appeared. During the intermission, however, after the first act, he did come in. "It was impossible to reach you," he said, "by telephone, or in time by telegram, so I have come to explain that Mrs. Clemens is so unwell this evening that I ought not to be away." He was an old man then; and he went out again into the storm and took the railway journey into the country, having remained true to the laws of courtesy, as his high standard conceived those laws.

Norman Hapgood, from *The Changing Years* (New York: Farrar & Rinehart, 1930), 202–11.

"Mark Twain from an Italian Point of View" (1904)

RAFFAELE SIMBOLI

> Raffaele Simboli, one of the editors of *Nuova Antologia*, visited Twain at the Villa di Quarto near Florence in the spring of 1904. Livy would die there on 5 June 1904.

HE IS A PASSIONATE LOVER of Italy, in which for years a number of American authors and artists have pitched their tents. Florence is the city especially affected by the Americans and English, who flock there in great numbers every year.

The most important personage in this group is Mark Twain, as the villa of his selection is the most sumptuous of them all. The Villa di Quarto lies in a charmingly picturesque spot not far from Florence. It has sheltered the most illustrious people, and all of them have admired its beauty, both natural and artificial—its magnificent grounds with broad avenues, fountains, and smiling gardens. An idea of its size—the circumference of the park is over two miles—may be given by saying that at one time a Russian princess lived there with a suite of one hundred persons. Victor Emmanuel II visited it frequently, as it is close to the royal country-seat of La Petraia.

Mark Twain was in Genoa in 1869, on his way back from Egypt and the Holy Land, and has spoken of it at some length in his *Innocents Abroad,* not forgetting some flattering words for its beautiful women. But Florence is the city of his choice—not because it is the birthplace of Dante, but because its delightful climate renews youth and gives health to the invalid. Ten years ago he spent some time at Settignano, where Gabriele d'Annunzio's villa is situated. Mr. Clemens came there worn out and ill, and went away in robust health of body and mind. He has now come back with his family in the hope of effecting a speedy and permanent improvement in his wife's health. He has leased the villa for a year, at the rental of twenty thousand francs—a figure which makes a deep impression on our Italian writers, who have never succeeded in getting rich, even when they have had their little quarter of an hour of celebrity or have taken a firmer hold on fame.

Mr. Clemens has a very retiring temperament, and the intimates who pass the gates of his villa are not many. At the end of November he completed his sixty-eighth year, but his old age has an extraordinary vigor and freshness. He is a remarkable person, who binds others to him by a sentiment which is almost more than friendship.

Mark Twain's life is regulated by a system. He takes but one meal a day, in the evening. All day long he is at work; during a good part of the night he strolls alone about the immense grounds of the villa, meditating and shaping in his mind the sketches which are destined to make future generations laugh and—to enrich his publishers. If you met him, you might think he was one of the ordinary people who are weary of life, and that he was turning over in his mind a plan for ending it once and for all. Instead of that, the brain of the man who walks there, silent amid the stillness of the night, is occupied by a rapid procession of memories of all the things which he has observed on the varied stages of human life. Out of this confused mass of visions and recollections, Mark Twain picks out the most delicious comic figures, which in the morning he will fix on paper with two or three of those sure touches that are the secret of his success as a writer. When the amount of his work becomes oppressive, he has a secretary, an intelligent American girl,[1] to whom he dictates letters and articles. Sometimes, if the day promises to be fine, he comes down into Florence with Clara and Jean, his idolized daughters, to enjoy the poetical beauty of the Arno and of the children playing on its bank. Often he stops and asks them some question; and the little Tuscan boys, lively and self-possessed, answer him in their charming dialect, of which the great humorist is very fond. This is his favorite method of learning Italian. . . .

It is uncertain how long the famous humorist will remain in Italy. His lease of the Villa di Quarto is only for a year, but Signora Massiglia, the owner, thinks that he will renew it when it expires, since he is so well and comfortable in Florence, and since his wife's health has already shown a marked improvement.[2]

Mrs. Clemens, his faithful companion for twenty-five [*sic*] years, unlike her husband, is an enthusiastic student of the masterpieces of art and of historical associations. Mark Twain has his own ideas about art, which are a subject of frequent controversy with his wife. She is a great admirer of Botticelli, while he stoutly maintains that the Pre-Raphaelite painters represent the infancy of art. "What would you say to the cook," so he puts it,

[258]

"if she still persisted in providing you, at your present age, with nothing but milk for breakfast, dinner, and supper?"

Few of Mark Twain's numerous volumes are known in Italy, outside of the *Personal Recollections of Joan of Arc,*[3] which met with considerable success. Translation, however accurate and conscientious, fails to render the special flavor of his work; and the result is only a lame copy in which the sparkle of true wit is lamentably absent. And then in Italy, where humorous writing generally either rests on a political basis or depends on risky phrases, Mark Twain's sketches are not appreciated because the spirit which breathes in them is not always understood. The story of the "Jumping Frog," for instance, famous as it is in America and England, has made little impression in France or Italy. Still, its author holds an unquestioned sovereignty in the realm of humor, and the newspapers have a stock of old things of his on hand, which they present to their readers as choice morsels. Even this is an homage on the part of Italy to the great writer who is sojourning within her gates; and everyone hopes that the sunny climate of the peninsula may restore Mrs. Clemens's health, and inspire her husband to give us another masterpiece.

Notes

1. Isabel Van Kleek Lyon (1863–1958), Twain's private secretary from 1902 until 1909.

2. Simboli was profoundly mistaken. Twain disparaged his American landlady, Countess Massiglia, in autobiographical dictation in January 1904: "She is excitable, malicious, malignant, vengeful, unforgiving, selfish, stingy, avaricious, coarse, vulgar, profane, obscene, a furious blusterer on the outside and at heart a coward. . . . It is good to be a real noble, it is good to be a real American, it is a calamity to be neither the one thing nor the other, a politico-social bastard on both counts" (Hill, *God's Fool,* 72). On 25 and 26 February 1904 he wrote Henry Rogers: "Well, we have been in a sweat for a month! The Countess Massiglia (the American bitch who owns this Villa) found that she could afflict me with all sorts of trivial and exasperating annoyances" (*Mark Twain's Correspondence with Henry Huttleston Rogers* 557–58).

3. Probably *Racconti Americani,* ed. Enrico Thovez (Milan: Edizione del Corriere della Sera, 1900).

Raffaele Simboli, "Mark Twain from an Italian Point of View," *Critic* 44 (June 1904): 518–24.

"Mark Twain on Friends and Fighters" (1906)

Samuel P. Davis

Twain and his daughters returned to the United States with Livy's body aboard the *Prince Oskar,* sailing from Naples on 28 June and arriving in New York on 12 July, 1904. She was buried in the family plot in Elmira on 14 July. Twain's publisher George B. M. Harvey (1864–1928) hosted 172 guests at a celebration of Twain's seventieth birthday at Delmonico's on Broadway in New York on 5 December, 1905. The proceedings were subsequently published as a supplement to the issue of *Harper's Weekly* for 23 December. Samuel Post Davis (1850–1920), owner and editor of the *Carson Daily Appeal,* attended the dinner and reminisced with Twain about Nevada over lunch a few days later.

AT THE RECENT DINNER given by Colonel Harvey in honor of the seventieth birthday of Mark Twain, the orator of the evening was, of course, the honored guest, and he was in his happiest vein of humor, philosophy, and pathos. His humor made us howl, his philosophy made us think, and his pathos made us cry. Regarding the sedate individuals who attempted to be funny because they thought the occasion required it, I have nothing to say. It is sufficiently sad even to think of them.

A few days later Mr. Twain was kind enough to invite me to lunch with him and asked me to bring along Mr. Philip Mighels,[1] as we were the only representatives of Nevada at the dinner, and he wanted to hear something of the old State where he had first begun to wake the laughter of the world.

As we started to find a little saloon on Fourteenth street, he wore a shocking battered hat and carried an umbrella that had a suspicious look, although he may have bought it somewhere.

We finally found the spot, and it looked for all the world like an old-time Nevada corner grocery with a little sawdust snuggery in the rear.

The proprietor nodded and smiled as Twain entered, and called him

Mark. He slid in behind a little round table, and then fitted his back into the corner and seemed like one braced there for the afternoon.

"Bring us everything you've got," he said, "and plenty of it. This cuisine is rather limited," he remarked, "and for that reason you have to order about everything to get much variety."

I made some inquiries regarding the sort of "variety" we might expect, and learned after a confidential talk with the waiter that the menu consisted of beer and ham sandwiches, and then more beer and more ham sandwiches.

After we had drained the first round of schooners Twain asked abruptly: "Is Steve Gillis still alive?"

"Yes, indeed, and as full of fight as ever."

"He was the most competent fighter I ever knew," continued Twain, in a reminiscent tone. "No man living could ever lick him of his weight, and it was seventy-five pounds when I last saw him."

"It is yet," I responded.

"Strange he never growed any. Kept fightin', so I guess he had no chance to gain any flesh. No seventy-five-pound man in the world ever had any business with Steve. Then there was a fellow named Furlong that was just as handy and just as willing, and he weighed seventy-five pounds, too, I think, if my memory is right."

"Weighs seventy-five and no more yet," remarked Mr. Mighels. "Saw him last summer on Winter's ranch in Washoe County."

"It's also true that no man of his weight could ever lick Furlong," continued Twain. "Now, I often wondered why those two pugnacious little bantams never bumped into each other. They would have made an interesting scrap."

"It would have been an interesting question to decide."

"What question were you speaking of?" asked Twain.

"As to which was the better man."

"How could there be any better man? No man of seventy-five pounds could lick Steve, and didn't you both admit that no seventy-five-pound man could lick Furlong? Then no question could have been decided. If they had started in when I lived there they'd been fightin' yet. No one in Nevada would ever interfere in such a fight. They'd be fightin' yet. I can't see any other logical outcome. I guess they had sense enough to realize that while they were occupied in that sort of a fight they couldn't be licking any other people and got shy of it."

This question having been so logically determined, some more beers and sandwiches were ordered, and the question of contracts arose.

"You can't be too careful in contracts," said Twain. "Every possible contingency should be covered. You have to rivet 'em on both sides and hammer the edges down tight and plug all the holes two or three times, and then if the d----- thing holds water you're in luck."

"You didn't have any such copper-riveted contract with Frank Mayo when he adapted *Pudd'nhead Wilson* to the stage?"[2]

"Of course not. No contract at all. I was speaking of contracts between mere people, but between *friends*—that's different. When they *are* friends. No contract needed there. The ink of contracts between friends smudges the friendship. Pity we don't find more people that we could do business with on a friendship basis. They are getting scarcer of late years. In the old days in Nevada a man's word went the route and all that a man's word implied. I read in the papers not long ago how a man named Jim Butler leased one hundred and fifty mining claims to one hundred and fifty miners, and all the leases were verbal and they all held. No trouble about any of them, and when the leases were up, although the miners were many of them clearing thousands a day out of their leases, they all quit at midnight, and there wasn't a word of dispute. Beautiful, wasn't it? They haven't forgotten to be men out there in that State where I spent so many pleasant days. Denis McCarthy, Joe Mallon, Sandy Baldwin, Rollin Daggett, Dan De Quille, all dead. God bless old Dan. I remember once that Rose Sissa, our landlady, took Dan to task for making such a noise when he got Daggett upstairs to bed. Dan said: 'Rose, if you can get a barrel of whiskey upstairs with any less noise than I do, just try it tomorrow night.' I never shall forget that."

Notes

1. Philip Verrill Mighels (1869–1911), a western American author.

2. A dramatic adaptation of *Pudd'nhead Wilson* starring Frank Mayo (1839–96) opened in Hartford on 8 April 1895 and in New York a week later.

Samuel P. Davis, "Mark Twain on Friends and Fighters," *Philadelphia North American*, 1 January 1906, 14.

From *Hardly a Man Is Now Alive* (1939)

DAN BEARD

> After returning to the United States, Twain lived first in a cottage in the Berkshires and then in a hotel near Washington Square before moving into a house at 21 Fifth Avenue. Dan Beard visited him there in early 1905.

WHEN I WAS EDITOR of *Recreation,* I heard that Mark Twain was ill. He then lived near Washington Square, and I immediately went down to see him. When the butler opening the door of the old-fashioned mansion I asked to see Mr. Clemens but was told very bluntly that Mr. Clemens was receiving *no* visitors. "Please take this card to him," said I, "and tell him I heard that he was ill and called to see how he is getting on." The butler left me standing and disappeared with the card, but when he returned he was bowing and smiling as he announced that Mr. Clemens wished to see me in his bedroom.

"Hello, D-a-a-n," was the drawling salutation I heard before I had entered the doorway of the bedchamber. "Come in. Take a cigar. I know they are good. I pay six dollars a barrel for them." The weather was cold, there was no fire in the old-fashioned open fireplace, but the butler appeared with Mr. Clemens's overcoat, which the white-haired philosopher donned over his pajamas as he arose. Then, slipping his feet into a pair of heelless slippers, he walked up and down the room, reading to me from a manuscript.

I exclaimed, "You are going to publish that, are you not, Mr. Clemens?"

"No, Dan," he replied. "I am telling the truth in that manuscript, and no man dares tell the truth until after he is dead. That will be published after I am buried." Speaking of the manuscript he had just read, he said that he had tried it on his daughter, his secretary, and his butler, and they were all shocked, declaring that the thing was sacrilegious and should never be published. "But," he continued, "without changing a word in the manuscript I tacked on a small paragraph, stating that a maniac had visited the church, and then everybody declared it was fine!" The title of the manuscript was "The Prayer."[1] . . .

While serving as president of that talented group of men known as the Society of Illustrators,[2] I launched a banquet to Mark Twain, but a note from his secretary to Mr. [Henry S.] Fleming, our secretary, said that Mr. Clemens could not attend. A smuggled note to Mark Twain himself, however, brought an immediate and cordial acceptance. I suggested to my fellow artists that we should have Joan of Arc there in full armor, with a real laurel wreath for Samuel Clemens. I insisted that we must get the prettiest girl in New York to act the part of the Maid of Orleans.

When the illustrators gave a banquet there was no dearth of celebrities. All invited were glad to come. Among those present on this occasion were Thomas A. Janvier, Frank Vanderlip, Norman Hapgood, Rollo Ogden, Sir C. Purdon Clarke, Arthur H. Scribner, Dr. E. L. Keyes, Willis Abbott, Andrew Carnegie, and Arthur Brisbane. Prominent among the illustrators were Charles Dana Gibson, Lucius Hitchcock,[3] E. W. Kemble, T. De Thulstrup,[4] A. B. Wenzell, and a jolly bunch of newspaper artists.

With such a crowd there was lots of life and gayety, even before Mark Twain entered the banquet hall. But everybody was anxiously waiting for Mark Twain himself to appear, which he did when coffee was being served and the orchestra was playing "My Old Kentucky Home." As he came through the curtains he was greeted with a spontaneous outburst of cheers.

When Mark Twain started to speak in his own inimitable manner he was interrupted by a medieval fanfare of trumpets, and suddenly and miraculously there appeared a lovely vision of a girl in a magnificent suit of glistening white armor. Proudly she bore a white satin cushion on which rested a classic wreath of laurel. Following Jeanne D'Arc was a page bearing a replica of the famous flag of old France dotted with the fleur-de-lis.

I thought that this would bring a roar of applause, but one never knows what the effect to such a spectacle will be. There was a sudden hush, no applause, only a deep and awed silence. Mark Twain stared at the girl as if he were gazing at a materialized spirit; his prominent Adam's apple worked up and down as if it were trying to pump air into his lungs, while he stood open-mouthed, transfixed by the vision. Sir C. Purdon Clarke, in mute astonishment, half arose from his chair, as did Arthur Brisbane, while Andrew Carnegie stood bolt upright, with big tears coursing down his chubby cheeks and splashing on his shirt front. Mark Twain could not utter a word until the spell was broken by the beautiful Maid of Orleans, who made a simple little speech as she handed the wreath to our guest of honor. I took the wreath and placed it on his frosty old head.

Notes

1. "The War Prayer" was rejected for publication by *Harper's Bazar* (as it was spelled at the time) in 1905. Twain wrote Beard soon afterward that "I don't think the prayer will be published in my time. None but the dead are permitted to tell the truth" (quoted in Zwick xxvii).

2. The Society of Illustrators dined at the Aldine Association on 21 December 1905. See also "Joan of Arc Appears to Startle Mark Twain," *New York Times,* 22 December 1905, 9.

3. Lucius Wolcott Hitchcock (1868–1942) illustrated Twain's "A Double Barrelled Detective Story" (1902) and "A Horse's Tale" (1907).

4. Thure de Thulstrup (1848–1930) illustrated Twain's *A Tramp Abroad.*

Dan Beard, from *Hardly a Man Is Now Alive* (New York: Doubleday, 1939), 342–43, 348–49.

"Innocents at Home" (1925)

ALBERT BIGELOW PAINE

> Paine later incorporated this essay into his authorized biography of Twain.

LIKE MOST BOYS of my time I was brought up in the company of Mark Twain. . . . That I should ever meet him, or even see him, never occurred to me. I would as soon have expected to meet Hercules. I was, in fact, well along in the middle years when I first saw him. A good many things had happened in the meantime, so that after all it came about naturally enough, at the Players' Club to which I belonged and where he had been invited to deliver the Founders' Night address. . . .

During a discussion of the matter he had told me of some autobiographical chapters which he had written, or dictated, from time to time, suggesting that these might be used as material. He had put aside the notion of an autobiography, but when on the morning of January 9, 1906, I arrived with a stenographer at 21 Fifth Avenue, his New York City home, he had been characteristically revising his plans, and proposed to continue dictating reminiscence instead of a sequence of notes, as we had arranged. He could not stick to the consecutive idea, he said; he could talk only of the thing interesting to him at the moment. At his suggestion the stenographer was already setting down his remarks. The dictation which was to continue intermittently through four years, the final years of his life, had begun. "This is no holiday excursion," he said. "It is a journey." And then he added:

"We will try this—see whether it is dull or interesting—whether it will bore us and we will want to commit suicide. I hate to get at it, I hate to begin, but I imagine if you are here to make suggestions from time to time we can make it go along, instead of having it drag."

He dictated that morning some memories of the Big Bonanza mine, of Nevada, an episode of the early seventies,[1] of which he had been a part.

Perhaps I should have stated earlier that he was in bed when we arrived, in a handsome dressing-gown, propped against snowy pillows—an antique bed, vast and magnificent, and the dull red walls forming a rich background for his striking figure. He seldom got up before noon, and most of the early dictations were set down at his bedside. He found the easy luxury of it inspiring; that and tobacco, for he smoked pretty continuously, fragrant domestic cigars which I early learned to shun because of their potency. The glow of a reading lamp on a little table beside him laid a sheen on his snowy hair, and made more vivid his brilliant coloring. As I think of him now that luminous picture is the one that oftenest presents itself.

He was likely to shift his position. Generally he lay at ease against the pillows, but there were moments when he sat erect and tense, folding and refolding one cuff of his dressing gown about his wrist, as an aid to thought. Now and again he would lean over his little table and handle the things on it, his cigars, his pipe, his watch or pencils, even when he had no occasion for them. Then flinging his arm behind his head he would settle against the great pillows, and looking back across the years would formulate the phrases that, whatever their purport, bore his unmistakable imprint. We were watching one of the great literary creators of his time in the very processes of his architecture. I thought myself the most fortunate biographer in the world, as indeed I was.

It never occurred to me to make the suggestions he had invited, and there was no need—no "drag" in his dictation. Sometimes—usually, in fact—he was very, very deliberate; that was his habit. Sometimes he did not speak for a full minute or more; then perhaps the sentences came so fast that the stenographer's pencil must fly to keep up with him. When, on this first day, he turned to me at last and inquired the time we were all amazed that two hours had slipped away.

"And how much I have enjoyed it," he said. "It is the ideal plan for this kind of work. Narrative *writing* is always disappointing. The moment you pick up a pen you begin to lose the spontaneity of the personal relation, which contains the very essence of the interest. With shorthand dictation one can talk as if one were at one's own dinner table, always a most inspiring place. I expect to dictate all the rest of my life if you good people are willing to come to listen to it."

The dictations thus begun continued from week to week, and with steadily increasing charm. Often he did not know what he was going to talk about until the moment of beginning. Frequently he had a memorandum or a news clipping to serve as a starting point, but as likely as not something else would present itself at the very instant of beginning, and the small reminder once put aside was likely never to be thought of again. If, as sometimes happened, he wanted it, there would be trouble in finding it. The great bed had a large capacity for concealment. Once, after diving about in it for several moments, he invited Miss Hobby, the stenographer,[2] to leave the room for a time, in order, as he said, that he might swear. He got up and began to explore the bed, his eloquence enlarging impressively with each moment.

"One could lose a *dog* in this bed!" he declared.

It occurred to me to suggest that he turn over a clipping that he held in his hand. He did so, and it proved to be the one he wanted. A series of explosions followed. Then he said:

"There ought to be a room in this house to swear in. It's dangerous to have to repress an emotion like that."

But when a moment later Miss Hobby returned he was serene and happy again. He was usually gentle during the dictations, and patient with those about him—remarkably so, I thought.

But there were moments that involved risk. He had requested me to interrupt him at any time that I found him repeating or contradicting himself, or misstating some fact known to me. At first I hesitated to do this, cautiously mentioning the matter when he had finished. Then he was likely to say:

"Why didn't you stop me? Why did you let me go on making a jackass of myself when you could have saved me?"

So then I would take the risk of getting struck by lightning, and make an effort to stop him in time. But if it happened that I upset his thought the thunderbolt was apt to fly. He would say:

"Now you've knocked everything out of my head!"

Then, of course, I was sorry, and would say so, which would remedy matters, though half an hour later it might happen again. I became lightning-proof at last; also I learned better the psychological moment for the interruption. There was always a humorous slant in the dictations, however grave or pathetic the subject. Humor was his natural medium of expression, and was almost never wholly absent. I do not mean by this that he intended to be funny—he rarely meant to be that—but he conveyed his thought in that quaint phrase which was the very breath of his utterance.

[268]

I have mentioned his acknowledged tendency to self-contradiction and misstatement. His memory, marvelous in some ways, had been always somewhat capricious as to casual events, dominated by a vigorously exercised imagination. He meant to set down the literal and unvarnished facts—to record, to confess, and to condemn without stint or deviation. If you wanted to know the worst about Mark Twain you only had to ask him for it. He would give it to the last syllable. But he would do more: his imagination would magnify it and adorn it with new iniquities, and if he gave it again, or a dozen times, he would improve it each time; and he would do all these things for another person just as willingly.

Yet in relating an occurrence, whatever his variation of detail, he reproduced an atmosphere and a coloring as true as life itself, as true as that in the Mississippi book, or in the story of Huck Finn. More than once he said:

"This autobiography of mine is not a revenge record," and though from time to time he dealt rather severely with those who had crossed his path unrighteously, he usually modified his remarks with some comment on the "cussedness" of human nature in general, some confession of his own shortcomings, or he half humorously relented. Once, when he had been chastising some old offender, he concluded:

"However, he's dead, and I forgive him." Then after a moment's reflection: "No, strike that last sentence out." When we laughed he added: "We can't forgive him—yet."

He became infatuated with his methodless method of autobiography, and assured William Dean Howells, a frequent visitor, that it was the only way in which autobiography should be done, declaring that he intended to go on until he had dictated a library, some of which would not be published for at least a thousand years. I think he had seldom been happier in his library work than when we arrived and lit a cigar and began to talk.

I usually remained for a time when the stenographer had gone, and in the talks we had I gathered much that was of special value to my own undertaking. He had then no thought of literary effect, but only of the idea, or the incident, of the moment.

In May we moved our "plant" to New Hampshire for the summer, to the Upton House, near Dublin, on the Monadnock slope.[3] Work was begun in his bedroom, but the call of the outside was too compelling, and a day later he was walking up and down a long veranda, clad all in white, against a far-lying background of unbelievable beauty, a combination of forest and lake and purple hills. He wore loose slippers, and their shuffling sound made a low accompaniment to his easy, drawling speech. Sometimes he sat in one of the big porch rockers. As the days grew warmer he did this more and more.

Perhaps the glory of the summer distracted him, for he was not always in the mood for work and we had frequent holidays. To Howells he wrote:

> The dictating goes lazily and pleasantly on. (With intervals.) I find I've been at it, off & on, nearly two hours a day for 155 days, since Jan. 9. . . . I've added 60,000 words in the month I've been here; which indicates I've dictated during 20 days of that time—40 hours, at an average of 1,500 words an hour. It's a plenty, & I'm satisfied.[4]

It was not until well into September that we returned to New York, and to a new regime. Soon after his arrival at 21 Fifth Avenue, Mrs. H. H. Rogers, wife of his closest business adviser and friend, presented him with a handsome billiard and pool table. Billiards had been Mark Twain's earlier passion, and it now returned with renewed force. On the day that the gift had been installed, at the end of the dictation, he said:

"Have you any special place to lunch today?"

I replied that I had not.

"Lunch here," he said, "and we'll try the new billiard table."

I protested that I was a poor player.

"No matter," he answered. "The poorer you play the better I shall like it."

He had been planning a trip to Egypt, but at the end of our first billiard session he said:

"I'm not going to Egypt. There was a man here yesterday who said it was bad for bronchitis, and besides it's too far away from this billiard table."

After dinner we played again—until midnight. The game was "Cowboy," in which both pockets and caroms count. I had "nigger" luck, as he called it, and at one point made a carom, followed by most of the balls falling into the pockets.

"Well," he said, "when you pick up that cue this dam' table drips at every pore."

The dictations became secondary. Like a boy he looked forward to his afternoon of play, which never came quick enough. He seldom ate luncheon, but he would get up and dress, snatch a game or two beforehand, then walk up and down the dining-room, talking that marvelous talk of his which later I did my best to record. To him it was only a method of killing time. Once, when he had been discussing the Japanese question,[5] he suddenly noticed that the meal was ending.

"Now," he said, "we'll proceed to more serious matters. It's your shot."

He was not an even-tempered player. When his game was going badly his language sometimes became violent, and he was likely to be critical of his opponent. Then reaction would set in, and remorse. He would become gentle and kindly, hurrying the length of the table to set up the balls as I knocked them into the pockets, as if to show in every way except by actual confession in words that he was sorry for what no doubt seemed to him an unworthy display of temper.

Once, when luck seemed to have quite deserted him and he was unable to make any of his favorite shots, the air became fairly charged, the lightning fierce and picturesque. Finally with a regular thunderblast he seized the cue with both hands and literally mowed the balls across the table, landing some of them on the floor. I do not recall his remarks during that performance—I was chiefly concerned in getting out of the way. Then I gathered up the balls and we went on playing as if nothing had happened, only he was very gentle and sweet, like a sunny meadow after a storm has passed by. After a little he said:

"This is a most—amusing game. When you play—badly, it—amuses *me*. And when I play badly, and lose my temper, it certainly *must*—amuse—*you*."

How we played! All of every afternoon and far into the night! His endurance was superhuman. I was comparatively a young man, and by no means an invalid, but when I was ready to drop from exhaustion he was still as fresh and buoyant as at the moment of beginning. He smoked continuously and followed the endless track around the table with the light step of youth. Dressed always in white, his cheeks aglow, his hair like spun silver, he made a beautiful picture. At three in the morning he would urge just one more game and taunt me with my weariness.

"You don't sleep enough," he would say. "You should sleep—more."

Often as I looked at him I tried to realize that he was in fact the half-mythical hero of my boyhood. To me he was still heroic, still half a myth, and such he remains to this day.

His seventieth birthday had been marked by great celebration, but on his seventy-first it happened that we were entirely alone, and played billiards from morning until far into the night. Flowers and telegrams came and a string of callers. Only one or two intimate friends were admitted. We dined quite alone and played that night a new game which he had invented for the occasion.

He was in his loveliest mood throughout, and when at last we set up on cues he said:

"I have never had a pleasanter day at this game."

I answered: "I hope ten years from now we shall still be playing it."

"Yes," he said, "still playing the best game on earth."

In June of the following year he was summoned to Oxford to receive the literary doctor's degree.

"I don't know why they gave me that," he said quaintly. "I never doctored any literature; I wouldn't know how."

His month in England was such a splendid personal triumph as the world has seldom seen. Echoes of it all came across the Atlantic, and I confess that when on the evening of his arrival I was summoned to 21 Fifth Avenue I went with a certain degree of awe, prepared to sit a good way off and listen to the tale of this returning conqueror. But when I arrived he was already in the billiard-room knocking the balls about—his coat off, for it was a hot night. As I entered he said:

"Get your cue—I've been inventing—a *new game*."

And there were scarcely ten words exchanged before we were at it. The pageant was over; the curtain was rung down; business was renewed at the old stand.

Notes

1. Twain had left the West in 1867 and was nowhere near Nevada in the 1870s. He may have been reminiscing about Dan De Quille's book about the Comstock, *The Big Bonanza,* published in Hartford by the American Publishing Co. in 1876.

2. Josephine S. Hobby worked as a stenographer for Twain from 1906 until 1908.

3. Twain spent the summers of 1905 and 1906 at the Upton House near Dublin, New Hampshire.

4. Twain to Howells, 17 June 1906 (*Twain-Howells Letters* 810).

5. In October 1906 the San Francisco school board provoked a crisis between the United States and Japan by adopting a policy requiring children of Asian descent to attend segregated schools.

Albert Bigelow Paine, "Innocents at Home," *Collier's Weekly,* 3 January 1925, 5–6, 45.

From *My Mark Twain* (1910)

W. D. HOWELLS

The Russian writer Maxim Gorky (1868–1936) had arrived in New York on 28 March 1906 with his mistress, Maria Andreeva, a Moscow Art Theater actress, to solicit support for the faltering Russian Revolution. Twain was sympathetic to the cause, Howells recalled, but he also understood that Gorky had ruined his credibility as a fund-raiser.

HE CAME ONE SUNDAY AFTERNOON to have me call with him on Maxim Gorky, who was staying at a hotel a few streets above mine. We were both interested in Gorky, Clemens rather more as a revolutionist and I as a realist, though I too wished the Russian Tsar ill, and the novelist well in his mission to the Russian sympathizers in this republic. But I had lived through the episode of Kossuth's visit to us and his vain endeavor to raise funds for the Hungarian cause in 1851, when we were a younger and nobler nation than now, with hearts if not hands opener to the "oppressed of Europe"; the oppressed of America, the four or five millions of slaves, we did not count. I did not believe that Gorky could get the money for the cause of freedom in Russia which he had come to get; as I told a valued friend of his and mine, I did not believe he could get twenty-five hundred dollars, and I think now I set the figure too high. I had already refused to sign the sort of general appeal his friends were making to our principles and pockets because I felt it so wholly idle, and when the paper was produced in Gorky's presence and Clemens put his name to it I still refused. The next day Gorky was expelled from his hotel with the woman who was not his wife, but who, I am bound to say, did not look as if she were not, at least to me, who am, however, not versed in those aspects of human nature.

I might have escaped unnoted, but Clemens's familiar head gave us away to the reporters waiting at the elevator's mouth for all who went to see Gorky. As it was, a hunt of interviewers ensued for us severally and jointly. I could remain aloof in my hotel apartment, returning answer to such guardians of the public right to know everything that I had nothing to say of Gorky's domestic affairs; for the public interest had now strayed far from the revolution, and centred entirely upon these. But with Clemens it was different; he lived in a house with a street door kept by a single butler, and he was constantly rung for. I forget how long the siege lasted, but long enough for us to have fun with it. That was the moment of the great Vesuvian eruption, and we figured ourselves in easy reach of a volcano which was every now and then "blowing a cone off," as the telegraphic phrase was. The roof of the great market in Naples had just broken in under its load of ashes and cinders, and crushed hundreds of people;[1] and we asked each other if we were not sorry we had not been there, where the pressure would have been far less terrific than it was with us in Fifth Avenue. The forbidden butler came up with a message that there were some gentlemen below who wanted to see Clemens.

"How many?" he demanded.

"Five," the butler faltered.

"Reporters?"

The butler feigned uncertainty.

"What would you do?" he asked me.

"I wouldn't see them," I said, and then Clemens went directly down to them. How or by what means he appeased their voracity I cannot say, but I fancy it was by the confession of the exact truth, which was harmless enough. They went away joyfully, and he came back in radiant satisfaction with having seen them. Of course he was right and I wrong, and he was right as to the point at issue between Gorky and those who had helplessly treated him with such cruel ignominy. In America it is not the convention for men to live openly in hotels with women who are not their wives. Gorky had violated this convention and he had to pay the penalty; and concerning the destruction of his efficiency as an emissary of the revolution, his blunder was worse than a crime.[2]

Notes

1. Mount Vesuvius near Naples, Italy, had erupted from 4 to 8 April 1906, causing the roof of the Monteoliveto market to collapse, killing eleven and injuring thirty.

2. For Twain's response to the reporters, see "Gorky Evicted Twice in a Day from Hotels," *New York World,* 15 April 1906, 1–2; repr. in Scharnhorst 541–43.

W. D. Howells, from *My Mark Twain* (New York: Harper & Bros., 1910), 93–95.

From *Mark Twain* (1910)

Archibald Henderson

In his biography of Twain (1910), Archibald Henderson (1877–1963) remembered the essay Twain published without signature in 1906 entitled *What Is Man?*

"IT HAS BEEN A VERY SERIOUS and a very difficult matter," Mr. Clemens once said to me, "to doff the mask of humor with which the public is accustomed, in thought, to see me adorned. It is the incorrigible practice of the public, in this or in any country, to see only humor in the humorist, however serious his vein. Not long ago I wrote a poem, which I never dreamed of giving to the public, on account of its seriousness; but on being invited to address the women students of a certain great university, I was persuaded by a near friend to read this poem. At the close of my lecture I said 'Now, ladies, I am going to read you a poem of mine'—which was greeted with bursts of uproarious laughter. 'But this is a truly serious poem,' I asseverated—only to be greeted with renewed and, this time, more uproarious laughter. Nettled by this misunderstanding, I put the poem in my pocket, saying, 'Well, young ladies, since you do not believe me to be serious, I shall not read the poem'—at which the audience almost went into convulsions of laughter."

Several years ago, when we were crossing the Atlantic on the same ship, Mr. Clemens told me that while he was living in Hartford in the early eighties, I think, he wrote a paper to be read at the fortnightly club [the Monday Evening Club] to which he belonged. This club was composed chiefly of men whose deepest interests were concerned with the theological and the religiously orthodox. One of his friends, to whom he read this paper in advance, solemnly warned him not to read it before the club. For he felt confident that a philosophical essay, expressing candid doubt as to the existence of free will, and declaring without hesitation that every man was under the immitigable compulsion of his temperament, his training, and his environment, would appear unspeakably shocking, heretical and blasphemous to the orthodox members of that club. "I did not read that paper,"

Mr. Clemens said to me, "but I put it away, resolved to let it stand the corrosive test of time. Every now and then, when it occurred to me, I used to take that paper out and read it, to compare its views with my own later views. From time to time I added something to it. But I never found, during that quarter of a century, that my views had altered in the slightest degree. I had a few copies published not long ago; but there is not the slightest evidence in the book to indicate its authorship." A few days later he gave me a copy, and when I read that book, I found these words, among others, in the prefatory note:

"Every thought in them (these papers) has been thought (and accepted as unassailable truth) by millions upon millions of men—and concealed, kept private. Why did they not speak out? Because they dreaded (and could not bear) the disapproval of the people around them. Why have I not published? The same reason has restrained me, I think. I can find no other."

What is Man? propounds at length, through the medium of a dialogue between a Young Man and an Old Man, the doctrine that "Beliefs are acquirements; temperaments are born. Beliefs are subject to change; nothing whatever can change temperament." He enunciates the theory, which seems to me both brilliant and original, that there can be no such person as a permanent seeker after truth.

Archibald Henderson, from *Mark Twain* (New York: Stokes, 1910), 121–22, 208–9.

From *Uncle Joe Cannon* (1927)

JOSEPH G. CANNON AND L. WHITE BUSBEY

Joseph Gurney (aka Uncle Joe, aka "Czar") Cannon (1836–1926) was Speaker of the U.S. House of Representatives from 1903 until 1911, and L. White Busbey (1852–1925) was his private secretary. In his ghostwritten autobiography of Cannon, Busbey recalled Twain's visit to Washington in early December 1906 to lobby Congress and President Theodore Roosevelt on behalf of international copyright. The occasion was also memorable because for the first time Twain wore the iconic white linen suit that would be identified with him for the rest of his life.

WHEN I HAVE READ the books of Mark Twain and laughed over some of his characters there has been a dim recollection of something close akin to them I have known in real life. Tom Sawyer is the most natural boy I ever met between the covers of a book, and Colonel Mulberry Sellers is a daily visitor to the national capital. In fact, the last time I met Mark Twain he admitted that he was playing the part of Colonel Sellers and trying to make me see there were millions in it, for he had come to Washington to lobby for the copyright bill. He had not aversion to the term lobbyist, but recognized his temporary vocation while in the capital just as he recognized men in their various disguises all through his life.

He was an author asking protection for his work. He took over a part of the enthusiasm of Colonel Sellers as he talked to Members of Congress about the great benefits of the copyright bill, and he showed some dissatisfaction, if not disgust, when he discovered that other people were taking advantage of his efforts and his influence. He came into the Speaker's Room one day, as he was accustomed to do every morning, and said, "See here, Uncle Joe, does every fellow who comes here get hitched up to a train he does not want to pull? I came down here to pull the copyright bill through Congress because I want the copyright on my literary work extended so that I can keep the benefits to myself and family and not let the pirates get it. I hitched my locomotive to that car, and just when the locomotive got under way it had to be halted to attach a new car, then another and another, until now the steam is getting low and the train is so long I don't know whether it will move or not. And I don't know that I want to pull it now with all sorts of cars attached which have no possible relation to the purpose I had in coming to Washington or the legislation I believe necessary for the protection of my literary work."

I told him he had had the usual experience of men who want to reform the world by legislation according to their own views. There are always people ready to help them. He had that understanding of human nature that made him quick to see the difficulties that surround legislative effort without making him suspicious that the other fellows' efforts were not just like his own—wisely selfish—but he insisted that there ought to be several classes of trains in legislation as there are on the railroads so that real inspiration and "canned goods" should not be hooked up together in the same train. I agreed with him, but those who were insisting on cooperating with him did not. They were all determined to get on the same train with so popular an engineer.

He had influence with Members of Congress and he was frank to admit his purpose. He came to lobby for a bill and was not ashamed to admit that he had an interest in the legislation he sought. There was no altruistic humbug about him. He wanted to go on the floor of the House to lobby, but those confounded "Cannon Rules" prohibited him, and they likewise so bound the Speaker that he could not recognize another Member to ask unanimous consent to admit Mark Twain or any other man to the floor. Mark studied those rules and discovered that the only exception made was to those who had received the thanks of Congress. So he wrote to me and, acting as his own messenger, came to my room one cold morning and laid the letter on my desk. It was as follows:

Dec. 7, 1906

Dear Uncle Joseph:

Please get me the thanks of Congress—not next week, but right away! It is very necessary. Do accomplish this for your affectionate old friend—and right away! By persuasion if you can, by violence if you must. For it is imperatively necessary that I get on the floor for 2 or 3 hours and talk to the members, man by man, in behalf of the support, encouragement, and protection of one of the nation's most valuable assets and industries—its literature. I have arguments with me—also a barrel. With liquid in it.

[278]

Get me a chance! Get me the thanks of Congress. Don't wait for the others—there isn't time—furnish them to me yourself, and let Congress ratify later. I have stayed away and let Congress alone for seventy-one years, and am entitled to the thanks. Congress knows this perfectly well; and I have long felt hurt that this quite proper and earned expression of gratitude has been merely felt by the House and never publicly uttered.

Send me an order on the Sergeant-at-Arms.

Quick!

When shall I come?

With love and a benediction,

Mark Twain.[1]

After reading his letter I repeated what I said about the embarrassment of those rules not only as affecting him but also the Speaker, and he laughed as he said his joke must have been pretty clear for me to catch the point at the first reading. I called my messenger and said to Twain, "I am in full sympathy with you and will help you lobby. Neal will take you to the Speaker's private room, which is larger, more comfortable, and more convenient than this one. That room and the messenger are yours while you stay, and if you don't break a quorum of the House it will be your own fault."

He installed himself and the messenger went on the floor whispering to Champ Clark, Adam Bede, and others on both sides of the House, and in a few minutes there was not a quorum on the floor. They were all crowding into the Speaker's private room to see Mark Twain and promise him to vote for the copyright bill, for he allowed no admirer to escape. After the day's session Mark came to me to say that those confounded rules were not so bad after all and that he didn't object to a "Czar" who abdicated and allowed him to occupy the throne room.

Note

1. A slightly different version of this letter appeared in the *New York Times*, 1 December 1910, 3.

Joseph G. Cannon and L. White Busbey, from *Uncle Joe Cannon* (New York: Holt, 1927), 270–75.

"Mark Twain's Exclusive Publisher
Tells What the Humorist Is Paid" (1907)

JAMES B. MORROW

George Harvey, president of Harper & Bros. from 1900 to 1915, signed Twain
to a lucrative contract in 1900.

WHO IS THE BEST PAID WRITER in the United States? George Harvey, publisher of books and editor of magazines, ought to know. The foremost authors of the day are on his payroll.

"Mark Twain," he instantly replied when I asked the question. "No other
man in the history of letters, either here or in Europe, has ever received
30 cents a word on a contract that is practically unlimited as to time, and
absolutely without conditions as to subjects, treatment, or anything else.
It is unthinkable that Mark Twain should write a story or article and have
it rejected. Even in that inconceivable event, however, he would be paid
30 cents a word just the same. Put into language easily understood, 30 cents
a word is equivalent to $360 per column in an average-sized newspaper.

"After he returned from his trip around the world, a journey he undertook when he failed in business as a publisher, Clemens could barely earn
$6,000 a year. I had a talk with him which resulted in a contract to pay
30 cents a word for everything he wrote, whether it was printed or thrown
away. No author had ever received more than 10 cents a word on a long contract. A. Conan Doyle, the Scotch writer and physician, was paid $1 a word
within a year or two for a new series of detective stories, but the engagement
was short, and a number of publishers were concerned. Mark Twain earns
$59,000 a year. Indeed. I think his income in 1907 will reach $70,000.

"Until recently he wrote wholly by hand. Quite unexpectedly he found
that he could dictate to a secretary. He was as pleased over the discovery as
was President Roosevelt when he happened upon Mount Sinai, Moses, and
the Ten Commandments. Now he lights a cigar after breakfast, sits down

in his library and dictates for three hours on his autobiography. When he gets up he has earned $1,000. He is a great man, and will live longer than Thackeray, who was verbose, for one thing, and whose vision was confined to a single phase of social development in a single country. Twain is world-wide in his breadth of view. A man of critical judgment said not long since that he is the first novelist of the age. Whatever his rank may be, I am sure he will remain in our literature when brighter stars have lost some of their splendor. He is now free from the worry about money, and is at his best."

James B. Morrow, "Mark Twain's Exclusive Publisher Tells What the Humorist Is Paid," *Washington Post,* 3 March 1907, A12.

"Letters to the Editor" (1944)

George Bernard Shaw

In early May 1907 Twain accepted an invitation to receive an honorary Litt. D. from Oxford University. He sailed from New York on 8 June and arrived in London on 18 June. By chance, George Bernard Shaw (1856–1950) was introduced to him at St. Pancras station upon his arrival. See also Scharnhorst 612–14.

ON ONE OF THE VISITS to London made by my biographer, Archibald Henderson, I met him at the railway station, and found that Mark had come over in the same boat and was in the same train. There was a hasty introduction amid the scramble for luggage which our queer English way of handling passengers' baggage involves; and after a word or two I tactfully took myself and Henderson off.

Some days later Clemens walked into our flat in Adelphia Terrace. Our parlor-maid, though she did not know who he was, was so overcome by his personality that she admitted him unquestioned and unannounced, like the state of the Commandant.

Whether it was on that occasion or a later one that he lunched with us, I cannot remember, but he did lunch with us, and told us stories of that old Mississippi storekeeper. He presented me with one of his books, and autographed the inside of the cloth case on the ground that when he autographed fly leaves they were *taken out and sold.*

He had a complete gift of intimacy which enabled us to treat one another as if we had known one another all our lives, as indeed I had known him through his early books, which I read and reveled in before I was twelve years old.

George Bernard Shaw, "Letters to the Editor," *Saturday Review of Literature,* 12 August 1944, 15.

"Mark Twain, Some Personal Reminiscences" (1938)

Sir George Ian MacAlister

> In one of the highlights of his life, Twain received an honorary Litt.D. from Oxford on 26 June 1907. Sir George Ian MacAlister (1878–1957) advised him about the ceremonial protocol.

THE UNIVERSITY OF OXFORD wrote to him and offered him an Honorary Degree, and he was tickled to death. He was more pleased and proud of that than of anything of the kind that had ever happened to him, particularly because no American University had ever thought of it.[1] . . . American Universities did not think of him as a possible holder of a Degree. He was not in that class. But Oxford, the oldest and finest University in the world, had offered him its greatest honor, and he came with joy to receive it. He asked me to see him at his hotel. He was stopping at Brown's Hotel. I went to see him in the afternoon. He was in bed. He had developed a habit of going to bed whenever he felt tired. It was not so much that he felt the need of going to bed, but he found, being a victim of reporters and so on, that the only way to protect himself was to have his clothes off and be in bed. So when he was tired he undressed, put on a white nightshirt, and went to bed, in the morning, afternoon, or anytime that he felt tired.

So he invited me in. I can see him to this day—the white hair, the bushy eyebrows and the wonderful eagle face and keen eyes, and this white silk nightgown open at the breast, and the old boy balanced on the pillows. He had sent for me for this reason. He was going to take this Honorary Degree and he wanted to know about the ceremony—what he was to do and say and all about it. He had an idea that on these occasions there was a great crowd of undergraduates who ragged the people who got the Degrees, and he wanted to get ready. He had got it into his head that he had to exchange witticisms with them, and stand up for himself. I had to explain to him that I was sorry there was nothing of that kind. He must not say a word. He must look quite solemn and dignified and quite ignore the gallery. I think he was really a bit disappointed. I think he had been looking forward to a kind of duel off with these fellows in the gallery. But he promised to be good. And he loved the whole affair, the mediæval scene, the robes, the procession, and all the dignity of it. And it was rather a striking affair. In the same procession, unless I am mistaken, there were Lord Kitchener, Rudyard Kipling, and General [William] Booth. That was a remarkable combination. Can you think of four more extraordinary people in the world to be in a procession at Oxford getting these Degrees?

He said after that, "Now, if Harvard offers me an Honorary Degree, I shall say, 'No, thank you. Oxford is good enough for me.'"

Note

1. Twain had in fact received honorary Doctor of Letters degrees from Yale in 1901 and the University of Missouri in 1902.

Sir George Ian MacAlister, "Mark Twain, Some Personal Reminiscences," *Landmark* 20 (March 1938): 141, 143–45.

"E. V. Lucas and Twain at a '*Punch* Dinner'" (1910)

E. V. Lucas

Edward Verrall Lucas (1868–1938), a popular English writer, met Twain at a special dinner hosted by *Punch* on his behalf on 9 July 1907. He was also greeted on this occasion by Joy Agnew, the young daughter of the composer Philip L. Agnew, who presented him with a copy of a cartoon that had appeared in *Punch* for 26 June 1907.

I MET MARK TWAIN only once. It was on his last visit to London, when he was present at the special *Punch* dinner given in his honor. Under any conditions, there could not have been a more appreciative or interesting guest; but, as it happened, a pretty little incident at the very outset of the evening touched a chord of tenderness that enabled those of us who were present to realize a completer Mark Twain than perhaps many of his fellow convivialists on such occasions were in the habit of doing. Immediately upon entering the dining-room, before we had time to sit down, three knocks sounded on an inner door, and there emerged little Miss Agnew bearing in her hands Bernard Partridge's cartoon of a week or so before, representing a welcome to Mark Twain, and this she offered to him in a few simple words. Whether it was the cumulative effect of the kindness of everyone with whom he had come in contact since landing, or whether he was overcome by the fresh candor of this child and the dramatic unexpectedness of the gift, I do not know, but Mark Twain was visibly touched, almost melted—and I was conscious throughout the evening that the scene was very near his thoughts. He referred to it more than once in his informal speech, which swung between recollections of London in the 'seventies, the wildest chaff of his old friend Sir Henry Lucy,[1] and passages that were almost too emotional.

In meeting him at last face to face, I was surprised by his size. I had always thought of him as long and gaunt; but he was quite a small man, and his lines were soft. I was surprised also by the almost tremulous gentleness of his expression; but that I imagine was a late acquisition: it had come with age and bereavement. His voice a little disappointed me. One had heard so

[285]

much of the famous drawl; but, possibly through careful cultivation of a similar mechanism by humorists of our own, I was not carried away by it. But everything that he said was good, and his choice of words seemed to me extremely felicitous.

Not long afterwards I had occasion to write to him about something, and recalled the evening to his mind. In reply, he asked me to go and stay with him at Stormfield, but as his letter began "My dear Lucy" I did not go.

Note

1. Sir Henry W. Lucy (1843–1924), English journalist.

E. V. Lucas, "E. V. Lucas and Twain at a '*Punch* Dinner,'" London *Bookman* 38 (June 1910): 16–19.

"A Little Girl's Mark Twain" (1935)

DOROTHY QUICK

> Twain met Dorothy Quick (1900–1962) aboard the SS *Minnetonka* while re-
> turning from England in mid July 1907. He soon recruited her for his "aquar-
> ium" of "angelfish." See also their correspondence in Cooley.

A LITTLE GIRL WALKED round and round the deck of an ocean liner. On the starboard side she fairly flew along, but when she turned the corner and came to the port side of the vessel, she walked slowly and her feet dragged, her eyes lost in admiration of a man who stood at the rail, talking to another man. Both of them were staring out towards the far horizon line, and didn't see the little girl, whose gaze was riveted on the older of the two, the one with the great shock of snowy white hair and a keen, kindly observant face. He was Mark Twain.

I can still remember the thrill I had when, after walking past him five or six times, he suddenly turned, held out his hand and said in a slow, drawly voice, "Aren't you going to speak to me, Little Girl?" His companion faded away into space, as far as I was concerned, when I took his place. In a few seconds I was at the rail, standing beside the Mark Twain whom only yesterday I had seen walking down the platform of a London station sur-rounded by literally hundreds of admirers. He hadn't seen me hanging half out of the compartment window to catch a glimpse of him, nor had I at that moment dreamed that the next morning I should be standing beside him on the deck of a steamer bound for New York—standing beside him and actually talking to him.

It was too wonderful; and I shall never forget how proud and happy I was. It wasn't very long before he asked me if I knew who he was. I re-plied, "Of course, you're Mark Twain, and I've read all your books." This, of course, was, as he said about the report of his own death, slightly exag-gerated, but in the main it was true enough. My grandfather had recited Shakespeare and *Tom Sawyer* to me in my cradle, and had read me not only

Tom Sawyer, Huckleberry Finn, but *Innocents Abroad* and *A Tramp Abroad,* as a preparation for the trip from which I was now returning.

I don't think Mark Twain, or Mr. Clemens, as I later preferred to call him, quite believed my elaborate statement, because he began asking me questions. If I hadn't actually read the books, this would soon have proved the fact; however, as I had not only read them, but they had been read to me, he soon found (as he laughingly said) that I knew more about his books than he did himself.

We got along famously and the time slipped by completely unnoticed. It wasn't until the luncheon gong sounded that I remembered my family with a guilty start. Mr. Clemens said he wanted to meet my mother very much. So hand in hand we walked along the decks of the *S.S. Minnetonka* until we finally got to the lower deck, where my mother and grandparents had ensconced themselves in a sunlit corner. I began to explain my long absence, but Mr. Clemens said it would be better if I did some introducing instead, so the explanations dropped. As I found out later, they weren't necessary. Mother had been worried about me and had gone on a searching tour. When she had seen how utterly absorbed I was, and in what good hands, she had gone contentedly back to the steamer chairs to wait until I came.

Almost before I knew it, Mr. Clemens had arranged to have his steamer chair by ours, and I discovered that without doubt I had made a new friend. That night, as usual, I wore a white sailor suit to dinner. Being only nine [*sic*], I had my dinner very early, so I didn't see Mr. Clemens; but just as I was getting into bed there was a knock on the door and it was my new friend clad in one of his famous white suits, come to see me in mine! Someone had told him about my costume.

Unfortunately, I was attired in pajamas so I could only promise, as he especially requested, to wear the white sailor suit the next day. Fortunately, I had a large supply of them, for he insisted I wear them throughout the rest of the voyage. So we both appeared each day in white. Mark Twain's were made of white flannel and mine of serge but everyone assured us that we looked very well together.

The second night out we had an accident. About five o'clock in the morning, in a dense fog, a fishing schooner ran into us—knocking a huge hole in the side of the boat. The Captain ordered all the life boats down, and for a few moments there was wild confusion. Then it was discovered that the hole was above the water line and, as the sea was calm, there was practically no danger. The news was circulated about, and the people who had rushed up on deck began to return to their cabins.

Then for a moment the fog lifted and showed the schooner which had rammed us, with her bow completely gone. There was only time for a glimpse when the fog closed in again. Our Captain sent down lifeboats to see if they could pick up anyone, or be of any assistance to the schooner; but though we waited there for several hours there was never another sign of the boat or its crew.

Later, when we returned to New York, all the papers made much of the accident, and said Mark Twain put on his Oxford gown (he had just had a degree conferred upon him by Oxford University) and rushed down to my stateroom and carried me up on deck. As a matter of fact, Mr. Clemens and I had both slept serenely through the whole affair—even the crash. I think we were about the only two people on the entire ship who had. Mr. Clemens's secretary had reported the incident to him after the suspense was over, and Mr. Clemens sent the steward down to my cabin to see if I was all right, and to tell me not to worry.

The report went back to him that I was still asleep. The next morning he told my mother that my sleeping through the affair was a sure sign that I was a genius. As he was one, and he'd slept, it naturally followed that I was going to be one as I'd done the same thing.

Mother was afraid the idea of an accident might make me nervous (there were people who slept in their clothes the rest of the voyage) so I was told nothing about it. But Mother neglected to warn Mr. Clemens to keep the secret, so the next day, as I took a morning promenade with him, I saw the men on pulleys over the side, mending the hole, and in answer to my questions Mr. Clemens told me all about the mishap. Instead of being frightened, I was rather pleased at the importance of having been in an accident; but Mr. Clemens laughed and said, "It didn't do you much good to be in it as you slept all through it."

Mr. Clemens became interested in getting up a statement to the directors of the Line, completely exonerating the Captain of all blame for the accident, and was not only one of the first to sign the document but personally saw that everyone else did also.

We were inseparable for the rest of the voyage; he literally wouldn't let me out of his sight. If I was late in appearing, he would come down to the stateroom to "fetch" me; and whenever I played shuffleboard he would have his chair moved where he could superintend, and put my coat around my shoulders between plays. He was much interested in my skill at shuffleboard or "Horse Billiards" as he called it. And even though I was eliminated from the Junior Tournament quite early in the games, he gave me his book, *Eve's Diary,* with this inscription: "To Dorothy with the affectionate regards of the Author. Prize for good play in Horse Billiards Tournament, July 19, 1907." At the same time he called me to his cabin and told me to pick out whichever photograph of him I liked best from a selection of twenty or so, and when I had made the choice he autographed it for me.

The only time during the day when we were separated was at meals, Mr. Clemens, of course, being at the Captain's table. But quite often he would leave his table and come over to sit with us. Then the Captain would send him over a plate of baked potatoes, done in a way of which Mr. Clemens was especially fond, declaring that they were better at his own table than at any other. And Mr. Clemens, who had already ordered a portion at our table, would eat both platefuls and swear they tasted exactly alike, which he considered a good joke on the Captain.

Mr. Clemens laughingly called me his business manager; so when they were getting up the concert program and a group of men approached him to see if he would speak, he said that they would have to ask me. "I never do anything unless my business manager says I may. So you'll have to ask her." I, of course, was only too delighted to give the required permission as I wanted above everything to hear him speak myself, and had already received permission to sit up for the occasion. Imagine my pride and delight when I saw printed on the concert program, which is to this day one of my most prized possessions: "S. L. Clemens (Mark Twain) *by courtesy of Miss Dorothy Quick.*"

As he talked about the improvement of the condition of the adult blind— and repeated the story told in *A Tramp Abroad* of having been caught with a companion in Berlin in the dark for an hour or more, and of his horror at not being able to see for even so short a time[1]—my head literally swam with the joy that this great man, who was holding all the people that were crowded into the ship's lounge literally breathless with the magic of his words, was my friend, and that he was saying them through the "courtesy of Dorothy Quick." He said that he would devote much of his life to the subject of aiding the blind, and the passengers promised their aid in anything he undertook. I remember his telling me that shortly before the trip he had met Helen Keller, and had been particularly impressed with the wonderful things her teacher had done to improve her condition.

It was like Mr. Clemens to take every opportunity of helping a cause in which he was interested. I recollect that I was staying with Mr. Clemens, at 21 Fifth Avenue, on a night when the Pleiades Club was giving a dinner in his honor.[2] He had for some reason refused to go. It was a bitter disappointment to me, because my mother was going to be there, and as I had been visiting Mr. Clemens I hadn't seen her for several days. The dinner was at the Hotel Brevoort, very near Mr. Clemens's house. As the time for the dinner drew nearer I became more and more downcast. Finally Mr. Clemens asked what was the matter. I stammered out something about the dinner. "Did you want to go?" he questioned. I nodded. "Then we'll go!" He began roaring up the stairs for his secretary to telephone the Master of Ceremonies we were coming, and when the secretary said, "I thought you'd decided not to go," he replied simply, "Dorothy wants to go and I've just remembered there's something I wanted to talk about."

I wish I could remember what it was, but the excitement of the evening— sitting next to Mark Twain at the Speakers' table, in a chair he had brought specially for me—was too much for my youthful memory. I know everyone said it was one of the best speeches he'd ever made; but the two things that stand out in my mind, apart from actually getting to the dinner, was my mother waiting at the door for us, as we came into the hotel, and whisking me off to fix my long braids—a small detail which Mr. Clemens and I had completely overlooked, and which kept the whole dinner waiting at least twenty minutes—and then being taken home by Mr. Clemens just as a sweet lady who had made a great fuss over me all evening was about to play the piano. I would much rather have remembered what Mr. Clemens spoke of, but I think it was something about making a collection of compliments instead of autographs, or cats and dogs. Anyway I've taken the idea to heart and collected them ever since, just because Mark Twain said, "The paying of compliments is an art by itself."

But I have strayed away from the ocean voyage. When, after the most thrilling and eventful nine days of my life, we arrived in New York, a swarm of reporters surrounded Mr. Clemens, who refused to be photographed unless I would be taken with him. He sent to ask Mother's permission, and once it was granted we went to the sun-deck and let the cameramen have full sway. Both Mr. Clemens and I had on our white suits, and the next day there wasn't a paper in New York that didn't have one of the pictures in. As it was rather unusual for Mr. Clemens to pose for the newspapers, they made the most of it; and even now they always bring forth the pictures we had taken that day whenever there is a call for pictures of Mark Twain.

Later, the *American* did a special article called "Me and Mark Twain," in which there was a sketch of Mr. Clemens and myself seated on the bow of an ocean liner, I very comfortably ensconced in his lap. Mr. Clemens liked this the best of all the things that appeared, and said it had given him a new idea. He'd never traveled on the bow of a ship, but he thought he would like to try it sometime, if I'd go along.

All the papers made much of our friendship. "Mark Twain Home— Captive of Little Girl" was one of the headlines.[3] And they carried long paragraphs about me. I have them all and with them another souvenir of the trip, a drawing of Buster Brown with sprouting wings looking at the following: "Resolved, that Mark Twain has deserted the entire ship's company for Dorothy Quick. I wish my name was Twain. Buster." This is pasted in my scrapbook, next to the concert program.

Notes

1. Quick alludes to a passage in *A Tramp Abroad,* chapter 13 (118–21). The episode is set in Heilbronn, Germany, not Berlin.

2. Twain spoke at the Pleiades Club dinner on 22 December 1907. His speech is reproduced in Fatout, *Mark Twain Speaking* 600–602.

3. *New York World,* 23 July 1907, 18.

Dorothy Quick, "A Little Girl's Mark Twain," *North American Review* 240 (September 1935): 342–48.

From *Mark Twain and the Happy Island* (1914)

Elizabeth Wallace

> Twain traveled to Bermuda four times during the final three years of his life
> in vain attempts to recover his health. There he met Elizabeth Wallace (1865–
> 1960), who recorded her memories about his visit in the autumn of 1909.

ONCE IN A WHILE it rained on the Happy Island, and when it did, it did it thoroughly. The water came down in sheets and torrents, sweeping in from the sea, across the harbor, blotting out the islands and filling the air indoors with moisture. At such times it was impossible to brave the weather, for the most impermeable protection became soaked. One compensation, however, was that the instant the rain ceased, the hard, white coral roads were as passable as ever. You could walk out, holding your head high, and with no fear of ending up in a mud puddle.

One Sunday morning the weather was thus comporting itself, and it was hard to mark the dividing line between sea and rain-drenched atmosphere. We went out on the veranda, where we found a protected spot and some capacious chairs. Margaret[1] had been condemned to write letters, and Mr. Clemens missed her. He came out on the veranda and joined us. He was dressed, as he always was in daytime the last few years of his life, in white serge. The only color about him was the dark brown of a row of cigars in either breast-pocket. The row diminished as the morning progressed. He was always immaculate, although he wore his clothes easily, and there was never anything about him to suggest that he himself cared how he looked. His beautiful white hair curled softly in the dampness, and he was the image of picturesque comfort as he pulled at his cigar and talked.

It may have been the suggestion of the day, but, whatever it was, something moved him to discuss missionaries. This subject, together with old-fashioned orthodoxy, were topics that invariably stirred him to satiric loquacity. He gave the poor missionaries no quarter, he made no exceptions, they were all impaled upon the sharp brochette of his keen diction and grilled by the fire of his contempt. And all that he said, he said in his quiet slow drawl, with a twinkle of the eye, once in a while—a twinkle that one did not often see, unless one looked carefully, for his bushy eyebrows almost concealed the deep gray green eyes. He often made us wait for a word, but when it came it was the only one in the *Century Dictionary* that could so exactly have conveyed to us what he wanted to say.

There sat not far from us a sweet soul whose heart was deeply interested in the missionary cause. All unconscious of this, Mr. Clemens went on. A long time afterward he learned that she had overheard the conversation and the quick expression of his regret showed that his kind heart saw no humor in that situation.

After an exhaustive arraignment of missionaries and their weaknesses, something was said about Mr. Clemens's recent story of "Captain Storm-field's Heavenly Experiences," which had shortly before appeared in magazine form. Mr. Clemens chuckled as he asked us if we remembered the picture of Heaven as presented in Elizabeth Stuart Phelps's book, *Gates Ajar.* He said that when he read that book he was deeply impressed by what seemed a sentimental and foolish idea. He resolved to satirize it, and wrote the first draught of "Captain Stormfield." The result did not quite suit him, and, besides, he hesitated to publish it so soon after the appearance of Miss Phelps's book. So he put the manuscript aside, and it was almost forgotten. Then one day he came across it, thought it worth publishing, and sent it to the magazine where it appeared.

His cigars were not all smoked, and the rain continued to fall prodigiously and so we led him on to talk of other books he had written. One that he loved best of all, perhaps, and that is not nearly so widely read as his others, was *Personal Recollections of Joan of Arc.* He said that for years he had been impressed by the spirit of the French heroine, and year by year, for twelve years, he had laid by in his memory, and in his notes, every impression he could get of her. The most thrilling historical document he had ever read, he said, was the official account of her trial. And he regretted that he had not traveled in the parts of France where she had lived. Finally the time came when he could write of her, and he found that she stood forth in his mind, a clear, convincing figure.

There was a silence as he finished speaking of her, and we looked almost reverently on this man, who had seen into the heart of a simple peasant maid, and had understood the inspiration that had transformed her into the savior of France, and yet had kept her girlishly gay and womanly sweet.

Note

1. Margaret Blackmer, daughter of the New England lawyer Henry Myron Blackmer.

Elizabeth Wallace, from *Mark Twain and the Happy Island* (Chicago: McClurg, 1914), 21–25.

"Mark Twain Lands an Angel Fish" (1967)

Dorothy Sturgis Harding

> Returning from Bermuda to New York in April 1908 aboard the *Bermudian*, Twain met Dorothy Sturgis (1891–1978), who became another of his "angelfish." See also their correspondence in Cooley.

ON OUR WAY HOME from Bermuda my new companion and I became inseparable. He and his dear friend, Mr. H. H. Rogers, and I spent a good deal of time huddled under rugs in our deck chairs, but Mr. Clemens and I also used to walk the decks. . . .

On the day of the storm we were walking around the deck, arm in arm, glorying in the elements, when the "wop" occurred. We were approaching the stern, and so, when the wave came aboard, were knocked down and washed into the scuppers. Helping each other to our feet, we returned laughing and dripping to our respective mentors, and thought no more about the matter. He, I think, got a scolding for taking such chances with his precious person, but Mama was well used to my being her despair for my reckless ways with wind, water, and horses, and I recollect no undue reprimand. However, on docking in New York, the reporters swarmed around the famous author, as the story of the storm had apparently preceded us, and I was separated from my new-found playmate. We read in the papers next day a garbled and highly dramatized version of the event, which pictured him as "carrying the swooning girl to her cabin."[1] What an insult! I was too much of a tomboy to tolerate the stigma of being rescued by anybody! In fact, I had supported him against the wind, for he was well along in years and I was concerned about his shivering in the white suit which by then had become his habitual wear. We went our ways to our respective homes, but he did not forget, and started a brisk correspondence about exchanging snapshots, not of course of the actual adventure—that would have been priceless—only of Mr. Rogers and ourselves in the deck chairs.

It all culminated in an invitation to visit him in Redding, Connecticut, at the new house designed by John Mead Howells, son of William Dean, and also a friend of my father's. Built on the lines of an Italian villa, it was first called "Innocents at Home," a perfect name, I thought. Later it was changed to "Stormfield," at the insistence of his daughter Clara—presumably because of his article in *Harper's*, "Capt. Stormfield's Visit to Heaven," the money from which had been used to build the loggia wing at the west end of the house. I was allowed to accept the invitation and for the first time in my life left home under the sole care of my dear old English "Nandy."

So we arrived at the beautiful house, white stucco I think, with its overhanging eaves and arched doorways, standing on a slight rise, the grounds at the back sloping away in a field left, by Mr. Clemens's wish, unlandscaped, with the rough grass and wildflowers as nature had intended. I seem to remember goldenrod and spirea, probably since it was autumn when I was there. The inside of the house was redolent of the then new era, recently broken away from the Victorian monstrosities and tinged with Edwardian Taste, not yet influenced by a revival of the still older Colonial. I have a dim recollection of dark wood paneling, gold raw-silk curtains in spacious rooms and a little figure standing in the entrance, with dark, wavy hair and a sallow, almost Spanish complexion. This was Miss Isabel Lyon, Mr. Clemens's secretary, waiting to greet me while my host descended the stairs, in his white suit, with his white and bushy eyebrows almost glowing in the dark interior. . . .

We soon settled into an informal, family relationship. There was the "Aquarium," official home of the Angel-Fish Club though actually the billiard room, and I was introduced to the cats, "Tammany" and "Sinbad," whose favorite resting place was the green-baize top of the billiard table, and they had to be played around when he showed me the intricacies of the game—odd entertainment for a little girl—but he loved it and so did I, for that matter. Also there was Mr. Ashcroft,[2] known as "Benares" because of *The Servant in the House,* a very popular current play by Charles Rann Kennedy. This "Benares" seemed always hovering, helpfully, in the background, as Mr. Clemens's general secretarial factotum, but he must have been busy elsewhere, for he later married Miss Lyon. Besides billiards, in the evening, I was allowed, rashly I think, to perform on his Aeolian orchestrelle, a thing you pump with your feet, and I produced the "Erl Koenig"[3] with all the stops out! The instrument now rests in the museum at Mark Twain's birthplace in Hannibal. . . .

For a few days Albert Bigelow Paine was at Stormfield, always, seemingly, up on a ladder in the library doing research for his coming biography of Mark Twain. Also daughter Clara came with Ossip Gabrilowitsch for a weekend and he actually played the piano for us, to my great delight. I learned, only later, that he was Clara's fiancé. I heard him again years afterwards, once, when my father drove John Sargent out to Martin Loeffler's studio for a private concert, and I was allowed to go along, as a special treat. The famous pianist playing in Redding had put my efforts on the orchestrelle to shame, but entertainment was provided in other ways for the rest of the visit. One day Mr. Clemens took us all into New York to see Billie Burke in *Love Watches*.[4] He took us backstage to meet her in the "green room." . . .

I do not remember getting back to Redding, and think we must have spent the night in New York, not at his own house, 21 Fifth Avenue, but perhaps at the old Brevoort which he habitually patronized because of the good food. However, we wound up at Stormfield again, where, all too soon, good-byes were said and I was shipped back to Boston.

Notes

1. "Mark Twain a Hero? He Won't Admit It," *New York World,* 14 April 1908, 16: "Miss Sturgis was swept away from her protector and the two were washed against the railing. Mr. Clemens got to his feet first, grabbed the girl and held her until the flood subsided." See also "Mark Twain Rescues a Girl as Huge Sea Sweeps the Bermudian," *New York Herald,* 14 April 1908, 5; repr. in Scharnhorst 664–67: "Miss Sturgis was swept from her grasp on the rail and was floundering on the lee scuppers when Mr. Clemens rescued her."

2. Ralph W. Ashcroft (1875–1947), Twain's business adviser from 1907 to 1909, married Isabel Lyon in March 1909.

3. Goethe's poem "Der Erlkönig" was set to music by Franz Schubert.

4. The American actress Billie Burke, aka Mary William Ethelbert (ca. 1885–1970), opened in *Love Watches* at the Lyceum Theatre in New York on 27 August 1908 and closed there on 23 January 1909. She is perhaps best known today for her role as Glinda the Good Witch in the film *The Wizard of Oz* (1939).

Dorothy Sturgis Harding, "Mark Twain Lands an Angel Fish," *Columbia Library Columns* 16 (February 1967): 5–10.

"Mark Twain at Stormfield" (1909)

ALBERT BIGELOW PAINE

> Twain moved into his new house in rural Connecticut on 18 June 1908. Paine
> would reprint his memories of the occasion in chapters 268–272 of *Mark
> Twain: A Biography* (1912).

IT WAS THE LATE AFTERNOON of a June day that Mark Twain first saw his
new home at Redding—a day such as those who were responsible for that
home had hoped for, and would have prayed for, perhaps—if they had
had time.

For there had been a great getting ready—a multitude of last things to
do—a marshalling and counter-marshalling of workmen and tradesmen of
every sort, in order that the last touch might be added, the last bit of furnishing be put in place—that the cat might indeed be "purring upon the
hearth-rug"[1] when he entered the door, according to his desire: for here
be it remembered that Mark Twain had never seen that house before, had
never even seen Redding until that day, and had no more than a hazy notion of the place and habitation which awaited him.

Redding recognized the occasion as historic, and June 18, 1908, became
a sort of holiday. When the train with Mark Twain aboard stopped at the
Redding platform (it had been a through express train up to that time) there
was a varied assemblage of vehicles and gala array to offer a gallant country
welcome. It was then a little before six o'clock of that long June day still and
dreamlike, and to the people assembled there was something which was
not quite reality in the scene. There was a tendency to be very still. They
nodded, waved their hands to him, smiled and looked their fill, but a spell
lay upon them, and they did not cheer. It would have been a pity if they
had done so. The picture was perfect. A noise, and the illusion would have
shattered.

His carriage led away on the three-mile drive to the house on the hilltop, and the floral turnout fell in behind. There had been drought, but two
days before a rain had laid the dust and washed the vendure clean. No first

impression of a fair land could have come at a sweeter time. Hillsides were green; fields were white with daisies; dogwood and laurel shone among the trees. And over all was the blue sky, and everywhere the fragrance of June.

He was very quiet as he drove along. Once with gentle humor, looking over a white daisy field, he said:

"That is buckwheat. I always recognize buckwheat when I see it. I wish I knew as much about other things as I know about buckwheat. It seems to be very plentiful here; it even grows by the roadside;" and a little later, "This is the kind of a road I like; a good country road through the woods."

The water was flowing over the mill-dam where the road crossed the Saugatuck, and he expressed approval of that clear, picturesque little river, one of the most charming of Connecticut waters. A little farther on, a brook cascaded down the hillside, and he compared it with some of the tiny streams of Switzerland. The lane that led to the new home opened just above, and as he entered the little leafy way he said:

"This is just the kind of a lane I like," thus completing his approval of everything except the house itself and its location.

The last of the procession had dropped away at the entrance of the lane, and he was alone with those who had most anxiety for his verdict. They had not long to wait. As they ascended higher to the open view he looked away, across the Saugatuck valley to the nestling village and church spire and farmhouses, and to the distant hills, and declared the land to be a good land and beautiful—a spot to satisfy one's soul. Then came the house— simple and severe in its architecture—an Italian villa, such as he had known in Florence, adapted now to American climate and needs. The scars of building had not all healed yet, but close to the house waved green grass and blooming flowers that might have been there always. Neither did the house itself look new. The soft gray stucco had taken on a tone that melted into the blue sky and foliage of its background. At the entrance his domestic staff waited to greet him, and then he stepped across the threshold into the wide hall and stood in his own home for the first time in seventeen years. It was an anxious moment, and no one spoke immediately. But presently when his eye had taken in the soft, satisfying harmony of the place and followed on through the wide doors that led to the dining-room—on through the open French windows to the most wonderful vista in America—he said, very gently:

"How beautiful it all is! I did not think it could be as beautiful as this."

They showed him the rooms; the great living-room at one end of the hall—a room on the walls of which there were no pictures, but only color harmony—and at the other end of the hall the splendid, glowing billiard-room, where hung all the pictures in which he took delight. Then to the floor above, with its spacious rooms and a continuation of color welcome and concord, the windows open to the pleasant evening hills.

And when he had seen it all—the natural Italian garden below the terraces; the loggia, whose arches framed enchanting vistas and formed a rare picture-gallery of myriad and eternal things; when he had completed the round and stood in the billiard-room—his especial domain—once more he said, as a final verdict:

"It is a perfect house—perfect, so far as I can see, in every detail. It might have been here always."

He was at home there from that moment—absolutely, marvelously at home, for he fitted the setting perfectly, and there was not a hitch or a flaw in his adaptation. To see him over the billiard table, five minutes later, one could easily fancy that Mark Twain, as well as the house, had "been there always."

There were guests that first evening—a small home dinner-party—and all so perfect were the appointments and service that one not knowing would scarcely have imagined it to be the first dinner served in that lovely room. A little later, at the foot of the garden of bay and cedar, neighbors set off some fireworks, and he stepped out on the terrace and saw rockets climbing through the summer sky to announce his arrival.

"I wonder why they all go to so much trouble for me," he said, softly; "I never go to any trouble for anybody"—a statement which all who heard it and all his multitude of readers in every land stood ready to deny.

That first evening closed with billiards—boisterous, triumphant billiards—and when with midnight the day ended and the billiard cues were set in the rack, there was none to say that Mark Twain's first day in his new home had not been without a flaw.

He had named it "Innocence at Home" before he saw it—a pleasant name, suiting his first week's occupancy, for his guests (there are usually guests) were two members of his "Aquarium," a society of which he is the founder and patron saint, composed of "Angel Fish"—that is to say, girls in their early teens. For Mark Twain is fond of children. He loves to see them on the premises, to provide entertainment for them, and to mingle with their games. That first week—a rare week in June—was idyllic, and had there been always fair weather and Angel Fish the house on the hilltop might have remained "Innocence at Home."

But by and by summer storms gathered over that rock-bound open hill with its wide reaches of vine and shrub—wild fierce storms that bent the birch and cedar and strained at the bay and huckleberry; glaring lightning and turbulent wind and thunder, followed by the charing phalanx of the rain. Standing with head bared to the tumult, his white hair tossing in the blast, and beholding the wide splendor of the spectacle, he recalled one of his later and briefer titles and rechristened the place "Stormfield."

Yet, within, the house is a house of beatitudes. No gentler westering sun ever illumined the afternoon of life than sheds its tranquil peace at Stormfield. There are those whom time embitters and hardens. There are others who, like rare and genuine art productions, grow mellow and more precious with the years. So tenderly have the seasons with their sweetness and their sorrows laid their kindliness on Mark Twain that today there is benediction in his very presence. He is seventy-three, but he is not old, and he never will be. He could not be old if he tried. His manner, his speech, his movement, his point of view—they are all young. His complexion is of exquisite coloring; he runs lightly upstairs; he skips like a lad of ten. One never feels that he is old—that he ever could be old. His hair is snow-white, but then so is his dress, and there is as much of freshness and youth and joy in the one as in the other. He is the embodiment of eternal youth, with youth's eternal charm.

How peacefully the days go by! There are no special morning regulations at Stormfield. One may have his breakfast at any time and at almost any place. He may have it in bed if he likes, or in the loggia or living-room or billiard-room. He may even have it in the dining-room, or on the terrace, just outside. The company—there is likely to be company—may suit their convenience in the matter; they are under no restrictions—no published restrictions—though on the mantel of the billiard-room there is a card of requests, to burglars. But other guests—invited guests—may rely upon their conscience and judgment for guidance. This applies mainly to the forenoon; in the afternoon there are games—that is, billiards—provided one knows billiards—otherwise, hearts. These two games are Mark Twain's safety-valves, and while there are no printed requirements relating to them, the unwritten code of Stormfield provides that guests of whatever age or previous convictions shall engage in one or both of these diversions.

The master of Stormfield himself is likely to spend his forenoon in bed, with his reading, his letters, and his literary labors, and he comes to the green table of skill and chance eager for the onset. If the fates are kindly, he approves of them generously. If not—well, the fates are old enough to know better and must take the consequences. Sometimes, when the weather is fine and there are no games (this is likely to be on Sunday afternoons), there are long drives among the hills, and along the Saugatuck, through the Redding Glen.

The cat is always "purring on the hearth" at Stormfield—several cats— for Mark Twain's fondness for this clean, cunning, intelligent domestic animal is one of his happiest characteristics. He is naturally gentle and tender-hearted toward all animals, and the grace and beauty and playfulness of the cat make a peculiar appeal to his nature. There are never too many cats at Stormfield, and the "hearth" takes in the entire house, including the billiard table. When, as is likely to happen at any time during the game, Sinbad or Danbury or Billiards may decide to hop up and play with the balls, the game simply adds this element of chance, and the uninvited player is not disturbed. The cats really own Stormfield; anyone could tell that from their deportment. Mark Twain will continue to pay the taxes and to keep up the repairs, but it is Danbury and Sinbad and the others that hold the place in fee simple and trouble themselves not at all with the blight of tribute and the waste of wear and tear. They possess themselves of any portion of the house or its furnishings at will, and they never fail to attract attention. Mark Twain is likely to be preoccupied and indifferent to the comings and goings of other members of the household. But no matter what he is doing, let Danbury appear on the horizon and he is observed and greeted with due deference and complimented and made comfortable. Mark Twain has been known to rise from the dinner table and carry certain choice food out on the terrace to Tammany—now late and lamented—and to be satisfied with almost no acknowledgement in the way of appreciation. One could not imagine any home of the great humorist where the cats were not supreme.

At the close of the day, particularly when there are no guests and he wants only the repose of meditation, Mark Twain likes music. A great orchestrelle at the end of the living-room supplies this need, and lying on a couch or in an easy chair, with eyes closed and cigar dimly alight, he listens half unconsciously to the stately measures of Chopin and Schubert and Beethoven, and mingles unusual philosophies and majestic speculations with long, long backward dreams.

Mark Twain came to his new home in Redding expecting to pass only the summer and autumn there. He changed his mind on the day after his arrival.

"I am sorry on one account that I did not see the place before," he said. "Had I done so, I should have brought everything I possess to this house, and I never would leave it again. It is a perfect home."

He has passed a full round of seasons in the house since then, but his verdict of those first days has not changed. Harmonious and gratifying throughout, amid surroundings that cannot be surpassed in all the beautiful hill country of New England; arranged in every detail for comfort and use and welcome, it is still the perfect home to him, and will so remain. It has been said that Mark Twain has had many homes, and that he tired of them all—that he would soon tire of this one. The statement is not well founded. Mark Twain has lived in many places, but he has had only three homes: the first in Buffalo—a house of sorrow which he abandoned soon; the second in Hartford—a beautiful home that sheltered him during the period of his most active literary labors, those rare early years of his married life. The stress of circumstances made it impossible for him to remain there, and still more impossible for him to return.[2] Stormfield is the third of Mark Twain's homes, and it is likely there will be no other. It is a quiet and beautiful harbor, despite its name, and it is not likely that its owner will slip the moorings again.

Notes

1. Paine alludes to the poem "Nothing to Do" in the children's book *Careless Kate* (1889) by William Taylor Adams, aka Oliver Optic (1822–97).

2. Paine implies that Langdon Clemens died in 1872 in Twain's Buffalo home, but in fact he had died in Hartford. Susy Clemens died in the mansion in Hartford in 1896.

Albert Bigelow Paine, "Mark Twain at Stormfield," *Harper's Monthly* 118 (May 1909): 955–58.

From *Hardly a Man Is Now Alive* (1939)

DAN BEARD

> Twain's old friend Dan Beard was his near-neighbor in rural Connecticut.

I SPENT THE DAY that Mr. Clemens was to arrive painting a chicken coop. My neighbor, Harry Lounsbury,[1] came over to the house to ask me to help him set off some fireworks. I replied, "Harry, I will do this for you and Mark Twain, but the last time I set off fireworks was in 1884, and it was six months before I could work again." So we climbed up on the mountain to a pergola where the fireworks were stored. There were rockets taller than myself, and everything else in proportion. We started things going. The rockets soared to an immense height, and the sticks dropped in Meeker Jones's pasture, stampeding horses and cattle. The red fire illuminated the distant mountains. Harry and I were having great fun when someone stepped out on the piazza with a megaphone, saying, "Mr. Clemens wants Mr. Beard and Mr. Lounsbury up at the house." Up to that time we had not realized that the red, blue and green fires and flares had illuminated the pergola so that we were plainly discernible from the house.

When we reached the house the drawing room was filled with people in evening clothes, ladies with décolleté gowns with long trains, while we were powder-blackened and bedaubed with paint. However, no one seemed to notice it. I was brought up to greet Mr. Clemens. We clasped hands. Then he turned to the assembly and said, "A toast." Everybody held their glasses aloft. "To Dan Beard!" cried the host. The party was a surprise party, but the biggest surprise that evening was my presence there. However, as no one seemed to know that I was not dressed in evening clothes, my embarrassment soon vanished. . . .

The sheriff had to go to Stormfield one day when the cook had gone a little crazy with drink. He asked me to go along to help. As we approached the house we could hear loud screaming, terrible oaths and base obscenity. Clad in a pink kimono, Mark was standing out in front of the pergola, placidly smoking his pipe. "Good morning, Dan," he greeted me. "Come and take a walk with me."

I agreed and he went in to change his clothes. We met on the lawn after I'd satisfied my curiosity about the appalling racket in the house. The cook had barricaded herself in her room, while the sheriff and a deputy were letting her spend her strength before going in to take her back to town. Mr. Clemens proposed a walk down to see Albert Bigelow Paine, so down we went. As distance increased the sounds from the house became fainter and fainter. But not once, by word, speech or action, did Mark Twain show that he was conscious that anything unusual was going on.

There was always something doing up at Stormfield. Gabrilowitsch would give an exhibition of his wonderful skill on the piano or play the accompaniment while his fiancée, Clara Clemens, sang. The guests came from long distances. No distance seemed too great for them to drive, but the one Mark Twain seemed to long for most and inquire about most frequently was W. D. Howells. He was very fond of Howells and very fond of [Richard Watson] Gilder, also his friend Rogers, the financier. Mark had been writing about financial pirates when Paine asked him, "How about your friend Rogers?"

Mark smiled. "He's a pirate all right, but he owns up to it and enjoys being a pirate. That's the reason I like him." . . .

While on my farm at Redding, Connecticut, John Burroughs, John Muir, and Edwin Markham all promised to visit me, my intention being to bring this delightful group of men into personal touch with Mark Twain, who lived on the hill just above my farmhouse. I considered them then, and still do, a wonderful and typical group, the product of American environment and institutions, each one very different in character from the other, yet all bearing an unmistakable family resemblance. I had planned to have the group photographed at Stormfield, but Mark Twain was rather suddenly taken ill and never recovered, and so my party was called off.

Mark went to Bermuda for his health, but he grew worse instead of better. He telegraphed to Albert Bigelow Paine to come down and get him. On the way home, every once in a while he said, "Paine, we won't make it, we won't make it." But he did. As soon as the big dailies learned that he was dangerously ill they sent their reporters to Redding, so that they would be on hand when his death occurred. These reporters said that they knew they were turkey buzzards but that that was part of their duty as reporters.

There was not one among them who was not a loyal clansman of the sick man up at Stormfield.

These newspapermen and myself accompanied Mark Twain's body to New York as a sort of voluntary guard of honor. Had he been conscious of the presence of the loyal representatives of the press the knowledge would no doubt have pleased him. Mark Twain left us at exactly the right moment—midst the glory of his career, with the sounds of the plaudits of the multitude ringing in his ears, and when he was glad to go.

Note

1. Harry A. Lounsbury, the general contractor who built Stormfield.

Dan Beard, from *Hardly a Man Is Now Alive* (New York: Doubleday, 1939), 346–50.

"Mark Twain" (1929)

HELEN KELLER

Among the visitors to Stormfield during the winter of 1909–10 were Helen Keller (1880–1968) and her tutor, Anna Sullivan Macy (1866–1936). See also Chambliss.

ONE OF THE MOST memorable events of my life was my visit to Mark Twain.

My memory of Mr. Clemens runs back to 1894, when he was still vigorous, before the shadows began to gather. Such was the affection he inspired in my young heart that my love for him has deepened with the years. More than anyone else I have ever known except Dr. Alexander Graham Bell and my teacher, Mrs. Macy, he aroused in me the feeling of mingled tenderness and awe. I met him many times at the home of my friend, Laurence Hutton, in New York, and later in Princeton; also at the residence of Mr. H. H. Rogers and at his own home at 21 Fifth Avenue, and last of all in Stormfield, Connecticut. Now and then I received letters from him. We were both too busy to write often, but whenever events of importance in our lives occurred we wrote to each other about them.

He knew with keen and sure intuition many things about me; how it felt to be blind and not to be able to keep up with the swift ones—things that others learned slowly or not at all. He never embarrassed me by saying how terrible it is not to see, or how dull life must be, lived always in the dark. He wove about my dark walls romance and adventure which made me feel happy and important. Once when Peter Dunne, the irrepressible Mr. Dooley, exclaimed, "God! How dull it must be for her; every day the same, and every night same as the day," Mr. Clemens said, "You're damned wrong there. Blindness is an exciting business, I tell you. If you don't believe it, get up some dark night on the wrong side of your bed when the house is on fire and try to find the door."

The second time I met Mr. Clemens was in Princeton during a spring vacation when we were visiting the Huttons in their new home. We had many happy hours together at that time. One evening, in the library, he lectured to a distinguished company—Woodrow Wilson was present—on the situation in the Philippines. We listened breathlessly. He described how six hundred Moros—men, women, and children—had taken refuge in an extinct crater bowl near Jolo, where they were caught in a trap and executed by the Americans. A few days afterwards, the Americans captured Aguinaldo by disguising their military marauders in the uniform of the enemy and pretending to be friends of Aguinaldo's officers. Upon these military exploits Mr. Clemens poured out a volume of invective and ridicule. Only those who heard him can know his deep fervor and the potency of his flaming words. All his life he fought injustice wherever he saw it in the relations between man and man, in politics, and in war. I loved his views on public affairs, perhaps because they were so often the same as my own.

He thought he was a cynic, but his cynicism did not make him indifferent to the sight of cruelty, unkindness, meanness, or pretentiousness. He would often say, "Helen, the world is full of unseeing eyes—vacant, staring, soulless eyes." He would work himself into a frenzy over dull acquiescence in any evil that could be remedied. True, sometimes it seemed as if he let loose all the artillery of Heaven against an intruding mouse. But even then his "resplendent vocabulary" was a delight. Even when his ideas were quite wrong they were expressed with such lucidity, conviction, and aggressiveness that one felt impelled to accept them—for the moment at least.

He was interested in everything about me—my friends and little adventures and what I was writing. I loved him for his beautiful appreciation of my teacher's work. Of all the people who have written about me, he is almost the only one who has realized the importance of Mrs. Macy in my life; the only one who has appreciated her "brilliancy, penetration, wisdom, character, and the fine literary competences of her pen."

He often spoke tenderly of Mrs. Clemens and regretted that I had not known her.

"I am very lonely. Sometimes, when I sit by the fire after my guests have departed," he used to say, "my thoughts trail away into the past. I think of Livy and Susy and I seem to be fumbling in the dark folds of confused dreams. I come upon memories of little intimate happenings of long ago that drop like stars into the silence. Some days everything breaks and crumbles. It did the day Livy died." Mr. Clemens repeated with emotion and inexpressible tenderness the lines which he had carved on her tombstone:

> Warm summer sun,
>   Shine kindly here;
> Warm Southern wind,
>   Blow softly here;
> Green sod above,
>   Lie light, lie light,
> Good night, dear heart,
>   Good night, good night.[1]

The year after her death, he said to me: "This has been the saddest year I have ever known. If it were not that work brings forgetfulness, life would be intolerable." He expressed regret that he had not accomplished more. I exclaimed, "Why, Mr. Clemens, the whole world has crowned you. Already your name is linked with the greatest names in our history. Bernard Shaw compares your work with that of Voltaire, and Kipling has called you the American Cervantes." "Ah, Helen," he replied, "you have a honeyed tongue: but you don't understand. I have only amused people. Their laughter has submerged me."

There are writers who belong to the history of their nation's literature. Mark Twain is one of them. When we think of great Americans, we think of him. He incorporated the age he lived in. To me he symbolizes the pioneer qualities—the large, free, unconventional, humorous point of view of men who sail new seas and blaze new trails through the wilderness. Mark Twain and the Mississippi River are inseparable in my mind.

When I told him that *Life on the Mississippi* was my favorite story of adventure, he said, "That amazes me. It wouldn't have occurred to me that a woman could find such rough reading interesting. But I don't know much about women. It would be impossible for a person to know less about women than I do." After some badinage back and forth about women, Mr. Clemens's manner changed. A sadness came into his voice. "Those were glorious days, the days on the Mississippi. They will come back no more, life has swallowed them up, and youth will come no more. They were days when the tide of life was high, when the heart was full of the sparkling wine of romance. There have been no other days like them," he said.

It was just after he had read my book, *The World I Live In,* that he sent a note to me saying, "I command you and Mrs. Macy to come and spend a few days with me in Stormfield." It was indeed the summons of a beloved King. His carriage met us at Redding station. If my memory serves me, it was in February; there was a light snow upon the Connecticut hills. It was a glorious five-mile drive to Stormfield; little icicles hung from the edges of the leaves and there was a tang in the air of cedar and pine. We drove rapidly along the winding country roads; the horses were in high spirits. As we approached the Italian villa on the very top of the hill, they told me Mr. Clemens was standing on the veranda waiting. As the carriage rolled between the huge granite pillars, he waved his hand; Mrs. Macy told me he was all in white and that his beautiful white hair glistened in the afternoon sunshine like the snow spray on the gray stones.

We were in the land of enchantment. We sat by the fire and had our tea and buttered toast, and he insisted that I must have strawberry jam on my toast. We were the only guests. Miss Lyon, Mr. Clemens's secretary, presided over the tea table.

It was obvious that Mr. Clemens took great satisfaction in his unusual house. He told us that it had been designed by the son of my lifelong friend, William Dean Howells. Delightedly he pointed out that the architecture was exactly suited to the natural surroundings; that the dark cedars and pines, which were always green, made a singularly beautiful setting for the white villa. Mr. Clemens particularly enjoyed the sunlight that came through the great windows and the glimpse of field and sky that could be seen through them. "You observe," he said to us, "there are no pictures on the walls. Pictures in this house would be an impertinence. No artist," he added, going to the window and looking out, "has ever equaled that landscape."

Our suite of rooms was next to his. On the mantelpiece, suspended from a candlestick, was a card explaining to possible burglars where articles of value were in the room. There had recently been a burglary in the house, and Mr. Clemens said that this was a precaution against being disturbed by intruders.[2]

We stayed in our room till dinner was announced—dinner in Mr. Clemens's house was always a function where conversation was important, yes, more important than the food. It was a rule in that house that guests were relieved of the responsibility of conversation. Mr. Clemens said that his personal experience had taught him that you could not enjoy your dinner if the burden of finding something to say was weighing heavily upon you. He made it a rule, he said, to do all the talking in his own house, and expected when he was invited out that his hosts would do the same. He talked delightfully, audaciously, brilliantly. His talk was fragrant with tobacco and flamboyant with profanity. I adored him because he did not temper his conversation to any femininity. He was a play-boy sometimes and on occasions liked to show off. He had a natural sense of the dramatic and enjoyed posing as he talked. But in the core of him there was no make-believe. He never attempted to hide his light under a bushel.

I think it was Goethe who said, "Only clods are modest." If that is true, then in all the world there was not less of a clod than Mr. Clemens. He ate very little himself, and invariably grew restless before the dinner was finished. He would get up in the midst of a sentence, walk round the table or up and down the long dining-room, talking all the while. He would stop behind my chair and ask me if there was anything I wanted; he would sometimes take a flower from a vase, and if I happened to be able to identify it, he showed his pleasure by describing in an exaggerated manner the powers that lie latent in our faculties, declaring that the ordinary human being had not scratched the surface of his own brain. This line of observation usually led to a tirade upon the appalling stupidity of all normal human beings. Watching my teacher spelling to me, he drawled, "Can you spell into Helen's left hand and tell her the truth!" Sometimes the butler called his attention to a tempting dish and he would sit down and eat.

To test my powers of observation, he would leave the room quietly and start the self-playing organ in the living-room. My teacher told me how amusing it was to see him steal back to the dining-room and watch stealthily for any manifestations on my part that the vibrations had reached my feet. I did not often feel the musical vibrations, as I believe the floor was tiled, which prevented the sound waves from reaching me, but I did sometimes feel the chord vibrations through the table. I was always glad when I did, because it made Mr. Clemens so happy.

We gathered about the warm hearth after dinner and Mr. Clemens stood with his back to the fire talking to us. There he stood—our Mark Twain, our American, our humorist, the embodiment of our country. He seemed to have absorbed all America into himself. The great Mississippi River seemed forever flowing, flowing through his speech, through the shadowless white sands of his thought. His voice seemed to say, like the river, "Why hurry? Eternity is long; the ocean can wait."

When the time came to say good night, Mr. Clemens led me to my room himself and told me that I would find cigars and a thermos bottle with Scotch whisky, or bourbon if I preferred it, in the bathroom. He told me that he spent the morning in bed writing, that his guests seldom saw him before lunch-time; but if I felt like coming in to see him about ten-thirty, he would be delighted, for there were some things he would like to say to me when my Guardian Angel was not present.

About ten o'clock the next morning, he sent for me. He liked to do his literary work in bed, dictating his notes to a stenographer. Propped up among his snowy pillows, he looked very handsome in his dressing gown of rich silk. He said if doing my work that way appealed to me, I might have half the bed, provided I maintained strict neutrality and did not talk. I told him the price was prohibitive, I could never yield woman's only prerogative, great as the temptation was.

It was a glorious bright day and the sun streamed through the great windows. Mr. Clemens said if I did not feel inclined to work after lunch (which was by way of sarcasm, he having previously remarked that I did not look industrious and that he believed I had somebody write my books for me), he would take a little walk with us and show us the "farm." He said he would not join us at lunch, as his doctor had put him on a strict diet. He appeared, however, just as dessert was being served. He said he had smelled the apple pie and could not resist. Miss Lyon protested timidly, "Oh, Mr. Clemens—" "Yes, I know," he conceded, "but fresh apple pie never killed anybody. But if Helen says I can't, I won't." I did not have the heart to say he couldn't, so we compromised on a very small piece, which was later augmented by a larger piece, after a pantomimic warning to the others not to betray him. I suspected what was going on and said, "Come, let us go before Mr. Clemens sends to the kitchen for another pie." He said, "Tell her I suspected she was a psychic. That proves she is."

After luncheon, he put on a fur-lined greatcoat and fur cap, filled his pockets with cigars, and declared himself ready to start on the walk.

He picked out a winding path which he thought I could follow easily. It was a delightful path, which lay between rock and a saucy little brook that winter had not succeeded in binding with ice fetters. He asked Mrs. Macy to tell me that there was a tall white building across an intervening valley from where we were standing. "Tell her it's a church," he said. "It used to stand on this side of the brook; but the congregation moved it last summer when I told them I had no use for it. I had no idea that New England people were so accommodating. At that distance it is just what a church should be—serene and pure and mystical."

We crossed the brook on a little rustic footbridge. He said it was a prehistoric bridge, and that the quiet brown pool underneath was the one celebrated in the Songs of Solomon. I quoted the passage he referred to: "Thine eyes like the fishpools in Heshbon by the gate of Bathrabbim." It was a joy being with him, holding his hand as he pointed out each lovely spot and told some charming untruth about it. Once he said, "The book of earth is wonderful. I wish I had time to read it. I think if I had begun it in my youth, I might have got through the first chapter. But it's too late to do anything about it now."

We wandered on and on, forgetful of time and distance, beguiled by stream and meadow and seductive stone walls wearing their autumn draperies of red and gold vines a little dimmed by rain and snow, but still exquisitely beautiful. When we turned at last and started to climb the hill, Mr. Clemens paused and stood gazing over the frosty New England valley; he said, "Age is like this; we stand on the summit and look back over the distance and time. Alas, how swift are the feet of the days of the years of youth."

We realized that he was very tired. Somebody suggested that one member of the party should return cross-lots and meet us on the road with a carriage. Mr. Clemens thought this a good idea and agreed to pilot Mrs. Macy and me to the road, which he had every reason to suppose was just beyond that elephant of a hill. Our search for that road was a wonderful and fearsome adventure. It led through cowpaths, across ditches filled with ice-cold water into fields dotted with little islands of red and gold which rose gently out of the white snow. On closer inspection, we found that these islands were composed of patches of dry goldenrod and huckleberry bushes. We picked our way through treacherously smiling cart-roads. He said, "Every path leading out of this jungle dwindles into a squirrel track and runs up a tree." The cart roads proved to be ruts that ensnared our innocent feet. Mr. Clemens had the wary air of a discoverer as he turned and twisted between spreading branches of majestic pines and dwarfed hazel-bushes.

I remarked that we seemed to be away off our course. He answered, "This is the uncharted wilderness. We have wandered into the chaos that existed before Jehovah divided the waters from the land. The road is just over there," he asserted with conviction.

"Yes," we murmured faintly, wondering how we should ever ford the roaring, tumbling imp of a stream which flung itself at us out of the hills. There was no doubt about it: The road was just there "where you see that rail fence." Prophecy deepened into happy certainty when we saw the coachman waiting for us. "Stay where you are," he shouted. In a few seconds, he had dismembered the rail fence and was transporting it over the field. It did not take long to construct a rough bridge, over which we safely crossed the Redding Rubicon. And sure enough, there was the narrow road of civilization winding up the hillside between stone walls and clustering sumachs and wild cherry trees on which little icicles were beginning to form like pendants. Halfway down the drive, Miss Lyon met us with tearful reproaches. Mr. Clemens mumbled weakly, "It has happened again—the woman tempted me."

I think I never enjoyed a walk more. Sweet is the memory of hours spent with a beloved companion. Even being lost with Mr. Clemens was delightful, although I was terribly distressed that he should be exerting himself beyond his strength.

The last evening of our visit we sat around a blazing log fire, and Mr. Clemens asked me whether I should like to have him read me *Eve's Diary*. Of course, I was delighted. He asked, "How shall we manage it?" "Oh," I replied, "you will read aloud, and my teacher will spell your words into my hand." He said, "I had thought you would read my lips." "I should like to," I answered, "but I am afraid you will find it very wearisome. We'll start that way, anyhow, and if it doesn't work, we'll try the other way."

This was an experience, I am sure, no other person in the world had ever had. "You know, Mr. Clemens," I reminded him, "that we are going home tomorrow, and you promised to put on your Oxford robe for me before I go."

"So I did, Helen," he agreed, "and I will—I will do it now before I forget." Miss Lyon brought the gorgeous scarlet robe which he had worn when England's oldest university conferred upon him the degree of Doctor of Letters. He put it on and stood there in the firelight, the embodiment of gracious majesty. He seemed pleased that I was impressed. He drew me towards him and kissed me on the brow, as a cardinal or pope or a feudal monarch might have kissed a little child.

How I wish I could paint the picture of that evening! Mr. Clemens sat in his armchair, dressed in his white serge suit, the flaming scarlet robe draping his shoulders, and his white hair gleaming and glistening in the light of the lamp which shone down on his head. In one hand he held *Eve's Diary,* in a glorious red cover. In the other he held his pipe. "If it gets in the way," he said, "I'll give it up, but I feel embarrassed without it."

I sat down near him in a low chair, my elbow on the arm of his chair, so that my fingers could rest lightly on his lips. And then the play began. Everything went smoothly for a time. I had no difficulty getting the words from his lips. His pleasant drawl was music to my touch. But when he began gesticulating with his pipe, the actors in the drama got mixed up with the properties and there was confusion until the ashes were gathered into the fireplace. Then a new setting was arranged. Mrs. Macy came and sat beside me and spelled the words into my right hand, while I looked at Mr. Clemens with my left, touching his face and hands and the book, following his gestures and every changing expression.

As the reading proceeded, we became utterly absorbed in the wistful, tender chronicle of our first parents. Surely the joy, the innocence, the opening mind of childhood are among life's most sacred mysteries, and if young Eve laughs she makes creation all the sweeter for her heaven-born merriment. The beauty of Mr. Clemens's voice when Eve sighed her love, and when Adam stood at her grave grieving bitterly, saying, "Wheresoever she was, there was Eden," caused me to weep openly and the others to swallow audibly.

To one hampered and circumscribed as I am, it was a wonderful experience to have a friend like Mr. Clemens. I recall many talks with him about human affairs. He never made me feel that my opinions were worthless, as so many people do. He knew that we do not think with eyes and ears, and that our capacity for thought is not measured by what we take in through our five senses. He kept me always in mind while he talked, and he treated me like a competent human being. That is why I loved him.

Perhaps my strongest impression of him was that of sorrow. There was about him the air of one who had suffered greatly. Whenever I touched his face his expression was sad, even when he was telling a funny story. He smiled, not with the mouth but with his mind—a gesture of the soul rather than of the face. His voice was truly wonderful. To my touch, it was deep, resonant. He had the power of modulating it so as to suggest the most delicate shades of meaning, and he spoke so deliberately that I could get almost every word with my fingers on his lips. Ah, how sweet and poignant the memory of his soft, slow speech playing over my listening fingers! His words seemed to take strange, lovely shapes on my hands. His own hands were wonderfully mobile and changeable under the influence of emotion. . . .

The affluence of Mr. Clemens's mind impressed me vividly. His felicitous words gushed from it with the abundance of the Shasta Falls. Humor was on the surface, but in the center of his nature was a passion for truth, harmony, beauty. Once he remarked, in his pensive, cynical way, "There is so little in life that is not pretense."

"There is beauty, Mr. Clemens," I reminded him.

"Yes," he agreed, "there is beauty, and beauty is the seed of spirit from which we grow the flowers that shall endure."

Time passed at Stormfield as it passes everywhere else, and the day came when we had to say good-by. The kindly white figure stood on the veranda waving us farewell, as he had waved his welcome when we arrived. Silently, through Mrs. Macy's eyes, I watched the stately villa on the white hilltop fading into the purple distance. We said to each other sadly, "Shall we ever see him again?" And we never did. But we knew that we had a picture of him in our hearts which would remain there forever. In my finger tips was graven the image of his dear face with its halo of shining white hair; and in my memory his drawling, marvelous voice will always vibrate.

I have visited Stormfield since Mark Twain's death. The flowers still bloom; the breezes still whisper and sough in the cedars, which have grown statelier year by year; the birds still sing, they tell me. But for me, the place is bereft of its lover. The last time I was there, the house was in ruins. Only the great chimney was standing erect, a charred shaft of bricks in the bright autumn landscape.

Notes

1. This poem, adapted from the final stanza of the poem "Annette" by Robert Richardson, was not inscribed on Livy's gravestone in 1904 but on Susy's in 1896.

2. Stormfield had been burglarized the evening of 18 September 1909. See also "Burglar Chase at Mark Twain's Ends in Shooting," *New York World*, 19 September 1908, 3; repr. in Scharnhorst 669–73.

Helen Keller, "Mark Twain," *American Magazine* 108 (July 1929): 51, 80–81.

"Mark Twain as His Secretary
at Stormfield Remembers Him" (1925)

MARY LOUISE HOWDEN

Mary Louise Howden immigrated from England in 1908. She alludes in her
memoir to the burglary at Stormfield in September 1908 shortly before she
went to work for Twain as a stenographer.

ALL THE WAY UP the hill to Stormfield it seemed as if the rustling of meadow grass, the roar of the waterfall down in the hollow, the twittering of the birds and the shrilling of the locusts were drowned out by the persistent beating of her much perturbed heart.

The butler[1] opened the front door and directed her to go to the study. Mr. Clemens, he said, would be down in about fifteen minutes.

The Neophyte put her hat and sweater in the place indicated. She selected a notebook and sharpened a couple of pencils with meticulous care. Then, hardly knowing what she was doing, she took the cover off the typewriter and began mechanically to clean it, although it was in perfect order and never had been used.

A measured tread sounded in the hall outside and the trembling Neophyte rose to her feet. All her life she had been familiar with pictures of her new employer. But no picture, it seemed to her, had ever done justice to the picturesqueness of the figure who appeared in the doorway—the mane of snow white hair, the white suit against the dark background of the hall, the busy eyebrows that gave to the deepest blue eyes a look of fierceness that was belied by the humorous curves of the mouth under the drooping mustache. But there was something else. Mr. Clemens was not a very tall man, yet there was a dignity, a majesty about the figure in the doorway that no picture has ever succeeded in reproducing. For the rest he was ruddy featured, spare and rather rugged of frame—not a superfluous ounce of flesh on him in spite of his seventy-two years—and he was regarding the flus-

[318]

tered Neophyte with an expression that was quite kindly. Maybe he wasn't so very terrible after all!

He shook hands gravely and inquired the Neophyte's name. It was given him. He requested to have it written for him. This was done, and he frowned over it while the Neophyte shook. Then he waved the paper on one side and said abruptly:

"You take notes—in shorthand?" The Neophyte admitted that she did.

"Good," he said, his face clearing. "I would like to dictate right now." As the Neophyte sat down and opened her notebook he walked over to the window and stood there. Minutes passed, but no sound came from him. The Neophyte ventured a look. He was standing gazing dreamily out, puffing little clouds from his pipe. Presently he turned and said:

"You've heard of our burglary?" She had—first from the driver coming up from the station; and it had been the mainstay of the conversation at the farmhouse supper the night before.

"Very well," said the humorist. "Now, take this," and he dictated the following:

NOTICE

To the Next Burglar

There is nothing but plated ware in this house now and henceforth.

You will find it in the brass thing in the dining room over in the corner by the basket of kittens.

If you want the basket put the kittens in the brass thing. Do not make a noise; it will disturb the family.

You will find rubbers in the front hall by that thing which has the umbrellas in it—chiffonier, I think they call it, or pergola, or something like that.

Please close the door when you go away! Very truly yours,

S. L. CLEMENS.

Who would take down a thing like that and not want to laugh? The Neophyte's shoulders were shaking, but she dared not make a sound. She stole another glance at him. He was still gazing out of the window, not a smile on his face, and speaking in a rather deliberate drawl. Once or twice he took a restless turn or two away from the window, but always returned to it again as if the little study were too restricted for him, as indeed it was. After the first morning he rarely dictated in the study, as there was not enough room to pace up and down, as he liked to do.

He finished the "notice," gave some directions for its typing and its fu-

ture position on the front door. Then he proceeded to dictate a highly humorous account of the burglary, which account he said was intended for
his autobiography. The Neophyte was enjoying herself. She had made a
valuable discovery. Mark Twain dictated so slowly, with such long pauses
between the sentences that, green beginner as she was, she could take notes
with perfect ease and in the pauses could read back and make sure she had
not forgotten anything in the previous sentence.

His restlessness increased and the pauses between the sentences became
longer. During one of them he strolled out into the hall and vanished for
several seconds, leaving the Neophyte in grave doubt as to whether he were
finished or not. She was to learn that this was characteristic of him when he
was getting tired.

He finished on this occasion by politely hoping he had not given her too
much to do! The Neophyte could have laughed aloud at that. There was
so little that it was typed and ready before she went home to lunch. In the
afternoon she returned and took from the social secretary her first lesson in
handling the mail. She was told that on mornings when Mr. Clemens did
not wish to dictate she could attend to the letters instead, and in that case
she did not need to return in the afternoon unless Mr. Clemens wanted her.

It was the Neophyte's first introduction to the enormous mass of letters
that a famous author receives, and she was at first amazed and appalled by
it. There were letters from budding authors who wanted him to read their
books; letters from near-poets who wished him to read their poems; letters
from people who wanted to invest his money for him; letters from people
who objected to his books; letters from people who enjoyed his books;
letters from people who wanted copies of his books; letters from people
who wanted copies of his photograph, of his autograph; letters from people
who wanted everything under the sun. Letters pertinent and impertinent;
amusing letters, abusive letters, pathetic letters, and letters that were merely
futile and boring. The new stenographer was moved to indignation. "They
pester him!" she said to the social secretary.

Mr. Clemens never saw most of it—did not wish to see it. Letters from
his daughters, relatives, and close friends he read and answered himself,
sometimes by hand, sometimes by dictation. Letters from strangers that
were more than ordinarily interesting and amusing sometimes got through
the barrier. People that required to be tactfully "headed off" were dealt
with by the social secretary. The majority of the importunate correspon-

dents received a polite form letter which could be altered a little to suit each particular case. The Neophyte soon learned to handle these. Requests for autographs were taken care of by the simple method of catching the great man when he happened to be in a good humor, seating him in front of a large sheet of paper and having him write his name all over it. These were afterward cut out in little squares and kept in a handy desk drawer ready to be slipped into an envelope when a request came. A request for an autograph was never refused. Autographed photographs were kept on hand in the same way, but were dealt out much more sparingly.

One terrible day—terrible because of her feeling when she found out what she had done—the Neophyte let an effusion in *vers libre* from an utterly unheard of poet "get through" to Mr. Clemens. He dictated in bed that morning, and when she entered the room he had the verses in his hand and was reading them with an expression of intense boredom. She shook in her shoes waiting for a storm, which, however, never came. He dropped the manuscript wearily on the counterpane and lit his pipe. After a few soothing puffs he flicked the offending papers on one side and remarked gently and meditatively:

"We know God made this poet, but we don't know what He did it for!"

He dictated in bed many mornings and made as complete a picture there, with his leonine head outlined against the enormous mahogany four-poster, as he did everywhere else. In bed he could not escape when she produced her unfailing sheet of paper with a request for many autographs. The whimsical patience with which he granted the request always surprised her a little. It was touching, too. There was a sort of pathetic patience about him at times as if he found the penalties of fame very burdensome but knew that nothing could be done about it.

On other mornings the dictation took place in the billiard room. The Neophyte, sitting on the dais with pencil poised over her notebook, used to watch with keenest appreciation the white figure contrasted against the crimson walls of the billiard room—pacing, pacing restlessly. Sometimes there were four or five minute pauses between sentences. But the phrase when it came was always perfectly formed.

He put in the punctuation himself. His stenographer was never allowed to add so much as a comma. His humor was a delight, but the Neophyte from the beginning rigidly suppressed her tendency to immoderate mirth. It required considerable self control at times to keep from spluttering.

Mark Twain's gravity in dictating was a continual surprise to her. "He doesn't seem to think he's funny," she said to herself. A slightly heightened and more deliberate drawl was the only indication that something more than usually delightful was about to fall from him. The dictations were all too short for her. She would have liked much more of them. But there were mornings when he would detain her only about fifteen minutes. Then he would say with a twinkle, "Well, I guess I've done enough work for today." And in a few minutes he would be heard outside whistling like a school boy.

The typewritten manuscript she left on the study table when she went home to lunch. Mr. Clemens would find it and look it over at his leisure. If he had criticisms or corrections to make he wrote little notes and left them on the typewriter where she could find them next morning.

He was not a distinctively humorous person in his everyday life. To the Neophyte he was always rather a tragic figure, lonely in his fame. To a casual observer he seemed just a kindly, gentle, rather sad old man with a courteous Old World dignity all his own. Outside of his dictation his flashes of spontaneous wit were only for those he liked best. Irritable he could be, furious he could certainly become; but his courtesy and consideration for those who served him made it a pleasure to work for him. . . .

If Mr. Clemens was seized with an inspiration in the afternoon he never telephoned for her, as he was supposed to do, but wrote out what he had to say in longhand and left it on the study table to be typewritten next day.

On the few occasions on which this happened the Neophyte was conscience-stricken and would spend two or three succeeding afternoons at Stormfield on the chance that she might be wanted. But she generally drew a blank. Mr. Clemens preferred to go for drives or play billiards in the afternoon. But on at least two such afternoons she stayed late and counted herself in luck, though she did not catch a glimpse of any of the household. She sat on the stairs in the gathering winter twilight, thrilled to the very marrow by the harmonies that poured through the house—harmonies interpreted by a master hand. Ossip Gabrilowitsch, who afterward became Mark Twain's son-in-law, was spending the weekend. The glorious sounds would stop for a while and Mr. Clemens's sonorously clear voice could be heard reading some passages from *Tom Sawyer*. Afterward the cataract of melody would fill the house again. These two masters of technique, each in his own line, were entertaining each other. It was an entertainment an outsider would have given many dollars to hear. And the little outsider sitting curled up on the dark staircase shivered with sheer bliss.

That was a red letter day. Another was when Mr. Clemens gave the address at the formal opening of the new little library in Redding, for which he had donated most of the books. If it is possible to be ill through sheer unadulterated enjoyment, the Neophyte came very near being incapacitated that day. As most of his audience were farmers, Mark Twain began by telling them how he adored farming. That year, of course, he hadn't done much, the bananas hadn't ripened and he hadn't planted very much sugar cane. But next year, why they should see what he would do.

He went on to tell them how in the day of his youth he had once edited an agricultural paper for a short time—for a very short time.[2] The day the paper first came out under his guidance people were sitting on the office railings and crowding up the stairs to catch a glimpse of the man who was doing the editing. The editorial page was devoted to turnips. Millions of turnips, it declared, were spoiled every year by being picked before they were ripe. The proper way to do was to send a boy up to shake the tree.

When the real editor for whom Mark Twain had been substituting returned he was annoyed about it and remonstrated vigorously. But Mark Twain told him that any fool would have known he meant to say "shake the vine," of course. However, the editor took exception to his remarks anent "the molting season for cows" and he had to resign. But he felt sure that he could have sent the circulation of that paper up by leaps and bounds if he had been allowed to stay with it!

The faces of his audience were a study at first. None of them had ever had the privilege of hearing the king of humorists before. Most of them were elderly country people with all the New England taciturnity and dislike of giving themselves away, and Mark Twain's drawling speech and gravity, his inimitable way of apparently not considering himself funny, puzzled them at the outset. But long before he got through they were rocking with delight.

The Neophyte did not need to draw on the Redding library for books. She could revel to her heart's content in the well-stocked book shelves that lined the living room at Stormfield, and borrow any book she pleased therefrom.

Mr. Clemens's favorite books were not to be found there. They were kept in his room, some of them beside his bed. The *Memoirs* of St. Simon were there, Carlyle's *French Revolution*[3] and *Pepys's Diary*. His reading covered an extremely wide range, but he was especially fond of biography and letters. It was his habit to make copious annotations on the margin of his favorite books, and these comments were sometimes caustic to a degree, but always illuminating. Lying in bed he would read and read, sometimes pausing to jot down his ideas on the margin and smoke copiously and constantly. Or, dictating, he would lie back against the pillows with his eyes half shut, blowing clouds of smoke and weaving a fabric of the most delicate fantasy, or speaking vividly of men and deeds of by-gone days. He seemed to ponder each sentence before uttering it, but whatever it was—sometimes humorous, sometimes cynical, sometimes deeply and cuttingly sarcastic— it was always of absorbing interest. He was building up his autobiography for posthumous publication. . . .

The Neophyte's chief feeling during the year that she spent at Stormfield was that there was so pitifully little she could do for the humorist. Watching him she often sensed the tragedy in the life of the man who made fun for the whole world. Deprived by death of those he had loved best, much separated by circumstances from the other members of his family, and dependent upon paid help, he appeared, for all his fame, a somewhat sad and lonely figure. He could be gay at times, he could be funny; he was always intensely alive, interested in the things of the moment, but there were depths of sadness in him which welled up frequently.

There was a difference between Mark Twain and his books. The public saw the humorist, but only those who were privileged to be much with him knew the dignity and seriousness and depth of the man.

Those who know only *Tom Sawyer* and *Huckleberry Finn* and *The Innocents Abroad* do not know Mark Twain. He was very versatile. *Joan of Arc* contains depths of pathos and tenderness not reached in his other books, and it was his own favorite brain child. In moments of anger or of deep sorrow he would find relief in writing, and it was to one of the latter moments that the world owes one of the most tenderly beautiful and heartrending things that ever was written—"The Death of Jean."[4]

On Christmas Eve of 1909 the Neophyte, waiting for a suburban train in a New York terminal, picked up a newspaper and read of the death of Jean Clemens. Jean had come home to be her father's secretary after the Neophyte's departure for Florida. She was the only one of his family left him in his old age, for his daughter Clara had married Ossip Gabrilowitsch a few months before and had gone with her husband to Europe. Jean had been found dead of heart failure in her bathtub on the morning before Christmas. And the thought of that lonely old man in that big house, surrounded by preparations for Christmas festivities, with the dead body of his daughter lying upstairs, was too much for the Neophyte. The tears flowed down her cheeks as she cried openly and unashamed there in the terminal and heeded not the curious looks of homebound commuters.[5]

Mr. Clemens eased the pain in his heart by putting the account of Jean's death down on paper and when he had finished he said, "I shall never write any more." It was his swan song, and when, four months later, the Neophyte heard that the end had come she could not but be glad for him. Mark Twain had coveted death. He had reached the zenith of his fame. His heart was buried in the graves of those whom he had loved so faithfully, and the world could give him nothing that he wanted any more. And those who knew the man and cared for him could only be thankful that he had got his wish in spite of their own sorrow.

Notes

1. Claude Joseph Beuchotte (1877–1941?), Twain's last butler.

2. At the opening of the library in Redding on 28 October 1908, Twain read a version of his essay "How I Edited an Agricultural Paper Once," originally published in *Galaxy* 10 (July 1870): 133–35.

3. Twain described Carlyle's *History of the French Revolution* in a letter to Mary Mason Fairbanks on 6 August 1877 as "one of the greatest creations that ever flowed from a pen" (*Mark Twain to Mrs. Fairbanks* 207).

4. "The Death of Jean" was Twain's last significant writing. Originally published in *Harper's Monthly* 122 (January 1911): 210–15, Twain chose to end his *Autobiography* with it.

5. According to the inventory of letters to Twain, Howden wrote him that day to express her condolences.

Mary Louise Howden, "Mark Twain as His Secretary at Stormfield Remembers Him," *New York Herald,* 13 December 1925, VII 1–4.

From *My Mark Twain* (1910)

W. D. HOWELLS

> Howells came to Stormfield for the wedding of Clara Clemens and Ossip Gabrilowitsch on 6 October 1909. It was the last time he saw Twain alive.

MY VISIT AT STORMFIELD came to an end with tender relucting on his part and on mine. Every morning before I dressed I heard him sounding my name through the house for the fun of it and I know for the fondness; and if I looked out of my door, there he was in his long nightgown swaying up and down the corridor, and wagging his great white head like a boy that leaves his bed and comes out in the hope of frolic with some one. The last morning a soft sugarsnow had fallen and was falling, and I drove through it down to the station in the carriage which had been given him by his wife's father when they were first married, and been kept all those intervening years in honorable retirement for this final use. Its springs had not grown yielding with time; it had rather the stiffness and severity of age; but for him it must have swung low like the sweet chariot of the negro "spiritual" which I heard him sing with such fervor, when those wonderful hymns of the slaves began to make their way northward. "Go Down, Daniel" was one in which I can hear his quavering tenor now. He was a lover of the things he liked, and full of a passion for them which satisfied itself in reading them matchlessly aloud. No one could read *Uncle Remus* like him; his voice echoed the voices of the negro nurses who told his childhood the wonderful tales. I remember especially his rapture with Mr. Cable's *Old Creole Days,* and the thrilling force with which he gave the forbidding of the leper's brother when the city's survey ran the course of an avenue through the cottage where the leper lived in hiding: "Strit must not pass!"

Out of a nature rich and fertile beyond any I have known, the material given him by the Mystery that makes a man and then leaves him to make himself over, he wrought a character of high nobility upon a foundation of clear and solid truth. At the last day he will not have to confess anything, for all his life was the free knowledge of anyone who would ask him of it.

The Searcher of hearts will not bring him to shame at that day, for he did not try to hide any of the things for which he was often so bitterly sorry. He knew where the Responsibility lay, and he took a man's share of it bravely; but not the less fearlessly he left the rest of the answer to the God who had imagined men.

It is in vain that I try to give a notion of the intensity with which he pierced to the heart of life, and the breadth of vision with which he compassed the whole world, and tried for the reason of things, and then left trying. We had other meetings, insignificantly sad and brief; but the last time I saw him alive was made memorable to me by the kind, clear judicial sense with which he explained and justified the labor-unions as the sole present help of the weak against the strong.

Next I saw him dead, lying in his coffin amid those flowers with which we garland our despair in that pitiless hour. After the voice of his old friend Twichell had been lifted in the prayer which it wailed through in broken-hearted supplication, I looked a moment at the face I knew so well; and it was patient with the patience I had so often seen in it: something of puzzle, a great silent dignity, an assent to what must be from the depths of a nature whose tragical seriousness broke in the laughter which the unwise took for the whole of him. Emerson, Longfellow, Lowell, Holmes—I knew them all and all the rest of our sages, poets, seers, critics, humorists; they were like one another and like other literary men; but Clemens was sole, incomparable, the Lincoln of our literature.

W. D. Howells, from *My Mark Twain* (New York: Harper & Bros., 1910), 99–101.

Works Cited

"About Mark Twain." *New York World,* 12 January 1877, 5.

Ade, George. *One Afternoon with Mark Twain.* Chicago: Mark Twain Society, 1939.

Alden, Henry M. "Mark Twain: Personal Impressions." *Book News Monthly* 28 (April 1910): 582.

Aldrich, Lilian. *Crowding Memories.* Boston: Houghton Mifflin, 1920.

Andrews, Kenneth. *Nook Farm: Mark Twain's Hartford Circle.* Cambridge, Mass.: Harvard University Press, 1950.

Austin, Franklin H. "Mark Twain Incognito—A Reminiscence." *Friend* 96 (September 1926): 201; 96 (October 1926): 250–52.

B., R. C. "Mark Twain on the Platform." *Critic* 25 (April 1896): 286.

Bacheller, Irving. *Opinions of a Cheerful Yankee.* Indianapolis, Ind.: Bobbs-Merrill, 1926.

Barnes, George E. "Mark Twain as He Was Known during His Stay on the Pacific Slope." *San Francisco Morning Call,* 17 April 1887, 1.

———. "Memories of Mark Twain." *Overland Monthly* 66 (September 1915): 263–65.

Bassford, Homer. "Mark Twain as a Cub Pilot: A Talk with Captain Horace Bixby." *Saturday Evening Post,* 16 December 1899, 515.

Beard, Dan. *Hardly a Man Is Now Alive.* New York: Doubleday, 1939.

Bigelow, Poultney. *Seventy Summers.* London: Edward Arnold, 1925.

Bowden, Betsy. "Gloom and Doom in Mark Twain's *Connecticut Yankee* from Thomas Malory's *Morte D'Arthur.*" *Studies in American Fiction* 28 (Autumn 2000): 179–202.

Branch, Edgar M., ed. *Clemens of the Call.* Berkeley: University of California Press, 1969.

Brooks, Noah. "Mark Twain in California." *Century* 57 (November 1898): 97–99.

Budd, Louis J., ed. *Mark Twain: The Contemporary Reviews.* New York: Cambridge University Press, 1999.

———. *Our Mark Twain.* Philadelphia: University of Pennsylvania Press, 1983.

Buinicki, Martin T. "Staking a Claim: Samuel L. Clemens' Pragmatic Views on Copyright Law." *American Literary Realism* 37 (Fall 2004): 59–82.

Bush, Harold K., Jr. "The Mythic Struggle Between East and West: Mark Twain's Speech at Whittier's 70th Birthday Celebration and W. D. Howells' *A Chance Acquaintance.*" *American Literary Realism* 27 (Winter 1995): 53–73.

Butcher, Philip. "Mark Twain's Installment on the National Debt." *Southern Literary Journal* 1 (Spring 1969): 48–55.

Cannon, Joseph G., and L. White Busbey. *Uncle Joe Cannon.* New York: Holt, 1927.

Carnegie, Andrew. *Autobiography.* Boston: Houghton Mifflin, 1920.

Chambliss, Amy. "The Friendship of Helen Keller and Mark Twain." *Georgia Review* 24 (Fall 1970): 305–10.

Churchill, Winston. *A Roving Commission.* New York: Scribner's, 1930.

Clark, Charles H. "Mark Twain at 'Nook Farm' (Hartford) and Elmira." *Critic,* 17 January 1885, 25–26.

Clemens, Clara. *My Father Mark Twain.* New York: Harper & Bros., 1931.

Clemens, James Ross, M.D. "Some Reminiscences of Mark Twain." *Overland Monthly and Out West Magazine* 87 (April 1929): 105, 125.

Clemens, Samuel L. [Mark Twain]. *Adventures of Huckleberry Finn.* Ed. Victor Fischer et al. Berkeley: University of California Press, 2003.

———. *The Adventures of Tom Sawyer.* Ed. John C. Gerber et al. Berkeley: University of California Press, 1980.

———. *The American Claimant.* New York: Webster, 1892.

———. *Autobiography.* Ed. Albert Bigelow Paine. New York: Harper and Bros., 1924.

———. *Autobiography.* Ed. Charles Neider. New York: Harper, 1959.

———. *Christian Science.* New York: Harper, 1907.

———. *A Connecticut Yankee in King Arthur's Court.* Ed. Bernard L. Stein. Berkeley: University of California Press, 1979.

———. *Early Tales and Sketches.* Ed. Edgar Marquess Branch and Robert H. Hirst. 2 vols. Berkeley: University of California Press, 1979–81.

———. *Following the Equator.* Hartford, Conn.: American Publishing, 1897.

———. *How to Tell a Story and Other Essays.* New York: Harper, 1897.

———. *The Innocents Abroad; or, The New Pilgrim's Progress.* Hartford, Conn.: American Publishing, 1869.

———. *King Leopold's Soliloquy.* Boston: Warren, 1905.

———. *Life on the Mississippi.* Boston: Osgood, 1883.

———. *Mark Twain in Eruption.* Ed. Bernard De Voto. New York: Harper, 1940.

———. *Mark Twain's Correspondence with Henry Huttleston Rogers, 1893–1909.* Ed. Lewis Leary. Berkeley: University of California Press, 1969.

———. *Mark Twain's Letters.* 6 vols. Ed. Edgar Marquess Branch et al. Berkeley: University of California Press, 1988–2002.

———. *Mark Twain's Letters from Hawaii.* Ed. A. Grove Day. New York: Appleton-Century, 1966.

———. *Mark Twain's Own Autobiography.* Ed. Michael J. Kiskis. Madison: University of Wisconsin Press, 1990.

———. *Mark Twain to Mrs. Fairbanks.* Ed. Dixon Wecter. San Marino: Huntington Library, 1949.

———. *Personal Recollections of Joan of Arc.* New York: Harper, 1895.

———. *Roughing It.* Ed. Elinor Smith et al. Berkeley: University of California Press, 1993.

———. *Sketches, New and Old.* Hartford, Conn.: American Publishing, 1875.

———. *The Tragedy of Pudd'nhead Wilson.* Hartford, Conn.: American Publishing, 1894.

———. *A Tramp Abroad.* Hartford, Conn.: American Publishing, 1880.

———. *What Is Man?* New York: De Vinne, 1906.

Clemens, Samuel L. [Mark Twain], and W. D. Howells. *Mark Twain–Howells Letters.* Ed. Henry Nash Smith and William Gibson. Cambridge, Mass.: Belknap, 1960.

Clemens, Samuel L. [Mark Twain], and Charles Dudley Warner. *The Gilded Age.* Hartford, Conn.: American Publishing, 1874.

Clemens, Susy. *Papa: An Intimate Biography of Mark Twain.* Ed. Charles Neider. Garden City, N.Y.: Doubleday, 1985.

Clemens, Will M. "Mark Twain on the Lecture Platform." *Ainslee's* 6 (August 1900): 25–32.

Conway, Moncure D. *Autobiography.* Boston: Houghton Mifflin, 1904.

———. "Mark Twain in London." *Cincinnati Commercial,* 10 October 1872, 4.

Cooley, John, ed. *Mark Twain's Aquarium: The Samuel Clemens Correspondence 1905–1910.* Athens: University of Georgia Press, 1991.

Dam, Henry J. W. "A Morning with Bret Harte." *McClure's* 4 (December 1894): 38–50.

David, Beverly R. "The Pictorial *Huck Finn:* Mark Twain and His Illustrator, E. W. Kemble." *American Quarterly* 26 (October 1974): 331–51.

———. "The Unexpurgated *A Connecticut Yankee:* Mark Twain and His Illustrator, Dan Beard." *Prospects* 1 (1975): 99–118.

Davis, Sam. "Mark Twain on Friends and Fighters." *Philadelphia North American,* 1 January 1906, 14.

De Quille, Dan. "Salad Days of Mark Twain." *San Francisco Examiner,* 19 March 1893, 13–14.

Eggleston, George Cary. *Recollections of a Varied Life.* New York: Holt, 1910.

Fairbanks, Mary Mason. "The Cruise of the *Quaker City.*" *Chautauquan* 14 (January 1892): 429–32.

Fanning, Philip. *Mark Twain and Orion Clemens: Brothers, Partners, Strangers.* Tuscaloosa: University of Alabama Press, 2003.

Fatout, Paul. "Mark Twain: Litigant." *American Literature* 31 (March 1959): 30–45.

———, ed. *Mark Twain Speaking.* Iowa City: University of Iowa Press, 1976.

Fields, Annie Adams. *Memories of a Hostess: A Chronicle of Eminent Friendships.* Ed. M. A. DeWolfe Howe. Boston: Atlantic Monthly Press, 1922.

Fitch, Tom. "Fitch Recalls Mark Twain in Bonanza Times." *San Francisco Chronicle,* 30 March 1919, 6F.

———. *Western Carpetbagger: The Extraordinary Memoirs of "Senator" Tom Fitch.* Reno: University of Nevada Press, 1978.

Flagg, James Montgomery. *Roses and Buckshot.* New York: Putnam's, 1946.

Frazer, Laura. "Mark Twain's Childhood Sweetheart Recalls Their Romance." *Literary Digest,* 23 March 1918, 70, 73–75.

French, Bryant Morley. *Mark Twain and the Gilded Age.* Dallas: Southern Methodist University Press, 1965.

Frohman, Daniel. *Daniel Frohman Presents: An Autobiography.* New York: Claude Kendall & Willoughby Sharp, 1935.

Garland, Hamlin. *Companions on the Trail: A Literary Chronicle.* New York: Macmillan, 1931.

———. *Roadside Meetings.* New York: Macmillan, 1931.

Gillis, William R. *Memories of Mark Twain and Steve Gillis.* Sonora, Calif.: Banner, 1924.

Goodwin, C. C. *As I Remember Them.* Salt Lake City: Special Committee of the Salt Lake Commercial Club, 1913.

Hammond, John Hay. *Autobiography.* New York: Farrar & Rinehart, 1935.

Hammond, Natalie. *A Woman's Part in a Revolution.* New York: Longmans, Green, 1897.

Hapgood, Norman. *The Changing Years.* New York: Farrar & Rinehart, 1930.

Harding, Dorothy Sturgis. "Mark Twain Lands an Angel Fish." *Columbia Library Columns* 16 (February 1967): 5–10.

Harper, J. Henry. *I Remember.* New York: Smith, 1934.

Harris, Frank. *Contemporary Portraits, Fourth Series.* New York: Brentano's, 1923.

Henderson, Archibald. *Mark Twain.* New York: Stokes, 1910.

Hill, Hamlin. "Ashcroft-Lyon Manuscript." In *The Mark Twain Encyclopedia,* ed. J. R. LeMaster and James D. Wilson, 43–44. New York: Garland, 1993.

———. *Mark Twain: God's Fool.* New York: Harper & Row, 1973.

House, Edward H. "Mark Twain as a Lecturer." *New York Tribune,* 11 May 1867, 2.

Howden, Mary Louise. "Mark Twain as His Secretary at Stormfield Remembers Him." *New York Herald,* 13 December 1925, VII 1–4.

Howells, W. D. *My Mark Twain.* New York: Harper & Bros., 1910.

"Jos. Goodman's Memories of Humorist's Early Days." *San Francisco Examiner,* 22 April 1910, 3.

Keller, Helen. "Mark Twain." *American Magazine* 108 (July 1929): 51, 80–81.

Kemble, E. M. "Illustrating Huck Finn." *Colophon,* part 1 (1930): n.p.

King, Grace. *Memories of a Southern Woman of Letters.* New York: Macmillan, 1932.

Kiskis, Michael J. "Introduction" to *Mark Twain's Own Autobiography,* xv–xl. Madison: University of Wisconsin Press, 1990.

Kordecki, Lesley C. "Twain's Critique of Malory's Romance: *Forma Tractandi* and *A Connecticut Yankee.*" *Nineteenth-Century Literature* 41 (December 1986): 329–48.

Langdon, Jervis. *Samuel Langhorne Clemens.* Elmira, N.Y.: privately printed, 1910.

Larned, J. N. "Mark Twain." *Buffalo Evening Express,* 26 April 1910, 5.

Lawton, Mary. *A Lifetime with Mark Twain: The Memories of Katy Leary.* New York: Harcourt, Brace, 1925.

Lucas, E. V. "E. V. Lucas and Twain at a '*Punch* Dinner.'" London *Bookman* 38 (June 1910): 16–19.

MacAlister, Sir George Ian. "Mark Twain, Some Personal Reminiscences." *Landmark* 20 (March 1938): 141–45.

"Mark Twain's Boyhood: An Interview with Mrs. Jane Clemens." *Chicago Inter-Ocean,* 5 April 1885, III 17.

"Mark Twain's Childhood Sweetheart Recalls Their Romance" *Literary Digest,* 23 March 1918, 70, 73–75.

Marsh, Grant. "Mark Twain." *St. Louis Missouri Republican,* 8 December 1878, 7.

Matthews, Brander. "Memories of Mark Twain." *Saturday Evening Post,* 6 March 1920, 14–15, 77–78, 81.

McEwen, Arthur. "In the Heroic Days." *San Francisco Examiner,* 22 January 1893, 15.

Morrow, James B. "Mark Twain's Exclusive Publisher Tells What the Humorist Is Paid." *Washington Post,* 3 March 1907, A12.

Paine, Albert Bigelow. "Innocents at Home." *Collier's Weekly,* 3 January 1925, 5–6, 45.

———. *Mark Twain: A Biography.* New York: Harper, 1912.

———. "Mark Twain at Stormfield." *Harper's Monthly* 118 (May 1909): 955–58.

Pond, James B. *Eccentricities of Genius.* New York: Dillingham, 1900.

Quick, Dorothy. "A Little Girl's Mark Twain." *North American Review* 240 (September 1935): 342–48.

Rideing, William H. "Mark Twain in Clubland." *Bookman* 31 (June 1910): 379–82.

Roberts, Taylor. "The Recovery of Mark Twain's Copy of *Morte D'Arthur.*" *Resources for American Literary Study* 23 (1997): 166–80.

Scharnhorst, Gary, ed. *Mark Twain: The Complete Interviews.* Tuscaloosa: University of Alabama Press, 2006.

Shaw, George Bernard. "Letters to the Editor." *Saturday Review of Literature,* 12 August 1944, 15.

Simboli, Raffaele. "Mark Twain from an Italian Point of View." *Critic* 44 (June 1904): 518–24.

Skandera Trombley, Laura. *Mark Twain in the Company of Women.* Philadelphia: University of Pennsylvania Press, 1994.

———. "Mark Twain's *Annus Horribilis* of 1908–1909." *American Literary Realism* 40 (Winter 2008): 114–36.

Smith, Henry Nash. "That Hideous Mistake of Poor Clemens." *Harvard Library Bulletin* 9 (1955): 145–80.

Stewart, William M. *Reminiscences of Senator William M. Stewart of Nevada.* Ed. George Rothwell Brown. New York: Neale, 1908.

Stoddard, Charles Warren. "In Old Bohemia." *Pacific Monthly* 19 (March 1908): 262–63.

Turner, Arlin. *Mark Twain and George W. Cable: The Record of a Literary Friendship.* East Lansing: Michigan State University Press, 1960.

Wallace, Elizabeth. *Mark Twain and the Happy Island.* Chicago: McClurg, 1914.

Watterson, Henry. "Mark Twain—An Intimate Portrait." *American Magazine* 70 (July 1910): 372–75.

White, Frank Marshall. "Mark Twain as a Newspaper Reporter." *Outlook* 96 (December 1910): 961–67.

Yates, Edmund. *Celebrities at Home,* vol. 3. London: Office of the World, 1879.

Zwick, Jim, ed. *Mark Twain's Weapons of Satire.* Syracuse, N.Y.: Syracuse University Press, 1992.

Index

A. B. Chambers (steamboat), 13
Abbey, Edwin Austin, 139, 140n5, 157
Abbott, Willis, 264
Aberdeen, Lord, 199
Adams, William Taylor, 304n1
Ade, George, xx, 246–50
Agnew, Joy, 285
Agnew, Philip L., 285
Aguinaldo, Emilio, 239, 240n1, 309
Albert, Prince, 84, 86n2
Alden, Henry M., xx, 253–54
Aldrich, Lilian, 95–98
Aldrich, Thomas Bailey, 80, 81, 95,
    96–97, 129, 141, 142, 184, 187
Aleck Scott (steamboat), 10, 12n3
Allen, James Lane, 139
Alonzo Child (steamboat), 10, 12n3
American Anti-Imperialist League, xix
"American Authors and British Pi-
    rates," 158, 161n3
American Copyright League, 157
American Publishing Co., 77, 272n1
Anderson, Rufus, 61
Andreeva, Maria, 273
angelfish, 287, 296–98, 301–2
Anthony, James, 54
anti-imperialism, xix
Appleton, Tom, 99, 102, 104n1
Ashcroft, Ralph, xvi, 297, 298n2
Atlantic Monthly, 80, 101, 107, 108,
    111n4

Aurora (Nevada), 16, 22
Austen, Jane, 116, 132
Austin, Franklin H., 55–58
Austin (Nevada), 40, 41
Austin, Samuel L., 55–58
Australia, 202–4
Authors' Club, 150

Bacheller, Irving, xx, 154–56
Bacon, Francis, 81, 116
Badeni, Kasimir Felix, 218, 220n2
Baldwin, Sandy, 262
Barnes, George E., xx, 40–41, 47–49,
    52, 54, 59–62
Barnes, W. W., 40–41
Barrett, Lawrence, 157, 183
Barstow, William H., 16
Bassford, Homer, 8–12
Bayreuth (Germany), 182n2
Beard, Dan, xv, xx, 163–68, 176–77,
    263–65, 305–7
Bede, Adam, 279
Beecher, Henry Ward, 104n7, 187
Beethoven, Ludwig von, 304
Belasco, David, 169
Bell, Alexander Graham, 208
Bellingham (Washington), 198
Berlin (Germany), 178, 179, 290
Bermuda, 174, 293–96, 306
Bermudian (steamship), 296
Bernhardt, Sarah, 164

Bettington, Rowland Albemarle, 207, 209n2

Beuchotte, Claude Joseph, 318, 325n1

Big Bonanza mine, 266, 272n1

Bigelow, Poultney, 210–12, 241

billiards, 115, 128–29, 154, 170, 270–72, 297, 301, 321, 322

Birrell, Augustine, 187–88

Bixby, Horace, xx, 8–12

Blackmer, Margaret, 293, 295n1

Bliss, Elisha, 124, 126n4

Boer War, 237

Boldrewood, Rolf, 204

Booth, Edwin, 183

Booth, William, 284

Boston (Massachusetts), 80–81, 100, 109, 118, 141

Botticelli, 258

Bowman, James F., 59, 60

Brevoort House, 94, 291, 298

Brisbane, Arthur, 264

British Museum, 84, 85

Brontë, Charlotte, 125n3

Brooks, Noah, xx, 67–68, 77–78

Brooks, Van Wyck, 126n5

Brown, George McL., 200

Brown, William, 10, 11n2

Browne, Charles Farrar, 25

Browne, Thomas Alexander, 204

Budd, Louis J., xiii, xv, xvii

Buffalo Express, xix, 79

Buffalo (New York), xix, 79, 304

Bunyan, John, xviii, 206

Burke, Billie, 298

Burke, Martin, G. J., 47

Burroughs, John, 306

Burton, Richard, 116, 117n4

Busbey, L. White, 277–79

Bushnell, Horace, 129

Butte (Montana), 194

Byrne, Michael, 235n1

Byron, Lord, 37n6, 86

Cable, George Washington, xx, 129, 139, 141, 142n1, 143, 145–47, 189, 326

Caine, Hall, 125

Cairo (Illinois), 13

Californian, 25, 47, 48, 52, 53

Cambridge (Massachusetts), 109–10

Cannon, Joseph G., xx, 277–79

Capetown (South Africa), 209, 213

Carlyle, Thomas, 324, 325n3

Carnegie, Andrew, xviii, xx, 221n4, 238–40, 264

Carson City (Nevada), 16, 20, 30, 31, 260

Carson Daily Appeal, 260

Castro, Thomas, 94n1

cats, 194, 297, 299, 303

Century, 138–39, 140n2, 142n1, 166

Cervantes, 205

Ceylon, 202

Charles L. Webster & Co., xiv, 137, 139, 152, 168n1, 189, 227

Chase, W. G., 200

Chatto and Windus, 222

Cheever, Henry T., 61

Chelsea (England), 211, 213, 217, 222

Chicago (Illinois), 20, 21, 248

Chicago Record, 248

Child, Francis James, 121

Choate, Joseph H., 187

Choate, Rufus, 104n8

Chopin, Frederic, 304

Christian Science, 231, 232n5, 232n6, 252

Christian Union, 148

Churchill, Winston, xx, 237

Cincinnati Commercial, 82, 92

Cincinnati (Ohio), 8, 82, 92, 145

Civil War, xviii, 11, 14–15, 209n1

Clare, Ada, 25, 35–36

Clark, Champ, 279

Clark, Charles H., 127–30

Clarke, C. Purdon, 264

Clay, Henry, 136

Clemens, Clara (daughter), xvi, xx, 111n2, 128, 131–32, 149, 178, 181, 190, 193, 194, 211, 212n2, 213, 235, 251, 252, 253, 255, 258, 260, 297, 298, 306, 324, 326

Clemens, Henry (brother), 3, 10, 11n2

Clemens, James Ross (cousin), xx, 219, 220n3, 222–24

Clemens, Jane (mother), xiv, xx, 1–3, 9, 44

Clemens, Jean (daughter), 100, 128, 131, 132n2, 165, 178, 181, 182n3, 251, 252, 253, 258, 260, 324–25

Clemens, John Marshall (father), 1, 2, 3, 7, 12n1

Clemens, Langdon (son), 106, 304n2

Clemens, Mollie (sister-in-law), 1, 13

Clemens, Olivia Langdon (wife), xix, 2, 79, 97, 99–100, 103, 104, 107, 110, 111n2, 126n5, 127, 128, 132, 133, 148, 149, 165, 178, 179–81, 191, 193, 194, 199, 200, 211, 213–14, 226, 227, 235, 239, 241, 243, 244, 252–58, 260, 309, 317n1

Clemens, Orion (brother), xviii, 1, 13, 15, 16

Clemens, Samuel. *See* Mark Twain

Clemens, Susy (daughter), xx, 100, 128, 131, 132n1, 148–49, 178, 180, 181–82, 213, 254, 304n2, 309, 317n1

Clemens, Will M., 143–44

Cleveland (Ohio), 69, 143, 190; *Cleveland Herald*, 69

Cody, Buffalo Bill, 145, 166

Collier's Weekly, 116

Collins, John A., 35

Collins, Wilkie, 125n3

Colt, Elizabeth Jarvis, 102, 104n9

Columbia (Missouri), 252n1

Columbus, Christopher, 205

Conway, Moncure D., 82–88

Coolbrith, Ina, 89

Cooper, James Fenimore, 125n3

copyright, xv–xvi, 157–59, 224, 277–79

Corbett, Jim, 171, 175n1

Crane, Stephen, 154

Crane, Susan Langdon, 127, 128, 131

Crane, Theodore W., 127, 128, 132

Crookston (Minnesota), 193

Cross, Samuel, 4, 6

Daggett, Roland M., 17, 19n4, 26, 27, 44–46, 48, 262

Dakin, Edwin Franden, 252

Dam, Henry J. W., 52–53

Dana, Richard Henry, 100

d'Annunzio, Gabriele, 257

Dante, 257

Darwin, Charles, 117

Davis, Samuel P., xx, 260–62

Dawson, George F., 29, 30

Day, Alice Hooker, 104n7

De Quille, Dan, xx, 16, 17, 22, 23, 24, 25–39, 262, 272n1

de Thulstrup, Thure, 264

De Voto, Bernard, xvi

Deane, William Henry, 30

Delmonico's, 260

Denver (Colorado), 188n1

Depew, Chauncey M., 216

Dickens, Charles, 91n1, 125n3, 202

Dickinson, Anna, 100

Dolby, George, 89, 91n1

Dowie, John Alexander, xvii

Doyle, A. Conan, 280

Dublin (New Hampshire), 269, 272n3

Duluth (Minnesota), 190, 192

Dumas père, Alexandre, 125n3

Duncan, C. C., xvii, xx, 69, 71–72

Dunne, Finley Peter, 308

Duse, Eleonora, 256

earthquakes, 18, 19n6, 19n7

Eddy, Mary Baker, xvii, 231, 232n5, 252

Edward, King, 125

Edwards, Harry Stilwell, 139

Eggleston, George Cary, 150–51

Egypt, 257, 270

Elmira (New York), 79, 127–29, 131, 133, 134, 181, 182, 190, 193, 246

Emerson, Ralph Waldo, 107, 109, 111n3, 118–21, 327

Emmanuel, Victor, 257

Fairbanks, Mary Mason, xx, 69–70, 191, 201n3, 325n3

Falls City (steamboat), 10, 12n3

Field, Kate, xvii

Fields, Annie Adams, 99–104

Fields, James T., 80, 81, 99, 103, 104n8

Fitch, Tom, xx, 14–15, 22, 27, 42–46, 63

Flagg, James Montgomery, xvi, 241–42

Fleming, Henry S., 264

Fleming, Marjorie, 254

Florence (Italy), 178–80, 257–59, 300

Florida (Missouri), 1

Foo, Wong Chin, 168n2

Franklin, William Buel, 207, 209n1

Fraser, W. Lewis, 138–39

Frazier (also Frazer), Laura, xx, 4–7

Frohman, Daniel, xiv, 169–70

Frost, A. B., 140

Funston, Frederick, xvii, 185, 188n1

Gabrilowitsch, Ossip, xvi, 212n2, 298, 322, 324, 326

Galaxy, 325n2

Gamble, Hamilton Rowan, 15n2

Garland, Hamlin, xx, 225–28, 251–52

Genoa (Italy), 257

Gerhardt, Karl, 152, 153n1, 230

Gibson, Charles Dana, 264

Gilder, Richard Watson, 138, 139, 140n3, 150, 166, 306

Gillette, William, 116, 117n2, 223, 230

Gillis, Jim, xx, 52

Gillis, Steve, 28, 29, 37n1, 42, 47, 50, 261

Gillis, William G., 50–51

Gilman, Charlotte Perkins, 104n7

Goerz, Adolf, 210–12

Goethe, 297, 298n3, 311

Gold Hill (Nevada), 21

Golden Era, 47, 48

Goldman, Moses, 26

Goldsmith, Oliver, 37n9

Goodman, Joseph T., xx, 16, 17, 20–21, 22, 26, 28, 30, 97

Goodwin, C. C., 16–19

Gorky, Maxim, xiv, 273–74

Graham-Dewey, E. H., 217, 218

Grant, Fred, 226

Grant, Ulysses, 148, 152, 153n1, 187, 190, 225–27, 228n1, 242

Great Falls (Montana), 193

Gridley, Reuel Colt, 40, 41

Griffin, George, 96, 98n3, 242

Griller, J. Adolphe, 201n1

Hale & Norcross mine, 47

Hall, Fred, 163, 168n1, 176, 177

Halstead, Murat, 92, 94

Hamersley, William, 99, 104n4

Hamilton, Alexander, 136

Hamilton (Ohio), 145

Hammond, John Hay, 207–9

Hammond, Natalie, 205–6, 207, 209n3

Hannibal (Missouri), 1, 4–7, 14, 41, 134, 248–49, 251, 252n1, 297

Hapgood, Charles H., 255

Hapgood, Fanny Powers, 255

Hapgood, Norman, 116–17, 255–56, 264

Harding, Dorothy Sturgis, xx, 296–98

Hardy, Thomas, 222

Harper & Bros., xiv, 151n1, 175n4

Harper, J. Henry, xx, 134–36, 150, 151n1, 171–75

Harper, John, 151n1

Harper's Bazar, 265

Harper's Monthly, 59, 60, 171, 172, 218, 253, 325n4

Harper's Weekly, 116, 175n4, 260

Harris, Frank, xvii, 123–26

Harris, Joel Chandler, 142n1, 326

Harte, Bret, xvii, xviii, xx, 52–53, 59, 60, 77, 80, 81, 89, 112, 123–25, 126n4

Hartford (Connecticut), 92, 95, 99, 105–6, 108, 112–13, 116–17, 121, 127–29, 154, 181, 182, 207, 233, 253, 275, 304

Hartford Courant, 92, 127

Harvey, George B. M., xx, 174, 175n4, 260, 280–81

Hawaii, 54, 55–58, 59–60

Hawkins, Laura. *See* Frazier, Laura

Hawkins, Willis, 154, 156n2

Hawthorne, Sophia, 99

Hay, John, 92, 143

Hayes, Rutherford B., 123

Heidelberg (Germany), 25, 123–25

Heilbronn (Germany), 292n1

Henderson, Archibald, 275–76, 282

Henry, Caleb Sprague, 129, 130n2

Herrick, Robert, 139

Hitchcock, Lucius, 264, 265n3

Hobby, Josephine, 268, 272n2

Holland, George, 188n3

Holmes, Oliver Wendell, 118–21, 187, 327

Honolulu Pacific Commercial Advertiser, 61

Horatio G. Wright (steamboat), 9

Horr, Elizabeth, 4, 6

Hotten, John Camden, xvii

Houghton, H. O., 107

Houghton Mifflin, 118, 137

House, Edward H., xiii–xiv, 64–66, 169

Howden, Mary Louise, 318–25

Howells, John Mead, 297

Howells, W. D., xvii, xx, 80–81, 95, 96, 105–11, 118–22, 126n5, 127, 129, 130n1, 140n5, 141–42, 150, 152–53, 160, 172–73, 184, 229–32, 241, 242–43, 248, 269, 270, 273–74, 297, 306, 311, 326–27

Howland, Robert, 16, 19n2

Hugo, Victor, 125n3

humor, 44, 115, 166, 172

Hutton, Laurence, 157, 308

international copyright, xv–xvi, 157–59, 224, 277–79

Irving, Henry, 129

Jackson, Claiborne Fox, 15n2
James, Henry, xvii–xviii
Jameson, Leander Starr, 205; and
    Jameson raiders, 205–9
Janvier, Thomas A., 264
Japanese question, 271
Jardin Mabille (Paris), 84
Jefferson, Joseph, 99
Jefferson, Thomas, 136
Joan of Arc, xiv, 171, 172, 181, 200, 259,
    264–65, 294, 324
Joel, Solomon Barnato, 208, 209n4
Johannesburg (South Africa), 207, 210
Johnson, Samuel, 223
Johnston, Richard Malcolm, 139
Jonson, Ben, 37n2
Joubert, Petrus Jacobus, 208, 209n7
Jouffroy, François, 153n1

Kate Adams (steamboat), 134
Keeler, Ralph, 80, 81
Keller, Helen, xx, 291, 308–17
Kemble, E. W., xv, xx, 137–40, 264
Kenealy, Edward Vaughan, 93, 94n2
Kennan, George, 192
Kennedy, Charles Rann, 297
Keokuk, Iowa, 1
Kerr, Orpheus C., 25, 35, 36, 37
Keyes, E. L., 264
King, Grace, xx, 178–82
Kinsmen, 157
Kipling, Rudyard, 246, 250n1,
    284, 310
Kitchener, Lord, 284
Kittery Point (Maine), 244
Klinefelter (or Kleinfelter), John S., 10,
    11n2
Kossuth, Louis, 273
Krüger, Paul, 208, 209n5

La Shelle, Kirke, 242n2
La Shelle, Maisie, 242
Laffan, W. M., 157
Laird, James L., 42–43
Lampton, James, 92, 93
Langdon, Jervis (the elder), xix,
    25, 79
Langdon, Jervis (the younger), xx, 133
Larned, J. N., 79
Lawton, Mary, 233–36
Leary, Katy, xx, 233–36
lectures, xviii, 141–47, 189, 202–4,
    229
Leo, Pope, 152
Leopold, King (of Belgium), 185
Life, 137, 140
Lincoln, Abraham, 15n3, 80, 135, 166,
    327
Locke, David Ross, 63
Loeffler, Martin, 298
London (England), 82–87, 89, 112,
    175, 187, 202, 211, 213–14, 222, 225,
    282–85; London *Evening Globe*,
    222; London *World*, 112
Longfellow, Henry Wadsworth,
    118–21, 327
Lotos Club, 241
Louisville (Kentucky), 141; *Louisville
    Courier-Journal*, 92
Lounsbury, Harry, 305, 307n1
Lowell, James Russell, 327
Lucas, E. V., 285–86
Lucy, Henry, 285, 286
Lyon, Isabel, xvi, 258, 259n1, 263, 289,
    297, 298n2, 311, 313, 315, 320

MacAlister, George Ian, 283–84
Macaulay, Thomas, 114
Mackay, Clarence, 139, 140n4

Mackay, Katherine Duer, 139, 140n4, 174
Mackinac (Michigan), 191
Macy, Anna Sullivan, 308–17
Madison Square Garden, 171, 175n1
Maguire's Academy of Music, 59, 60, 61
Mallon, Joe, 262
Malory, Thomas, 147
Manhattan Club, 92
Marion Rangers, 14
Mark Twain Company, xv
Mark Twain Papers, xv
Mark Twain's Library of Humor, 137
"Mark Twain's Scrapbook," 130
Mark Twain's Speeches, 160–61, 162n4
Markham, Edwin, 306
Marsh, Grant, 13
Marshall, Edward, 154, 156n1
Massiglia, Countess, 258, 259n2
Matthews, Brander, xx, 157–62, 225
Mauna Loa, 61, 62
Mauritius, 202
Mayo, Frank, 262
McAleer, Patrick, 96, 98n2, 109
McAllister, Ward, 166–67, 168n3
McCarthy, Denis, 28, 29, 37n1, 61, 262
McClure's Magazine, 227
McComb, John, 67, 68n1
McCord, J. H., 10
McDowell's Cave, 5–6, 7
McElhinney, Jane, 25
McEwen, Arthur, 22–24
McGuinn, Warner, 108, 111n7, 230
McKinley, William, xvii
Mead, Mary Gertrude, 140n5
Melbourne (Australia), 204
Melville, Herman, xviii
Memphis (Tennessee), 3

Menken, Adah Isaacs, 25, 35–37
Meredith, George, 132
Michelet, Jules, 181
Mighels, Philip, 260, 261, 262n1
Millet, Frank, 157
Milton, John, 54, 106, 111n1
Milwaukee (Wisconsin), 190
mining, 16, 50–51
Minneapolis (Minnesota), 192, 201n4; *Minneapolis Journal*, 201n4; *Minneapolis Times*, 192, 201n4
Minnehaha (steamship), 229
Minnetonka (steamship), 287, 288
Missoula (Montana), 195, 196
Modesto (California), 41
Moffett, Pamela, xiv, 6, 7n3
Moffett, Samuel E., 196, 201n5
Monday Evening Club, 104n4, 129–30, 275
Montreal (Canada), 141
Morris, Cort, 137
Morrison, George, 164
Morrow, James B., 280–81
Mount Davidson, 35
Mount Vesuvius, 274n1
Muir, John, 306
Munro, David Alexander, 186–87, 188n4
Myers, W. F., 26

Naples (Italy), 255, 260, 274
Napoleon I, 30
Nasby, Petroleum V., 63
Nelson, Lord, 84
New Orleans (Louisiana), 8, 9, 134, 175n1
New Princeton Review, 158, 161n2, 161n3
New York American, 22, 255, 292

New York Herald, 220–21, 298n1
New York Journal, 213
New York Sun, 182n2
New York Times, 108, 111n5, 279n1
New York Tribune, xiv, 79, 92, 126n5, 140n2
New York *World*, xiv, 72n1, 92, 94, 218, 292n3
New Zealand, 202
Newell, Robert Henry, 25
North American Review, xvii, 42, 183, 188n4
Nuova Antologia, 257
Nye, James W., 16, 19n1

Oakland (California), 18
Ogden, Rollo, 264
Olympia (Washington), 196, 197
Onteora Park (New York), 159
Optic, Oliver, 304n1
Oregonian, 197
O'Reilly, Bernard, 152
Orton, Arthur, 94n1
Osgood, James R., 95, 134
Overland Monthly, 52
Oxford University, xix, 272, 282, 283, 289, 315

Page, Thomas Nelson, 139
Paige typesetter, xix, 228
Paine, Albert Bigelow, xvi, xvii, xx, 4, 7n1, 228, 266–72, 298–304, 306
Paris (France), 190
Paris (Kentucky), 145
Partridge, Bernard, 285
Patti, Adelina, 242
Paul Jones (steamboat), 8, 9
Pease, Lute, 197, 201n7
Pennsylvania (steamboat), 3, 10, 11n2

Pension Fund for University Professors, 238
Pepys, Samuel, 324
Perkins, Charles Enoch, 104n7
Perkins, Lucy Maria, 101, 104n7
Petoskey (Michigan), 191–92
Phelps, Elizabeth Stuart, 294
Philadelphia (Pennsylvania), 8, 169
Philippines–American War, 230, 240, 309
piloting, 2, 8–13
Planché, James Robinson, 104n2
plasmon, xviii, 230, 231
Players' Club, 161, 170, 183, 186, 266
Pleiades Club, 291, 292n2
Pond, James B., xx, 141, 142n2, 189–201
Pope, Alexander, 37n7
Port Elizabeth (South Africa), 209n6
Porter, Horace, 173, 175n3
Portland (Oregon), 196, 197, 201n6
Potter, Edward Tuckerman, 104n5
Pre-Raphaelites, 258
Pretoria (South Africa), 205
Price, H. Sterling, 14, 15n1
Prince Oskar (steamship), 260
Princess Irene (steamship), 255
Princeton University, 308
Punch, 285

Quaker City voyage, xvii, xx, 67, 69–73, 77, 133, 191
Quarles, John A., 39
Quarry Farm, 127, 131
Quick, Dorothy, 287–92
Quincy (Illinois), 134

Racconti Americani, 259n3

race, xviii, 33–34, 230

Raymond, John T., 92, 93

Read, Opie, 134

Redding (Connecticut), 296, 298, 299, 304, 306, 310–11, 322–23

Redpath, James, 95, 98n1, 189

Reid, Whitelaw, xiv, 126n5

Reinhart, Charles S., 140

Remington, Frederic, 140

Rhodes, Cecil, 205, 207

Rice, Clarence C., 246–49

Richardson, Abby Sage, 169

Richardson, Robert, 317n1

Rideing, William H., 183–88

Riverdale (New York), 231, 232n4, 244, 247, 251, 256

Rochester (New York), 145, 146

Rogers, Henry H., xviii, 239, 240n2, 259n2, 270, 296, 306, 308

Roosevelt, Theodore, 176, 251, 277, 280

Routledge, George, 82

Russell, Annie, 164

Russian Revolution, 273

Sabine, William T., 185, 188n3

Sacramento Union, 54, 58, 59

St. Louis (Missouri), 8, 9, 10, 11, 108, 111n5, 130n1, 134, 251, 252n1; *St. Louis Democrat*, 108, 111n5

St. Nicholas, xv, 176

St. Paul (Minnesota), 141, 192

St. Simon, 323

San Diego (California), 38

San Francisco (California), xiii, 20, 42, 47, 48, 54, 59, 60, 63, 64–65, 67, 73, 77, 190, 196, 272n5; *San Francisco Alta California*, 67, 73, 77; *San*

Francisco Examiner, 196; San Francisco *Morning Call*, 47, 48, 54, 60

Sandwich Islands, 54, 59, 63, 87

Sargent, John, 298

Saturday Press, 53, 64

Saturday Review, 157, 161n1

Sault Ste. Marie, 190

Savage Club, 82–83, 85

Schubert, Franz, 304

Scott, Walter, 108, 111n6, 230, 231n2, 239

Scribner, Arthur H., 264

Seattle (Washington), 196, 198

Shakespeare, William, 81, 116, 199, 201n10, 287

Shaw, George Bernard, xx, 125, 282, 310

Shelley, Percy Bysshe, 185

Sidgwick, Henry, 185

Simboli, Raffaele, 257–59

Singleton, Henry, 10

Siskiyou (California), 38

Sloane, William M., 158

Smedley, W. T., 140

Smith, Helen Yale, 99, 104n3

Smith, Hopkinson, 172, 175n2

smoking, 10, 56–58, 74–75, 105, 113, 128, 132, 156, 164, 166, 168, 180, 183, 199, 200, 211, 243, 248, 263, 294, 313, 324

Smythe, R. S., 202

Society of Illustrators, 264, 265n2

South Africa, 202, 205–13, 237

Spanish-American War, 230

Spenser, Edmund, 37n3

Spokane (Washington), 195–96

Springfield (Massachusetts), 95

Standard Oil Co., xviii, 240n2

Steamboat Springs (Nevada), 48

Stevenson, Robert Louis, 125

Stewart, William M., xx, 73–76

Stoddard, Charles Warren, 59, 89–91

Stormfield, 297, 298, 299–304, 306, 307, 308, 310, 317, 318, 322, 326

Stowe, Harriet Beecher, 104n7, 109, 116, 119, 129

Sturgis, Dorothy, xx, 296–98

Sub-Rosa Club, 173

Sullivan, Anna, 308–17

Sullivan, John L., 171, 175n1

Sullivan, Tim, xvii

"Susy's Diary," 254

Sydney (Australia), 202–4

Tacoma (Washington), 196, 197

Talmadge, DeWitt, xvii

Taylor, Bayard, 129

telephone, xviii

Tennyson, Alfred, Lord, 37n8, 102

Thackeray, William Makepeace, 281

Tichborne trial, 93, 94n1

Ticknor & Fields, 80

Titian, 116

Toole, John L., 82–83, 86

Toronto (Canada), 145, 146

translation, 259

Trumbull, J. Hammond, 129, 130n3

Tupper, Martin, 125

Twain, Mark: *Adventures of Huckleberry Finn*, xiv, xviii, xix, 2, 39, 116, 117n1, 125, 127, 137–40, 141, 143, 144n1, 148, 157, 161n1, 188n1, 201n4, 202, 203, 269, 288, 324; *Adventures of Tom Sawyer*, xix, xx, 2, 4, 5, 7n2, 110, 116, 125, 127, 251, 277, 287–88, 322, 324; "Ah Sin" (play), xviii; *American Claimant*, xviii, 163; "At the Shrine of St. Wagner," 182n2;

Autobiography, xvi–xvii, 7n2, 20, 42, 92, 100–1, 228n4, 244–45, 254, 266, 268–69, 320, 325n4; "Awful German Language," 144n2, 203; "Baker's Blue-Jay Yarn," 146, 147n1; "Bloody Massacre Near Carson," 38; "Celebrated Jumping Frog of Calaveras County," 52–53, 57, 64, 69, 86, 125, 179, 183–85, 201n4, 203, 248, 259; "Christian Science and the Book of Mrs. Eddy," 232n5, 232n6; *Connecticut Yankee in King Arthur's Court*, xiv, xix, 127, 147, 163–64; "Curious Republic of Gondour," 101; "Death of Jean," 324, 325n4; "Defense of General Funston," 188n1; "Die Schrecken der Deutschen Sprache," 160, 162n5; "Double Barrelled Detective Story," 265n3; *Eve's Diary*, 290, 315, 316; "Extract from Captain Stormfield's Visit to Heaven," 149n1, 294, 297; *Following the Equator*, 201n9, 219; "Fortifications of Paris," 79; "Forty-three Days in an Open Boat," 59; "Frightful Accident to Dan De Quille," 25; "Full and Reliable Account of the Extraordinary Meteoric Shower of Last Saturday Night," 25; *Gilded Age* (novel), xiii, xix, 3, 92, 123, 124, 189, 201n1, 277; "Gilded Age" (play), 76, 92, 93, 102, 117n3; "Golden Arm," 144n2; "Horrors of the German Language," 160, 162n5; "Horse's Tale," 265n3; "How I Edited an Agricultural Paper Once," 323, 325n2; *How to Tell a Story and Other Essays*, 144n2; *Innocents Abroad*, xix, xx, 69, 70, 71–72, 75, 77–78, 80, 86n1, 112, 115n1, 123,

250n2, 257, 288, 324; "Jim Blaine and His Grandfather's Old Ram," 201n4; "Jim Smiley and His Jumping Frog" (*See* "Celebrated Jumping Frog of Calaveras County"); *King Leopold's Soliloquy,* 188n2; *Letters from the Earth,* xvi; "Life on the Mississippi," xix, 7n2, 8, 12n2, 108, 111n4, 111n6, 130n1, 134, 310; "My Debut as a Literary Person," 59; "My Late Senatorial Secretaryship," 73; "Mysterious Stranger," 245n1; "Old Times on the Mississippi," 8, 108, 111n4, 134; *Personal Recollections of Joan of Arc,* xiv, 171, 172, 181, 200, 259, 294, 324; "Petrified Man," 25; *Prince and the Pauper* (novel), xiv, xix, 127; "Prince and the Pauper" (play), 169; "Private History of a Campaign That Failed," 14; *Pudd'nhead Wilson,* 176–77, 223, 262; *Roughing It,* xix, 19n6, 40, 41, 44, 47, 56, 58, 61, 75, 76n3, 112, 114, 115n1; *1601,* xv; "Small Piece of Spite," 49; "Stirring Times in Austria," 218, 220n1; "Terrible Accident to Dan De Quille," 32, 37n5; *Tom Sawyer Abroad,* xv, xviii, 163, 176, 201n4; "Tragic Tale of the Fishwife and Its Sad Fate," 143, 144n2; *Tramp Abroad,* xix, 144n2, 202, 265n4, 288, 292n1; "Trying Situation," 143, 144n2; "War Prayer," xv, 263, 265n1; "Weather of New England," 160, 162n5; "What Goes with the Money?" 48; *What Is Man?,* 275–76; "What Ought He to Have Done?" 148, 149n2; "Whittier Birthday Speech," xv, 118–21, 160, 162n5

Twichell, Joseph H., 106, 111n2, 116–17, 129, 327

University of Missouri, 252n1, 284n1
U.S. Sanitary Commission, 40–41

Vance, Zebulon, 135–36
Vancouver (B.C.), 190, 198, 199
Vanderlip, Frank, 264
Victoria (B.C.), 189, 199, 200
Victoria, Queen, 213–16, 241
Vienna (Austria), 108, 162n5, 210, 213, 218
Virginia City (Nevada), 16, 17, 18, 19n4, 19n7, 20, 21, 22, 23, 25, 26, 28, 29, 30, 31, 32, 33, 35, 37n1, 38, 40, 41, 42, 44–46, 47, 73; Virginia City *Chronicle,* 22; Virginia City *Territorial Enterprise,* 16, 17, 18, 19n4, 19n7, 20, 21, 23, 25, 26, 29, 30, 31, 32, 33, 37n1, 38, 40, 41, 47, 73; Virginia City *Union,* 40, 41, 42; *Virginia City Weekly Occidental,* 44–46
Voltaire, 310

Wadhams, Albion V., 197, 201n8
Wagner, Richard, 181, 182n2
Waldorf-Astoria, 237
Waldstein, Charles, 124, 125n2
Walker, William Wallace, 241
Wallace, Elizabeth, 293–95
Ward, Artemus, 25, 32–35, 37n7, 63, 65, 86, 87
Warner, Charles Dudley, xix, 92, 95, 96, 105, 116, 117n2, 120, 125n1, 129, 182
Warner, George, 116, 117n2
Warrimoo (steamship), 198, 199, 200, 201n9
Washington, D.C., 73, 277, 278

Washoe City (Nevada), 63

Watterson, Henry, 92–94

Webb, Charles, 48

Webster, Charles, xv, 168n1

Wellington, Duke of, 84

Wells, Virginia, 74–75, 76n2

Wenzell, A. B., 264

Whatcom (Washington), 198

Whistler, James McNeill, 175

White, Frank Marshall, xv, 213–21

Whitman, Walt, 25

Whitney, Henry M., 61

Whittaker, Johnson C., 108, 111n8

Whittier, John Greenleaf, 118, 119

Wildman, Edwin, 240n1

Wilhelm, Kaiser, II, 179, 182n1

William, Prince (of Hohenzollern), 241, 242n1

Williams, Dimond & Co., 55, 58

Wilson, Woodrow, 309

Winnipeg (Manitoba), 192

Wood, Charles E. S., 197, 201n6

Wright, William H. *See* De Quille, Dan

Yale University, 284n1

Yates, Edmund, 112–15

York Harbor (Maine), 244

WRITERS IN THEIR OWN TIME BOOKS

Alcott in Her Own Time
Edited by Daniel Shealy

Emerson in His Own Time
Edited by Ronald A. Bosco and Joel Myerson

Fuller in Her Own Time
Edited by Joel Myerson

Hawthorne in His Own Time
Edited by Ronald A. Bosco and Jillmarie Murphy

Poe in His Own Time
Edited by Benjamin F. Fisher

Stowe in Her Own Time
Edited by Susan Belasco

Twain in His Own Time
Edited by Gary Scharnhorst

Whitman in His Own Time
Edited by Joel Myerson